MEMOIRS OF
EMMA, LADY HAMILTON
The Friend of Lord Nelson

AND THE COURT OF NAPLES

*With a Special Introduction
and Illustrations*

VIGILANS ET AUDAX

University Press of the Pacific
Honolulu, Hawaii

Memoirs of Emma Lady Hamilton, The Friend of
Lord Nelson, and The Court of Naples
(Memoirs of the Court of Europe Series)

by
Emma Lady Hamilton

ISBN: 0-89875-374-0

Copyright © 2001 by University Press of the Pacific

Reprinted from the 1910 edition

University Press of the Pacific
Honolulu, Hawaii
http://www.universitypressofthepacific.com

CONTENTS

INTRODUCTION

"AMONG the lovely faces that haunt history none, surely, is lovelier than that of Emily Lyon, who abides undying as Emma, Lady Hamilton. Yet it was never the mere radiance of rare beauty that entitled her to such an empire over the hearts and wills of several remarkable men and of one unique genius, or which empowered a girl humbly bred and basely situated to assist in moulding events that changed the current of affairs. She owned grace and charm as well as triumphant beauty; while to these she added a masculine mind, a native force and sparkle; a singular faculty, moreover, of rendering and revealing the thoughts and feelings of others, that lent an especial glamour to both beauty and charm."

Walter Sichel thus strikes the keynote to the remarkable life-story here presented—a story which transcends the bounds of romance and fascinates and baffles the reader by turns. Indeed, no two critics of this famous beauty and confidante of Lord Nelson have ever agreed as to her place in history. To one she is an adventuress, luring Nelson on by the sheer power of her physical charm; to another, she is his guiding star, his inspiration; while others see in her merely an astute politician, eager for power. To quote Mr. Sichel again:

"It will be found that Lady Hamilton, by turns fulsomely flattered and ungenerously condemned, was a picturesque power and a real influence. She owned a fine side to her puzzling character. She was never mercenary, often self-abandoning, and at times actually noble. Her courage, warm-heartedness and gift of staunch friendship, her strength in conquering, her speed in assimilating circumstances, the firmness mixed with her frailty, were conspicuous; and it was the blend of these that, together with her genuine grit, appealed so irresistibly to Nelson. She must be largely judged by her capabilities. Her faults were greatly those of her antecedents and environment. She rose suddenly to situations and fulfilled them, while these again led her both to climax and catastrophe. She .worked long and hard, and with success; she took a strong line and pursued it. She became a serious politician in correspondence with most of the leaders in the European death-grapple with Jacobinism. So far, as has been represented, from having proved the mere tool of an ambitious queen, it will appear that more than once she swayed that beset and ill-starred woman into decision. So far from having craftily angled for Nelson's love, it will be shown that the magnet of *her* enthusiasm first attracted *his*. She was indeed singularly capable of feeling enthusiasm, and of communicating and enkindling it. It is as an enthusiast that she must rank."

"The story of her wonderfully checkered career from her cradle to her grave," writes W. H. Long in an earlier edition of her Memoirs, "and her connection with the greatest naval commander the world has ever seen, is as attractive and thrilling as a romance, and will serve for all time 'to point a moral or adorn a tale.'" We find in these pages the life history of a girl of obscure but honest parentage beginning her career as a household servant, then practically cast adrift in the streets seeking a precarious living in doubtful ways; thence rising from the very edge of circumstance by successive stages to become the inspiration of artists and Bohemians, the protegée of ministers, the wife of an ambassador, the trusted confidante of a queen, and the all-absorbing passion of a nation's hero. Rapid as this ascent to power was, the descent was no less swift, and the poverty which accompanied her early years again greets her at the end of the journey. The bare outline of such a career exhibits its remarkable contrasts of light and shadow. We can only explain it in part by a study of the woman herself—the same woman who, as an untutored girl of nineteen, sighed: "If I only had a good education, what a woman I might have been!"

Lady Hamilton rose to power not merely through beauty of face—many other women have been thus endowed—but through a combination of rare qualities which astounded such critics as Goethe, Sir Horace Walpole, the artists Romney and Madame Le Brun, and men and women in every walk of life. These qualities were a naturally fine mind, a magnetic personality, an overflowing sympathy and generosity, and a boundless enthusiasm. One may also characterize her as naturally theatrical. She did not pose, she was the living personification of the emotions she typified; and this natural adaptiveness became intensified by the scenes into which the untutored girl was so suddenly cast.

And what a theatre it was! England, just recovering from the American War of Independence, was facing a conflict with France. The latter country had emerged from the throes of Revolution only to plunge into a Titanic struggle with every other European nation. Napoleon marched through Italy, overran Egypt and swept the Mediterranean with his ships, preparatory to wider conquests. The Mediterranean thus became a seething caldron, and in its very centre the kingdom of the Two Sicilies struggled for existence. It was at Naples, the capital of this kingdom, that Emma, Lady Hamilton, as wife of the English Ambassador spent the momentous years of her life, and here her peculiar genius found full scope. She stirred her sluggish ambassador husband to action. She became the real power behind the Sicilian throne, through the friendship of Maria Carolina the Queen (sister of the ill-fated Marie Antoinette of France). And when the fleet of Nelson drew near in pursuit of the French, she it was who procured water and provision for it, enabling Nelson to fight and win his famous Battle of the Nile. Upon the return of the victor began his remarkable intimacy with *both* the Hamiltons, which was to endure through the lifetime of each and all. And of the three, the chivalrous attitude of the elderly Sir William is alone meritorious. His regard for his wife and his friend never wavered; while they, carried mutually onward by a wave of irresistible love, forgot the one his wife, the other her husband in the *liaison* so widely known to history.

That Lady Hamilton's influence upon Nelson was permanent and paramount is never disputed. He idealized her and strove to live up to the fond ideal which he cherished. His letters constantly attest his devotion, and his dying message confided her and her child to the care of his country—a charge which ungrateful England wholly neglected. Nelson, indeed, always hoped to have been able to legalise this union of hearts. Emma was his "wife before God," his "pride and delight." While to her, Nelson was "the dearest husband of her heart," her "hero of heroes," her "idol." They lived for each other, and died in the hope that they should meet again. "Nelson's unselfishness transfigured her to herself; she became capable of great moments. And she was born for friendship. 'I would not be a lukewarm friend for the world,' she wrote to him at the outset; 'I cannot make friendships with all, but the few friends I have I would die for them.' She was always warm-hearted to a fault, as will amply appear as her character grows up in these pages. So far from numbing Nelson, she nerved him; nor did she debase any within the range of her influence."

The earliest "Memoirs of Lady Hamilton" appeared shortly after her death, in 1815, from the pen of an anonymous author, and were published by H. Colburn, London. They were widely read, a second enlarged edition appearing a few months later. Frequent printings were made, and finally W. H. Long brought out a revised edition in 1891. But other and more authentic memoir material meanwhile became available—all of which has been utilised by the present editor. The first of these sources is a volume of "Letters of Lord Nelson to Lady Hamilton," published by Thomas Lovewell & Co., London, 1814. The reader of the present book will note how these cherished letters were stolen from Lady Hamilton, while she was ill and in trouble, and how she stoutly denied any responsibility for their publication. Nevertheless, they are undoubtedly genuine, many of the originals having been preserved, and they furnish an important basis for these Memoirs. They include letters by Lady Hamilton, her husband, Greville, Bristol, but chiefly a long series of private letters from Nelson himself. The editor has also drawn upon various recent manuscript collections in the British Museum, such as the correspondence of Lady Hamilton with Nelson in the autumn of the year 1798, after the Nile Victory, and letters between Lady Hamilton and Mrs. William Nelson, during 1801, relative to the Prince of Wales episode which created such a scandal in officialdom. The latter collection was not obtained by the Museum until 1896, and has therefore not been available to preceding biographers. Besides the above there are other important sources, such as the Nelson family papers, the Acton-Hamilton correspondence, the manuscript letters of Maria Carolina, Queen of Naples, in the British Museum, and numerous state documents and private papers. Mr. Sichel has left no bit of evidence unturned, basing his story closely upon contemporary evidence, with the result that he has here given the first complete and accurate pen portrait of Lady Hamilton which has yet appeared.

"It is a career of widespread interest and unusual fascination," he finds, "a human document of many problems that well repay the decipherer and the discoverer. My aim throughout has been to quicken research into life, and to furnish a new study of her striking temperament and the temperaments which became so curiously interwoven both with each other and with history. I venture also to hope," he adds, "that Nelson's own character and achievements stand more fully revealed by the fresh lights and side-lights which serve to bring his extraordinary individuality into relief, to explain his policy, and to clear up some vexed passages both in his private and his public actions."

Whatever sentence the reader may pronounce on the evidence to be submitted, he cannot fail to mark the psychological problems of her being. In any case, with all her blots and failings, Lady Hamilton presents one of the most fascinating studies in the eternal duel of sex. To her may well be applied the line which her husband quoted in his book of 1772:—"The heroine of a thousand things."

My Dear Lady Hamilton—

  I have kissed the Queens letter pray say I hope for the honor of kissing her hand when no fears will intervene, assure her majesty that no person has her felicity more at heart than myself, and that the Sufferings of her family will be a Tower of Strength on the day of Battle, fear not the event, God is with us, God bless you and Sir William pray say I cannot Stay to answer his letter her

  Yours faithfully

17th May 6PPM Horatio Nelson.

LETTER FROM LORD NELSON TO LADY HAMILTON
[See next page, also pp. 197-199]

NOTE ON NELSON'S LETTER

(Reproduced on foregoing page)

The circumstances calling for this remarkable letter are given in full in Chapter VII. "Nelson was in chase of Buonaparte's fleet," it begins. The English admiral's instructions were to water and provide his fleet in any Mediterranean port, except in Sardinia, if necessary by arms. The success of his expedition absolutely depended upon it. The various ports, however, were so dominated by Napoleon, then at the height of his power, that they dared not welcome the English, even if willing.

At this critical juncture, the woman's hand succeeded where the mailed fist might have failed. Lady Hamilton's husband was Ambassador to Naples, and she herself exerted a vital influence in affairs of that little kingdom, not so much through her husband's position, as her own close friendship with Queen Carolina of Naples. She obtained secret permission from the Queen to obtain supplies for the fleet, in a personal note so jealously guarded that when it is forwarded to Nelson, Lady Hamilton entreats him to "kiss it, and send it back by Bowen, as I am bound not to give any of her letters."

The overjoyed Admiral hastened to kiss the precious missive; his ships were quickly supplied; and not long thereafter the news that the French fleet had been destroyed in the Battle of the Nile thrilled the world.

EMMA, LADY HAMILTON

CHAPTER I

THE CURTAIN RISES—1765-1782

On the morning of January 10, 1782, the punctilious and elegant Honourable Charles Francis Greville, gloomy still over the loss of his Warwick election, but consoled by a snug, if unsafe, post in the Board of Admiralty, much exercised, too, in his careful way, about minerals, animals, science, the fine arts, and the flickering out of the American war, was even more exercised by a missive from a poor young girl who had already crossed his path. Fronting him in the dainty chamber of his mansion in the new and fashionable Portman Square, hung the loaned "Venus" attributed to Correggio, and slightly retouched with applied water-colour. This over-prized picture had been for years the cherished idol of his uncle and *alter ego,* Sir William Hamilton, K.B., Fellow of the Antiquarian and the Royal Societies, member of the Dilettanti, the Tuesday, and other clubs, foster-brother of the now George III., and sometime both his and his brother's equerry; the busy man of pleasure, the renowned naturalist and virtuoso of Portland vase celebrity, and already for about eighteen years His Britannic Majesty's amiably-grumbling Ambassador at the Court of the King of the two Sicilies. Greville's natural *sangfroid* was not easily ruffled, but this letter almost excited him. It was franked by himself on a wrapper in his own neat handwriting, bore the Chester postmark, and contrasted strongly with the tasteful tone of the room and its superfine owner.

It ran as follows: " Yesterday did I receve your kind letter. It put me in some spirits for, believe me, I am allmost distracktid. I have never hard from Sir H.,[1] and he is not at Lechster now, I am sure. I have wrote 7 letters, and no anser. What shall I dow? Good God what shall I dow. . . . I can't come to toun for want of mony. I have not a farthing to bless my self with, and I think my friends looks cooly on me. I think so. O. G. what shall I dow? What shall I dow? O how your letter affected me when you wished me happiness. O. G. that I was in your posesion or in Sir H. what a happy girl would I have been! Girl indeed! What else am I but a girl in distres—in reall distres? For God's sake, G. write the minet you get this, and only tell me what I am to dow. Direct same whay. I am allmos mad. O for God's sake tell me what is to become on me. O dear Grevell, write to me. Write to me. G. adue, and believe [me] yours for ever Emly Hart.

" Don't tel my mother what distres I am in, and dow afford me some comfort.

" My age was got out of the Reggister, and I now send it to my dear Charles. Once more adue, O you dear friend."

Who was this girl in " reall distres," what her past? who were the friends who looked " cooly " on her, and for what reasons? These questions will shortly be answered so far as replies admit of real proof. But first a brief space must be devoted to Greville himself,

---

[1] Sir Harry Fetherstonehaugh, of Up Park, Sussex, who lived to correspond in middle age with her in terms of deferential friendship. His name is thus spelt in his letters.

since his individuality is as necessary to the coming plot as her own.

The Honourable Charles Francis Greville was now thirty-two.

The second son of the Right Honourable Francis, Earl of Brooke (afterwards Earl of Warwick), and of Elizabeth Hamilton, one of Sir William's sisters, he was born at Fulham on May 12, 1749, and baptised on June 8 following. He was born prematurely old, parsimoniously extravagant, and cautiously careless. His cradle should have been garlanded with official minutes, and draped with collectors' catalogues. From his earliest days he was prim, methodical, and pedantic beyond his years. The unlikelihood of surviving his eldest brother had been ever before his eyes, and he was set on the emoluments of a political career, promising much to one so highly connected. While still in his teens he began amassing *virtu* with discernment, and specimens of mineralogy on a " philosophical " system. Some years before his majority he had struck up a brotherly affection with his freehearted uncle, nearly twenty years his senior, who relied on a precocious judgment, invaluable to one compelled by long absences to entrust to others the management of his wife's Pembrokeshire property, indispensable also to both in the keen pursuit of their common tastes, the one in Italy, the home of art, the other in England, the nursery of science. From a very early date the student of beauty and curios, the investigator of shells, marine monsters, and volcanoes, " Pliny the Elder," as he came to be called, was always exchanging rarities with " Pliny the Younger," or commissioning him to buy, sell, or raffle Dutch and Italian pictures, Etruscan urns, Greek torsos, and Roman vases.

Hamilton was a true man of science, and a really

great archæologist. When he first came to Naples in
1764 he spent months in his Villa Angelica, on the
slopes of Mount Vesuvius, taking observations and ex-
cavating antiquities. He was far less a trafficker in
objects of art and learning than his nephew. He presented both books and specimens of value to the British
Museum. His aim, in his own words, was that of
" employing his leisure in use to mankind." [1] Not
quite so, however, was that of Pliny the Younger, who
in his turn bought crystals and works of art with equal
zest of connoisseurship. Greville was barely twenty-
one when he went the Italian tour, stayed with his
uncle at Naples, then in the full fever of unearthing
buried *chefs-d'œuvre* at Herculaneum and Pompeii,
which were so soon to experience many fresh escapes
from re-destruction by earthquakes and eruptions.
From Rome, in this year, the nephew indited two of
the most self-assured letters of grave gossip and counsel that any youngster has ever addressed to one nearly
twice his age. They are so like himself that a small
part of one must be given: " I begin with a subject
that I have resolved every time I have wrote to mention, and now particularly I am under an obligation
to remember, as for the first time my handkerchief

---

[1] *Observations on Mount Vesuvius,* etc. (1772). The villa was
probably called after the artist. Hamilton constantly ran great
danger in observing and recording violent eruptions. He was
indefatigable in superintending excavations, and he mentions
being present at Pompeii when a horse with jewelled trappings
and its rider were unearthed. He was a munificent patron alike
of discoverers, travelers, scientists, and artists, including Flaxman and Wedgwood. He was a trustee of the British Museum,
and a vice-president of the Society of Antiquaries. A big book
on his Greek and Roman antiquities was written by D'Harcau-
ville (Naples, 1765-1775; Paris, 1787). Besides the book already
mentioned, supplemented in 1779, Hamilton wrote *Campi
Phlegræi* (Naples, 1776-77), and the famous work on Greek
and Etruscan urns, etc., illustrated by Bartolozzi. A *Life*
worthy of him ought to be written.

has been knotted on the occasion. It is to desire you
to enquire for two books I left in my room at your
house; 2 pocket volumes of Milton's works. I borrowed them, and left them with an intention they
should be sent to Mrs. Harfrere to whom they belong. . . . The ink bottle has this moment oversett,
but you see I am not disconcerted, so pray don't make
observations, and the letter is as good as it was. Pray
let me beg you to avoid every mention of prices, I
have done so once before. Pray let me send and be
favoured with the acceptance of some baubles. . . ,
I am in the best of humours. I received this morning
a line from Lord Exeter, who informed me of the
Douglas cause being decided in his favour. . . . I
am running about the antiquities from 9 to 11 with
Byres, from 11-12 with Miss A., so you see I gain
Horace's happiness, *omne tulit punctum qui miscuit
utile dulci.* . . . Pray let me lay on you a disagreeable task, choose me a handsome pattern for an
applicée, have it wrought for me instantaneously, and
sent to Rome. I wish an Etrusc vase could be introduced. It must be handsome and rich; as to its elegance, anything, particularly Etrusc, conducted by
your taste cannot fail to be elegant. If a contrivance
could be hit on for making it less regular and straight,
. . . I should be pleased. Yours is charming, but
rather too much like a lace. . . . The spangles must
be caution'd against and well fastened. There have
been some fine conversations since the Emperor has
been here. The Grand Duke asked after you of me.
. . . The E. has lessened the talk about the D.
However I like the D. best: more of engaging and
gentlemanlike deportment, and more of the world.
. . . By the Bye if you can pick up any vases, of
which you have duplicates, lay them aside for me, and
don't buy them if not well conserv'd and good; nor

many of a shape, a few elegant and good. Adieu my dear Hamilton."

Certainly Greville proved the Horatian mixer of pleasure with profit; and since he, like his far franker uncle, was ever complaining of a narrow purse tantalised by the temptations of *virtu*, that other trite Horatian maxim, *Virtute me involvo*, would also admirably fit them. Wrapped in their mantles of *Virtu*, they both bewailed means far too slender for their tastes. The richer Sir William, indeed, expending in antiquities what he retrenched elsewhere, seems in his correspondence all debt and Correggio; while Greville removed to his mansion under pretext of its size being a bargain. Each sought to serve the other, and Greville in his youth persistently charged his uncle to be his *député*. As time proceeded, Sir William with an ailing wife and a buried daughter, his nephew ever on his watch-tower for an heiress, confided to each other their little gallantries, and peccadilloes also. As for Greville, just as in the case of the " applicée," " contrivances " were soon " hit on " for making him " less regular and straight." Already, in 1781, this solemn frequenter of new Almack's had acquired the Reynolds picture of " Emily in the character of Thais," which had been left on Sir Joshua's hands. His character was that of a free-living formalist, the reverse of austere, but with all austerity's drawbacks.

Yet there were some excellent points in this queer compound of the Pharisee and the Publican, something between a Charles and a Joseph Surface. If none was more prone to sin with self-righteousness, and to excuse to himself half-shabbiness as unselfish generosity, if none could write more glibly of a " good heart," he was not consciously a hypocrite; though *par excellence* the man of taste rather than the man of feeling.

He displayed scrupulous honour in all money transactions, much dignity and reticence, with grace of demeanour (if not always of behaviour); independence too of mind, and a public-spirited industry that often kept him sitting on important committees six hours at a stretch. He was a steadfast friend, and the early death of his Pylades, the brilliant Charles Cathcart, was a real blow to him and an irretrievable loss. He was an ideal trustee. He could say with truth, "I am a good jobber for a friend, but an awkward one for myself." He was worthy of his uncle's confidence, and to the last superintended his affairs and those of others with integrity and tact. Nor did he neglect the welfare of Hamilton's tenants at Milford. He was capable of limited disinterestedness as well as of true patriotism. His father's death and his brother's accession to estates and title in 1773 reduced his allowance afresh, and all his resource was needed to repair the deficiency.

Socially a disciple of the old-fashioned Chesterfield, and affecting to flout the opinion of a world that he was far from despising, politically he was a trimming Whig, but an unbending supporter of all authority and establishment. He throve on coalitions, and lamented with reason the nearing end of that coalition ministry which was still in power when this chapter opened.

Such is an epitome of the man who still holds the *soi-disant* "Emily Hart's" letter in his hands. It is her origin and past that now demand re-investigation. In view of her instinctive independence and her native appetite for glory, the notion of which grew with her expanding horizon, these trivial beginnings are not unimportant, while some of her cousins played a prominent part in the later scenes of her life.

Emily (or "Emy") Lyon was born on April 26 in 1765, the year of her baptism, unless, without reason, we are to assume her illegitimacy. The Neston parish registers prove the marriage of her parents to have taken place on June 11, 1764. The rumours and fictions about her early adventures, seemingly requiring a longer space than her extreme girlhood affords, have impelled certain biographers to antedate her birth by so much as four years. But many references, both in Greville's letters and Hamilton's, with other evidence outside them, entirely tally with the date that I have assigned. She was christened " Emily " (of which " Emy " and not " Amy," as has been alleged, is the contraction), though from the " Emy " she may in childhood have been called " Amy " at times. The copy of the baptismal register sent to Greville is incorrect, as will be seen in the note below. Her marriage register, it is true, is signed " Amy Lyons " according to the Marylebone clerk's information, but this again seems a natural misreading of her rapid and often indistinct handwriting for " Emy Lyon."

Her father was Henry Lyon, " Smith of Nesse," and her mother Mary Kidd of Hawarden, Flintshire. In their marriage register both sign by marks, although her mother soon afterwards became " a scholar." Her father died, it is said, in the year of her birth; but there is no vestige of her mother's remarriage to one " Doggan " or " Doggin," to which has been attributed her after-name of Mrs. Cadogan from the present period in London to that when she became " La Signora Madre dell'Ambasciatrice," and the esteemed friend both of Hamilton and of Nelson. " Emy " has always been described as an only child, but she seems to have had a brother or half-brother, " Charles." Thomas Kidd, an old salt and cousin, writing from Greenwich in 1809, to thank for past and beg for future favours, observes: " I have to inform you that *your brother Charles* is in Greenwich College and has been here since the 6th inst.;" but I can find no further trace of this "brother," nor is there any record of relatives on the father's side.[1] This Thomas Kidd may well have been the son of a William Kidd, "labourer," who, as "widower" in September, 1769, in the Hawarden registers, married one "Mary Pova." And William Kidd is possibly Lady Hamilton's cousin or uncle, who was at one time a publican, and who used to complain that he was "never brought up to work." If this be so, something of the paternal strain seems to have descended to the son, who, in the letter just mentioned, excuses his remissness in calling, as requested, by the insinuating remark that "I declare my small cloaths are scandolous, and my hat has the crown part nearly off"; while he speaks pointedly of the attentions of a "Mr. Ingram," who in turn refers to his "justifiable character" in "His Majesty's service," and suggests that, since both the porter of the west gate and the "roasting cook" of the college are infirm and ill, there is a choice of probable promotions awaiting him. In after years it was not only her humble kinsfolk, whom she never forsook, that were to importune Emma for advancements.

The Kidds were mostly sailors or labourers. Lady Hamilton's grandmother, with whom in girlhood she often stayed, and whom she always cared for and cherished, dwelt in one of some thatched cottages, two of which still remain. That Mary Lyon, *née* Kidd, was a superior woman, is shown by her after-acquirements. Tradition associates her both with dressmaking and with domestic service. If tradition again is trustworthy, she may have been cook in the household of Lord Halifax, who is also reported to have educated both her and her child. But Lady Hamilton herself,

---

[1] At the last moment I have been informed that Emma had a sister "Anna."

writing to Mr. Bowen of Portman Square (and of
Merton?) in 1802 about Charlotte Nelson's education,
declares that her own did not begin till she was seventeen—that is to say, under Greville's auspices. I have
read none of her mother's letters before 1800, and it
is not improbable that mother and daughter began their
education together. She was always an energetic
housekeeper and a most resourceful home-physician.
Her letters to Emma, to George Rose, and others, seem
neither ill-worded nor ill-spelt. At Naples and Palermo we shall find her visited by the Queen. The
King of Naples was in the December of 1798 to call
her an " angel " for her services during the hurricane
attending the royal escape to Palermo, though he also,
if we may trust the Marchioness of Solari, had before dubbed her " Ruffiana." The Duke of Sussex
highly esteemed her. Nor can the accomplished Miss
Cornelia Knight have found her intolerable, for on
the return of Nelson, the Hamiltons, and herself to
London after the ill-starred continental tour of 1800,
she drove straight off and stayed with Mrs. " Cadogan " at the hotel in St. James's. There is no evidence
as to how this homely and trustworthy woman came
by her grand name. Doggin, her second husband,
however, may not be a myth; although the Marchioness
of Solari mentions that " Codogan " was the name by
which " Emma's reputed mother " caused her to be
known at Naples before her marriage; and at any rate
it is a singular coincidence that Earl Nelson's companion when he went to Calais to fetch Horatia away,
after Lady Hamilton's death in 1815, was to be a
Mr. Henry Cadogan, a relation of the late and well-
known Mr. Rothery.

Only two sisters of Emma's mother are generally
mentioned. Both of these seem also to have risen
above their station. The one married a Mr. John

Moore, afterwards, it would seem, successful in business at Liverpool, but at one time addressed by Emma at the house of a Mr. Potter in Harley Street. The other was a Mrs. Connor, who had six children, all of them long supported by Lady Hamilton: one of them, Sarah, to be the governess both at Merton and Cranwich, was well educated; another, Cecilia, became an accomplished singer, and also a (though a less capable) preceptress. Ann, the eldest, and Eliza both rose above their sphere, though they proved most ungrateful; while Charles, who entered the Navy under Nelson's protection, could write an excellent letter, but unfortunately went mad, for, as Lady Hamilton recorded in a very curious statement regarding four of them, "there was madness in the family." Ann's showed itself in eventually asserting that she was Lady Hamilton's daughter, for which there is no evidence; indeed, to her must be traced the unfounded rumour spread by the *chronique scandaleuse* of the time that Ann, Eliza, and Charles were Greville's three children. Mary, too, was to be popular, and with all her sisters intimate with the whole Nelson and Hamilton family, as well as with Sir William Hamilton's relations.

Lady Hamilton's mother had also a third sister, Ann, who married "Richard Reynolds, Whitesmith," in 1774. The Sarah (misspelt "Reynalds") who finds a mention as grateful to her titled cousin in the Morrison correspondence, was probably his daughter. She may further have had another brother or cousin, William, an entry regarding whom and his wife Mary finds place also in the Hawarden parish books. There were the "Nicolls," whom, just before her own bankruptcy, Emma is found continuously maintaining with the rest of her connections. And finally there are traces of friends—of her Parkgate landlady in 1784

Mrs. Downward, and of a Mrs. Ladmore whom she seems to have known.

When we remember the bright and intelligent letters that remain of this Connor family, their acquirements, and the way in which they were treated and received, the fairy-tale of Lady Hamilton's conquest over circumstance seems to have extended also to her relations.

Nothing can be proved of Emma's childhood but that it was passed at Hawarden in extreme poverty, that she was a madcap, and that she blossomed early and fairly into stature and ripeness beyond her age. At sixteen (or perhaps thirteen) she was already a grown woman, which explains the puzzled Greville's inquiry for the register of her baptism. The most ridiculous romances were spread during her lifetime and after it. Hairbreadth escapes and *Family Herald* love-stories, regardless of facts or dates, adorn the pages of a novel published in the fifties, and professing to be circumstantial;[1] while Alexandre Dumas has embroidered his *Souvenirs d'Une Favorite* with all the wild scandals of a teeming imagination. The earliest certainty is that at some thirteen years of age she entered the service of Mr. Thomas of Hawarden, the father of a London physician, and brother-in-law of the famous art patron, Alderman Boydell of London. Miss Thomas was the first to sketch Emma while she was their nurse-maid. The drawing survives at Hawarden, and the Thomases always remained her friends. Whether it is possible that the roving Romney may have seen her there must be left to fancy. It is at least a curious fact that she came so early into indirect touch with art. The loose rumour ascribing her departure from Hawarden to the severity of her first master or mistress is entirely without foundation.

[1] *Nelson's Legacy.*

A far more probable conjecture is that she left Hawarden for London because her mother left also. It seems probable from the letter to Greville, already quoted, as well as from Greville's answer, which will soon follow, that Mrs. " Cadogan " was already in some London situation known to and approved of by Greville.

About the end, then, of 1779 or the beginning of 1780, when Emma was some fifteen years of age, she repaired with her mother to the capital; and there seems little doubt that she found employment with Dr. Budd, a surgeon of repute, at Chatham Place, near St. James's Market. A comrade with her in this service was the talented and refined woman afterwards famed as the actress, Jane Powell, who is not to be confused with the older Harriet Powell, eventually Lady Seaforth. When Sir William and Lady Hamilton returned home in 1800, they attended a performance at Drury Lane, where Emma and her old fellow-servant were the cynosure of an audience ignorant of their former association. When Lady Hamilton was at Southend in the late summer of 1803 she again met her quondam colleague. Pettigrew possessed and quoted a nice letter from her on this occasion. It is assuredly not among the least of the many marvels attending Emma's progress that an eminent surgeon should have harboured two such belles in his area.

And now Apocrypha is renewed. Gossip has it that she served in a shop; that she became parlourmaid elsewhere, and afterwards the risky " companion " of a vicious " Lady of Quality." The Prince Regent, who was years afterwards to solicit and be repulsed by her, used to declare that he recollected her selling fruit with wooden pattens on her feet; but he also used to insist, it must be recollected, on his own presence at the battle of Waterloo. It was said, too,

that she had been a model for the Academy students.
For such *canards* there is no certainty, and for many
rumours there is slight foundation. But there is a
shade of evidence to show that somewhere about 1781
she was in the service of the manager of Drury Lane
Theatre, Sheridan's father-in-law, Thomas Linley the
elder, and that she suddenly quitted it from grief at
the death of his young son, a naval lieutenant, whom
she had nursed. Angelo in his *Reminiscences* has
drawn the pathetic picture of his chance meeting with
her in Rathbone Place, a dejected figure clad in deep
mourning; he has added an earlier encounter and an
allusion to her brief sojourn with the " Abbess " of
Arlington Street, Mrs. Kelly, who may be identical
with the " Lady of Quality." If so, destitution must
have caused her downfall. Hitherto this girl of sixteen, so beautiful that passers-by turned spellbound to
look at her, had rejected all overtures of evil. Writing to Romney after her marriage, in a letter which
seems to imply that she had known him even before her
acquaintance with Greville, Lady Hamilton thus recalls
her past: " You have seen and discoursed with me in
my poorer days, you have known me in my poverty and
prosperity, and I had no occasion to have lived *for
years* in poverty and distress if I had not felt something of virtue in my mind. Oh, my dear friend, for
a time I own through distress my virtue was vanquished, but my sense of virtue was not overcome."
Some two years earlier, when she had insisted on accompanying Sir William on a shooting expedition,
and he had evidently remonstrated about hardship,
rough lodging did not deter her; she had been accustomed to it.

From Angelo's story it would appear that her
earliest admirer was Fetherstonehaugh, who will soon
cross the scene, and who in her later years was to

emerge friendly and even respectful. But the name of
her first betrayer has been so constantly given as that
of " Captain," afterwards Rear-Admiral, " Jack " Willet-Payne, man of fashion, member of Parliament, and
eventually treasurer of Greenwich Hospital, that the
story cannot be wholly discredited. Tradition has
added that she first encountered him in a bold attempt
to rescue a cousin from being impressed into the
service. This may or may not be. The sole sidelight, afforded by an unnoticed letter from Nelson of
1801, which proves that she had confided much of her
past to her hero, more probably refers to Greville:
" That other chap did throw away the most precious
jewel that God ever sent on this earth."

Her relations with the Captain can scarcely have
lasted more than about two months. If she was his
Ariadne, he sailed away in haste, nor does he darken
her path again. It was perhaps on his sudden departure that this lonely girl fell in with Dr. Graham,
the empiric and showman. How she met him is unknown: that he was anything to her but an employer
has never been suggested; that he ever employed her
at all rests merely on a story, so accredited by Pettigrew, who had known several of her early contemporaries, that one can hardly doubt it. The sole evidence that she ever " posed " for him is to be found
in Greville's reply to Emma's appeal already cited: in
it Greville speaks of the last time you came to " G.,"
which Mr. Jeaffreson guesses to mean " Graham." It
may, however, at once be noted that his living adver-
tisement of the goddess of health and beauty, " Hebe
Vestina," did not figure in his museum of specifics
until 1782, when he had removed from the Adelphi to
Pall Mall, and had there opened his " Temple of
Hymen " in the eastern part of Schomberg House, the
western side of which had been leased to Gainsborough

by the eccentric artist and adventurer, Jack Astley.
The strong probability is that Emma was first engaged
by him as a singer in those miniature mock-oratorios
and cantatas, composed by himself, which played such
a part in his miscellany, and were supposed to attune
the souls of the faithful; while her expressive beauty
may have soon tempted him to exhibit her as the
draped statue of " Hygieia," or Goddess of Health,
though certainly not as his later *tableau vivant* of
" Hebe Vestina."

Dr. Graham was no common impostor. He belongs
to the class of charlatan that unites pseudo-mysticism
and pseudo-piety to real skill—in short, a High Priest
of Pompeian Isis. He was no mere conjurer; he effected genuine cures besides dealing in quack remedies.
At this time he was about forty years of age. He
may have qualified in Edinburgh University; he had
certainly travelled in France and America, and received testimonials from personages at home and
abroad. He knew his classics, which he quoted
profusely in those curious " lectures " combining puff
with literary, satirical, scriptural, philanthropic, and
scientific allusion. His brother had married the " historian," Mrs. Catharine Macaulay, who often figures
in his florid catalogues of cures. That authoress is
depicted in mezzo-tints as a sickly-looking lady, pen
in hand, with a row of her volumes before her, trying
apparently to draw inspiration from the ceiling. He
was never tired of assuring the public that she was own
sister to " Mr. John Sawbridge, M.P. for London."
He posed as a sort of prayerful alchemist, eradicating
and healing at once the causes of vice, and its consequences. His advertisements are a queer union of
cant earnestness, travestied truth, sensible nonsense,
humour and the lack of it, effrontery and belief—
especially in himself. After he had closed his costly

and ruinous London exhibitions, he turned " Christian Philosopher " at Bath and Newcastle, anticipated the modern open-air cure, " paraphrased " the Lord's Prayer for the public, the Book of Wisdom for the Prince of Wales, and hastened to lay on the pillow of the suffering George III. one of his numerous " prayers." His specialty in 1780 (and throughout his career) was the then derided but now accepted electricity and mud-baths. By their means he claimed to restore and preserve beauty, to prolong existence, to enable a decayed generation to repair its losses by a vigorous, comely, and healthful progeny. He had opened a pinchbeck palace enriched with symbolical paintings, gilt statues, and coloured windows, where up to ten o'clock nightly he advertised his wares to the sound of sweet music, in his " Temple of Æsculapius " at the Royal Terrace, Adelphi. His pamphlets, sermons, hymns, exhortations, and satires, were rained on the town. In one of these pieces of fulsome *réclame* he describes his museum of elixirs as Emma may have viewed it in 1780 or 1781. Over the porch stood the inscription " Templum Æsculapio Sacrum." There were three gorgeously decorated rooms with galleries above, and pictures of heroes and kings, including Alfred the Great. Crystal glass pillars enshrined the costly electrical apparatus for reviving youth and strength. The third chamber was the tinsel " Temple of Apollo " with its magnetic " celestial bed," with its gilt dragons, overarching " Pavilion," and inscription, " Dolorifica res est si quis homo dives nullum habet domi suæ successorem." " But on the right of the Temple," he says, " is strikingly seen a beautiful figure of Fecundity," holding her cornucopia and surrounded by reclining children; and above all, an " electric " " celestial glory," which, mellowed by the stained windows, shed a dim and solemn light. Strains of majestic melody filled the air; and here also were sold his " Nervous Balsam " and " Electrical Æther "; while in the mornings this reverse of " seraphic " doctor punctually attended consultations in the dwelling-rooms adjoining.

Whether such ambrosial tomfoolery yielded Emma an intermittent livelihood at all, and whether before she loved Willet-Payne or after, remains doubtful; the latter is more probable. The blatant novelty-monger offered prizes for emblematic pictures, and it is possible that Tresham, or even his friend Romney, might have been pressed into his service. It may well be, too, that here the young blood and baronet, Sir Henry Fetherstonehaugh, became her admirer. As we see him in his letters some thirty years afterwards, this worthy appears as a silly old beau and sportsman, indulging in compliments pompous as his political reflections, and interlarding his correspondence with superfluous French. In his old age he educated and married a most worthy peasant girl, and brought her sister (also educated in France) to reside with them at Up Park, while from Lady Fetherstonehaugh the estate passed into that sister's possession.

Up Park (like Willet-Payne) was fraught with dreams of the fleet, for from its lofty position on the steep Sussex Downs it commands a prospect of Portsmouth and the Isle of Wight. Here this erring and struggling girl, for a brief space, it may be in 1781, became the mistress of the mansion and its roystering owner, both Nimrod and Macaroni. Here she " witched the world with noble horsemanship," for she was always a fearless rider. Here, among rakes, she could not rest, as she sighed for the artistic admiration which her *tableau vivant* in the Adelphi had already aroused among clever Bohemians. Here, perhaps in despair, she became so reckless and capricious, so hopeless of that peace of mind and happy innocence which, ten years later, she joyfully assured Romney had been restored to her by marriage, that she was ejected and cast adrift at the very moment when she found herself soon to become a mother. That she was " a girl in reall distres " for the *first* time (and not, as has often been presumed, for the second) will be shown when we come to " little Emma," and it is here evidenced by her entreaty that Greville would spare her mother any knowledge of this fresh and crushing blow.

At Up Park, most probably, Greville had first met her in the autumn of 1781, on one of those shooting-parties in great houses which he always frequented more from fashion than amusement. She had doubtless contrasted him with Sir Harry's stupid and commonplace acquaintances. Greville always took real interest in people who interested him at all, and at least he never acted below his professions. He was nobly bred, considerate, and composed; he was good-looking, prudent, and ever liberal—in advice. No wonder that his condescension seemed ideal to this girl of sixteen, who had lost yet coveted self-respect; who had already suffered from degrading experience, and yet had ever " felt something of virtue " in her " mind." He had afterwards (as his letter will show) befriended and scolded her headstrong sallies, though his warnings must have passed unheeded. On her retirement in disgrace and despair to her loving grandmother at Hawarden, he doubtless gave her the franked and addressed papers enabling her to communicate with him should need compel her. Just as evidently, she had written and been touched with the kind tone of his answer. It seems obvious also from Greville's coming reply that, as was her way, she would neither cajole Sir Harry into renewed favour nor be dependent on anything but sincere kindness. But at last she was trembling on a precipice from the brink of which she besought him to rescue her.

To him and to Fetherstonehaugh she was known as Emily Hart; nor, in spite of Greville's advice, would she, or did she, change that name till her wedding. Whence it was assumed is unknown. In the Harvey family there lingered a tradition that " Emma Hart " was born at Southwell, near Biggleswade, and with her mother had served at Ickwell Bury, where she was first seen and painted by Romney. But this is wholly unfounded, though Romney appears to have painted portraits in that house, and it is curious that, about forty years ago, one Robert Hart—still living—was a butler in their service and professed to be in some way related to Lady Hamilton. A guess might be hazarded that " Hart " was derived from the musician of that name who visited Hamilton's house at Naples in 1786 as her old acquaintance. Not one of the parish registers offers any solution through the names of her kindred. The " Emily " became Emma through the artists and the poets, through Romney and Hayley.

It is " Emly Hart's " pleading and pathetic note, then, that Charles Greville still holds in his fastidious hands on this winter morning. With a glance at his statues, specimens, and the repaired Venus, and possibly with a pang at the thought of the plight to which this " modern piece of *virtu* " was reduced, he sits down most deliberately to compose his answer. How deliberately, is shown by the fact that of this letter he kept a " pressed copy " done in the ink just invented by James Watt; it was a minute of semi-official importance. The letter is long, and extracts will suffice; it will be gathered that he was more prig than profligate, and he had evidently formed the delightful design of being her mentor:—

"My dear Emily,—I do not make apologies for Sir H.'s behaviour to you, and altho' I advised you to deserve his esteem by your good conduct, I own I never expected better from him. It was your duty to deserve good treatment, and it gave me great concern to see you imprudent the first time you came to G., from the country, as the same conduct was repeated when you was last in town, I began to despair of your happiness. To prove to you that I do not accuse you falsely, I only mention five guineas and half a guinea for coach. But, my dear Emily, as you seem quite miserable now, I do not mean to give you uneasiness, but comfort, and tell you that I will forget your faults and bad conduct to Sir H. and myself, and will not repent my good humor if I find that you have learned by experience to value yourself, and endeavor to preserve your friends by good conduct and affection. I will now answer your last letter. You tell me you think your friends look cooly on you, it is therefore time to leave them: but it is necessary for you to decide some points *before* you come to town. You are sensible that for the next three months your situation will not admit of a giddy life, if you wished it. . . . After you have told me that Sir H. gave you barely money to get to your friends, and has never answered one letter since, and neither provides for you nor takes any notice of you, it might appear laughing at you to advise you to make Sir H. more kind and attentive. I do not think a great deal of time should be lost, for I have never seen a woman clever enough to keep a man who was tired of her. But it is a great deal more for me to *advise you* never to see him again, and to write only to inform him of your determination. You must, however, do either the one or the other. . . . You may

easily see, my dearest Emily, why it is absolutely necessary for this point to be completely settled *before I can*
move one step.   If you love Sir H. you should not give
him up. . . . But besides this, my Emily, I would not
be troubled with your connexions (excepting your
mother) and with Sir H.('s) friends for the universe.
My advice then is to take a steady resolution. . . . I
shall then be free to dry up the tears of my lovely
Emily and to give her comfort.   If you do not forfeit
my esteem perhaps my Emily may be happy.   You
know I have been so by avoiding the vexation which
frequently   arises   from   ingratitude   and   caprice.
Nothing but your letter and your distress could incline
me to alter my system, but remember I never will give
up my peace, or continue my connexion one moment
after my confidence is betray'd.   If you should come
to town and take my advice . . . You should part
with your maid and take another *name*.   By degrees
I would get you a new set of acquaintances, and by
keeping your own secret, and no one about you having
it in their power to betray you, I may expect to see you
respected and admired.   Thus far as relates to yourself.   As to the child . . . its mother shall obtain it
kindness from me, and it shall never want.   I inclose
you some money; do not throw it away.   You may
send some presents when you arrive in town, but do
not be on the road without some money *to spare* in
case you should be fatigued and wish to take your time.
I will send Sophy anything she wishes for. . . . God
bless you, my dearest lovely girl; take your determination and let me hear from you once more.   Adieu, my
dear Emily." [1]

And with this salutation Greville folds his paper
with precision and addresses it, in the complacent belief that it is irresistible.   Truly an impeccable shep-

[1] Morrison MS. 114, January 10, 1782.

herd of lost sheep, a prodigious preacher to runagates continuing in scarceness; a Mr. Barlow-Rochester with a vengeance! And yet real goodwill underlies the guardedness of his disrespectable sermon. As, however, he sinks back in his chair, and plumes himself on the *communiqué*, it never strikes him for an instant that this wild and unfortunate girl is quite capable of distancing her tutor and of swaying larger destinies than his. His main and constant object was never to appear ridiculous. So absurd a forecast would have irretrievably grotesqued him in his own eyes and in those of his friends. His attitude towards women appears best from his reflections nearly five years later, which read like a page of La Rochefoucauld tied up with red tape:—

". . . With women, I observe they have only resource in Art, and there is to them no interval between plain ground and the precipice; and the springs of action are so much in the extreme of sublime and low, that no absolute dependence can be given by·men. It is for this reason I always have anticipated cases to prepare their mind to reasonable conduct, and it will always have its impression, altho' they will fly at the mere mention of truth if it either hurts their pride or their intrest, and the latter has much more rarely weight with a young woman than the former; *and therefore it is like playing a trout to keep up pride to make them despise meaness, and not to retain the bombast which would render the man who gave way to it the air of a dupe and a fool.* It requires much conduct to steer properly, but it is to be done when a person is handsome, and has a good heart; *but to do it without hurting their feelings requires constant attention; it is not in the moment of irritation or passion that advice has effect;* it is in the moment of reason and good nature. It reduces itself to simple subjects; *and when a woman can see more than one alternative of comfort or despair, of attention and desertion, they can take a line."* [1]

Thus Greville—the prudent psychologist of womankind and the nice moralist of the immoral. His metaphor of the " trout " must have appealed to that keen fisherman, his " dear Hamilton." Greville angled for " disinterested " hearts with a supple rod. His " system " was to attach friendship rather than to rivet affection; to " play " a woman's heart in the quick stream of credulous emotion past the perilous eddies of headlong impulse with the bait of self-esteem, till it could be safely landed in a basket, to be afterwards transferred for the fish's own benefit to a friend. If the trout refused thus to be landed, it must be dropped into the depths of its own froward will; but the sportsman could at least console himself by the thought that, as sportsman, he had done his duty and observed the rules of his game. Greville was already contemplating a less expensive shrine for his minerals and old masters. He was anxious to be quit of Portman Square, and a light purse proverbially makes a heavy heart.

He must be left calculating his chances, while his Dulcinea books places in the Chester coach, weeps for joy, and kisses her Don Quixote's billet with impetuous gratitude.

[1] Morrison MS. 156, November(?) 1786.

CHAPTER II

March 1782—*August* 1784

A GIRLISH voice, fresh as the spring morning on Paddington Green outside, with its rim of tall elms, and clear as the warbling of their birds, rings out through the open window with its bright burden of " Banish sorrow until to-morrow." The music-master has just passed through the little garden-wicket, the benefactor will soon return from town, and fond Emma will please him by her progress. Nature smiles without and within; " Mrs. Cadogan " bustles over the spring-cleaning below, and to-morrow the radiant housewife will take her shilling's-worth of hackney coach as far as Romney's studio in Cavendish Square. She is very happy; it is almost as if she were a young bride; perchance, who knows, one day she *may* be Greville's wife. In her heart she is so now; and yet at times that hateful past will haunt her. It shall be buried with the winter; " I will have it so," as she was to write of another matter. And is it not

> " Spring-time, the only pretty ring time,
> When birds do sing hey ding a-ding a-ding"?

Edgware Row a hundred and twenty-three years ago was the reverse of what it looks to-day. Its site, now a network of slums, was then a country prospect. It fronted the green sward of a common, abutting on the inclosure of a quaint old church, in a vault of

which, when the crowning blow fell, Lady Hamilton
was to lay the remains of her devoted mother. That
church had for many years been associated with artists,
singers, and musicians, British and foreign. Here in
March, 1733, the apprentice Hogarth had wedded Jane
Thornhill, his master's daughter. Here lay buried
Matthew Dubourg, the court violinist; and Emma
could still read his epitaph :—

> "Tho' sweet as Orpheus thou couldst bring
> Soft pleadings from the trembling string,
> Unmoved the King of Terror stands
> Nor owns the magic of thy hands."

Here, too, lay buried George Barret, "an eminent
painter and worthy man." Here later were to lie Lolli,
the violinist; the artists Schiavonetti and Sandby; Nol-
lekens and Banks the sculptors; Alexander Geddes the
scholar; Merlin the mechanic; Caleb Whiteford the
wine-merchant wit; and his great patron, John Henry
Petty, Marquis of Lansdowne, who descends to history as the Earl of Shelburne. Here once resided the
charitable Denis Chirac, jeweller to Queen Anne.
Here, too, were voluntary schools and the lying-in hospital. The canal, meandering as far as Bolingbroke's
Hayes in one direction, and Lady Sarah Child's Nor-
wood in the other, was not finished till 1801, when
Lady Hamilton may have witnessed its opening ceremony.

Greville, still saddled with his town abode, at once
economised. The Edgware Row establishment was
modest in both senses of the word. He brought repu-
table friends to the house, and a few neighbouring ladies
seem to have called. The household expenses did not
exceed some £150 a year. Emma's own yearly allowance was only about £50, and she lived well within it.
Her mother was a clever manager, whose services the
thrifty prodigal appreciated. The existing household

accounts in Emma's handwriting only start in 1784, but from them some idea may be formed of what they were in the two years preceding. They belong to the Hamilton papers inherited by Greville in 1803, and they were evidently deemed worthy of preservation both by nephew and uncle.

It is clear from these accounts that all was now " retrenchment and reform "; that all was not plenty, is equally apparent. But Emma was more than satisfied with her lot. Had not her knight-errant (or erring) dropped from heaven? From the first she regarded him as a superior being, and by 1784 she came to love him with intense tenderness; indeed she idealised him as much as others were afterwards to idealise her.

All was not yet, however, wholly peace. Her character was far from being ideal, quite apart from the circumstances which, by comparison, she viewed as almost conjugal. Her petulant temper remained unquelled long after her tamer undertook to " break it in," and there were already occasional " scenes " against her own interest. Yet how soon and warmheartedly she repented may be gathered from her letters two years onwards, when she was sea-bathing at Parkgate: " So, my dearest Greville," pleads one of them, " don't think on my past follies, think on my good, little as it has been." And, before, " Oh! Greville, when I think on your goodness, your tender kindness, my heart is so full of gratitude that I want words to express it. But I have one happiness in view, which I am determined to practice, and that is eveness of temper and steadin[e]ss of mind. For endead I have thought so much of your amable goodness when you have been tried to the utmost, that I will, endead I will manege myself, and try to be like Greville. Endead I can never be like him. But I will do all I can towards it, and I am sure you will not desire more. I think if the time would come over again, I would be differant. But it does not matter. There is nothing like bying expearance. I may be happyer for it hereafter, and I will think of the time coming and not of the past, except to make comparrasons, to shew you what alterations there is for the best. . . . O Greville! think on me with kindness! Think on how many happy days weeks and years—I hope—we may yett pass. . . . And endead, did you but know how much I love you, you wou'd freely forgive me any passed quarrels. For I now suffer from them, and one line from you wou'd make me happy. . . . But how am I to make you amends? . . . I will try, I will do my utmost; and I can only regrett that fortune will not put it in my power to make a return for all the kindness and goodness you have showed me."

Conscious of growing gifts, she had chafed by fits and starts at the seclusion of her home—for home it was to her, in her own words, " though never so homely." On one occasion (noted by Pettigrew and John Romney too substantially to admit of its being fiction) Greville took her to Ranelagh, and was annoyed by her bursting into song before an applauding crowd. His displeasure so affected her that on her return she doffed her finery, donned the plainest attire, and, weeping, entreated him to retain her thus or be quit of her. This episode may well have been the source of Romney's picture " The Seamstress."

The accounts omit any mention of amusements, and it must have been Greville alone who (rarely) treated her. She may have seen " Coxe's Museum," and the " balloonists " Lunardi and Sheldon, the Italian at the Pantheon, the Briton in Foley Gardens. She may

have been present, too, when in the new " Marylebone
Gardens " Signor Torre gave one of his firework displays of Mount Etna in eruption. If so, how odd
must she afterwards have thought it, that her husband was to be the leading authority on Italian and
Sicilian volcanoes! But what at once amazed Greville
—the paragon of *nil admirari*—was the transformation
that she seriously set herself to achieve. " She does
not," observed this economist of ease three years later,
" wish for much society, but to retain two or three
creditable acquaintances in the neighbourhood she has
avoided every appearance of giddiness, and prides
herself on the neatness of her person and the good
order of her house; these are habits," he comments,
" both comfortable and convenient to me. She has
vanity and likes admiration; but she connects it so
much with her desire of appearing prudent, that *she is
more pleas'd with accidental admiration than that of
crowds which now distress her*. In short, this habit,
of three or four years' acquiring, is not a caprice, but is
easily to be continued. . . ." " She never has wished
for an improper acquaintance," he adds a month later.
" She has dropt everyone she thought I could except
against, and those of her own choice have been in a
line of prudence and plainness which, tho' I might have
wished for, I could not have proposed to confine her
[to]."

Their visitors seem to have included his brother and
future executor, Colonel the Honourable Robert Fulke-
Greville, with perhaps, too, his kinsmen the Cathcarts;
afterwards, the sedate Banks, a Mr. Tollemache, the
Honourable Heneage Legge, whom we shall find meeting her just before her marriage, and oftener the artist
Gavin Hamilton, Sir William's namesake and kinsman.
He at once put Emma on his " list of favorites," re-
minding him, as she did, of a Roman beauty that he

had once known, but superior to her, he said, in the lines of her beautiful and uncommon mouth. Her main recreation, besides her study to educate herself, were those continual visits to Romney, which indeed assisted it. His *Diaries* contain almost three hundred records of " Mrs. Hart's " sittings during these four years, most of them at an early hour, for Emma, except in illness, was never a late riser. One portrait of her, unmentioned in our previous list, represents her reading the *Gazette* with a startled expression. I have been informed (though at first I thought otherwise) that this is really a likeness of her in the character of Serena reading scandal about herself in the pages of a journal. " While," remarks the sententious John Romney, " she lived under Greville's protection, her conduct was in every way correct, except only in the unfortunate situation in which she happened to be placed by the concurrence of peculiar circumstances such as might perhaps in a certain degree be admitted as an extenuation. . . . Here is a young female of an artless and playful character, of extraordinary Elegance and symmetry of form, of a most beautiful countenance glowing with health and animation, turned upon the wide world. . . . In all Mr. Romney's intercourse with her she was treated with the utmost respect, and her demeanour fully entitled her to it." He adds that she " sat " for the " face " merely and " a slight sketch of the attitude," and that in the " Bacchante " he painted her countenance alone; while Hayley, in his *Life* of the painter, speaks of " the high and constant admiration " with which Romney contemplated not only the " personal " but the " mental endowments of this lady, and the gratitude he felt for many proofs of her friendship," as expressed in his letters. " The talents," he continues, " which nature bestowed on the fair Emma, led her to delight in the two kindred arts of music and painting; in the first she acquired great practical ability; for the second she had exquisite taste, and such expressive powers as could furnish to an historical painter an *inspiring* model for the various characters either delicate or sublime. . . . Her features, like the language of Shakespeare, could exhibit all the gradations of every passion with a most fascinating truth and felicity of expression. Romney delighted in observing the wonderful command she possessed over her eloquent features." He called her his "inspirer." To Romney, as we have already seen, she "first opened her heart." At Romney's she met those literary and artistic lights that urged her native intelligence into imitation. A sketch by Romney of his studio displays her seated as his model for the "Spinstress" by her spinning-wheel. A figure entering and smiling is Greville; of two others seated at a table, the one appealing to her would seem to be Hayley, to whom she always gratefully confessed her obligations.

William Hayley, the "Hermit" of Eartham, the close ally both of Romney and Cowper, must have been far more interesting in his conversation than his books, though his *Triumphs of Temper* created a sensation now difficult to understand. He was a clever, egotistical eccentric, who successively parted from two wives with whom he yet continued to correspond in affectionate friendship. Curiously enough, Hayley's rhymed satirical comedies [1] are much the best of his otherwise stilted verses. He must have remembered Hamilton and Greville when, in one of them, he makes "Mr. Beril" account for his ownership of a lovely Greek statue:

[1] *The Happy Prescription* (1784) and *The Two Connoisseurs* are brilliant *vers de société*. For Horace Walpole's poor opinion of his authorship, cf. *Letters*, vol. viii. pp. 235, 236, 251.

> "I owe it to chance, to acknowledge the truth,
> And a princely and brave Neapolitan youth,
> Whom I luckily saved in a villainous strife
> From the dagger of jealousy aimed at his life:"

and when his " Bijou " ironically observes to " Varnish " :

> "I protest your remark is ingenious and new,
> You have gusto in morals as well as *virtu*:"

His unfamiliar sonnet on Romney's " Cassandra " may be here cited, since it may have suggested to Greville his estimate of Emma—" piece of modern *virtu* " :

> "Ye fond idolaters of ancient art,
>   Who near Parthenope with curious toil,
> Forcing the rude sulphureous rocks to part,
>   Draw from the greedy earth her buried spoil
> Of antique entablature; and from the toil
>   Of time restoring some fair form, acquire
> A fancied jewel, know 'tis but a foil
>   To this superior gem of richer fire.
> In Romney's tints behold the Trojan maid,
>   See beauty blazing in prophetic ire.
> From palaces engulphed could earth retire,
>   And show thy works, Apelles, undecay'd,
> E'en thy Campaspe would not dare to vie
> With the wild splendour of Cassandra's eye."

In a late letter to Lady Hamilton the poet assures her that an unpublished ode was wholly inspired by her, and there are traces of her influence even in his poor tragedies. But since " Serena " influenced her often, it may be of interest to single out a few lines from the *Triumphs of Temper* (composed some years before its author first met her) as likelier to have arrested her attention than his triter commonplaces about " spleen " and " cheerfulness " :

> "Free from ambitious pride and envious care,
> To love and to be loved was all her prayer."

"Th' imperishable wealth of sterling love."

" . . . She's everything by starts and nothing long,
But in the space of one revolving hour
Flies thro all states of poverty and power,
All forms on whom her veering mind can pitch,
Sultana, Gipsy, Goddess, nymph, and witch.
At length, her soul with Shakespeare's magic fraught,
The wand of Ariel fixed her roving thought."

And

"But mild Serena scorn'd the prudish play
To wound warm love with frivolous delay;
Nature's chaste child, not Affection's slave,
The heart she meant to give, she frankly gave."

The August of 1782 brought about an event decisive
for Emma's future—the death of the *first* Lady Hamilton, the Ambassador's marriage with whom in 1757
had been mainly one of convenience, though it had
proved one also of comfort and esteem. She was a
sweet, tranquil soul of rapt holiness, what the Germans
call "*Eine schöne Seele,*" and she worshipped the very
earth that her light-hearted husband, far nearer to it
than she was, trod on. He had set out as a young
captain of foot, who, in his own words, had "known
the pinch of poverty"; but during the whole twenty-
five years of their union she had never once reproached
him, and had dedicated to him all "that long disease"
she called "her life." So far, though intimate with
the young Sicilian King and friendly with the Queen,
Hamilton had weighed little in diplomacy. In a
sprightly letter to the Earl of Dartmouth some six
years earlier, he observes: "It is singular but certainly
true that I am become more a *ministre de famille* at
this court than ever were the ministers of France,
Spain, and Vienna. Whenever there is a good shoot-
ing-party H.S. Majesty is pleased to send for me, and
for some months past I have had the honour of dining

with him twice or three times a week, nay sometimes
I have breakfasted, dined, and supped . . . in their
private party without any other minister." He next
descants on his exceptional opportunities of helping the
English in Naples. He hits off a certain Lady Boyd
among them as " Like Mr. Wilkes, but she has [such]
a way of pushing forward that face of hers and filling
every muscle of it with good humour, that her homeli-
ness is forgot in a moment "; and he concludes with the
usual complaint that—unlike his predecessor, Sir William Lynch—he has not yet been made " Privy Coun-
cillor." So dissatisfied was he that in 1774 he had
tried hard on one of his periodical home visits to exchange his ambassadorship at Naples for one at
Madrid; and hitherto science, music, pictures, archæol-
ogy, sport, and gallantry had occupied his constant
leisure—indeed he was more of a Consul than of an
Ambassador. General Acton's advent, however, as
Minister of War and Marine in 1779 proved a passing
stimulus to his dormant energy. If a dawdler, he was
never a trifler; and he was uniformly courteous and
kind-hearted. His frank geniality recommended him
as bear-leader to the many English visitors who flocked
annually to Naples, often stumbled lightly into scrapes
that caused him infinite trouble, and prompted his
humorous regret that Magna Charta contained no
clause forbidding Britons to emigrate. It was not till
Emma dawned on his horizon that he woke up in
earnest to the duties of his office. His wife made
every effort, so far as her feeble health admitted, to
grace his hospitalities. She shared his own taste for
music, and sang to the harpsichord before the Court of
Vienna. The sole regret of her unselfish piety was
that he remained a worldling. She studied to spare
him every vexation and intrusion; and while he pursued his long rambles, sporting, artistic, or sentimental,

she sat at home praying for her elderly Pierrot's eternal welfare. Her example dispensed with precepts, and hoped to win her wanderer back imperceptibly. How little she deserved the caricature of her as merely " a raw-boned Scotchwoman " may be gleaned from some of the last jottings in her diary and her last letters to her husband :—

" How tedious are the hours I pass in the absence of the beloved of my heart, and how tiresome is every scene to me. There is the chair in which he used to sit, I find him not there, and my heart feels a pang, and my foolish eyes overflow with tears. The number of years we have been married, instead of diminishing my love have increased it to that degree and wound it up with my existence in such a manner that it cannot alter. How strong are the efforts I have made to conquer my feelings, but in vain. . . . No one but those who have felt it can know the miserable anxiety of an undivided love. When he is present, every object has a different appearance; when he is absent, how lonely, how isolated I feel. . . . I return home, and there the very dog stares me in the face and seems to ask for its beloved master. . . . Oh! blessed Lord God and Saviour, be Thou mercifully pleas'd to guard and protect him in all dangers and in all situations. Have mercy upon us both, oh Lord, and turn our hearts to Thee."

" A few days, nay a few hours . . . may render me incapable of writing to you. . . . But how shall I express my love and tenderness to you, dearest of earthly blessings. My only attachment to this world has been my love to you, and you are my only regret in leaving it. My heart has followed your footsteps where ever you went, and you have been the source of all my joys. I would have preferred beggary with you to kingdoms without you, but all this must have an end—forget and forgive my faults and remember me with kindness. I entreat you not to suffer me to be shut up after I am dead till it is absolutely necessary. Remember the promise you have made me that your bones should lie by mine when God shall please to call you, and leave directions in your will about it."

That promise was kept, and the man of the world sleeps by the daughter of heaven, re-united in the Pembrokeshire vault. A possibly adopted daughter—Cecilia—who is mentioned in the greetings of early correspondents, had died some seven years before.

Could any Calypso replace such pure devotion? Yet Calypsos there had been already—among their number the divorced lady who became Margravine of Anspach, the " sweet little creature *qui a l'honneur de me plaire,*" and whom he pitied; a " Madame Tschudy "; a " Lady A.," contrasted by Greville in 1785 with Emma; and, perhaps platonically, those gifted artists Diana Beauclerk, once Lady Bolingbroke, and Mrs. Damer, who was to sculpture one of the two busts of Nelson done from the life. In England as well as Naples flirtation was the order of the day. Yet about Sir William there must have been a charm of demeanour, a calm of ease and good nature, and a certain worldly unselfishness which could fasten such spiritual love more surely than the love profane. He was a sincere worshipper of beauty, both in art and nature; while Goethe himself respected his discriminating taste. He was a Stoic-Epicurean, a " philosopher." His confession of faith and outlook upon existence are well outlined in a letter to Emma of 1792 which deserves attention. " My study of antiquities has kept me in constant thought of the perpetual fluctuation of everything. The whole art is, really, to live all the *days* of our life; and not, with anxious care, disturb the sweetest hour that life affords—which is.

the present. Admire the Creator, and all His works to us incomprehensible; and do all the good you can upon earth; and take the chance of eternity without dismay."

Absent since 1778, he came over at the close of 1782 to bury his wife. It is just possible that even then he may have caught a flying glimpse of the girl whom he was to style two years later " the fair tea-maker of Edgware Row." Greville, of course, was punctual in condolence: " You have no idea how shocked I was. . . . Yet when I consider the long period of her indisposition and the weakness of her frame, I ought to have been prepared to hear it. I am glad that her last illness was not attended with extraordinary suffering, and I know you so well that I am sure you will think with affection and regret, as often as the blank which must be felt after 25 years society shall call her to your memory, and it will not be a small consolation that to the last you shew'd that kindness and attention to her which she deserved. *I have often quoted you for that conduct which few have goodness of heart or principle to imitate.*" He had hoped to hasten to his dearest Hamilton's side in the crisis of affliction, but his brother's affairs, the troubles of trusteeships, and the bequest by Lord Seaforth of a rare cameo, alas! intervened, and therefore he could not come. So Mount Vesuvius-Hamilton hurried to Mahomet-Greville, and doubtless, after a little *virtu* and more business, returned for the autumn season at Naples and his winter sport at Caserta.

But meanwhile Greville grew ruffled and out-at-elbows. He was once more member for his family borough. He needed larger emolument, yet the coalition was on the wane. For a brief interval it returned, and Greville breathed again, pocketing a small promotion in the general scramble for office. In 1783, however, the great Pitt entered on his long reign, and Greville's heart sank once more. His post, however, was confirmed, despite his conscientious disapproval of reforms for England and for Ireland, and new India bills in the interval. Still, his tastes were so various that even now he pondered if, after all, an heiress of *ton* (none of your *parvenues*) were not the only way out; and, pending decision, he went on collecting crystals, exchanging pictures of saints, and lecturing Emma on the *convenances*—perhaps the least extravagant and most edifying pastime of all. Every August he toured in Warwickshire after his own, and to Milford and Pembrokeshire after his uncle's affairs (for Milford was being " developed "); nor was he the man to begrudge his *élève* a few weeks' change in the dull season during his absence. In 1784 she was to require it more than usual, for sea-baths had been ordered, while her first thought was then to be for her " little Emma," now being tended at Hawarden.

In the early summer of this very year Sir William Hamilton had reappeared as widower, and crossed the threshold of Edgware Row to the flurry, doubtless, of the little handmaidens, whose successors, " Molly Dring " and " Nelly Gray," were so regularly paid their scanty wages, as registered in the surviving accounts.

The courtly connoisseur was enraptured. Never had he beheld anything more Greek, any one more naturally accomplished, more uncommon. What an old slyboots had this young nephew been these last two years, to have concealed this hidden treasure while he detailed everything else in his letters! The demure rogue, then, was a suburban *amateur* with a vengeance! The antiquarian-Apollo, carrying with him a new work on Etruscan vases, and a new tract on volcanic phenomena, flattered himself that here were volcanoes and vases indeed. Here were Melpomene and Thalia, and Terpsichore and Euterpe and Venus, all combined and breathing. Did he not boast the secret of perpetual youth? After all, he was only fifty-four, and he looked ten years younger than his age. He would at least make the solemn youngster jealous. Not that he was covetous; his interest was that of a father, a collector, an uncle. The mere lack of a ring debarred him from being her uncle in reality. " My uncle," she should call him.

Greville's amusement was not quite unclouded; he laughed, but laughed uneasily. To begin with, he believed himself his uncle's heir, but as yet 'twas " not so nominated in the bond." Sir William might well remarry. There was Lord Middleton's second daughter in Portman Square, a twenty thousand pounder, weighing on the scales, a fish claimed by Greville's own rod. But with others, the Court of Naples, an alliance with a widower kinsman of the Hamiltons, the Athols, the Abercorns, and the Grahams, enriched too by recent death, were solidities that might well outweigh his paltry pittance of six hundred a year. And *if* the widower re-married?—As for Emma, it was of course absurd to consider her. She adored her Greville, and should uncle William choose to play light father in this little farce, he could raise no objection.

Emma herself felt flattered that one so celebrated and learned should deign to be just a nice new friend. He was so amiable and attentive; so discerning of her gifts; so witty too, and full of anecdote. This was no musty scholar, but a good-natured man of the very wide world, far wider than her pent-in corner of it. Indeed, he was a " dear." And then he laughed so heartily when she mimicked Greville's buckram brother, or that rich young coxcomb Willoughby, who had wooed her in vain already; no giddy youths for her. Was not her own matchless Greville a man of accomplishments, a bachelor of arts and sciences, a master of sentences? The uncle was worthy of the nephew, and so she was " his oblidged humble servant, or affectionate " niece " Emma," whichever he " liked the best."

And in her heart of hearts already lurked a little scheme. Her child, the child to whom Greville had been so suddenly, so gently kind, and after which she yearned, was with her grandmother. After she had taken the tiny companion to Parkgate, and bathed it there, why should not her divinity permit the mother to bring it home for good to Edgware Row? It would form a new and touching tie between them. The plan must not be broached till she could report on " little Emma's " progress, but surely then he would not have the heart to deny her.

Some evidence allows the guess that she had confided her desire to Sir William, and that he had favoured and forwarded her suit with Greville.

And so she left the smoke and turmoil, hopeful and trustful. Mother and child would at length be re-united under purer skies and by the wide expanse of sea. All the mother within her stirred and called aloud; her heart was ready to " break " at the summons. Fatherly Sir William saw her off as proxy for her absent Greville, whom he was to join, the happy man. " Tell Sir William everything you can," she wrote immediately, " and tell him I am sorry our situation prevented me from giving him a kiss, . . . but I will give him one, and entreat it if he will accept it. Ask him how I looked, and let him say something kind to me when you write."—" Pray, my dear Greville, do lett me come home as soon as you can;

. . . indeed I have no pleasure or happiness. I wish I could not think on you; but if I was the greatest lady in the world, I should not be happy from you; so don't lett me stay long."

Her first Parkgate letters, in the form of diaries, speak for themselves. After she had fetched away little Emma "Hart" from her grandmother's at Hawarden, she stopped at Chester. She had fixed on Abergele, but it proved too distant, fashionable, and dear. "High Lake" (Hoylake) was too uncomfortable; it had "only 3 houses," and not one of them "fit for a Christian." With her "poor Emma" she had bidden farewell to all her friends; she had taken her from "a good home"; she hoped she would prove worthy of his "goodness to her, and to her mother." Her recipe-book had been forgotten;—"parting with you made me so unhappy."—" My dear Greville, don't be angry, but I gave my granmother 5 guineas, for she had laid some [money] out on her, and I would not take her awhay shabbily. But Emma shall pay you. . . . My dear Greville, I wish I was with you. God bless you!"

By mid-June she was installed " in the house of a Laidy, whose husband is at sea. She and her granmother live together, and we board with her at present. . . . The price is high, but they don't lodge anybody without boarding; and as it is comfortable, decent, and quiet, I thought it wou'd not ruin us, till I could have your oppionon, which I hope to have freely and without restraint, as, believe me, you will give it to one who will allways be happy to follow it, lett it be what it will; *as I am sure you wou'd not lead me wrong*. And though my little temper may have been sometimes high, believe me, I have allways thought you right in the end when I have come to reason. I bathe, and find the water very soult. Here is a good many laidys batheing, but I have no society with them, as it is best not. So pray, my dearest Greville, write soon, and tell me what to do, as I will do just what you think proper; *and tell me what to do with the child.* For she is a great romp, and I can hardly master her. . . . She is tall, [has] good eys and brows, and as to lashes, she will be passible; but she has overgrown all her cloaths. I am makeing and mending all as I can for her. . . . Pray, my dear Greville, do lett me come home, as soon as you can; for I am all most broken-hearted being from you. . . . You don't know how much I love you, and your behaiver to me, when we parted, was so kind, Greville, I don't know what to do. . . ." And her next epistle seems to echo under circumstances far removed the voice of the first Lady Hamilton:—" How teadous does the time pass awhay till I hear from you. Endead I should be miserable if I did not recollect on what happy terms we parted— parted, yess, but to meet again with tenfould happiness. . . . Would you think it, Greville? Emma—the wild, unthinking Emma, is a grave, thoughtful phylosopher. 'Tis true, Greville, and I will convince you I am, when I see you. But how I am runing on. I say nothing abbout this guidy, wild girl of mine. What shall *we* do with her, Greville? . . . Wou'd you believe, on Sattarday we had a little quarel, . . . and I did slap her on her hands, and when she came to kiss me and make it up, I took her on my lap and cried. Pray, do you blame me or not? Pray tell me. Oh, Greville, you don't know how I love her. Endead I do. *When she comes and looks in my face and calls me ' mother,' endead I then truly am a mother,* for all the mother's feelings rise at once, and tels me I am or ought to be a mother, *for she has a wright to my protection;* and she shall have it as long as I can, and I will do all in my power to prevent her falling into the error her

poor miserable mother fell into. But why do I say
miserable? Am not I happy abbove any of my sex,
at least in my situation? Does not Greville love me,
or at least like me? Does not he protect me? Does
not he provide for me? Is not he a father to my child?
Why do I call myself miserable? No, it was a mistake, and I will be happy, chearful and kind, and do
all my poor abbility will lett me, to return the fatherly
goodness and protection he has shewn. Again, my
dear Greville, the recollection of past scenes brings
tears in my eyes. But the[y] are tears of happiness.
To think of your goodness is too much. But once for
all, Greville, I will be gratefull. Adue. It is near
bathing time, and I must lay down my pen, and I won't
finish till I see when the post comes, whether there is a
letter. He comes in abbout one o'clock. I hope to
have a letter to-day. . . . I am in hopes I shall be
very well. . . . But, Greville, I am oblidged to give a
shilling a day for the bathing horse and whoman, and
twopence a day for the dress. It is a great expense,
and it fretts me when I think of it. . . . At any rate
it is better than paying the docter. But wright your
oppinion truly, and tell me what to do. Emma is crying because I won't come and bathe. So Greville, adue
till after I have dipt. May God bless you, my dearest Greville, and believe me, faithfully, *affectionately,
and truly yours only.*"—" And no letter from my dear
Greville. Why, my dearest G., what is the reason you
don't wright? You promised to wright before I left
Hawarden. . . . Give my dear kind love and compliments to Pliney,[1] and tell him I put you under his care,
and he must be answereble for you to me, wen I see
him. . . . Say everything you can to him for me, and
tell him I shall always think on him with gratitude,
and remember him with pleasure, and shall allways

[1] Sir W. Hamilton.

regret loesing [h]is good comppany. Tell him I wish him every happiness this world can afford him, and that I will pray for him and bless him as long as I live. . . . Pray, my dear Greville, lett me come home soon. I have been 3 weeks, and if I stay a fortnight longer, that will be 5 weeks, you know; and then the expense is above 2 guineas a week with washing . . . and everything. . . ." "With what impatience do I sett down to wright till I see the postman. But sure I shall have a letter to-day. Can you, Greville—no, you can't—have forgot your poor Emma allready? Tho' I am but a few weeks absent from you, my heart will not one moment leave you. I am allways thinking of you, and cou'd allmost fancy I hear you, see you; . . . don't you remember how you promised? Don't you recollect what you said at parting? how you shou'd be happy to see me again?"

A belated answer arrived at last; Emma was very grateful. But this was not the letter for which she looked. What she wanted was omniscience's per-mission for "little Emma" to share their home, to let her be a mother indeed. After a week two "scold-ing" notes were his reply. "Little Emma" in Edg-ware Row was not on Greville's books at all. He would charge himself with her nurture elsewhere, but the child must be surrendered; he certainly knew how to "play" his "trout." Emma meekly kissed her master's rod. Greville being Providence, resignation was wisdom as well as duty. She was not allowed to remain a mother:—

"I was very happy, my dearest Greville, to hear from you as your other letter vex'd me; you scolded me so. But it is over, and I forgive you. . . . You don't know, my dearest Greville, what a pleasure I have to think that my poor Emma will be comfortable and happy . . . and if she does but turn out well, what a happyness it will be. And I hope she will for your sake. I will teach her to pray for you as long as she lives; and if she is not grateful and good it won't be my fault. But what you say is very true: a bad disposition may be made good by good example, and Greville wou'd not put her anywheer to have a bad one. I come into your whay athinking; hollidays spoils children. It takes there attention of[f] from there scool, it gives them a bad habbit. When they have been a month and goes back this does not pleas them, and that is not wright, and the[y] do nothing but think when the[y] shall go back again. Now Emma will never expect what she never had. But I won't think. All my happiness now is Greville, and to think that he loves me. . . . I have said all I have to say about Emma, yet only she gives her duty. . . . I have no society with anybody but the mistress of the house, and her mother and sister. The latter is a very genteel yong lady, good-nattured, and does everything to pleas me. But still I wou'd rather be at home, if you was there. I follow the old saying, home is home though 'tis ever so homely. . . . *P.S.*—. . . I bathe Emma, and she is very well and grows. Her hair will grow very well on her forehead, and I don't think her nose will be very snub. Her eys is blue and pretty. But she don't speak through her nose, but she speaks countryfied, but she will forget it. We squable sometimes; still she is fond of me, and endead I love her. For she is sensible. So much for Beauty. Adue, I long to see you." [1]

Empowered by the Sultan of Edgware Row, the two Emmas, to their great but fleeting joy, were suf-

[1] Morrison MS. 128. There is, of course, no conclusive evidence for identifying "little Emma" with the nameless child born early in 1782, but I can see no reason otherwise, or for supposing an earlier "Emma."

fered to return in the middle of July. Sir William and his nephew were still on their provincial tour, when Emma, who fell ill again in town, thus addressed him for the last time before his own return. It shall be our closing excerpt:—

" I received your kind letter last night, and, my dearest Greville, I want words to express to you how happy it made me. For I thought I was like a lost sheep, and everybody had forsook me. I was eight days confined to my room and very ill, but am, thank God, very well now, and a great deal better for your kind instructing letter, and own the justice of your remarks. You shall have your appartment to yourself, you shall read, wright, or sett still, just as you pleas; for I shall think myself happy to be under the seam roof with Greville, and do all I can to make it agreable, without disturbing him in any pursuits that he can follow, to employ himself in at home or else whare. For your absence has taught me that I ought to think myself happy if I was within a mile of you; so as I cou'd see the place as contained you I shou'd think myself happy abbove my sphear. So, my dear G., come home. . . . You shall find me good, kind, gentle, and affectionate, and everything you wish me to do I will do. For I will give myself a fair trial, and follow your advice, for I allways think it wright. . . . Don't think, Greville, this is the wild fancy of a moment's consideration. It is not. I have thoughroly considered everything in my confinement, *and say nothing now but what I shall practice.* . . . I have a deal to say to you when I see you. Oh, Greville, to think it is 9 weeks since I saw you. I think I shall die with the pleasure of seeing you. . . . I am all ways thinking of your goodness. . . . Emma is very well, and is allways wondering why you don't come home. She sends her duty to you. . . . Pray, pray come as soon as you come to town. Good by, God bless you! Oh, how I long to see you."

It should be at once remarked that Greville conscientiously performed his promise. He put "little Emma" to a good school, and several traces of her future survive. Meanwhile, having won his point, and having also "prepared" her mind for another separation, of which she little dreamed, he came back to his bower of thankful worship and submissive meekness. He can scarcely have played often with the child, whose benefactor he was—a dancing-master, so to speak, of beneficence, ever standing in the first position of correct deportment. In August he bade farewell to his indulgent uncle, whom, indeed, he had "reason" to remember with as much "gratitude and affection" as Emma did. Romney was commissioned to paint her as the "Bacchante" for the returning Ambassador, who had reassured his nephew about the distant future. He had appointed him his heir, and offered to stand security if he needed to borrow. He had also joined Greville's other friends in advising him to bow to the inevitable and console his purse with an heiress. Whether he also had already contemplated an exchange seems more than doubtful. But the secretive Greville had already begun to harbour an idea, soon turned into a plan, and perpetually justified as a piece of benevolent unselfishness. While the ship bears the unwedded uncle to softer climes and laxer standards, while Greville, with a sigh of relief, pores over his accounts, we may well exclaim of these two knowing and obliging materialists, *par nobile fratrum*—a noble brace of brothers indeed!

CHAPTER III

To March, 1786

" **I** REALY do not feel myself in a situation to accept favours." " I depend on you for some cristals in lavas, etc., from Sicily." These sentences from two long epistles to his uncle at the close of 1784 are keynotes to Greville's tune of mind. With the new year he became rather more explicit :— " Emma is very grateful for your remembrance. Her picture shall be sent by the first ship—I wish Romney yet to mend the dog.[1] She certainly is much improved since she has been with me. She has none of the bad habits which giddiness and inexperience encouraged, and which bad choice of company introduced. . . . I am sure she is attached to me, or she would not have refused the offers which I know have been great; and such is her spirit that on the least slight or expression of my being tired or burthened by her, I am sure she would not only give up the connexion, but would not even accept a farthing for future assistance."

Here let us pause a moment. In the " honest bargain " shortly to be struck after much obliquity, Greville's shabbiness consists, if we reflect on the prevailing tone of his age and set, not so much in the disguised transfer—a mean trick in itself—as in the fact

---

[1] In the first picture of the " Bacchante." Some trace of a goat as well as of a dog figures in all the known versions.

that, while he had no reproach to make and was avow-
edly more attached to her than ever, he practised upon
the very disinterestedness and fondness that he praised.
Had he been unable to rely on them with absolute confidence, so wary a strategist would scarcely have ventured on the attempt, since his future prospects largely
depended on her never disadvantaging him with Sir
William.   That she never did so, even in the first burst
of bitter disillusion; that she always, and zealously,
advocated his interests, redounds to her credit and
proves her magnanimity.   A revengeful woman, whose
love and self-love had been wounded to the quick,
might have ruined him, as the censor of Paddington
was well aware.   That he continued to approve his part
in these delicate negotiations is shown by the fact of
preserving these letters after they came into his possession as his uncle's executor. He never ceased to protest that his motives in the transaction were for her own
ultimate good.   He was not callous, but he was jesuit-
ical.   Let him pursue his scattered hints further :—

"This is another part of my situation.   If I was independent I should think so little of any other connexion that I never would marry.   I have not an idea
of it at present, but if any proper opportunity offer'd
I shou'd be much harassed, not know how to manage,
or how to fix Emma to her satisfaction; and to forego
the reasonable plan which you and my friends advised is not right.   I am not quite of an age to retire from bustle, and to retire into distress and poverty
is worse.   I can keep on here creditably this winter.
The offer I made of my pictures is to get rid of the
Humberston engagements which I told you of.   I have
a £1000 ready and 1000 to provide.   I therefore am
making money.   If Ross will take in payment from
me my bond with your security, I shall get free from
Humberston affairs entirely, and be able to give them

up. It is indifferent to me whether what I value is in
your keeping or mine. I will deposit with you gems
which you shall value at above that sum. . . . It will
be on that condition I will involve you, for favor I take
as favor, and business as business."

His subsequent communications dole out the growing plot by degrees and approaches; he works by sap
and mine. In March, 1785, after discussing politics
at large, he doubts if his uncle's "heart or his feet"
are "the lightest." He compliments him on his energy
in sport, flirtation, and friendship—"quests" not "in-
compatible" in "a good heart." He moots his design
in the light of Hamilton's welfare. "He must be a
very interested friend indeed who does not sincerely
wish everything that can give happiness to a friend."
He is convinced that each of them can sincerely judge
for the other. He does not, of course, venture to
"suppose" an "experiment" for the diplomatist; but
he himself has made the happiest though a "limited"
experiment, which, however, "*from poverty . . . cannot last*"; his poverty but not his will consents. And
then he opens the scheme. "*If you did not chuse a
wife, I wish the tea-maker of Edgware Rowe was
yours, if I could without banishing myself from a visit
to Naples. I do not know how to part with what I
am not tired with. I do not know how to go on, and
I give her every merit of prudence and moderation and
affection. She shall never want,* and if I decide sooner
than I am forced to stop by necessity, it will be that I
may give her part of my pittance; and, if I do so it
must be by sudden resolution and by putting it out of
her power to refuse it for I know her disinterestedness
to be such that she will rather encounter any difficulty
than distress me. I should not write to you thus, if I
did not think *you* seem'd as partial as I am to her. She
would not hear at once of any change, and from no

one that was not liked by her. I think I could secure
on her near £100 a year. It is more than in justice
to all I can do; but with parting with part of my *virtu*,
I can secure it to her and content myself with the remainder. I think· *you* might settle another on her.
. . . I am not a dog in the manger. If I could go on
I would never make this arrangement, but to be reduced to a standstill and involve myself in distress
further than I could extricate myself, and then to be
unable to provide for her at all, would make me miserable from thinking myself unjust to her. And as
she is too young and handsome to retire into a convent or the country, and is honorable and honest and
can be trusted, after reconciling myself to the necessity I consider where she could be happy. I know you
thought me jealous of your attention to her; I can assure you her conduct entitles her more than ever to
my confidence. Judge, then, as you know my satisfaction in looking on a modern piece of *virtu*, if I do not
think you a second self, in thinking that by placing her
within your reach, I render a necessity which would
otherwise be heartbreaking tolerable and even comforting."

Having prepared the ground, he wrote again in the
following May, " without affectation or disguise."
Delicacy had prevented him from writing about " Lady
C[raven] " who, Hamilton's friends were glad to
learn, had departed. Would not all of them prefer one
like Emma? The " odds " in their own two lives were
not " proportioned to the difference " of their years; he
was very " sensible " of his uncle's intentions towards
him. At what followed Sir William must have smiled.

The real reason for all his fencing emerges. Sir
William's joint security on the pledge of half his
minerals, the assurance that he was made his heir,
were mere credentials to be shown by Greville to a

prospective father-in-law. "Suppose a lady of 30,000 was to marry me," and so forth—a vista of married fortune. Even now the name of the lady thus honoured was withheld; but Hamilton must have known it perfectly: ". . . If you dislike my frankness, I shall be sorry, for it cost me a little to throw myself so open, and to no one's friendship could I have trusted myself but to yours, from which I have ever been treated with indulgence and preference."

A month more and he disclosed a positive, if "distant and imperfect," prospect. Lord Middleton's youngest daughter was the favoured lady—in the "requisites of beauty and disposition," "beyond the mark for a younger brother." The die was cast; he penned a formal proposal to her father. It may be gathered that the lady rejected him; Greville certainly never married. Often and often he must have wished his poor and unfashionable Emma back again, when she was poor and unfashionable no longer: his *amour propre* had been hurt, and, till he became vice-chamberlain in 1794, to Lady Hamilton's genuine pleasure,[1] his fortunes drooped.

Greville's·tentatives were now at an end. At length he laid a plain outline before Sir William:—"If you

[1] Cf. her letter of congratulation (Sept. 16, 1794), Morrison MS. 246, in answer to his letter of August 18 announcing his good fortune and claiming the approbation of such friends as herself, as the best reward for one who plumes himself on friendship [*Nelson Letters* (1814), vol. i. p. 265]: "I should not flatter myself so far," he writes, "if I was not very sincerely interested in your happiness and ever affectionately yours." "I congratulate you," she answers, "with all my heart on your appointment. . . . You have well merited it; and all your friends must be happy at a change so favourable not only for your pecuniary circumstances, as for the honner of the situation. May you long enjoy it with every happiness that you deserve! I speak from my heart. I don't know a better, honester, or more amiable and worthy man than yourself; and it is a great deal for me to say this, for, whatever I think, I am not apt to pay compliments."

could form a plan by which you could have a trial, and could invite her and tell her that I ought not to leave England, and that I cannot afford to go on; and state it as a kindness to me if she would accept your invitation, she would go with pleasure. She is to be six weeks at some bathing place; and when you could write an answer to this, and inclose a letter to her, I could manage it; and either by land, by the coach to Geneva, and from thence by *Veturine* forward her, or else by sea. I must add that I could not manage it so well later; after a month, and absent from me, she would consider the whole more calmly. If there was in the world a person she loved so well as yourself after me, I could not arrange with so much *sang-froid;* and I am sure I would not let her go to you, if any risque of the usual coquetry of the sex being likely to give uneasiness or appearance. . . ."

Sir William's "invitation" was to be perfectly innocent. She was to understand that her dear Greville's interest demanded a *temporary* separation; that she and her mother would be honoured guests at the Naples Embassy; that she could improve the delightful change of scene and climate by training her musical gifts under the best masters, by studying the arts in their motherland, by learning languages amid a cosmopolitan crowd; that by October her fairy-prince would reappear, and, like another Orpheus, bring back his Eurydice. And all this she was to be told, after absence, that makes the heart grow fonder, had inured her to separation, softened her heart to self-sacrifice, and reconciled her to his lightest bidding—when, in short, it would be easiest to practise on devotion. About these machinations Emma was presumably left in the dark; their windings took place behind her back. Her all-wise, all-powerful and tender Greville could never consult but for her good, while his real unselfishness towards the child forbade any suspicion of his purpose.

To Emma his prim platitudes were the loving eloquence of Romeo. And for the last few months he had been always preaching up to her the spotless example of a certain " Mrs. Wells," refined and accomplished, who, in Emma's own situation, had earned and kept both her own self-respect and that of more than one successive admirer; who had learned the art of retaining the lover as friend, while she accepted his friend as lover. These innuendoes may well have puzzled her. Had she not realised a dream of constancy, and could that pass? Had she not parted with the child she loved to please the man of her heart, and fasten his faith to hers? Yet all the time her dearest Greville could speak of " forwarding " her, just as if she were one of those crystals on which he doted.

The fact was that, added to his embarrassments, his need for fortune with a wife, his wish at once to oblige Sir William and to preclude him from wedlock, his genuine desire—which must be granted—to provide for Emma's future, arose the feeling that Emma herself was now too fond. It was hard to resign her; but, unless the choice was quickly made, it might become impossible ever to make it; and he might be entangled into a marriage which would hold him up to ridicule.

But for once Greville was in haste. Sir William, always leisurely, took time before he began to broach a scheme of life which filled his nephew with alarm. Greville had never doubted that, should his will prevail with Emma as well as with his uncle, the latter would sequester her in one of his villas near Naples— some Italian Edgware Row. His mind recoiled from the awful thought that she might ever dispense the honours of the Embassy. The Ambassador, however, could not agree. He had discerned powers in this singular woman passing Greville's vision, and the connoisseur longed to call them forth and create a work of art. He lived, too, in a land where the *convenances* were not so rigid as in his own. Did not the *bonne amie* of a distinguished diplomat and Knight of Malta grace his Roman house and circle?

Illness also made for postponement. When Greville returned to town after his summer outing, he found Emma, fresh from her sea-baths, " alarmed and distress'd " over her mother's " paralysis." " It was not so severe an attack," he told his uncle in November, " as I understood it to be when I informed you of it from Cornwall. . . . You may suppose that I did not increase Emma's uneasiness by any hint of the subject of our correspondence "; " at any rate," he sighs, " it cannot take place, and she goes on so well, . . . and also improv'd in looks, that I own it is less agreeable to part; yet I have no other alternative but to marry, or remain a pauper; I shall persist in my resolution not to lose an opportunity if I can find it, and do not think that *my* idea of sending her to Naples on such an event arises from my consulting my convenience only. I can assure you she would not have a scarcity of offers; she has refused great ones; but I am sure she would prefer a foreign country. . . . I know that confidence and good usage will never be abused by her, and that nothing can make her giddy. I was only ten days with her when I was call'd away to be Mayor of Warwick; it was not kindly meant, but it will turn out well. I have been at the castle; I have put myself on good terms with my brother, and I think I shall keep him passive, if not interested for me in the borough. . . ."

It was not, therefore, Emma only who had grown " much more considerate and amiable." Lord Warwick must be enlisted if Greville was to "stand high with both parties," and urge them into competition for his services, as he gravely proceeded to inform his uncle.

December brought Sir William's offer, and with it matured Greville's plans for the March ensuing. He would visit Scotland to retrench and profit by the lectures of Edinburgh dominies, while his "minerals" would remain his, thanks to Hamilton's generosity; Emma, she was assured, for a while only, would repair to Naples chaperoned by her mother, and the pleasant Gavin Hamilton, Romeward bound. All of them were to be couriered so far as Geneva by the Swiss Dejean; at Geneva Sir William's man Vincenzo—still his faithful servant in Nelson's day—would meet the party. For six months only Emma could cease her own course of incomparable lectures at Edgware Row; and a brief absence alone reconciled her to severance. A charming visit was to hasten a welcome re-union.

". . . The absolute necessity," explains the casuist once more, "of reducing every expence to enable me to have enough to exist on, and to pay the interest of my debt *without parting with my collection of minerals, which is not yet in a state of arrangement which would set it off to its greatest advantage,* occasion'd my telling Emma," with sudden artlessness, "that I should be obliged on business to absent myself for some months in Scotland. She naturally said that such a separation would be very like a total separation, for that she should be very miserable during my absence, and that she should neither profit by my conversation nor improve in any degree, that my absence would be more tolerable if she had you to comfort her, . . . *as there was not a person in the world whom she could be happy with, if I was dead,* but yourself, and that she certainly would profit of your kind offer, if I should die or slight her "—two equally improbable alternatives in Emma's purview. ". . . I told her that *I should have no objection* to her going to Naples *for 6 or 8 months,* and that if she really wish'd it I would forward any letter she wrote. . . . *That she would not fear being troublesome, as she would be perfectly satisfied with the degree of attention you should from choice give her, and that she should be very happy in learning music, Italian, etc.,* while your avocations imploy'd you. . . . I told her that she would be so happy that I should be cut out, and she said *that if I did not come for her, or neglected her, she would certainly be grateful to you; but that neither interest nor affection should ever induce her to change, unless my interest or wish required it."*

It should be noted that the previous sentences about Emma's alternatives are contradicted by those which set her down as only to be weaned from Greville by becoming a willing sacrifice to his " interest."

Enclosed was Emma's own missive. " Emboldened " by Sir William's kindness when he was in England, she recapitulated the circumstances. Greville, " whom you know I love tenderly," is obliged to go for four or five months in the " sumer " " to places that I cannot with propriety attend him to "—here surely it is Greville who dictates? She has too great a " regard for him to hinder him from pursuing those plans which," she thinks, " it is right for him to follow." As Hamilton was so good as to encourage her, she " will speak her mind." Firstly, she would be glad " to be a little more improv'd," and Greville " out of kindness " had offered to dispense with her for the few months at the close of which he would come to " fetch " her home, and stay a while there when he comes, " which I know you will be glad to see him."

He therefore proposed the 1st of March for his own departure northward and hers to the south. She would be " flattered " if Hamilton will " allot " her an apartment in " his house," " and lett Greville occupye those appartments when he comes ; you know that *must* be ; but as your house is very large, and you must, from the nature of your office, have business to transact and visiters to see,"—here Greville dictates again—" I shall always keep my own room when you are better engaged, and at other times I hope to have the pleasure of your company and conversation, which will be more agreable to me than anything in Italy. As I have given you an example of sincerity, I hope you will be equaly candid and sincere in a speedy answer. . . . I shall be perfectly happy in any arrangements you will make, as I have full confidence in your kindness and attention to me. . . ."

The *must* in this letter leaves no doubt that the permanence of separation never crossed her mind. Greville's crystals, however, required a sacrifice, which for him she prided herself on making.

On April 26—her birthday—she duly arrived at the Palazzo Sessa.[1]   But she at once felt wretched away from the man she loved, and her sole comfort lay in forwarding his interest. " It was my birthday, and I was very low spirited. Oh God! that day that you used to smile on me and stay at home, and be kind to me— that *that* day I shou'd be at such a distance from you! But my comfort is that I rely upon your promise, and September or October I shall see you! But I am quite unhappy at not hearing from you—no letter for me yet, . . . but I must wait with patience." " I dreaded," she continued later, " setting down to write, for I try to appear as chearful before Sir William as I could, and I am sure to cry the moment I think of

[1] Then the Embassy.

you.[1] For I feel more and more unhappy at being separated from you, and if my fatal ruin depends on seeing you, I will and *must* at the end of the sumer. For to live without you is impossible. I love you to that degree that at this time there is not a hardship upon hearth either of poverty, cold, death, or even to walk barefooted to Scotland to see you, but what I wou'd undergo. Therefore my dear, dear Greville, if you do love me, for my sake, try all you can to come hear as soon as possible. You have a true friend in Sir William, and he will be happy to see you, and do all he can to make you happy; and for me I will be everything you can wish for. I find it is not either a fine horse, or a fine coach, or a pack of servants, or plays or operas, can make [me] happy. It is *you* that [h]as it in your power either to make me very happy or very miserable. I respect Sir William, I have a great regard for him, as the uncle and friend of you, and he loves me, Greville. But he can never be anything nearer to me than your uncle and my sincere friend. He never can be my lover. You do not know how good Sir William is to me. He is doing everything he can to make me happy. . . ."

Her inmost soul speaks in these sentences. They ring true, and are without question outpourings of the heart on paper bedewed with tears. Sir William was indeed kind. He wanted to wean her from one who could thus have treated her. He was never out of her sight. He gazed on her; he sighed; he praised her

[1] Sir William had divined this probability the day before she arrived:—" However, I will do as well as I can and hobble in and out of this pleasant scrape as decently as I can. You may be assured I will comfort her for the loss of you as well as I am able, but I know, from the small specimens during your absence from London, that I shall have at times many tears to wipe from those charming eyes."—Morrison MS. 149, April 25, 1786.

every movement. He gave her presents and showed her all that romantic antiquity which he loved, understood, and explained so well. She had gazed on Posilippo, and was to revel in the villino at Caserta and the Posilippo villa, which soon bore her name. But carriage and liveries, "like those of Mrs. Damer," who had just left, a private boat, and baths under summer skies in summer seas—all these availed nothing with Greville absent. Her apartment was of four rooms fronting that enchanted bay. The Ambassador's friends dined with her, and she sang for them :— "Yes, last night we had a little concert. But then I was so low, for I wanted you to partake of our amusement. Sir Thomas Rumbold is here with [h]is son who is dying of a decline, . . . and poor young man! he cannot walk from the bed to the chair; and Lady Rumbold, like a tender-hearted wretch, is gone to Rome, to pass her time there with the English, and [h]as took the coach and all the English servants with her, and left poor Sir Thomas, with [h]is heart broken, waiting on [h]is sick son. You can't think what a worthy man he is. He dined with ous, and likes me very much, and every day [h]as brought [h]is carriage or phaeton . . . and carries me and mother and Sir William out." None the less her heart stays with Greville. She is always helping him with Sir William, whose good *will* (in both senses of that word) makes her "very happy for his sake. . . . But Greville, my dear Greville, wright some comfort to me." "Only remember your promise of October." This delusive October must have hung over Greville's head like a sword of Damocles, or Cæsar's inevitable Ides of March.

The sensation of Emma's first appearance in the kaleidoscope of Naples, with its King of the Lazzaroni and Queen of the Illuminati, together with the conjunctures of affairs and men first witnessed by her, will find place in the next chapter. It was not many months before she was to exclaim to Greville, " You do not know what power I have hear "; before Acton, the Premier, was to rally Sir William on " a worthy and charming young lady." But now and here the climax of her emotions, when she first fully realised Greville's breach of faith and his real purpose in exiling her, must be reached without interruption. Even on the first of May, when his uncle told her in reply to her solicitude for Greville's welfare, that she might command anything from one who loved them both so dearly, " I have had a conversation this morning," she wrote, " with Sir William that has made me mad. He speaks—no, I do not know what to make of it."

Three months went by, and still no letter came, except one to tell her how grateful was the nephew for the uncle's care; and still Sir William looked and languished. The truth began to dawn upon her, but even now she dare not face, and would not believe it. At the close of July, when Naples drowses and melts in dreamy haze, she made her last and piteous, though spirited, appeal. " I am now onely writing to beg of you for God's sake to send me one letter, if it is onely a farewell. Sure I have deserved this for the sake of the love you once had for me. . . . Don't despise me. I have not used you ill in any one thing. I have been from you going of six months, and you have wrote one letter to me, enstead of which I have sent fourteen to you. So pray let me beg of you, my much loved Greville, only one line from your dear, dear hands. You don't know how thankful I shall be for it. For if you knew the misery I feel, oh! your heart wou'd not be intirely shut up against me; for I love you with the truest affection. Don't let any body sett you against me. Some of your friends—your foes per-

haps, I don't know what to stile them—have long wisht
me ill.   But, Greville, you never will meet with anybody that has a truer affection for you than I have,
and I onely wish it was in my power to shew you what
I cou'd do for you.   As soon as I know your determination, I shall take my own measures.   If I don't
hear from you, and that you are coming according to
promise, I shall be in England at Cristmass at farthest.
Don't be unhappy at that, I will see you once more for
the last time.   I find life is insupportable without you.
Oh! my heart is intirely broke.   Then for God's sake,
my ever dear Greville, do write to me some comfort.
I don't know what to do.   I am now in that state, I
am incapable of anything.   I have a language-master,
a singing-master, musick, etc., but what is it for?   If
it was to amuse you, I shou'd be happy.   But, Greville,
what will it avail me?   I am poor, helpless, and forlorn.   I have lived with you 5 years, and you have
sent me to a strange place, and no one prospect but
thinking you was coming to me.   Instead of which I
was told. . . . No, I respect him, but no, never. . . .
What is to become of me?   But excuse me, my heart is
ful.   I tel you give me one guiney a week for everything, and live with me, and I will be contented.
But no more.   I will trust to Providence, and wherever
you go, God bless you, and preserve you, and may you
allways be happy!   But write to Sir William.   What
[h]as he done to affront you? " [1]

She awaited Greville's orders.   Sir William had
commissioned still another portrait of her from Romney; " Angelaca " was about to paint her; she was
" so remarkably fair " that " everybody " said she
" put on red and white "; Lord Hervey was her slave;
a foreign prince was in her train each evening; the
king was " sighing " for her.   It was Greville's orders

[1] Morrison MS. 152, July 22, 1786.

for which she waited.   She had just visited Pompeii
and viewed the wrecks of love and bloom and life unearthed by alien hands.   Was here no moral for this
distraught and heaving bosom?   And there that awful
mountain lowered and threatened ruin every day.   The
Maltese Minister's house hard by had been struck by
lightning.   Like lurid Nature, Emma too was roused
to fury, though, a microcosm of it also, she smiled
between the outbursts.   What could she do but
wait?

Twelve days more; the order comes—"*Oblige Sir
William.*"   Her passion blazes up, indignant:
". . . Nothing can express my rage.   Greville, to advise me!—you that used to envy my smiles!   Now
with cool indifference to advise me! . . . Oh! that is
the worst of all.   But I will not, no, I will not rage.
If I was with you I wou'd murder you and myself
boath.   I will leave of[f] and try to get more strength,
for I am now very ill with a cold. . . . I won't look
back to what I wrote . . . Nothing shall ever do for
me but going home to you.   If that is not to be, I will
except of nothing.   I will go to London, their go into
every excess of vice till I dye, a miserable, broken-
hearted wretch, and leave my fate as a warning to
young whomen never to be two good; for now you
have made me love you, you made me good, you
have abbandoned me; and some violent end shall finish
our connexion, if it is to finish.   But oh! Greville, you
cannot, you must not give me up.   You have not
the heart to do it.   You love me I am sure; and I am
willing to do everything in my power, and what will
you have more?   And I only say this is the last time
I will either beg or pray, do as you like."—" I always
knew, I had a foreboding since first I began to love
you, that I was not destined to be happy; for their is
not a King or Prince on hearth that cou'd make me

happy without you."—"Little Lord Brooke is dead. Poor little boy, how I envy him his happiness."

She had been degraded in her own eyes, and by the lover whom she had heroised. Was this, then, the reward of modesty regained; of love returned, of strenuous effort, of hopes for her child, and a home purified? Her idol lay prone, dashed from its pedestal, with feet of clay. And yet this did not harden her. Though she could not trust, she still believed in him as in some higher power who chastens those he loves. Her paroxysms passed to return again:—". . . It is enough, I have paper that Greville wrote on. He [h]as folded it up. He wet the wafer. How I envy thee the place of Emma's lips, that would give worlds, had she them, to kiss those lips! . . . I onely wish that a wafer was my onely rival. *But I submit to what God and Greville pleases.*" Even now she held him to his word. "I have such a headache with my cold, I don't know what to do. . . . I can't lett a week go without telling you how happy I am at hearing from you. Pray, write as often as you can. *If you come,* we shall all go home together. . . . Pray write to me, and don't write in the stile of a freind, but a lover. For I won't hear a word of freind. Sir William is ever freind. But we are lovers. I am glad you have sent me a blue hat and gloves. . . ."

For many years she cherished Greville's friendship. She wrote to him perpetually after the autumn of this year saw Sir William win her heart as well as will by his tenderness, and by her thought of advancing the ingrate nephew himself. Never did she lose sight of Greville's interests during those fourteen future years at Naples. She lived to thank Greville for having made Sir William known to her, to be proud of her achievements as his *élève*.

But at the same time in these few months a larger

horizon was already opening. She had looked on a bigger world, and ambition was awakening within her. She had seen royalty and statesmen, and she began to feel that she might play a larger part. Under Greville's yoke she had been ready to pinch and slave; with Sir William she would rule. " Pray write," she concludes one of her Greville letters, " for nothing will make me so angry, and it is not to your *intrest* to disoblidge me, for you don't know," she adds with point, " the power I have hear. . . . If you affront me, *I will make him marry me*. God bless you for ever." [1]

And amid all her tumult of disillusionment, of uncertainty, of bewilderment in the new influence she was visibly wielding over new surroundings, she remained the more mindful of those oldest friends who had believed her good, and enabled her to feel good herself. Sir William, wishful to retain for her the outside comforts of virtue, hastened to gratify her by inviting Romney and Hayley to Naples. The disappointment caused by Romney's inability to comply with a request dear to him [2] threw her back on herself and made her feel lonelier than ever; her mother was her great consolation.

And what was Greville's attitude? These Emma-letters would have been tumbled into his waste-paper basket with the fourteen others that remain, had he not returned them to Hamilton with the subjoined and private comment:—" *L'oubli de l'inclus est volant, fixez-le: si on admet le ton de la vertu sans la vérité,*

---

[1] Morrison MS. 153, August 1, 1786. Some of the sentences are quoted in the order of *feeling* and not of sequence. Emma seldom wrote long letters in a single day.

[2] Romney had been very ill. In his answer (August, 1786) he hopes " in a weke or to, to be upon my pins (I cannot well call them legs), as you know at best they are very poor ones."—Cf. Ward and Roberts's *Romney*, vol. 1. p. 67.

on est la dupe, et je place naturellement tout sur le pied vrai, comme j'ai toujours fait, et je constate l'état actuel sans me reporter à vous." One must not be duped by the tone without the truth of virtue! The " self-respect," then, instilled by him, was never designed to raise her straying soul; it was a makeshift contrived to steady her erring steps—a mere bridge between goodness and its opposite, which he would not let her cross; though neither would he let her throw herself over it into the troubled and muddy depths below: it was a bridge built for his own retreat. Greville recked of no " truth " but hard " facts," which he looked unblushingly in the face, nor did his essence harbour one flash or spark of idealism. And still he purposed her welfare, as he understood it; he had sought to kill three birds with one stone. Hamilton, for all his faults, was never a sophist of such compromise. For Emma he purposed a state of life above its semblance, and a strength beyond its frail supports; already he desired that she would consent to be, in all but name, his wife. Greville, certain of her good nature, had dreaded permanence; Hamilton, if all went smoothly, meant it. Yet Greville exacted friendship without affection. His French postscript was designed to escape Emma's comprehension, though a month or so later it could not have succeeded in doing so. But the letter itself contained some paragraphs which he probably intended her to study:—

" . . . I shall hope to manage to all our satisfaction, for I so long foresaw that a moment of separation must arrive, that I never kept the connexion, but on the footing of perfect liberty to her. Its commencement was not of my seeking, and hitherto it has contributed to her happiness. She knows and reflects often on the circumstances which she cannot forget, and in her heart she cannot reproach me of having acted otherwise than a kind and attentive friend. But you have now rendered it possible for her to be respected and comfortable, *and if she has not talked herself out of the true view of her situation she will retain the protection and affection of us both*. For after all, consider what a charming creature she would have been if she had been blessed with the advantages of an early education, and had not been spoilt by the indulgence of every caprice. I never was irritated by her momentary passions, for it is a good heart which will not part with a friend in anger; and yet it is true that when her pride is hurt by neglect or anxiety for the future, the frequent repition of her passion ballances the beauty of the smiles. If a person knew her and could live for life with her, by an economy of attention, that is by constantly renewing very little attentions, she would be happy and good temper'd, *for she has not a grain of avarice or self-interest.* . . . Knowing all this, infinite have been my pains to make her respect herself, and act fairly, *and I had always proposed to continue her friend, altho' the connexion ceased.* I had proposed to make her accept and manage your kind provision,[1] and she would easily have adopted that plan; it was acting the part of good woman, *and to offer to put her regard to any test, and to show that she contributed to MY happiness,* by accepting the provision . . . it would not have hurt her pride, and would have been a line of heroicks more natural, *because it arose out of the real situation,* than any which by conversation she might persuade herself suited her to act. Do not understand the word " act " other than I mean it. We all [act] well when we suit our actions to the real situation, and conduct them by truth and good intention. We act capriciously and incon-

[1] Sir William offered to settle £100 annually, and Greville a like sum, on her. Romney was to have been a trustee.

veniently to others when our actions are founded on an imaginary plan which does not place the persons involved in the scene in their real situations. . . . If Mrs. Wells had quarrell'd with Admiral Keppell, she would never have been respected as she now is. . . . If she will put me on the footing of a friend . . . she will write to me fairly on her plans, she will tell me her thoughts, and her future shall be my serious concern. . . . She has conduct and discernment, and I have always said that such a woman, if she controul her passions, might rule the roost, and chuse her station."

Thus Æneas-Greville, of Dido-Emma, to his trusty Achates. Surely a self-revealing document of sense and blindness, of truth and falsehood, one, moreover, did space allow, well worth longer excerpts. He excused his action in his own eyes even more elaborately, over and over again. He would conscientiously fulfil his duty to her and hers, if only she would accept his view of her own duty towards him: his tone admitted of few obligations beyond mutual interest. He never reproached either her or himself: he thought himself firm, not cruel; he remained her good friend and well-wisher, her former rescuer, a father to her child. "Heroicks" were out of place and out of taste. He again held up to her proud imitation the prime pattern of "Mrs. Wells." He was even willing that she should return home, if so she chose; but his terms were irrevocably fixed, and it was useless for her to hystericise against adamant.

But he did not reckon with the latent possibilities of her being. The sequel was to prove not "what Greville," but what "God pleases."

CHAPTER IV

1787-1791

WHAT was the new prospect on which **Emma's** eyes first rested in March, 1786? Goethe has described it. A fruitful land, a free, blue sea, the scented islands, and the smoking mountain. A population of vegetarian craftsmen busy to enjoy with hand-to-mouth labour. A people holding their teeming soil under a lease on sufferance from earthquake and volcano. An inflammable mob, whose king lost six thousand subjects annually by assassination, and whose brawls and battles of vendetta would last three hours at a time. An upper class of feudal barons proud and ignorant. A lower class of half-beggars, at once lazy, brave, and insolent, who, if they misliked the face of a foreign inquirer, would stare in silence and turn away. A middle class of literati despising those above and below them. A race of tillers and of fishermen alternating between pious superstition and reckless revel, midway, as it were, between God and Satan. The bakers celebrating their patron, Saint Joseph; the priests their child-like "saint-humorous," San Filippo Neri; high and low alike, their civic patrons, Saints Anthony and Januarius, whose liquefying blood each January propitiated Vesuvius. Preaching Friars, dreaming Friars; singing, sceptical, enjoying Abbés. A country luxuriant not only with southern growths, but garlanded even in February by banks of wild violets and tangles of wild heliotrope and sweet-peas. A spirit of Nature, turning dread to beauty, and beauty into dread.

She sits, her head leaned against her hand, and gazes through the open casement on a scene bathed in southern sun and crystal air—the pure air, the large glow, the light soil that made Neapolis the pride of Magna Græcia. Her room—it is Goethe himself who describes it—" furnished in the English taste," is " most delightful "; the " outlook from its corner window, unique." Below, the bay; in full view, Capri; on the right, Posilippo; nearer the highroad, Villa Reale, the royal palace; on the left an ancient Jesuit cloister, which the queen had dedicated to learning; hard by on either side, the twin strongholds of Uovo and Nuovo, and the busy, noisy Molo, overhung by the fortress of San Elmo on the frowning crag; further on, the curving coast from Sorrento to Cape Minerva. And all this varied vista, from the centre of a densely thronged and clattering city.

The whirlwind of passion sank, and gradually yielded to calm, as Greville had predicted. " Every woman," commented this astute observer, resenting the mention of his name at Naples, " either feels or acts a part"; and change of *dramatis personæ* was necessary, he added, " to make Emma happy " and himself " free." But his careful prescription of the immaculate " Mrs. Wells " only partially succeeded. True, the elderly friend was soon to become the attached lover, and the prudential lover a forgiven friend; but he ceased henceforward to be " guide " or " philosopher," and gradually faded into a minor actor in the drama, though never into a supernumerary. She felt, as she told Sir William, forlorn: her trust had been betrayed and rudely shaken. What she longed for was a *friend*, and she could never simulate what she did not feel.[1] His gentle respect, his chivalry, contrasting with Greville's cynical taskmastership, his persuasive endearments, eventually won the day; and by the close of the year Emma's heart assented to his suit. Her eyes had been opened. To him she " owed everything." He was to her " every kind name in one." " I believe," she told him early in 1787, " it is right I shou'd be seperated from you sometimes, to make me know myself, for I don't know till you are absent, how dear you are to me "; she implores one little line just that she " may kiss " his " name." Sir William at fifty-six retained that art of pleasing which he never lost; and she was always pleased to be petted and shielded. Already by the opening of 1788 she had come to master the language and the society of Naples. Disobedient to his nephew, and his niece Mrs. Dickinson, who remonstrated naturally but in vain, Sir William insisted on her doing the honours, which she astonished him by managing, as he thought, to perfection. Every moment spared from visits abroad or her hospitalities in the Palazzo Sessa was filled by strenuous study at home, or in the adjoining Convent of Santa Romita. Her captivating charm, her quick tact, her impulsive friendliness, her entertaining humour, her natural taste for art, which, together with her " kindness and intelligence," had already been acknowledged by Romney as a source of inspiration; her unique " Attitudes," her voice which, under Galluci's tuition, she was now beginning " to command," even her free and easy manners when contrasted with those of the

[1] Cf. her very striking letter to Hamilton, Morrison MS. 163: " . . . Do you call me your dear friend? . . . Oh, if I cou'd express myself! If I had words to thank you, that I may not thus be choked with meanings, for which I can find no utterance!"

Neapolitan *noblesse,* all seemed miracles, broke down
the easy barriers of susceptible southerners, and gained
her hosts of " sensible admirers." So early as February, 1787, Sir William reported to his nephew:
". . . Our dear Em. goes on now quite as I cou'd
wish, and is universally beloved "—a phrase which
Emma herself repeated ten months later to her first
mentor, with the proud consciousness of shining at a
distance before him. " She is wonderful," added
Hamilton, " considering her youth and beauty, and I
flatter myself that E. and her Mother are happy to be
with me, so that I see my every wish fulfilled." By
the August of this year, when she first wrote Italian,
she saw " good company," she delighted the whole
diplomatic circle; Sir William was indissociable; she
used the familiar " we "—" *our* house at Caserta is
fitted up," while Sir William followed suit. The very
servants styled her " Eccellenza." Her attached Ambassador " is distractedly in love "; " he deserves it,
and indeed I love him dearly." There was not a grain
in her of inconstancy. " He is so kind, so good and
tender to me," she wrote as Emma Hart, in an un-
published letter, " that I love him so much that I have
not a warm look left for the Neapolitans." His evenings, he wrote, were sweet with song and admiring
guests, while her own society rendered them a " comfort." Inclination went on steadily ripening, until it
settled within three years into deep mutual fondness.
He fitted up for her a new boudoir in the Naples house
with its round mirrors, as Miss Knight has recorded,
covering the entire side of the wall opposite the semi-
circular window, and reflecting the moonlit bay with
its glimmering boats, the glass tanks with their marine
treasures of " sea-oranges " and the like. Within a year
Hamilton tells Greville that she asks him " Do you
love me, aye, but as much as your new apartment? "—

both here and at Caserta. He did his best to " form " her, and in the course of time she was able to share his botanical studies, which they pursued not as " pedantical prigs " to air learning, but with zeal and pleasure in the early mornings and fresh air of the " English " gardens. Her aptitude and adaptiveness worked wonders. Within a year she could take an intelligent interest in the virtuoso's new volume, if we may judge from Sir J. Banks, who some years later again bade his old crony tell her that he hoped she admired Penelope in his work on Urns. She aided his volcanic observations; Sir William laughed, and said she would rival him with the mountain now. Both had already stayed with, and she had enchanted, the Duke and Duchess of St. Maître at Sorrento, the musical Countess of Mahoney at Ischia; cries of *" Una donna rara," " bellissima creatura,"* were on every mouth. The Duke of Gloucester begged Hamilton to favour him with her acquaintance. The Olympian Goethe himself beheld and marvelled. Her unpretending naïveté won her adherents at every step. "All the female nobility, with the queen at their head," were " distantly civil " to her already; none rude to Emma were allowed within the precincts. Meddlers or censors were sent roundly to the right-about, and informed that she was the sweetest, the best, the cleverest creature in the world. When he returned from his periodical royal wild-boar chases, it was Emma again who brewed his punch and petted him. Now and again there peeps out also that half voluptuous tinge in her wifeliness which never wholly deserted her. She had been Greville's devoted slave; Sir William was already hers. Her monitor had repulsed her free sacrifice and urged it for his own advantage towards his uncle; but her worshipper had now fanned not so much the flame, perhaps, as the incense of her unfeigned[1] attachment. The English dined with her while Sir William was away shooting with the king. She trilled Handel and Paisiello, learned French, Italian, music, dancing, design, and history. Hamilton, himself musical, used later on to accompany her voice—of which he was a good judge—on the viola. She laughed at the foibles and follies of the court; she retailed to him the gossip of the hour. She entered into his routine and protected his interests; she prevented him from being pestered or plundered. Only a few years, and she was dictating etiquette even to an English nobleman.

It was a triumphal progress which took the town by storm; her beauty swept men off their feet. The transformations of these eighteen months, which lifted her out of her cramped nook at Paddington into a wide arena, read like a dream, or one of those Arabian fairy-tales where peasants turn princes in an hour. Nor is the least surprise, among many, the thought that these dissolving views present themselves as adventures of admired virtue, and not as unsanctioned escapades. At Naples the worst of her past seemed buried, and she could be born again. Her accent, her vulgarisms mattered little; she spoke to new friends in a new language. The " lovely woman " who had " stooped to folly, and learned too late that men betray," seems rather to have " stooped to conquer " by the approved methods of the same Goldsmith's heroine.

The scene of her *début* is that of Opera, all moonlight, flutter, music, and masquerade. Escaping in

---

[1] Cf. Morrison MS. 164, 1787 (Emma to Sir William): " . . . My comforter in distress. Then why shall I not love you. Endead I must and ought whilst life is left in me or reason to think on you. . . . My heart and eyes fill. . . . I owe everything to you, and shall ever with gratitude remember it. . . ." And cf. *ibid*. 172, 1788: " . . . I love Sir William, for he renounces all for me."

the cool of the evening from her chambers, thronged by artists, wax-modellers, and intaglio-cutters, she attends Sir William's evening saunter in the royal gardens at the fashionable hour. Her complexion so much resembles apple-blossom, that beholders question it, although she neither paints nor powders. Dapper Prince Dietrichstein from Vienna ("Draydrixton" in her parlance as in Acton's) attends her as " *cavaliere servente,*" whispering to her in broken English that she is a "diamond of the first water." Two more princes and "two or three nobles" follow at her heels. She wears a loose muslin gown, the sleeves tied in folds with blue ribbon and trimmed with lace, a blue sash and the big blue hat which Greville has sent her as peace-offering. Beyond them stand the king, the queen, the minister Acton, and a brilliant retinue. That queen, careworn but beautiful, who already "likes her much," has begged the Austrian beau to walk near her that she may get a glimpse of his fair companion, the English girl, who is a "modern antique." "But Greville," writes Emma, "the king [h]as eyes, he [h]as a heart, and I have made an impression on it. But I told the prince, Hamilton is my friend, and she belongs to his nephew, for all our friends know it." [1] Only last Sunday that "Roi d'Yvetot" had dined at Posilippo, mooring his boat by the casements of Hamilton's country casino for a nearer view. This garden-house is already named the "Villa Emma," and there for Emma a new "music-room" is building. Emma and the Ambassador had been entertaining a "diplomatick party." They issue forth beneath the moon to their private boat. At once the monarch places his "boat of musick" next to theirs. His band of "French Horns" strikes up a serenade for the queen of hearts. The king re-

[1] Morrison MS. 152, July 22, 1786.

moves his hat, sits with it on his knees, and " when going to land," bows and says, " it was a sin he could
not speak English." She has him in her train every
evening at San Carlo, villa, or promenade; she is the
cynosure of each day, and the toast of every night.

Or, again, she entertains informally at Sorrento, all
orange-blossom in February, after an afternoon of
rambling donkey-rides near flaming Vesuvius, and
visits to grandees in villeggiatura. In one room sits
Sir William's orchestra; in the other she receives their
guests. At last her turn comes round to sing; she
chooses " Luce Bella," in which the Banti makes such
a *furore* at San Carlo, that famous Banti who had
already marvelled at the tone and compass of her
voice, when in fear and trembling she had been induced to follow her. As she ceases, there is a ten
minutes' round of applause, a hubbub of *" Bravas "*
and *" Ancoras."* And then she performs in " buffo "
—" that one " (and Greville knew it) " with a Tam-
bourin, in the character of a young girl with a raire-
shew [raree-show], the pretiest thing you ever heard."
He must concede her triumph, the hard, unruffled man!
She turns the heads of the Sorrentines; she leaves
" some dying, some crying, and some in despair. Mind
you, this was all nobility, as proud as the devil "; but
—and here brags the people's daughter—" *we* humbled
them "; " but what astonished them was that I shou'd
speak such good Italian. For I paid them, I spared
non[e] of them, tho' I was civil and oblidging. One
asked me if I left a love at Naples, that I left them so
soon. I pulled my lip at him, to say, ' I pray, do you
take me for an Italian? . . . Look, sir, I am English. I have one Cavaliere servente, and have brought
him with me,' pointing to Sir William." Hart, the
English musician, wept to hear her sing an air by Handel, pronouncing that in her the tragic and comic

Muses were so happily blended that Garrick would have been enraptured. These were the very qualities that even thus early distinguished her self-taught " Attitudes," by common consent of all beholders a marvel of artistic expression and refinement. Goethe, at this moment in Naples, and certainly no biassed critic, was an eye-witness. He had been introduced by his friends, the German artists,[1] to the Mæcenas Ambassador and " his Emma." He thus records his impressions :—

". . . The Chevalier Hamilton, so long resident here as English Ambassador, so long, too, connoisseur and student of Art and Nature, has found their counterpart and acme with exquisite delight in a lovely girl—English, and some twenty years of age. She is exceedingly beautiful and finely built. She wears a Greek garb becoming her to perfection. She then merely loosens her locks, takes a pair of shawls, and effects changes of postures, moods, gestures, mien, and appearance that make one really feel as if one were in some dream. Here is visible complete, and bodied forth in movements of surprising variety, all that so many artists have sought in vain to fix and render. Successively standing, kneeling, seated, reclining, grave, sad, sportive, teasing, abandoned, penitent, alluring, threatening, agonised. One follows the other, and grows out of it. She knows how to choose and shift the simple folds of her single kerchief for every expression, and to adjust it into a hundred kinds of headgear. Her elderly knight holds the torches for her performance, and is absorbed in his soul's desire. In her he finds the charm of all antiques, the fair profiles on Sicilian coins, the Apollo Belvedere himself. . . . We have already rejoiced in the spectacle

[1] Tischbein, Hackert, and Andreas, who, with others, were at this time painting in Naples.

two evenings. Early to-morrow Tischbein paints her." [1]

There are less familiar references also in the *Italian Journey*. On Goethe's return from Sicily in May, the author of *Werther,* occupied with the art, the peasant life, and the geology of the neighbourhood, renewed his acquaintance with the pair and acknowledges their kindnesses. He dined with them again. Sir William favoured him with a view of his excavated treasures in the odd " vault," where statues and sarcophagi, bronze candelabra and busts, lay disarranged and jumbled. Among them Goethe noticed an upright, open chest " rimmed exquisitely with gold, and large enough to contain a life-size figure in its dark, inner background." Sir William explained how Emma, attired in bright Pompeiian costume, had stood motionless inside it with an effect in the half-light even more striking than her grace as "moving statue." Goethe, ever curious, was now keenly interested in studying the superstitions of the Neapolitan peasantry, including the realistic shows of manger and Magi with which they celebrated Christmas-tide. In these, living images were intermixed with coloured casts of clay. And he hazards the remark—while deprecating it from the lips of a contented guest—that perhaps " Miss Harte " was at root not more than such a living image —a *tableau vivant*. Perchance, he muses, the main lack of his " fair hostess " is *"geist"* or soulfulness of mind. Her dumb shows, he adds, were naturally unvoiced, and voice alone expresses spirit. Even her admired singing he then thought deficient in " fulness." Had Goethe, however, known her whole nature, he would have owned that if she were *" geistlos "* in the highest sense, she was never dull, and was to prove the reverse of soulless; while he, of all men,

[1] Goethe, *Italienische Reise*, March 16, 1787.

would have admired not only her enthusiasm but her more practical qualities. Did he, perhaps, in after years recall this mute and lovely vision when her name, for good or ill, had entered history? At any rate, though neither Hamilton nor Emma has noticed him in existing letters, they both endure on Goethe's pages; and to have impressed Goethe was even then no easy task. That the creator of *Iphigenia* and *Tasso* was deeply impressed is proved by another and better known passage, where after praising Hamilton as "a man of universal taste, who has roamed through all the realms of creation," and has "made a beautiful existence which he enjoys in the evening of life," he adds that Emma is "a masterpiece of the Arch-Artist."

To resume our dissolving views: a priest begs her picture on a box, which he clasps to his bosom. A countess weeps when she departs. The Russian empress hears her fame, and orders her portrait. Commodore Melville gives a dinner to thirty on board his Dutch frigate in her honour, and seats her at the head as "mistress of the feast." She is robed "all in virgin white," her hair "in ringlets reaching almost to her heels," so long, that Sir William says she "look't and moved amongst it." She has soon learned by rote the little ways of the big world, and whispers to him that it is gala night at San Carlo, and *de rigueur* to reach their box before the royal party entered their neighbouring one. The guns salute; the pinnace starts amid laughter, song, and roses, while off she speeds to semi-royal triumphs—"as tho' I was a queen." Serena's wholesome lesson is being half forgotten.

Once more, Vesuvius "looks beautiful," with its lava-streams descending far as Portici. She climbs the peak of fire at midnight—five miles of flame; the peasants deem the mountain "burst." The climbers seek the shelter of the Hermit's cabin—that strange Hermit who had thus retired to solitude and exile for love of a princess.[1] Has she not spirit? Let Greville mark: "For me, I was enraptured. I could have staid all night there, and I have never been in charity with the moon since, for it looked so pale and sickly. And the red-hot lava served to light up the moon, for the light of the moon was nothing to the lava." Ascending, she meets the Prince-Royal. His "foolish tuters," fearful of their charge's safety and their own, escort him only halfway, and allow him but three minutes for the sight. She asks him how he likes it. "*Bella, ma poca roba,*" replies the lad. Five hundred yards higher he could have watched "the noblest, sublimest sight in the world." But the "poor frightened creatures" beat "a scared" retreat: "O, I shall kill myself with laughing!" And is not the plebeian girl schooling herself to be a match for crass blue blood? "Their [h]as been a prince paying us a visit. He is sixty years of age, one of the first families, and [h]as allways lived at Naples; and when I told him I had been at Caprea, he asked me if I went there by land. Only think what ignorance! I staired at him, and asked him who was his tutor," coolly remarks the *femme savante* who writes of "as" and "stair."

She cannot tear her eyes away from the volcano's awful pageant. She takes one of her maids—"a great biggot"—up to her house-top and shows her the conflagration. The contadina drops on her knees, calling on the city's patron saints: "*O Janaro mio, O Antonio mio!*" Emma falls down on hers, exclaiming, "*O Santa Loola mia, Loola mia!*" Teresa rises, and with open eyes inquires whether "her Excellency"

[1] Alexandre Sauveur, who dared to love the Princess Ferdinand, whose tutor he was.

doubts the saints. "No," replies her mistress in Italian, "it is quite the same if you pray to my own 'Loola.'" ". . . She look't at me, and said, to be sure, I read a great many books and must know more than her. But she says, 'Does not God favour you more than ous?' Says I, no. 'O God,' says she, 'your eccellenza is very ungrateful! He [h]as been so good as to make your face the same as he made the face of the Blessed Virgin's, and you don't esteem it a favour!' 'Why,' says I, 'did you ever see the Virgin?' 'O yes,' says she, 'you are like every picture that there is of her, and you know the people at Iscea fel down on their knees to you, and beg'd you to grant them favours in her name.' And, Greville, it is true that they have all got it in their heads that I am like the Virgin, and—do come to beg favours of me. Last night there was two preists came to my house, and Sir William made me put a shawl over my head, and look up, and the preist burst into tears and kist my feet, and said God had sent me a purpose."

Emma is in vein indeed. How buoyantly she swims and splashes on the rising tide! How exuberantly the whole breathes of "I always knew I could, if opportunity but walked towards me!" and of "I will show Greville what a pearl he has cast away!" Although she could be diffident when matched with genuine excellence or before those she loved, how the blare of her trumpet drowns all the still small voices! One is reminded of Woollett, the celebrated eighteenth century engraver, who was in the habit of firing off a small cannon from the roof of his house every time he had finished a successful plate. What a profuse medley of candour and contrivance, of simplicity and vanity, of commonness and elegance, of courtesy and challenge, of audacity and courage, of quick-wittedness and ignorance, of honest kindness and honest irreverence! She is already a born actress of realities, and on no mimic stage. Yet many of her faults she fully felt, and held them curable. " Patienza," she sighs, and time may mend them; in her own words of this very period, " I am a pretty woman, and one cannot be everything at once."

But a more delicate strain is audible when her heart is really touched.

At the convent whither she resorted for daily lessons during Sir William's absence, now transpired an idyl which must be repeated just as she describes it:—

" I had hardly time to thank you for your kind letter of this morning as I was buisy prepairing for to go on my visit to the Convent of Santa Romita; and endead I am glad I went, tho' it was a short visit. But to-morrow I dine with them in full assembly. I am quite charmed with Beatrice Acquaviva. Such is the name of the charming whoman I saw to-day. Oh Sir William, she is a pretty whoman. She is 29 years old. She took the veil at twenty; and does not repent to this day, though if I am a judge in physiognomy, her eyes does not look like the eyes of a nun. They are allways laughing, and something in them vastly alluring, and I wonder the men of Naples wou'd suffer the oneley pretty whoman who is realy pretty to be shut in a convent. But it is like the mean-spirited ill taste of the Neapolitans. I told her I wondered how she wou'd be lett to hide herself from the world, and I daresay thousands of tears was shed the day she deprived Naples of one of its greatest ornaments. She answered with a sigh, that endead numbers of tears was shed, and once or twice her resolution was allmost shook, but a pleasing comfort she felt at regaining her friends that she had been brought up with, and religious considerations strengthened her mind, and she parted with the world with pleasure. And since that time one of her sisters had followed her example, and another—which I saw—was preparing to enter soon. But neither of her sisters is so beautiful as her, tho' the[y] are booth very agreable. But I think Beatrice is charming, and I realy feil for her an affection. Her eyes, Sir William, is I don't know how to describe them. I stopt one hour with them; and I had all the good things to eat, and I promise you they don't starve themselves. But there dress is very becoming, and she told me that she was allow'd to wear rings and mufs and any little thing she liked, and endead she display'd to-day a good deal of finery, for she had 4 or 5 dimond rings on her fingers, and seemed fond of her muff. She has excellent teeth, and shows them, for she is allways laughing. She kissed my lips, cheeks, and forehead, and every moment exclaimed ' Charming, fine creature,' admired my dress, said I looked like an angel, for I was in clear white dimity and a blue sash." (This, surely, is scarcely the seraphic garb as the great masters imaged it.) ". . . She said she had heard I was good to the poor, generous, and nobleminded. ' Now,' she says, ' it wou'd be worth wile to live for such a one as you. Your good heart wou'd melt at any trouble that befel me, and partake of one's greef or be equaly happy at one's good fortune. But I never met with a freind yet, or I ever saw a person I cou'd love till now, and you shall have proofs of my love.' In short I sat and listened to her, and the tears stood in my eyes, I don't know why; but I loved her at that moment. I thought what a charming wife she wou'd have made, what a mother of a family, what a freind, and the first good and amiable whoman I have seen since I came to Naples for to be lost to the world—how cruel! She give me a sattin pocketbook of her own work, and bid me think of her, when I saw it, and was many miles far of[f]; and years hence when she peraps shou'd be no more, to look at it, and think the person that give it had not a bad heart. Did not she speak very pretty? But not one word of religion. But I shall be happy to-day, for I shall dine with them all, and come home at night. There is sixty whomen and all well-looking, but not like the fair Beatrice. 'Oh Emma,' she says to me, 'the[y] brought here the Viene minister's wife, but I did not like the looks of her at first. She was little, short, pinch'd face, and I received her cooly. How different from you, and how surprised was I in seeing you tall in statu[r]e. We may read your heart in your countenance, your complexion; in short, your figure and features is rare, for you are like the marble statues I saw when I was in the world.' I think she flattered me up, but I was pleased." [1]

The convent cloisters bordered on those "royal" or "English" gardens which Sir William and she were afterwards so much to improve; and here, if the Marchesa di Solari's memory can be trusted—and it constantly trips in her Italian record—happened, it would seem, about this time, another incident typical of another side, more comic than pathetic. It sounds like some interlude by Beaumarchais, and recalls Rosina of Figaro. Intrigue belongs to Naples. The young Goethe observed of the Neapolitan atmosphere: " Naples is a paradise. Every one lives, after his manner, intoxicated with self-forgetfulness. It is the same with me. I scarcely recognise myself, I seem an altered being. Yesterday I thought 'either you *were* or *are* mad.' " [2]

The madcap belle's stratagem was this. Walking

---

[1] Morrison MS. 160, January 10, 1787. It should here be commemorated that one of her first actions at Naples was to procure a post for Robert White, a protégé of Greville.

[2] Goethe, *Italienische Reise*, March 16, 1787.

there one afternoon under the escort of her duenna, she was accosted by a personage whom she knew to be King Ferdinand. He solicited a private interview, and was peremptorily refused. He succeeded, however, in bribing her attendant, and followed her to a remote nook, where they would be unobserved. He pressed his promises with fervour, but Emma refused to listen to a word, unless everything was committed to paper.[1] The monarch complied, and thereupon Emma hastened to the palace and urgently entreated an audience with the Queen. Sobbing on her knees, she implored her to save her from persecutions so great that unless they were removed she had resolved to quit the world and find shelter with the nuns. The Queen, touched by such beauty in such distress, urged her to disclose the name of her unknown importuner. Thereupon Emma handed her the paper, was bidden by the Queen to rise, and comforted. So far there seems ground for the tale. The Marchesa says that Sir William " partially " confirmed it; and this must allude to the sequel which represents Maria Carolina as urging the Ambassador to marry his Lucretia without delay. Whether it is true that the tears of affliction were caused by an onion, and that Emma was " on her marrow-bones " in the garden while the Queen was perusing the tell-tale document, depends upon the number of embellishments such a farce would probably receive. If true, it hardly redounds to Emma's credit.

But from Emma we must now part awhile to con-

[1] From indications in her letter. Cf. Morrison MS. 157, December 26, 1786 (Emma to Sir William) : " If I had the offer of *crowns*, I would refuse them and except you, and I don't care if all the world knows it. . . . Certain it is I love you and sincerely." And cf. *ibid*. 153 : "We are closely besieged by the King in a roundabout manner, but . . . we never give him any encouragement." In this very year the prima donna Banti was whisked off across the frontier by the Queen's orders for presuming to favour the amorous King's attentions.

sider the social and political conditions of the court of
Naples, very different now from what they were to
become a few years later under the new forces of the
French Revolution, and, afterwards, of the meteoric
Napoleon. It is a panorama which here can only be
sketched in outline. It was to prove the theatre of
Emma's best activities.

During the entire eighteenth century, from the War
of Succession to the Treaty of Utrecht, from the
Treaty of Utrecht to that of the Quadruple Alliance,
from that again to those of Vienna and of Aix, the
Bourbons and the Hapsburgs had been perpetually
wrestling for the rich provinces of central and southern Italy—a prize which united the secular appeal to
Catholic Europe with supremacy over the Mediterranean. The Bourbons, by a strange chain of coincidence, had prevailed in Spain, and in 1731 " Baby
Carlos " solemnly entered on his Italian and Sicilian
heritage, long so craftily and powerfully compassed by
his ambitious mother, Elizabeth Farnese. The Hapsburgs, however, never relinquished their aim, though
the weak and pompous Emperor, Charles VI., was reduced to spending his energies on the mere phantom of
the " Pragmatic Sanction " by which he hoped to
cement his incoherent Empire in the person of his masterful daughter; he died hugging, so to speak, that
" Pragmatic Sanction " to his heart. Maria Theresa
proved herself the heroine of Europe in her proud
struggle with the Prussian aggressor who for a time
forced her into an unnatural and lukewarm league
with the French Bourbons, themselves covetous of
the Italian Mediterranean. Even after the French
Bourbons were quelled, France, in the person of Napoleon, succeeded to their ambitions. Second only to
his hankering after Eastern Empire, was from the

first the persistent hankering after Naples and Sicily
of the would-be dominator of the sea, whose coast
had been his cradle.

Maria Theresa was therefore delighted when in
April, 1768, her eldest daughter, Maria Charlotte, better known as " Maria Carolina," espoused, when barely
sixteen years of age, Ferdinand, son of the Bourbon
Charles III. of Spain, then only one year her senior,
and already from his eighth year King of the Two
Sicilies. Still more did she rejoice when two years
later her other daughter, Marie Antoinette, married at
the same age the Duc de Berri, then heir-presumptive
to the French throne, which he ascended four years
afterwards. Both daughters were to fight manfully
with a fate which worsted the one and extinguished
the other, while the husbands of both were true Bourbons in their indecision and their love of the table;
for of the Bourbons it was well said that their chapel
was their kitchen.

" King " Maria Theresa educated all her children
to believe in three things: their religion, their race,
and their destiny. They were never to forget that
they were Catholics, imperialists, and politicians. But
she also taught them to be enlightened and benevolent,
provided that their faithful subjects accepted the grace
of these virtues unmurmuring from their hands. They
were to be monopolists of reform. They were also
to be monopolists of power; nor was husband or wife
to dispute their sway. Indeed, the two daughters
were schooled to believe that control over their con-
sorts was an absolute duty, doubly important from
the rival ascendency wielded by the Queens of the
Spanish Bourbons, who for three generations had been
mated with imbecile or half-imbecile sovereigns; they
had a knack of calling their husbands cowards. And
they were to be monopolists of religion even against

the Pope if he unduly interfered. These lessons were graven on the hearts of all but Marie Antoinette, who shared the obstinacy but lacked the penetration of her sister and brothers.

Maria Theresa's son and successor, Joseph II. of Austria, showed to the full this union of bigotry and benevolence, both arbitrary yet both popular. He and his premier, Kaunitz, were strenuous in education and reform, but also strenuous in suppressing the Jesuits. His brothers were the same. Archduke Ferdinand played the benevolent despot in Bohemia, while Leopold, afterwards Grand Duke of the Tuscan dominions, was even more ostentatious in his high-handed well-doing. Never was a dynasty politer, more cultivated, more affable. But never also was one haughtier, more obstinate, or more formal. All were martyrs to etiquette, but all were also enthusiastic freemasons, and Queen Maria Carolina's family enthusiasm for the secret societies of " Illuminati " sowed those misfortunes which were afterwards watered with blood, reaped in tears, and harvested by iron. In 1790 Leopold, for a space, succeeded to Joseph; and Maria Carolina was afterwards to see one of her sixteen children wedded to Francis, Leopold's successor on the Austrian throne, another to the King of Sardinia, a third, in the midst of her final calamities, united at Palermo to the future Louis Philippe. She thus became mother-in-law to an emperor of whom she was aunt, as well as to two monarchs; while already she had been sister to two successive emperors.

Her husband, Ferdinand IV., was a boor and *bon vivant,* good-natured on the surface, but with a strong spice of cruelty beneath it; suspicious of talent, but up to the fatal sequels of the French Revolution the darling of his people. As the little Prince of Asturias, he had been handed to the tutorship of the old Duke of San Nicandro, who was restricted by the royal commands to instruction in sport, and in his own learning to a bowing acquaintance with his breviary. Inheriting a throne, while a child, by the accident of his father's accession to the Spanish crown, he had been reared in Sicily—always jealous of Naples— under the tutelage of Prince Caramanico, a minister of opera bouffe, and of Tenucci, a corrupt vizier of the old-world pattern, who preferred place to statesman- ship, and pocket to power. The young King, how- ever, was by no means so illiterate or unjust as has often been assumed, and, if he was " eight years old when he began to reign," the rest of the Scripture cannot then, at any rate, be justly applied to him. He remained throughout his life a kind of Italianised Tony Lumpkin, addicted to cards and beauty, de- voted to arms and sport. Indeed, in many ways he resembled a typical English squire of the period, as Lord William Bentinck shrewdly observed of him some twenty-five years afterwards. Music was also his hobby. He sang often, but scarcely well; and Emma, when he first began to practise duets with her, humorously remarked, *" He sings like a King."*

The people that he loved, and who adored him, were the Neapolitan Lazzaroni--not beggars, as the name implies, but loafing artisans, peasants, and fish- ermen, noisy, loyal, superstitious, rollicking, unthrifty, vigorous, in alternate spasms of short-li·ed work and easy pleasure—the natural and ineradicable outcome of their sultry climate, their mongrel blood, their red- hot soil, and their pagan past. Motléy was their wear. As happens to all peculiar peoples, they could not suf- fer or even fancy alien conditions. When the Grand Duke and Duchess of Russia visited Naples in 1782 during an abnormal spell of February cold, they swore that the northerners had brought the accursed weather

with them.   They had their recognised leaders, their
acknowledged improvisatores, their informal functions and functionaries, like a sort of unmigratory
gypsy tribe.   They had their own *patois,* their own
customs, their own songs, their favourite monks.   Such
was the famous Padre Giordano, the six-foot portent
of a handsome priest, the best preacher, the best singer,
the best eater of macaroni in the King's dominions.
They had, too, their own feuds, in a country where
even composers like Cimarosa and Paisiello were always at loggerheads and made separate factions of
their own.   All that they knew of England before
1793 was that their own Calabria furnished the wood
for its vaunted ships.   With the Lazzaroni, Ferdinand
early became a prime favourite.   He was not only
their king, but their jolly comrade.   He was a Falstaff
king, even in his gross proportions; a king of mis-
rule in his boisterous humour.   He was a Policinello
king whose Bourbon nose won him the *sobriquet* of
" Nasone " from his mountebank liegemen.   He was
a Robin Hood king, who early formed his own free-
booting bodyguard; he was also King Reynard the
Fox, with intervals of trick and avarice, although, unlike that jungle-Mephistopheles, Ferdinand could never
cajole.   He was, in truth, both cramped and spirited—
" a lobster crushed by his shell," as Beckford once
termed him—despite his defects both real and imputed, his want of dignity, his phlegmatic exterior and
his rude antics.   Every Christmas saw him in his box
at San Carlo, sucking up macaroni sticks for their
edification from a steaming basin of burnished silver,
while the Queen discreetly retired to a back seat.
Every Carnival witnessed him in fisher's garb playing
at fish-auctioneer on the quay which served as market,
bandying personal jests, indulging in rough horse-
play, and driving preposterous bargains to their boister-

ous delight.   This picturesque if greasy court would
strike up the chorus in full sight of their macaroni
monarch :—

> "S'e levata la gabella alla farina!
> Evviva Ferdinando e Carolina."

He loved to play Haroun Alraschid—to do justice in
the gate—and, when hunting, to pay surprise visits
to the cabins of the peasantry and redress their
wrongs; though when the fit was on him he could
scourge them with scorpions.   In his rambles on the
beach the despot would toss the dirtiest of his rough
adherents violently into the sea, and if he could not
swim, would then himself plunge into the water and
bring him laughing from his first bath to the shore.
It was one of these sallies that suggested to Canova
his marble Hercules throwing Lichas into the sea, acquired by the bankers Torlonia before they were styled
princes; and, indeed, the coarser side of Hercules
as Euripides portrays him in the *Alcestis* bears
some resemblance to this uncouth and burly Nimrod.

While he was at first proud of his *femme savante*
and left affairs of state until 1799 almost entirely in
her hands and Acton's, his jealousy tended more and
more to treat her as a *précieuse ridicule,* and he grew
fond of asserting his mastery by playing the
Petruchio, sometimes to brutality.

For a long time he was pro-Spanish, while his
wife remained pro-Austrian, and came to abominate
Spanish policy more than ever when in 1778 Charles
IV. of Spain ascended the throne with a caballing
consort whom Maria Carolina detested.   Ferdinand
boasted that his people were happy because each could
find subsistence at home, and the time was still distant
when to the proverb on his name of " Farina " and

" Feste," " Forca " was superadded. If he pauper-
ised his people with farinaceous morsels and festivities, he did not as yet execute them. Nor was
he destitute of bluff wit and exceedingly *common*
sense.

There is a familiar anecdote which may illustrate his
rough and ready humour as well as his favourite
methods of government. On one occasion his pedantic
brother-in-law Leopold asked Ferdinand what he was
" doing " for the people. " Nothing at all, which is
the best," guffawed the King in answer; " and the
proof is that while plenty of your folk go wheedling
and begging in my territory, I will wager anything
you like that none of mine are soliciting anything in
yours." This was the same Leopold whom the royal
pair visited in their " golden journey " of 1785 which
paraded the new navy organised by Acton.

The Queen, however, was an " illuminata " by bent
and upbringing. She was always devising theories
and executing schemes, and besides literature, botany,
too, engrossed her attention. It is a mistake to judge
either her or him in the light of after occurrences, and
it is an error as misleading to judge even those events
by the evidence of Jacobin *littérateurs,* one at least
among the most violent of whom did not hesitate to
recant. It was only long afterwards that she became
lampooned, and that the " head of a Richelieu on a
pretty woman " was held up to execration in the words
of the ancient diatribe on Catherine of Médicis :—

> " Si nous faisons l'apologie
>   De Caroline et Jézabel,
> L'une fut reine en Italie,
>   Et l'autre reine en Israël.
> Celle-ci de malice extrême,
> L'autre était la malice même." [1]

[1] " Would casuists find excuses try

Neither King nor Queen, though both have much
to answer for at the bar of history, were ever the pan-
tomime-masks of villainy and corruption that resentment and rumour, public and private, have affixed to
their names.

The Queen's full influence was not apparent until
the birth of an heir in 1777, when by a clause of
her marriage-settlement she became entitled to sit in
council.   But long before, she had begun to inspire
reforms very distasteful to the feudal barons who at
first composed her court.   She endeavoured to turn a
set of antiquated prescriptions into a freer constitution, and to cleanse the Neapolitan homes.   She limited
the feudal system of rights—odious to the people at
large—to narrow areas, and this popular limitation
proved long afterwards the main cause of the nobility's share in the middle-class revolution of 1799.   The
marriage laws were re-cast much on the basis of Lord
Hardwick's Act in England.   The administration of
justice was purified.   Besides locating the University
in the fine rooms of the suppressed Jesuit monastery,
to some of which she transferred the magnificent antiques of the Farnese and Palatine collections, she
founded schools and new institutions for the encouragement of agriculture and architecture.   Even the
hostile historian Colletta admits that she drew all the
intellect of the age to Naples.   Waste lands were re-
claimed, colonies planted on uninhabited islands, existing industries developed, and the coral fisheries on
the African coasts converted into a chartered com-

> For Caroline and Jezebel,
> The one was queen in Italy,
>   The other, queen in Israel.
> Extremes of malice marked the second,
> Malice itself the first was reckoned."

Cf. *Crimes et Amours des Bourbons de Naples*, Paris, Anon.,
1861.

pany. The evils of tax-gathering were obviated; the ports of Brindisi and Baia restored; highways were made free of expense for the poor; tolerance was universally proclaimed; the Pope's right to nominate bishops was defied; nor was she reconciled to Pius VI. till policy compelled her to kneel before him in her Roman visit of 1791. At the period now before us, most of the pulpits favoured her. Padre Rocco, the blunt reformer of abuses, Padre Minasi, the musical archæologist, were loud in her praises. And this despite the fact that, though regular in her devotions and the reverse of a free-thinker, she resolutely opposed the "crimping" system which from time to time reinforced the Neapolitan convents. She also bitterly offended the vested rights of the lawyers and the army. An enthusiast for freemasonry (and long after her death the Neapolitan lodges toasted her memory), she assembled around her through these societies a brilliant throng of *savants* and poets, while it was her special aim to elevate the intellects of women. Among the circle of all the talents around her were the great economist and jurist Filangieri, revered by Goethe, but dead within two years after Emma's arrival; the learned and ill-starred Cirillo and Pagano, who both perished afterwards in the Revolution; Palmieri, Galanti, Galiani, Delfico, the scientists; Caravelli, Caretto, Falaguerra, Ardinghelli, Pignatelli, all lights of literature; and Conforti, the historian. But perhaps the most interesting of all, and the most typical, was Eleonora de Fonseca Pimentel, subsequently muse and victim of the outburst in 1799.

This remarkable poetess, Portuguese by origin, merits and has received a monograph. Up to 1793, indeed, this friend and disciple of Metastasio was the professed eulogist of the Queen. She styled her

"La verace virtute, e di lei figlio
Il verace valor." [1]

She joined her in denouncing "Papal vassalage" in
Italy. When the royal bambino died in 1778 she indited her "Orfeo" as elegy. When the "golden journey" was accomplished, the Miseno port re-opened,
and the fleet re-organised, her "Proteus and
Parthenope" celebrated the commencement of a golden
age. But what most aroused her enthusiasm was the
foundation of that singular experiment in monarchical
socialism—the ideal colony of San Leucio at Caserta
between the years 1777 and 1779. This settlement
was the first-fruits of the Queen's socialism, though its
occasion was the King's liking for his hunting-box—
built in 1773 at the neighbouring Belvedere, and on
the site of the ancient vineyard and palace of the old
Princes of Caserta. A church was erected in 1776
for a parish governed by an enlightened code of duties
"negative and positive," and even then numbering no
less than seventeen families. Some of the royal build-
ings were converted into schools; even the prayers and
religious ordinances were regulated, as were all observ-
ances of the hearth, and every distribution of property.
Allegiance was to be paid first to God, then to the
sovereign, and lastly to the ministers. Under Ferdinand's nominal authorship a book of the aims, orders,
and laws of the colony was published, of which a copy
exists in the British Museum. On its flyleaf Lady
Hamilton has herself recorded:—"Given to me by the
King of Naples at Belvedere or S. Leucio the 16th of
May, 1793, when Sir William and I dined with his
Majesty and the Duchess of Devonshire, Lady Webster,
Lady Plymouth, Lady Bessborough, Lady E. Foster,
Sir G. Webster, and Mr. Pelham. Emma Hamilton."

[1] "True virtue, and the birth of virtue true,
True courage."

These names are in no accidental association. The then and the future Duchesses of Devonshire headed a galaxy of which Charles James Fox was chief, and to which Sir William's devotees, Lady " Di " Beauclerk and the Honourable Mrs. Damer, also belonged.

Eleonora's ode in its honour hymns the " royal city " where " nature's noble diadem " crowns " the spirit of ancient Hellas."

But for all these undertakings, even before stress of invasion and vengeance for wrongs prompted large armaments and an English alliance, financial talent of a high order was needful; taxation had to be broadened, and it could not be enlarged without pressing heavily on the professional classes, for the Lazzaroni were always privileged as exempt. The necessities which led to the shameful tampering with the banks in 1792-93 had not yet arisen; but organising talent was needed, and organising talent was wanting. Tenucci proved as poor a financier as once our own Godolphin or Dashwood. Jealous of Carolina's manifest direction, he caballed, and was replaced as first minister in 1776 by the phantom Sambuca. Even then the pro-Spanish party among the grandees menaced the succession well-nigh as much as the pro-Jacobins did some five years later. Even then it was on very few of the numberless Neapolitan nobles (a " golden book " of whom would outdo Venice and equal Spain) that the perplexed Queen could rely. Caramanico was a mere monument of the past, and as such consigned to England as ambassador; while his young and romantic son Joseph was reputed the Queen's lover, and forbidden the court. The coxcomb and procrastinator, Gallo, who afterwards ratted to Napoleon, was already mismanaging foreign affairs. The old and respectable Caracciolo, father of that rebel admiral whom Nelson was to execute, was for the moment Minister of Finance, but approaching his end. That Admirable Crichton, Prince Belmonte, afterwards as "Galatone" ambassador at the crucial post of the Madrid Embassy, now preferred the office of Chamberlain to any active direction of affairs. Prince Castelcicala, twice ambassador to the court of St. James's, and nearly as acceptable to the Queen as Belmonte, had not yet been pressed into home concerns, nor had he disastrously earned his inquisitorial spurs of 1793. Sicigniano, who was to commit suicide when ambassador in London in the same year, belonged to the same category; the young and accomplished Luigi di Medici had not yet emerged into a prominence that proved his doom. Prince Torella was a nonentity; the Rovere family, which was to supply the Sidney or Bayard [1] of the Revolution, was not now of political significance. The professional classes were as yet excluded from government, and creatures like the notorious Vanni were denied power. Amid the general dearth the excitable Queen was at her wit's end for a capable minister. During her Vienna and Tuscan visits of 1778 she consulted, as always, her august relations; and the result was their recommendation of John Francis Edward Acton, whose younger brother had for some time been serving in the Austrian army. In consenting to the trial of an unknown man, middle-aged and a foreigner, the Queen hardly realised to what grave issues her random choice was leading.

Acton, third cousin of Sir Richard Acton of Aldenham Hall, Shropshire, to whose baronetcy and estates he most unexpectedly succeeded in 1791, was the son of a physician, Catholic and Jacobite, settled at Besançon. He was born in 1736, and may have first entered the French Navy, which he quitted probably as a cadet

[1] Prince Ettore Carafa.

in search of advancement, and not because of the
vague discredits afterwards imputed by the Jacobins.
The British Navy he could scarcely have contemplated,
because in the days of the Georges Catholicism and
Jacobitism were grave impediments to success. At
the age of thirty-nine he entered the naval service of
Carolina's brother, the Grand Duke Leopold of
Tuscany, and attracted Caramanico's notice by his
bravery as Captain on a Spanish expedition against
the Moors.   Summoned by a stroke of luck to control
a realm at once ambitious and sluggish, he infused
English energy at every step.   A martinet by training and disposition, shrewd, worldly, calculating, yet
sturdy, and for Naples, where gold always reigned,
inflexibly honest, he was well capable of defying and
brow-beating the supple Neapolitan nobility who detested his introduction.   A smooth-tongued adventurer, though good looks were not on his side, he
speedily won the favour of a Queen inclined to make
tools of favourites, and favourites of tools; but he
soon convinced her also that a mere tool he could never
remain.   He was naturally pro-British, and Britain
was already a Mediterranean power: Acton recommended the country of his origin to the Queen's notice
in the veriest trifles.   It was not many years before
Maria Carolina was driving in the English curricle
which Hamilton had provided for her.   Little else
than a stroke of destiny, under the conjunctures of the
near future, brought the new foreigner into close alliance with Sir William Hamilton, whose patriotism in
the very year when he was lolling with Sir Horace
Mann at Portici had expressed itself in a fervent wish
to see France " well drubbed," and a fury at the
non-support of Rodney by Government.   The different natures of the two perhaps cemented their friendship.   Hamilton for all his natural indolence could

rise to emergency; Acton, on the contrary, was all compromise and caution—a sort of Robert Walpole in
little, with " steady " for his motto.   Hamilton was
good-tempered to a fault: Emma wrote of him after
her marriage that he preferred " good temper to
beauty."   In Acton lay a strong spice of the bully,
and he could be very unjust if his authority was im-
pugned.   He was a born bureaucrat, and it was his
love of bureaucracy, as will appear, that ruined the
Queen.

Acton's only marriage occurred in his old age with
his young niece, by papal dispensation in 1805, as Pettigrew has recorded.   His brother Joseph's descendants are still at Naples.   But none of his family play
any part in the drama before us.   Starting as an Admiral of the Neapolitan Fleet, he soon became Minister both of Marine and War.   Caracciolo the elder's
opportune transference to diplomacy in Paris and London, which Acton's future libellers accused him of
contriving, as afterwards even of causing his death,
installed him as Minister of Finance.   He at once advised the institution of thirteen Commissioners who
could all be censured in event of failure; " divide et
impera " was his principle; and at first his resource
proved successful.   He was soon made also a Lieuten-
ant-General; while some ten years later, in his heyday,
he was appointed Captain-General, and at last a full-
blown Field-Marshal.   But long before, he blossomed
into power with the Queen, whose anti-Spanish policy
chimed with his own, and whose abhorrence of the
pro-Spanish functionaries around her required a
champion in council.   This created two camps in the
court, for up to 1796 the King was pro-Spanish to
the core.   But the Queen was already predominant,
and it was soon bruited that the Latin " hic, hæc, hoc "
meant Acton, the Queen, and the King thus derided

as neuter; indeed some added that Acton was "*hic,*
hæc, hoc" in one. In a brief space Acton had con-
solidated a powerful fleet—which in 1793 he was able
to despatch in aid of the English at Toulon—and a
formidable army. The French events of 1789 rendered him all the more indispensable to Maria Carolina, whose ears were terrified by the first rumblings
of an earthquake so soon to engulf her sister's family. The Bastille was taken, the Assembly held, and
fawning false-loyalty loomed fully as dangerous as up-
roarious Jacobinism. In the same year America established her "Constitution." Already the aunts of
Louis XVI., the two old "demoiselles de France,"
were on the verge of abandoning Paris for Rome;
already the charged air tingled with Liberty, Equality, Fraternity; already Carolina, masking hysterical
restiveness by imperious composure, was debating if
armed help were possible from Austria as well as
from Naples. But the irritated barons were unwar-
like, the King cared little, the lawyers still depended on
his favour, the intelligent middle-class was beginning
to welcome the Gallic doctrines. Austria, too, was by
no means ready. And yet in Carolina's ears the hour
of doom was already striking. She longed for an
untemporising deliverer, a self-sacrificing friend, a
leader of men and movements; and as she longed and
champed in vain, she could only wait and hope and
prepare. Her anxiety was not that of a normal
woman. Calm in mind, in love and hate her ardour
ran to extremes. Though she owned a far better head
than her unhappy sister, her heart, outside her home
and in spite of her passions, was far colder. She was
truly devoted to her children, she was fond of romp-
ing even with the children of strangers; and yet when
her sons-in-law grew lukewarm in aiding her, she
could rage against her daughters. Jealousy of her

ogling and dangling consort was often a prime motive for her actions; and yet she had often been
femme galante, and was ever bent on mystery and
intrigue. She harped on duty, but her notions of
duty rested on maintaining the royal birthright of
her house. Masterful as her mother, light-living as
her eldest brother, she was neither hard nor frivolous.
She could be both ice and fire. Her strange temperament combined the poles with the equator.

The year 1789 proved critical for Emma also. It
brought to Naples, among other illustrious visitors,
the good and gracious Duchess of Argyll, formerly
Duchess of Hamilton, who, as the beautiful Miss Gun-
ning, had years before taken England, and indeed
Europe, by storm. She had come southward for her
health. Her first marriage had related her to Sir
William, and no sooner had she set eyes on Emma than
she not only countenanced her in public but conceived
for her the most admiring and intimate friendship.
Hitherto the English *ladies* had been coldly civil, but
under the lead of the Duchess they now began to follow the Italian vogue of sounding her praises. Emma
became the fashion. It was already whispered that
she was secretly married to the Ambassador, and had
she been his wife she could scarcely have been more
heartily, though she would have been more openly, accepted. Her request that she might accompany Sir
William, the King, and Acton on one of their long
and rough sporting journeys had been gladly granted.
She had attended her deputy-husband on his equally
rough antiquarian ramble through Puglia, made in
the spring of 1789. " She is so good," he informed
Greville, " there is no refusing her." By the spring of
1790 not only the Duchess but the whole Argyll family lavished kindness on the extraordinary girl whom

they must have respected. The new Spanish ambassador's wife also had become her intimate friend. Madame Le Brun, too, repaired in the wake of the French troubles to Naples, and was besieged for portraits. Madame Skavonska, the Russian ambassador's handsome wife, so empty-headed that she squandered her time in vacancy on a sofa, was her first sitter. Emma, brought by the eager Hamilton, was the second, and during her sittings she was accompanied by the Prince of Monaco and the Duchess of Fleury. Madame Le Brun, herself by no means devoid both of jealousy and snobbishness, raved of her beauty, but formed no opinion of her brain, while she found her " supercilious." This is curious, for by common consent Emma gave herself no airs; she conciliated all. But though never a *parvenue* in her affections, she could often behave as such in her dislikes; and her self-assertiveness could always combat jealous or freezing condescension. Her improvement both in knowledge and behaviour had from other accounts enhanced her accomplishments. No breath of scandal had touched her; she was Hamilton's unwedded wife, and her looks had kept even pace with her forward path in many directions: she was fairer than ever and far less vain. The Queen herself already pointed to her as an example for the court, to which, however, Emma could not gain formal admittance until the marriage which she had predicted in 1786 had been duly solemnised. For that desired climax everything now paved the way. Each night in the season she received fifty of the *élite* at the Embassy, till in January, 1791, her success was crowned by a concert and reception of unusual splendour. The stars of San Carlo performed. The court ladies vied with each other in jewels and attire. The first English, as well as the first Neapolitans, thronged every room; there were some four hundred guests. Emma herself was conspicuously simple. Amid the blaze of gems and colours she shone in white satin, set off by the natural hues only of her hair and complexion.

And yet she was not elated. Her one study, her single aim, she wrote to Greville, were to render Sir William, on whom she "doated," happy. She would be the "horridest wretch" else. They had already passed nearly five years together, "with all the domestick happiness that's possible."

Was there any rift within the lute? If so, it lay in Greville's attitude. He opened his eyes and sighed as he read of Emma's virtuous glory; and he opened them still wider when she assured him of her "esteem" for "having been the means of me knowing him," and added "next year you may pay ous a visit." That Sir William should marry her quite passed the bounds of his philosophy; there would be an *éclat,* and *éclats* he detested; his uncle would make himself ridiculous. It seems likely, from an allusion in a letter from Hamilton of a full year earlier, that the nephew had already thrown out hints of suitable provision should chance or necessity ever separate the couple. Sir William, however, had been deaf to such suggestions, although, "thinking aloud," he *did* mention £150 a year to Emma, and £50 to her mother, "who is a very worthy woman." Such contingencies, however, could not apply to their present "footing," for "her conduct was such as to gain her universal esteem." The only chance for such a scheme hinged on her pertinacity in pressing him to marry her. "I fear," he continued, "that her views are beyond what I can bring myself to execute, and that when her hopes on this point are over, she will make herself and me unhappy." But he recoiled from the thought; despite the difference in their ages and antecedents, "hitherto her conduct is irreproachable, but her temper, as you must know, unequal."

And now all these obstacles had melted under the enchanter's wand, it would seem, of the charming Duchess, who may well have urged him to defy convention and make Emma his wife. Sir William's fears were not for Naples, nor wholly for Greville, who might laugh if he chose. They were rather for the way in which his foster-brother, King George, and his Draco-Queen, might receive such news, and how they might eventually manifest their displeasure; the Ambassador, however much and often he was wont to bewail his fate, had no notion of retiring to absurd obscurity. But these objections also seem to have been equally dispersed by the fairy godmother of a Duchess who was bent on raising Cinderella to the throne; and although Queen Charlotte eventually refused to receive Lady Hamilton, yet Sir William's imminent return was in fact signalised by the honour of a privy councillorship. Long afterwards, he assured Greville that his treatment when he was eventually replaced, and subsequently when he was denied reimbursement for his losses and his services (both to go fully as unrewarded as his wife's), was not due to the king but to his ministers. Moreover, his two old Eton School friends, Banks and the ubiquitous Lord Bristol, Bishop of Derry, had signified their approval. The latter in his peregrinations had already worshipped at Emma's Neapolitan shrine—a devotee at once generous and money-grubbing, cynical and ingenuous, constant and capricious, who (in Lady Hamilton's words) " dashed at everything," and who was so eccentric as to roam Caserta in a gay silk robe and a white hat. This original—a miniature mixture of Peterborough, Hume, and, one might add, Thackeray's Charles Honeyman—had braced Hamil-

ton's resolution by telling him it was " fortitude " and
a " manly part " to brave a stupid world and secure
Emma's happiness and his own.   Sir William, whose
inclination struggled with Greville's prudence, could
not gainsay his friends who echoed the wishes of his
heart.   And all this must have been furthered by the
Duchess of Argyll.

No wonder that her sad death at the close of 1790,
far away from the climate which had proved powerless to save her, desolated Emma.   " I never," she assured Greville, who already knew of their home-
coming in the spring, " I never had such a freind as
her, and that you will know when I see you, and recount . . . all the acts of kindness she shew'd to me:
for they where too good and numerous to describe in a
letter.   Think then to a heart of gratitude and sensibility what it must suffer. *Ma passienza: io ho
molto.*"

The marriage project was first to visit Rome, where
they would meet the Queen, about to be reconciled to
the Pope, on her homeward journey from Vienna.
Then to repair to Florence, where they could take a
short leave both of her and the King; and thence to
Venice, where they were to encounter, besides many
English, the cream of the flying French *noblesse,* including the Counts of Artois and Vaudreuil, the Poli-
gnacs, and Calonne.   Before May was over they would
be in London, and there, if things went smoothly, the
wedding should take place.   Emma's heart must have
throbbed when she reflected on the stray hazards that
might still wreck that happiness for which she had
long pined, and overthrow the full cup just as it
neared her lips.

Greville was unaware of the dead secret, but he implored Emma not to live in London as she had done in
Naples; he pressed the propriety of separate establish-

ments.   Emma laughed him to scorn.   The friend of
the late Duchess and her friends could afford to flout
insular opinion.   But she laughed too soon: had she
been wiser she might possibly have propitiated the
Queen of England by discretion.   It further happened
that Greville's official friend and Emma's old acquaintance, Heneage Legge, met and spied on the
happy pair at Naples, just before he and they left for
Rome; he promptly reported progress to Greville, who
had plainly asked for enlightenment.   The unsuspect-
ing Hamilton called on Legge immediately to proffer
him every friendly service.   Mrs. Legge was in delicate health, and Emma, too, kindly offered to act
as her companion, or even nurse.   Legge was embarrassed; his wife civilly declined Emma's attentions,
"kindly intended," but owing to Emma's "former
line of life" impossible to accept.   These proprieties
confirmed Sir William's determination, and aroused
Emma's ire.   The one was accustomed to observe that
the "reformed rake" proverb applied fully as much
to a woman as a man.   The other felt herself morti-
fied and insulted just when her virtues rang on every
lip.   If the frail Lady Craven, for instance, were good
enough to touch the hem of Mrs. Legge's garments,
why not Emma, who had rashly hastened to be kind?
Legge must tell the rest himself: "Her influence over
him exceeds all belief. . . . The language of both
parties, who always spoke in the plural number—we,
us, and ours—stagger'd me at first, but soon made me
determined to speak openly to him on the subject,
when he assur'd me, what I confess I was most happy
to hear, that he was not married; but flung out some
hints of doing justice to her good behaviour, if his
public situation did not forbid him to consider himself
an independent man. . . . She gives everybody to understand that he is now going to England to solicit

the K.'s consent to marry her. . . . I am confident she will gain her point, against which it is the duty of every friend to strengthen his mind as much as possible; and she will be satisfied with no argument but the King's absolute refusal of his approbation. Her talents and powers of amusing are very wonderfull. Her voice is very fine, but she does not sing with great taste, and Aprili [*sic*] says she has not a good ear; her Attitudes are beyond description beautifull and striking, and I think you will find her figure much improved since you last saw her. *They* say they shall be in London by the latter end of May, that their stay in England will be as short as possible, and that, having settled his affairs, he is determined never to return. She is much visited here by ladies of the highest rank, and many of the *corps diplomatique;* does the honours of his house with great attention and desire to please, but wants a little refinement of manners in which . . . I wonder she has not made greater progress. I have all along told her that she could never change her situation, and that she was a happier woman as Mrs. H. than she wou'd be as Lady H., when more reserved behaviour being necessary, she wou'd be depriv'd of half her amusements."[1]

Sound sense enough, but most unlikely to convince Emma's self-confidence. Mrs. Legge, too, and afterwards Queen Charlotte, were justified in excommunicating Emma *before* her marriage; such decencies are concerns of precedent, the etiquette of morality. But it is surely a cruel and un-Christian precedent, to set up without exception that a girl who had raised and trained herself as Emma had done should be debarred from the possibility of legitimate retrieval. Such standards savour far more of the world than of

[1] Morrison MS. 190; Legge to Greville, Naples, March 8, 1791.

Heaven. And, at all events, it must be conceded
that at this period Emma, who had been beloved not
only by the Duchesses of Argyll and Devonshire, but
by such young ladies as Miss Carr, could not possibly
have hurt or soiled the British matron. There may
well have been quite as much unamiable envy as injured innocence in the blank refusal to let her show
that she was a kind and helpful woman, even though
she had not always been irreproachable.

London was reached at last, and the King's reluctant sanction obtained. They were fêted and entertained by the Marquis of Abercorn, by Beckford at
Fonthill, and by the Duke of Queensberry, who gave
a brilliant concert at Richmond in their honour, where
Emma herself performed. But her chief delight was
her reunion with those art coteries where she had ever
felt herself freest and most at home. One of her first
visits was to Cavendish Square. On a June morning
she surprised Romney—an apparition in " Turkish
dress "—while he was ailing and melancholy. Neither
his trip in the previous year, nor the warm friendship
of Hayley, who had now fitted up a studio for him
at Eartham, could exorcise the demon of dejection
which brooded over him. The wonderful girl whose
career he had watched afar, cheered him back to his
former source of inspiration. His letters to Hayley
of this date are full of her. She was eager that her
old friend should recognise that she was " still the
same Emma." She sat for him constantly, and besides his many other studies and portraits of her, he at
once made her the model of his Joan of Arc, the idea
of which his recent journey across the Channel had
suggested. Both this and a " Magdalen " were commissioned by the Prince of Wales, who seems to have
met her at the Duke of Queensberry's. He painted
her as " Cassandra," he designed to paint her as " Con-

stance," he commenced a fresh "Bacchante." He
dined with her and Sir William, and they both dined
thrice with him, first in July and afterwards in August.
He broke his rule of solitude in order that "several
people of fashion" might behold the performances of
one whom he declared "superior to all womankind."
She in her turn begged him to let Hayley set about
writing his life. All that she did or said fascinated
him; and the fondest father, remarks his biographer,
could not have taken a keener pleasure in the marriage
of a favourite daughter than did Romney in her imminent wedding. Her acting and singing so transported him, that he was on the point of posting off
near midnight to fetch Hayley from Eartham. "She
performed both in the serious and comic to admiration: but her 'Nina'"—a part two years later the
especial delight of Maria Carolina—"surpasses everything I ever saw, and I believe, as a piece of acting,
nothing ever surpassed it. The whole company were
in an agony of sorrow. Her acting is simple, grand,
terrible, and pathetic." It was this power of moving
others that, according to a tradition often repeated
by the late Sir Francis Hastings Doyle, once so worked
on Nelson ten years afterwards, that he walked up
and down the crowded room muttering, "D——
Mrs. Siddons!" with whom somebody had contrasted
her. On the occasion just mentioned Gallini, the im-
presario, offered her £2000 a year and two benefits "if
she would engage with him"; but, in Romney's words,
"Sir William said pleasantly that he had engaged
her for life."

For a few weeks Romney fancied her attitude
towards him altered; the mere suspicion disquieted his
nerves, but the cloud was soon dispelled. Meanwhile
Hayley, who was to compose a fresh poem on her just
before her wedding, indited the following:

" Gracious Cassandra ! whose benign esteem
    To my weak talent every aid supplied,
Thy smile to me was inspiration's beam,
    Thy charms my model, and thy taste my guide.

But say ! what cruel clouds have darkly chilled
    Thy favour, that to me was vital fire?
O let it shine again ! or worse than killed,
    Thy soul-sunk artist feels his art expire."

On her very wedding day Emma sat for the last
time to the great artist for that noble portrait of her
as the " Ambassadress," and she and her husband
" took a tender leave " of one inseverable from her for
ever.

Hamilton and she were the talk of the town.   When
they drove out or went to parties, or entered the box
at Drury Lane, every eye was upon them, and it was
at Drury Lane that the acting of Jane Powell brought
together the two former mates in servitude as the admired of all beholders.

All this must have nettled Greville, of whose feelings at this time there is no record.   But his opposition does not seem to have been serious, for Sir William and Emma passed their time in a round of visits to
the whole circle of his relations, who were mostly
her keen partisans.   Lord Abercorn, indeed, went so
far as to protest that her personality had " made it
impossible " for him " to see or hear without making
comparisons "; and from this time forward Lord William Douglas also became Emma's lifelong upholder.
The summer of 1791 was unusually hot, and from the
latter part of July to mid-August they stayed with
relatives in the country, including Beckford, when
Emma for the first time beheld the Oriental and the
Gothic glories, the mounting spire, the magic ter-
races, the fairy gardens, and all the bizarre splendours,
including its owner, of Fonthill Abbey.

On the whole, this delicate experiment had succeeded, although Queen Charlotte's ban doubtless rankled in Emma's breast.[1] The King himself was more pained than offended, and had confirmed Hamilton in the security of his appointment.

Nor was it only grand folks or old friends that Emma had frequented. It is clear from allusions in shortly subsequent letters that both she and her mother visited that " poor little Emma " who had re-awakened the longings of motherhood in the old but unforgotten days of Parkgate.

On September 6th Sir William and " Emy," or " Emily," Lyon were duly wedded at Marylebone Church, long associated with the Hamilton family. The marriage was solemnised by the Rev. Doctor Edward Barry, rector of Elsdon, Northumberland. The witnesses were Lord Abercorn and L. Dutens, secretary to the English Minister at Turin, with whom Emma long maintained a faithful friendship. Her heart was overflowing. She felt, as she told Romney, so grateful to her husband, so glad in restored innocence and happiness, that she would " never be able to make " him " amends for his goodness." They started homeward by way of Paris, where they were to see for the first and last time that tortured Queen who was fast completing the tragedy of her doom. Henceforward the name of " Hart " is heard no more. Henceforward Emma is no longer obscure, but, as Lady Hamilton, passes into history.

[1] The Queen would never receive Lady Hamilton even after the return of the Hamiltons to England, and Nelson will be found angry that Sir William would go to court alone; cf. *post,* chap. xii.

CHAPTER V

TILL THE FIRST MEETING

1791-1793

L ADY HAMILTON returned to bask in social
favour. It was not only the Neapolitan *noblesse*
and the English wives that courted and caressed
her. Their young daughters also vied with each other
in attentions, and vowed that never was any one so
amiable and accomplished as this eighth wonder.
Among these was a Miss Carr, who not long afterwards married General Cheney, an Aide-de-Camp to
the Duke of York, during the next few years more
than once a visitor at Naples. The writer possesses
a miniature in water-colour, drawn by this young lady,
of the friend to whom she long remained attached.
Emma sits, clad all in white, with an air of sweetness
and repose. At the back of this memento she has
herself recorded : " Emma Hamilton, Naples, Feb. 11,
1792. I had the happiness of my dear Miss Carr's
company all day; but, alas, the day was too short."
There is nothing in this likeness to betoken the purpose and ambition which she was shortly to display
in the side-scenes of history. Horace Walpole had
written, " So Sir William has married his gallery of
statues." Emma soon ceases to be a statue, and becomes prominent in the labyrinth of Neapolitan intrigue; her rôle as patriot begins to be foreshadowed.
Throughout these three critical years of stress and
shock momentous issues were brewing, destined to

bring into sharp relief and typical collision the two giants of France and England, Napoleon and Nelson; while all the time, under fate's invisible hand, Nelson was as surely tending towards Naples and Emma, as Emma was being drawn towards Nelson. From the moment of her return in the late autumn of 1791 she began, at first under Hamilton's tuition, to study and understand the political landscape.

Nowhere outside France did the Revolution bode omens more sinister than at the Neapolitan court. The Queen clearly discerned that her French sister and brother-in-law trembled on the brink of destruction. She knew that the epidemic of anarchy must endanger Naples among the first, and might involve the possible extinction of its dynasty. She was not deceived by the many false prophets crying peace where no peace was; still less by the wild schemes for hairbreadth escapes which sent visionary deliverers scouring through Europe. Her one hope—soon rudely shattered—lay in Austria's power to effect a coalition of great powers and strong armies. She had just quitted the family council in Vienna, following on the death of her brother Joseph the Second, and the short-lived accession to the throne of her other brother Leopold, the pedantic philanthropist. Its object had been, in Horace Walpole's phrase, to " Austriacise " the position of the Italian Bourbons, by family inter-marriages and a betrothal. Her efforts were bent on a league against France, and it was for this that on her way home she had contrived a surprise meeting with the weak Pope Pius VI., penetrated the Vatican, abjured her anti-papal policy, and humiliated herself in the dust. And yet Louis XVI. besought her to suspend efforts which might rescue him, and shrank from embittering his false friends. Austria, too, was for seven years to prove a broken reed. Spain was never a whole-hearted enemy of France, and within three years was to become her ally. The Queen awoke to a fury of indignation and hopelessness. Her foes were those of her own household—her nobles, her husband, his Spanish brother and sister,—and herself. Hitherto she had been reckoned an enlightened patroness, compassing the equality and fraternity of subjects who had never required political liberty. She had stubbornly resisted the Spanish Machiavellianism which had manœuvred to undermine those very freemasonries which Maria Carolina had founded and forwarded. Spain was, in truth, the key of the present position. Spain was befooling Ferdinand and spiting his wife at every turn. The Spanish queen coveted Naples for her own offspring, and the two queens abominated each other. She was quite aware that the pro-Spanish party, abetted by her blockhead of a husband, covertly designed the transference of the Crown of the Two Sicilies to the Duke of Parma, while many of the Neapolitan nobles, affronted at the abolition of their feudal rights, were in secret confederation with it. She sprang from a house glorying in its despotic monopoly of popular principles, yet it was to such fatalities that these very principles were leading. Stability and authority had been her aims, yet the ground was fast slipping from beneath her feet. She was a true scion of the casuist Hapsburgs, who had always considered pride as a sacred duty, and who, if their system were imperilled, would be ready to defend it by conscientious crimes. In the refrain of her own subsequent letters, "*Il faut faire son devoir jusqu'au tombeau.*"

And added to all this was the shifting mood of her consort, whose infidelities she (like the queen of our own George the Second) only condoned in order that his good humour might enable her to rule. He had always twitted her with being an "Illuminata," he now derided her as the "Austrian hen." His advisers would prompt him to rely more than ever on his Spanish kindred, to slight the Hapsburgs and herself. When Emma long afterwards claimed to have "De-Bourbonised" the Neapolitan court, it was to these conditions that she referred.

Gallo, the foreign minister, leaned towards and upon Spain. Even Acton hitherto had been content to propitiate the King by taking his cue from Madrid. The King himself had regarded England merely as a market for dogs and horses, the Queen, only as an enemy of Spain. That the attitude of both was shortly to be transformed was partly due to Emma's enthusiasm as spokeswoman for her husband. Even in February, 1796, Emma wrote to Lord Macartney, who had just arrived at Naples, that "the Queen has much to do to persuade" Ferdinand, that "she is *wore out* with fatigue," and that "he approves of all *our prospects.*" She refers, I think, to his Spanish bias. The moot question soon became, Was Naples to be Spanish or English? The Austrian influence, so prized by an Austrian princess, was on the wane. As England's advocate the light-hearted Emma was drawn into the political vortex, and assumed the mysterious solemnity befitting her part.

In her perplexity it was to Acton that Maria Carolina turned. She thought him a man of iron, whereas he was really one of wood; but he was methodical, pro-Austrian, and at the core pro-English. Under the imminence of crisis, he and Hamilton—still a man of pleasure, but not its slave—both came to perceive that unless the whole system of Europe was to be reversed, an Anglo-Sicilian alliance was imperative. Hamilton, however, was slower to discern the necessity which Emma realised by instinct. Writing in

April, 1792, he says: "The Neapolitans, provided they can get their bellies full at a cheap rate, will not, I am sure, trouble their heads with what passes in other countries, and great pains are taken to prevent any of the democratic propaganda, or their writings, finding their way into this kingdom." Even in 1795 he was to be more concerned with the success of his treatises on Vesuvius than with the tangle of treaties fast growing out of the situation. It was not till 1796 that he took any strong initiative with Acton. The two Sicilies indeed were now a shuttlecock between the treacheries of Spain and the dilatoriness as well as venality of Austria.

But for England the French cataclysm meant something wholly different from its significance for the Continent. Great Britain stood alone and aloof from other powers. She was the nurse of traditional order and traditional liberty conjoined; disorder and license, although exploitable by political factions under specious masks, never appealed to the nation at large. Britain's upheavals had been settled by happy compromise more than a century before. Jacobinism menaced her "free" trade, and might strike even at her free institutions. She was a great maritime and a Mediterranean power whose coign of vantage in Gibraltar would prove useless if Naples and Sicily, Malta and Sardinia should fall to France. Sicily, indeed, had been one of her objectives in that great Utrecht Treaty which had transferred it to the friendly house of Savoy, while it secured Gibraltar and Port Mahon to Great Britain. And ever since, Spain had been England's sworn enemy. Spain was France's natural ally, nor would the revolutionary burst long deter the Spanish Bourbons from an anti-British policy. Spain had tricked Austria and braved Great Britain throughout the eighteenth century, yet it was on Spain that Maria

Carolina's husband habitually relied. From England, too, throughout that century, had rained those showers of gold which had subsidised the enemies of Bourbon preponderance. "Will England," wrote Acton some years later to Hamilton, when Emma, as the Queen's "minister plenipotentiary," had "spurred" them on, "see all Italy, and even the two Sicilies, in the French hands with indifference? . . . We shall perish if such is our destiny, but we hope of selling dear our destruction."

In England the remonstrant Burke forsook the pseudo-Jacobin Whigs. It was hoped, and not without reason, that Pitt as a great statesman might foresee the situation. But the difficulty all along in the British cabinet, and sometimes the obstacle, was to prove Lord Grenville, cold, stiff, timid, official to a fault; so cautious that he twice counselled the two Sicilies to make the best peace they could with Buonaparte, since they must go under; and so diplomatic that, even after Nelson's Mediterranean expedition had been concerted between the two courts, he begged Circello, the Neapolitan Ambassador, to pretend discontent in public with what had just been privately arranged. In the same year, defending the ministry against the Duke of Bedford's abortive motion for their dismissal, and praising the gallant navy "which had ridden triumphant at the same moment at the mouths of Brest and Cadiz and Texel," the Secretary for Foreign Affairs could only be wise after the event. He could only defend the prolongation of war by Barère's threat of "Delenda est Carthago," by Condorcet's opinion that under a peace we should have been relieved of Jamaica, Bengal, and our Indian possessions; by bemoaning England's vanished "power to control the Continent," by proclaiming that she was "at her lowest ebb," and by complaining that Austria had deserted the Alliance. Commenting on his attitude, thirteen years afterwards, towards Emma's claims, Canning, who warmly favoured them, dwells on the same characteristic of " coldest caution." Such a spirit could ill deal with the conjuncture. Mob-despotism was now the dread of Europe. Mob-rule was already rampant in France, though the time was still distant when the Marchioness of Solari could declare that the French had robbed her of all but the haunting memory of Parisian gutters swimming with blood.

Acton acceded to the Queen's request with rigour, but his weak point lay in the fact that he was a born bureaucrat; while the sort of bureaucracy that he favoured, one of secret inquisition, turned political offences into heresies, and Jacobins into martyrs. Bureaucracies may check, but have never stemmed, revolutions which are calmed—when they can be calmed—by commanding personality alone. A bureaucrat is never a trusted nor even a single figure, for he belongs to unpopular and unavailing groups and systems, which from their nature must at best be temporary stop-gaps. As Jacobinism throve and persevered, the Lazzaroni, who execrated it as a foreign innovation, cheered their careless King, but they came to hiss the Queen for her countenance of bureaucracy, until Nelson entered the arena, and Emma formed, in 1799, a " Queen's party," at the very moment when Maria Carolina dared not so much as show her face at Naples.

Already in the spring the French events began to affect Naples. Mirabeau dead, the abortive escape to Varennes, Louis XVI. in open and abject terror, Danton and Pétion bribed, the National Convention, the cosmopolitan cries of " Let us sow the ideas of 1789 throughout the world. . . . We all belong to our country when it is in danger. . . . Liberty and equality constitute country," spread their contagion broadcast. They did not yet inflame the Neapolitan middle class; they never caught the Neapolitan people; but their leaven had already touched the offended nobles and the ungrateful students. From the moment of Louis' imprisonment in the Temple, his sister-in-law changed her tack and resolved to go " Thorough." The pulpits were pressed into an anti-Jacobin crusade. The administration of the twelve city wards, hitherto supervised by elected aldermen, was transferred without warning to chiefs of police as judges and inspectors. Denouncers and informers were hired, although as yet the brooding Queen used her spies for precaution alone, and not for vengeance. The republican seed of the secret societies, sown by her own hands, had borne a crop of democracy ripening towards harvest. Her academic reformers were fast developing into open revolutionaries. The red cap was worn and flaunted. Copies of the French Statute were seized in thousands as they lurked in sacks on the rocks of Chiaromonte; two even found their way into the Queen's apartments. This conspiracy she hoped to nip in the bud. It had not assumed its worst proportions; nor as yet had disloyalty thrown off the mask, and appeared as a bribed hireling of the National Convention. The grisly horrors at Paris of 1792, preluding only too distinctly the crowning executions of 1793, called also for sterner measures. By July, Beckford, an eye-witness, remarks that even Savoy was " bejacobinised, and plundering, ravaging," were " going on swimmingly." The Queen bestirred herself abroad. A league was formed between Prussia and Austria. The Duke of Brunswick issued his manifesto that one finger laid on Louis would be avenged. Danton exclaimed, " To arms! " France, generalled by Dumouriez, hero of

Jemappes, and Kellermann of Valmy, was invaded.
The assassination of Gustavus of Sweden followed.
But the brief victory of the confederate arms at
Longwy soon yielded to the Valmy defeat. Monarchy
was on its trial.

Once more the Queen conferred with Acton, and
their deliberations resulted in the detestable Star Chamber of the " Camera Oscura." Force was to be met
by force, and cabal by cabal. Prince Castelcicala, a
far abler minister than Acton,·was recalled from London to assist in its councils; Ruffo, not yet Cardinal,
became its assessor; while the stripling Luigi di Medici,
under the title of " Regente della vicaria," was made
its head inquisitor. But mercy was still shown. She
does not indeed appear at this period to have entertained any idea of persecution. Most odious means,
however, were taken to crush a conspiracy of foreign
and unpopular origin. Some hundreds of the better
class, some thousands of the scum, were banished, or
confined in the prisons of Lampedusa and Tremiti.
Such is an imperfect outline of what happened in 1791
and 1792.

The interview of the Hamiltons with Marie Antoinette on their homeward journey has been already
noticed. Nearly twenty-four years afterwards Lady
Hamilton, never accurate, and constitutionally exag-
gerative, declared in her last memorial under the
pressure of sore distress, that she then presented to the
Queen of Naples her sister's *last* letter. There is small
disproof that substantially she told the truth. She
may well have carried a missive, for Marie Antoinette
neglected none of her now rare chances of communication. About the same time, however, the Marchioness
of Solari also repaired from Paris to Naples with
another communication, which was probably verbal,
and may possibly have preceded Lady Hamilton's al-

leged message. In the autumn of 1793, however, the Marchioness again visited Naples and brought with her what undoubtedly seems the last letter received by Maria from Marie. Emma's statement has been questioned on the ground that hers was not the *last* message. It is perhaps hardly worth while debating whether all credence should be denied to the bearer of an important letter simply on the ground of priority. Any such letter whatever would have recommended its bearer to the Queen of Naples.

Whether or no this incident fastened afresh the Queen's regard, certain it is that Maria Carolina gave the *mot d'ordre* for Lady Hamilton's acceptability. Nobody disputed her position, least of all the English. She was at once formally presented to the Queen. By mid-April of 1792 Sir William Hamilton could tell Horace Walpole, just acceding to his earldom, that the Queen had been very kind, and treated his wife " like any other travelling lady of distinction." " Emma," he adds, " has had a difficult part to act, and has succeeded wonderfully, having gained by having no pretensions the thorough approbation of all the English ladies. . . . You cannot imagine how delighted Lady H. was in having gained your approbation in England. . . . She goes on improving daily. . . . She is really an extraordinary being."

Within a month of her arrival in the previous autumn, and in the midst of successes, she sat down to write to Romney. The tone of this letter deserves close attention, for no under-motive could colour a communication to so old and fatherly a comrade: " I have been received with open arms by all the Neapolitans of both sexes, by all the foreigners of every distinction. I have been presented to the Queen of Naples by her own desire, she [h]as shewn me all sorts of kind and affectionate attentions; in short, I am

the happiest woman in the world. Sir William is
fonder of me every day, and I hope I [he?] will have
no corse to repent of what he [h]as done, for I feel
so grateful to him that I think I shall never be able
to make him amends for his goodness to me. But
why do I tell you this? You was the first dear friend
I open'd my heart to; you ought to know me.[1] . . .
How grateful then do I feel to my dear, dear husband
that has restored peace to my mind, that has given
me honors, rank, and what is more, innocence and
happiness. Rejoice with me, my dear sir, my friend,
my more than father; believe me, I am still that same
Emma you knew me. If I could forget for a moment what I was, I ought to suffer. Command me in
anything I can do for you here; believe me, I shall
have a real pleasure. Come to Naples, and I will be
your model, anything to induce you to come, that I
may have an opportunity to show my gratitude to you.
. . . We have a many English at Naples, Ladys
Malm[e]sbury, Malden, Plymouth, Carnegie, and
Wright, etc. They are very kind and attentive to me;
they all make it a point to be remarkably cevil to me.
Tell Hayly I am always reading his *Triumphs of Temper;* it was that that made me Lady H., for God
knows I had for five years enough to try my temper,
and I am affraid if it had not been for the good example Serena taught me, my girdle wou'd have burst,
and if it had I had been undone; for Sir W. minds
more temper than beauty. He therefore wishes Mr.
Hayly wou'd come, that he might thank him for his
sweet-tempered wife. I swear to you, I have never
once been out of humour since the 6th of last September. God bless you."

Romney, whose friend Flaxman, now in Rome,

[1] Here follows the passage about her " sense of virtue " not
being overcome in her earliest distresses, quoted *ante* in chap. ii.

counted himself among Emma's devotees, replied in terms of humble respect. He deprecated the liberty of sending a friend with a letter of introduction, and only wished that he could express his feelings on the perusal of her " happyness." " May God grant it may remain so to the end of your days."

How " attentive " to her Lady Plymouth and the English sisterhood were at this early period is shown by a letter which changed hands during the present year. It is couched not only in terms of affection, but of trust. If the French terror became actual at Naples, Lady Plymouth would take refuge with Lady Hamilton, and " creep under the shadow of " her " wings." The leaders of English society relished, as always, a new sensation, and, away from England, delighted to honour one so different from themselves.

While all this underground disturbance proceeded, the outward aspect of court and city was serenity itself. Ancient Pompeii could not have been more frivolously festive. Ill as they suited her mood, the Queen, from policy, encouraged these galas. They distracted the court from treason, they pleased her husband and people, and they attracted a crowd of useful foreigners, especially the English, who, during these two years, inundated Naples to their Ambassador's dismay. The distinguished English visitors of 1792 included the sickly young Prince Augustus, afterwards Duke of Sussex, whose delicate health and morganatic marriage [1] alike added to Hamilton's anxieties. But for the disturbed state of the Continent, " Vathek " Beckford—to whom Sir William was always kind— would have revisited his kinsman also. He had not

---

[1] With Lady Augusta Murray, to whom he was a devoted husband in the teeth of his father's and brother's opposition. Lady Hamilton continued to enjoy his friendship long afterwards.

long quitted his " dear " and queenly friend " Mary of Portugal," and was now travelling through Savoy with a retinue worthy of Disraeli's Sidonia and composed of half the *émigrés,* musicians, and cooks—*chefs d'orchestre et de cuisine*—of Versailles; and Emma's old friend Gavin Hamilton was also among the throng.

A correspondence between husband and wife during the January of this year, and his absence with the King at Persano, is pleasant reading, and pictures a happy pair. The Ambassador, who up to now had found his business in sport, cheerfully roughing it on bread and butter, going to bed at nine and rising at five, reading, too, " to digest his dinner," is affectionate and playful. He was " sorry," he writes on leaving, that his " dear Em " must " harden " herself to such little misfortunes as a temporary parting "; but he " cannot blame her for having a good and tender heart." " Believe me, you are in thorough possession of all mine, though I will allow it to be rather tough." His diary of the hour flows from a light heart and pen. He tells her the gossip : " Yesterday the courier brought the order of St. Stephano from the Emperor for the Prince Ausberg, and the King was desired to invest him with it. As soon as the King received it, he ran into the Prince's room, whom he found in his shirt, and without his breeches, and in that condition was he decorated with the star and ribbon by his majesty, who has wrote the whole circumstance to the Emperor. Leopold may, perhaps, not like the joking with his first order. Such nonsense should certainly be done with solemnity ; or it becomes, what it really is, a little tinsel and a few yards of broad ribbon." His watchful wife, in her turn, acquaints him with London cabals to dislodge him from office. " Our conduct," he answers with indignation, " shall be such as to be unattackable. . . . Twenty-seven years' service, having spent all the King's money, and all my own, besides running in debts, deserves something better than a dismission. . . . I would not be married to any woman but yourself for all the world." And again, " I never doubted your gaining every soul you approach. . . . Nothing pleases me more than to hear you do not neglect your singing. It would be a pity, as you are near the point of perfection." The very etiquette of the Embassy he leaves with confidence in her hands. " You did admirably, my dear Em., in not inviting Lady A. H[atton] to dine with the prince, and still better in telling her honestly the reason. I have always found that going straight is the best method, though not the way of the world. You did also very well in asking Madame Skamouski, and not taking upon you to present her [to the Queen] without leave. In short, consult your own good sense, and do not be in a hurry; and I am sure you will always act right. . . . As the Prince asked you, you did right to send for a song of Douglas's, but in general you will do right to sing only at home." He also politely deprecates his plebeian mother-in-law's attendance at formal receptions. But Emma, throughout her career, disdained to be parted for a moment. Unlike most *parvenues*, she never blushed for the homely creature who had stood by her in the day of trouble, and her intense love for her mother, even when it stood most in her way, ennobles her character.

The Neapolitan revelries were sometimes the reverse of squeamish: " Let them all roll on the carpet," he writes, " provided you are not of the party. My trust is in you alone."

It may be added that from stray allusions in this series it is evident that even thus early Lady Hamilton could translate letters and transact business. Sir William was naturally torpid, and his enthusiasm centred on the wife who bestirred him. His efforts to keep eternally young were already being damped by the deaths of contemporaries. That of his old intimate, Lord Pembroke, in 1794, was to evoke a characteristic comment:—"It gave me a little twist; but I have for some time perceived that my friends, with whom I spent my younger days, have been dropping around me."

The close of 1792 saw the first of those serious illnesses through which Emma was so often to nurse him. For more than a fortnight he lay in danger at Caserta. Lady Hamilton was "eight days without undressing, eating, or sleeping." The Queen and King sent constantly to inquire. Although Naples was distant sixteen miles, Ladies Plymouth, Dunmore, and Webster, with others of the British contingent, offered even to stay with her. She tells her dear Mr. Greville (how changed the appellation!) of her "great obligations," and of her grief. "Endead I was almost distracted from such extreme happiness at once to such misery. . . . What cou'd console me for the loss of such a husband, friend, and protector? For surely no happiness is like ours. We live but for one another. But I was too happy. I had imagined I was never more to be unhappy. All is right. I now know myself again, and shall not easily fall into the same error again. For every moment I feel what I felt when I thought I was loseing him for ever."[1] This is the letter concerning her grandmother to which reference has already been made. Since I lay stress on the fact that Emma was a typical daughter of the people both in scorn and affection, that she was warm-hearted, unmercenary, and grateful, and that she never lowered the natures of those with whom she was brought into contact, another excerpt may be pardoned:—"I will

[1] Morrison MS. 215; Caserta, December 4, 1792.

trouble you with my own affairs as you are so good
as to interest yourself about me.   You must know I
send my grandmother every Cristmas twenty pounds,
and so I ought.   I have 200 a year for nonsense, and it
wou'd be hard I cou'd not give her twenty pounds
when she has so often given me her last shilling.
As Sir William is ill, I cannot ask him for the order;
but if you will get the twenty pounds and send it to
her, you will do me the greatest favor; for if the time
passes without hearing from me, she may imagine I
have forgot her, and I would not keep her poor old
heart in suspense for the world. . . . Cou'd you not
write to her a line from me and send to her, and tell
her by my order, and she may write to you?   Send
me her answer.   For I cannot divest myself of my
original feelings.   It will contribute to my happiness,
and I am sure you will assist to make me happy.   Tell
her every year she shal have twenty pound.   The
fourth of November last I had a dress on that cost
twenty-five pounds, as it was Gala at Court; and believe me I felt unhappy all the while I had it on.   Excuse the trouble I give you."

The end of 1792 and the whole of 1793 loomed big
with crisis.   The new year opened with the judicial
murder of the French King, it closed with that of
Marie Antoinette.   Her execution exasperated all Europe against France.   England declared war; Prussia
retired from the first Coalition, and the second was
formed.   An Anglo-Sicilian understanding ensued.
Through the arrival of La Touche Tréville's squadron
at Naples, the French sansculottes shook. hands with
the Italian.   Hood's capture of Toulon, Napoleon's
undoing of it, and Nelson's advent in the *Agamemnon,*
opened out a death-struggle unfinished even when the
hero died.

To the Queen's promptings of temperament and hab-

its of principle were now to be added the goads of revenge. Jacobinism for her and her friends soon came
to mean the devil. And with this year, too, opened also
Lady Hamilton's intimacy with the Queen, her awakening of her listless husband, and her keen endeavours
on behalf of the British navy.

The worst hysteria is that of a woman who is able
to conceal it. Such was now the Queen's. The overture to this drama of 1793 was her formal dismissal of
Citizen Mackau, for a few months past the unwelcome
Jacobin representative of France at the Neapolitan
court; at the same time, the Queen's influence procured
the dismissal of Semouville, another " citizen " ambassador at Constantinople. Tréville's fleet promptly
appeared to enforce reparation. His largest vessel
dropped anchor in face of Castel Del Uovo, and the
rest formed in line of battle behind it. A council was
called. The Anglo-Sicilian treaty was yet in abeyance,
and with shame and rage Maria Carolina had to submit, and receive the minister back again. But this
was not all. No sooner had Tréville departed than a
convenient storm shattered his fleet, and he returned to
refit. His sailors hobnobbed with the secret societies,
and a definite revolution began. France had hoped
for attack; open war being refused, she renewed her
designs by stealth. The Queen, incensed beyond measure, redoubled her suspicions and her precautions. To
the secret tribunal she added a closed " Junta," and the
grim work of deportation and proscription set in.
All Naples, except the Lazzaroni, rose. Despite the
Neapolitan neutrality, Maria now organised a second
coalition against France, which was at first successful.
The French, too, were beaten off Sardinia. In August
she renewed her desperate attempts to save her sister; the jailor's wife was interviewed. Archduchess
Christine contrived to send the Marquis Burlot and

Rosalia D'Albert with *carte blanche* on a mission of rescue. It was too late: they were arrested. But Toulon was betrayed by Trogoff to Hood, who took possession of it for Louis XVII.

Meanwhile, repression reigned at Naples. Every French servant was banished; some of the English visitors, among them, as Mackau's friend, Mr. Hodges, who pestered Emma by his attentions, were implicated. The Queen, mistrustful of the crew who had played her false, turned to Emma in her misfortunes, for Lady Hamilton was now quite as familiar with the royalties as her husband. One of the Neapolitan duchesses long afterwards insinuated to the Marchioness of Solari that Emma's paramount influence was due to spying on them and the libertine King.[1] This may at first have been so (though envy supplies a likelier reason), but the real cause lies deeper. The Queen's correspondence commences in the winter of 1793, and it is quite clear that its mainspring was sympathy.

> " Par le sort de la naissance
>   L'un est roi, l'autre est berger.
> Le hasard fit leur distance;
>   L'esprit seul peut tout changer."[2]

The constraint of a traitorous and artificial court left the Queen without a confidante, and she welcomed a child of nature whom she fancied she could mould

---

[1] Abominable rumours, as to her and the Queen, passed current among the French Jacobins, who fastened the same filth with as little foundation on Marie Antoinette. Emma told Greville how she despised and ignored the lying scandals of Paris which Napoleon afterwards favoured from policy.

[2] It may thus be paraphrased:—

> " Random lot of birth can start
>   Peasant one, another Queen.
> Chance has placed them far apart;
>   Mother-wit can change the scene."

at will.   The more her pent-up hatred fastened on her
courtiers, the more she spited them by petting her new
favourite.   The friendship of queens with the lowly
appeals to vanity as well as to devotion.   It proved so
with both Sarah Jennings and even more with the
humbler Abigail Masham.   In still greater degree did
it now so prove with Emma.   It was not long before
she rode out regularly on a horse from the royal
stables, attended by a royal equerry, and enjoying
semi-royal privileges.   Maria's haughty ladies-in-
waiting, the Marchionesses of San Marco and of San
Clemente, can scarcely have been pleased.   Jealousy
must have abounded, but it found no outlet for her
downfall.   That the Neapolitan nobility, at any rate,
believed in her real services to England, is shown by
the rumour among them that she was Pitt's informer.
Henceforward dates the growth of an English party
and an Anglo-mania at the Neapolitan court which was
violently opposed alike by the pro-Spanish, the pro-
Jacobin, and the " down-with-the-foreigner " parties.
Emma, however, stood as yet only on the threshold of
her political influence.

In the June of that year, " for political reasons,"
Lady Hamilton informs Greville, " we have lived eight
months at Caserta," formerly only their winter abode,
but now the Queen's regular residence during the hot
months.   " Our house has been like an inn this winter."   (Sir William naturally sighed over the expense.)   ". . . We had the Duchess of Ancaster several days.   It is but 3 days since the Devonshire family has left; and we had fifty in our family for four
days at Caserta.   'Tis true we dined every day at
court, or at some casino of the King; for you cannot
immagine how good our King and Queen as been to
the principal English who have been here—particularly
to Lord and Lady Palmerston, Cholmondely, Devon-

shire, Lady Spencer, Lady Bessborough, Lady Plymouth, Sir George and Lady Webster. And I have carried the ladies to the Queen very often, as she as permitted me to go very often in private, which I do. . . . In the evenings I go to her, and we are *tête-à-tête* 2 or 3 hours. Sometimes we sing. Yesterday the King and me sang duetts 3 hours. It was but bad. . . . To-day the Princess Royal of Sweden comes to court to take leave of their Majesties. Sir William and me are invited to dinner with her. She is an amiable princess, and as lived very much with us. The other ministers' wives have not shewed her the least attention because she did not pay them the first visit, as she travels under the name of the Countess of Wasa. . . . Her Majesty told me I had done very well in waiting on Her Royal Highness the moment she arrived. However, the ministers' wives are very fond of me, as the[y] see I have no pretentions; nor do I abuse of Her Majesty's goodness, and she observed the other night at court at Naples [when] we had a drawing-room in honner of the Empress having brought a son. I had been with the Queen the night before alone *en famille* laughing and singing, etc. etc., but at the drawing-room I kept my distance, and payd the Queen as much respect as tho' I had never seen her before, which pleased her very much. But she shewed me great distinction that night, and told me several times how she admired my good conduct. I onely tell you this to shew and convince you I shall never change, but allways be simple and natural. You may immagine how happy my dear, dear Sir William is. . . . We live more like lovers than husband and wife, as husbands and wives go nowadays. Lord deliver me! and the English are as bad as the Italians, some few excepted.

"I study very hard, . . . and I have had all my

songs set for the viola, so that Sir William may accompany me, which as pleased him very much, so that we study together. The English garden is going on very fast. The King and Queen go there every day. Sir William and me are there every morning at seven a clock, sometimes dine there and allways drink tea there. In short it is Sir William's favourite child, and booth him and me are now studying botany, but not to make ourselves pedantical prigs and shew our learning like some of our travelling neighbours, but for our own pleasure. Greffer [1] is as happy as a prince. Poor Flint, the messenger, was killed going from hence. I am very sorry. He was lodged in our house and I had a great love for him. I sent him to see Pompea, Portici, and all our delightful environs, and sent all his daughters presents. Poor man, the Queen as expressed great sorrow. Pray let me know if his family are provided for as I may get something for them *perhaps.* . . . Pray don't fail to send the inclosed."

But more than such surface-life was now animating Emma. A peasant's daughter, at length in the ascendant over an Empress's, was receiving, communicating, intensifying wider impressions. When her Queen denounced, she abominated the Jacobins; her tears were mingled with Maria's over the family catastrophes. She preached up to her the English as the avengers of her wrongs. She rejoiced with her over the Anglo-Sicilian alliance concluded in July. She longed for some deliverer who might justify her flights of eloquence.

England had at last joined the allies and thrown

[1] Gräfer—a trusted agent of Hamilton's. He afterwards became the manager of Nelson's Bronte estates. His wife was a scheming woman who, in later years, gave much trouble both to Nelson and Lady Hamilton.

down the gauntlet in earnest. The 10th of September, 1793, brought Nelson's first entry both into Naples and into the Ambassador's house.

He had been despatched by Lord Hood on a special mission to procure ten thousand troops from Turin and Naples after that wonderful surrender of starved-out Toulon:—" The strongest in Europe, and twenty-two sail of the line . . . without firing a shot." [1]

The previous year had called forth two ruling strains in his nature: the one of irritable embitterment at his unrecognised solicitations for a command; the other of patriotic exultation when Chatham and Hood suddenly " smiled " upon him, thanks, it would seem, to the importunity of his early admirer and lifelong friend, the Duke of Clarence. For five years he had been eating out his heart on half-pay in a Norfolk village; and even when the long-delayed command had come, crass officialism assigned him only a " sixty-four " and the fate of drifting aimlessly off Guernsey with no enemy in sight. If proof be wanted of Nelson's inherent idealism, it is found in the fact that in these long days of stillness and obscurity he was brooding over the future of his country, and devising the means of combating unarisen combinations against her.

He was now almost thirty-five, and had been married six years and a half; his wife was five years younger than himself.

From his earliest years, at once restrained and sensitive, companionable and lonely, athirst for glory rather than for fame, simple as a child yet brave as a lion, he had experienced at intervals several passionate friendships for women. As a stripling in Canada he conceived so vehement an affection for Miss Molly Simpson that he was with difficulty withheld from

[1] Nelson to his wife, 11th September.

leaving the service. After a short interval, Miss An-
drews in France had rekindled the flame. His in-
tensest feeling in the Leeward Islands had been for
Mrs. Moutray, his "dear, sweet friend." His engagement to her associate, Frances Nisbet, had been
sudden—some suspected from pique. The young
widow of the Nevis doctor attracted him less by her
heart than what he called her "mental accomplishments, . . . superior to most people's of either sex."
These were rather of a second-rate boarding-school
order. Nelson's unskilled, uncritical mind and his
frank generosity always exaggerated such qualities
in women, and not least in Emma, more self-taught
than himself. His wife's virtues were sterling, but
her power of appreciation very limited. She was
perhaps more dutiful than gentle, less loving than
jealous; her self-complacent coldness was absolutely
unfitted to understand or hearten or companion genius.
She entirely lacked intuition. Her outlook was
cramped—that of the plain common-sense and un-
imaginative prejudice which so often distinguishes her
class. She was a nagger, and she nagged her son.
She was quite satisfied with her little shell and, ailing
as she was, perpetually grumbled at everything outside it. But directly success attended her husband, she
at once gave herself those social airs for which that
class is also distinguished when it rises. She became
ridiculously pretentious. This it was that seems to
have disgusted Nelson's sisters in later years, though
they were certainly prejudiced against her. Some disillusionment succeeded as time familiarised him with
the lady of his impulsive choice. She nursed him
dutifully in 1797; but, for her, duties were tasks. At
Bath, a short time before his eventful voyage of 1798,
he was to express his delight at the charms of the
reigning toasts; but in steeling himself against tempta-

tion, he got no further than the avowal of having
" everything that was *valuable* in a wife."

There are two sorts of genius, or supreme will: the
cold and the warm. The one commands its material
from sheer fibre of inflexible character and hard intellect; the other creates and enkindles its fuel by idealism. The former in England is signally illustrated in
differing spheres by Walpole and Wellington; the latter by Chatham and Nelson. Both of these shared
that keen faculty of vision, really, if we reflect, a form
of spiritual force, and allied to faith which, in volume,
whether for individuals or nations, is irresistible.
This sword of the spirit is far more powerful than
ethical force without it; still more so than merely
conventional morality, which, indeed, for good or for
ill, and in many partings of the ways, it has often by
turns made or marred. Both, too, were histrionic—
a word frequently misused. The world *is* a stage,
and of all nature there is a scenic aspect. The dramatic
should never be confused with the theatrical, nor attitude with affectation. And the visionary with a
purpose is always dramatic. He lives on dreams of
forecast, and his forecast visualises combinations,
scenes of development, characters, climaxes. When he
is nothing but a lonely muser, or, again, an orator
destined to bring other hands to execute his ideas, his
audience is the future—the " choir invisible." But
when he himself acts the chief part in the dramas
which he has composed, he needs the audience that he
creates and holds. He depends on a sympathy that
can interpret his best possibilities to himself.

In Nelson's soul resided from boyhood the central
idea of England's greatness. His intuitive force, his
genius, incarnated that idea, and what Chatham
dreamed and voiced, Nelson did. He realised situations in a flash, and, from first to last, his courage took

the risk not only of action, but of prophecy. Indeed, his own motto may be said to have been that fine phrase of the other which he quoted to Lady Hamilton in the first letter which counselled the flight of the royal family in 1798—" *The Boldest measures are the Safest.*" George Meredith's badge of true patriotism fits Nelson beyond all men: " To him the honour of England was as a babe in his arms; he hugged it like a mother."

Nelson, again, was eminently spontaneous. There was nothing set or petty about him. He never posed as " Sir Oracle." He dared to disobey the formalists. He despised and offended insignificance in high places; the prigs and pedants, the big-wigs of Downing Street, the small and self-important purveyors of dead letter, the jealous Tritons of minnow-like cliques. Above all, he abhorred from the bottom of his honest heart the " candid friend "—" willing to wound and yet afraid to strike "; but he honoured—to return from Pope's line to Canning's—" the erect, the manly foe." Clerical by association, the son of a most pious, the brother of a most worldly clergyman, his bent was genuinely religious, as all his letters with their trust in God and their sincere " amens " abundantly testify. To clergymen he still remains the great but erring Nelson. But his God was the God of truth, and justice, and battles—the tutelary God that watches over England; and he himself owns emphatically in one of his letters that he could never turn his cheek to the smiter. He liked to consecrate his ambitions, but ambition, even in childhood, had been his impulse. " Nelson will always be first " had been ever a ruling motive.

And, man of iron as he was in action, out of it he was unconstrained and sportive. He loved to let himself go; he delighted in fun and playful sallies. He formed a band of firm believers, and he believed in them with enthusiasm—an enthusiasm which accentuated his bitterness whenever it was damped or disappointed. A daredevil himself, he loved daredevilry in others. In Emma as he idealised her, he hailed a nature that could respond, encourage, brace, and even inspire, for she was to be transfigured into the creature of his own imaginings. She was his Egeria. It was a double play of enthusiastic zeal and idealisation. She fired him to achieve more than ever she could have imagined. He stirred her to appear worthier in his eyes. She wreathed him with laurel; he crowned her image with myrtle. Many to whom the fact is repugnant refuse to see that this idealised image of Emma in Nelson's eyes, however often and lamentably she fell short of it, was an influence as real and potent as if she had been its counterpart. Her nearest approach to it may be viewed in her letters of 1798.

It is idle to brand her as destitute of any moral standard; her *inward* standards were no lower than those of the veneered " respectables " around her. Her *outward* conduct, as Sir William's partner, had been above suspicion; the sin of her girlhood had been long buried. And in many respects her fibre was stronger than that of a society which broadened its hypocrisies some thirty years later, when Byron sang

> "You are *not* a moral people, and you know it,
>   Without the aid of too sincere a poet."

The radical defect in her grain was rather the complete lack of anything like spiritual aspiration. Hers, too, were the vanity that springs from pride, and the want of dignity bred of lawlessness. She had been a wild flower treated as a weed, and then transplanted to a hothouse; she was a spoiled child without being in the least childlike: she was self-conscious to the core.

But if she was ambitious for herself, she was fully as ambitious for those that she loved, and she admired all who admired them.

It is idle to dwell on the " vulgarity " of an adventuress. Adventure was the breath of Nelson's nostrils, and Emma's unrefined clay was animated by a spirit of reality which he loved. It is idle, again, to talk of his " infatuation," for that word covers every deep and lasting passion in idealising natures. It seems equally idle, even in the face of some uncertainty, to say that Nelson was a " dupe " in any portion of his claims for her " services " which lay within his own experience. With regard to these he was absolutely aware of what had actually transpired, and if it had not transpired he himself was a liar, which none have had the temerity to assert. The only sense in which Nelson could ever be styled the " dupe " of Emma would be that he was utterly cheated in his estimate of her. If she merely practised upon his simplicity, if there was nothing genuine about her, and all her effusiveness was a tinsel mask of hideous dissimulation; if she was a tissue of craft and cunning, then she was the worst of women, and he the most unfortunate of men. Wholly artless she was not; designedly artful, she never was. She was an unconscious blend of Art and Nature. In all her letters she is always the same receptive creature of sincere volitions and attitudes; and these letters, when they describe actions, are most strikingly confirmed by independent accounts. They are genuine. Her spirit went out to his magnetically; each was to hypnotise the other. Had she ever been artful she would have feathered her nest. Throughout her career it was never common wealth or prodigal youth that attracted her, and in her greatest dependence she had never been a parasite. It was talent and kindness that

she prized, and towards genius she gravitated.   It is
not from the bias either of praise or blame that her
character must be judged.   It is as a human document
that she should be *read*.   The real harm in the future
to be worked by her on Nelson was that of the falsehood, repugnant to them both, which, eight years
later, the birth of Horatia entailed—an evil aggravated
by reaction in the nature of a puritan turned cavalier,
and anxious to twist the irregularities of a " Nell
Gwynne defender-of-the-faith " into consonance with
the forms of his upbringing.

At Naples, Nelson and his men found a royal welcome in every sense of the word.   The King sailed
out to greet him, called on and invited him thrice
within four days.   He was hailed as the " Saviour of
Italy," and while he was fêted, his crew, who from
the home Government had obtained nothing but
" honour and salt beef," were provisioned and petted.
A gala at San Carlo was given in their honour; six
thousand troops were offered without hesitation; a
squadron   was   despatched.   The   atmosphere   of
despairing indecision was dispersed by his unresting
alertness, his lightning insight, his faith in Great
Britain and himself, and the heroic glow with which
he invested duty.

The phlegmatic Acton was impressed.   His only
fear was lest England's co-operation with Naples
should provoke the interference of the allies, and be
impeded by it.   He superintended all the arrangements, for he was eminently a man of detail; he
brought Captain Sutton (who stayed throughout the
autumn) to see the King.   Nelson he mis-styled " Admiral," and there for the moment his respect ended.
But the hospitable Hamilton, under the sway of
Emma's enthusiasm, was enraptured.   He brought
him to lodge at the Embassy in the room just pre-

pared for Prince Augustus, who was returning from
Rome.   He caught a spark of the young Captain's own
electricity, he mentioned him in despatches, and conceived friendship at first sight.   Here was a real man
at last, a central and centralising genius.   His wife
shared and redoubled his astonishment.   Here was
a being who, like herself, " loved to surprise people."
Here was one who, indefatigable in detail, and almost
sleepless in energy, took large views, was a statesman
as well as a sailor, and showed the qualities of a general besides; one, too, who, although a stern discipli-
narian, could romp and sing with his midshipmen, one
who made their health and his country's glory his chief
concern.   Moreover, his appearance, small, slight, wiry
in frame, and rugged of exterior, was nevertheless
prepossessing and imposing.   When he spoke, his face
lit up with his soul; nor had he yet lost an eye and an
arm.   And his contempt for Jacks-in-office, which seldom failed to show itself, chimed with her own—with
that of a plebeian who in after years constantly used
that Irish phrase, adopted by Nelson, " I would not give
sixpence to call the King my uncle."   Here was one
who might rescue her Queen and shed lustre on Britain;
who might prove the giant-killer of the Jacobin ogres.

What Emma thought of her guest may be gathered
from two facts, one of which is new.   Though they
were not to meet again until 1798, Nelson and Sir W.
Hamilton were in constant and most sympathetic correspondence for the next five years.   In 1796 Sir
William recommended him to the Government as " that
brave officer, Captain Nelson "; " if you don't deserve
the epithet," he told him, " I know not who does. . . .
Lady Hamilton and I admire your constancy, and hope
the severe service you have undergone will be handsomely rewarded."   And her first letter of our new
series in 1798, written hurriedly on June 17th while

Nelson, anchored off Capri, remained on the *Van-guard*, contains this sentence: " I will not say how glad I shall be to see you.   Indeed I cannot describe to you my feelings on your being so near us."   A woman could not so express herself to a man unseen for five years unless the twelve days or so spent in his company had produced a deep effect.   Every concern of his already enlisted her eagerness.   His stepson, Josiah, then a young midshipman, was driven about by her and caressed.   She laughingly called him her *cavaliere servente*.   As yet it was only attraction, not love for Nelson.   This very third anniversary of her wedding day had enabled her proudly to record that her husband and she were more inseparable than ever, and that he had never for one moment regretted the step of their union.   But she did fall in love with the quickening force that Nelson represented.   Infused by the ardour of her Queen, proud of the destiny of England as European deliverer, urged by her native ambition to shine on a bigger scale, she reflected every hue of the crisis and its leaders.   If *his* hour struck, hers might strike also.   He, she, and Sir William had for this short span already realised what the legend round Sir William's Order of the Bath signified, " *Tria juncta in uno* "—three persons linked together by one tie of differing affections.

The sole mentions of Emma by Nelson at this time are in a letter to his brother, and another to his wife, already noticed.   But that her influence had already begun to work is proved by the fact that he carefully preserved the whole series of her letters of the summer and autumn of 1798.   Three days only after he had started for Leghorn, he wrote as follows: " In my hurry of sailing I find I have brought away a butter-pan.   Don't call me an ungrateful guest for it, for I assure you I have the highest sense of your and Lady

Hamilton's kindness, and shall rejoice in the opportunity of returning it. . . . The sending off the prints
adds to the kindness I have already received from
you and Lady Hamilton." And when at the close of
August in the next year he stayed at Leghorn once
more, he assured Sir William how glad he would have
been to have visited them again, " had the state of the
Agamemnon allowed of it," but " her ship's crew are
so totally worn out, that we were glad to get into the
first port, . . . therefore for the present I am deprived of that pleasure."

When Nelson was not dining at court or concerting
operations with the Ministers, he was at the Embassy
or Caserta, meeting the English visitors, who included
the delicate Charles Beauclerk, whom the artistic Lady
Diana had commended to Emma's charge. All was
joy, excitement, preparation. " I believe," wrote Nelson, " that the world is now convinced that no conquests of importance can be made without us." Nelson had aroused Naples from a long siesta, and henceforward Emma sings " God save the King " and calls
for " Hip, hip, hurrah! " which she teaches the Queen,
at every Neapolitan banquet. Naples is no more a
hunting-ground for health or pleasure, but a focus of
deliverance. It is as though in our own days the
Riviera should suddenly wake up as a centre of patriotism and a rallying-ground for action. Within a few
years Maria Carolina could write to Emma of singing
the national anthem, and in the year of the Nile battle,
of the " brave, loyal nation," and of the " mag-
nanimous " English, whom she loves and for whose
glory she has vowed to act. As for Nelson, he was
in that year to be called her deliverer, her preserver,
and her " hero."

On September 24th Nelson purposed a slight mark
of gratitude for the hospitality and the substantial

reinforcements so liberally proffered.   The *Agamemnon* was all flowers and festivity.   He had invited the
King, the Queen, the Hamiltons, Acton, and the Ministers to luncheon.   The guests were awaiting the arrival of the court under a cloudless sky amid the flutter
of gay bunting and all the careless chatter of southern
mirth.   Suddenly a despatch was handed to the captain.   He was summoned to weigh anchor and pursue
a French man-of-war with three vessels stationed off
Sardinia.   Not an instant was lost.   The guests dispersed in excitement.   When Ferdinand arrived in
his barge, it was to find the company vanished, the
decks cleared, and the captain buried in work.   Within
two hours Nelson had set sail for Leghorn, which he
had immediately to quit for Toulon.   Calvi and its
further triumph awaited him afterwards.

But over the bright horizon was fast gathering a
cloud no bigger than a man's hand.   By the end of
the year the Queen was again in the depths.   Her
sister had been executed with infamy.   Buonaparte—
whom Nelson heard described at Leghorn as an " ugly,
unshaven little officer "—had shot into pre-eminence
and had worked his wonders; Toulon was evacuated.
At home fresh conspiracies were discovered, this time
among the nobles.   The best names were implicated.
The Dukes of Canzano, Colonna, and Cassano, the
Counts of Ruvo and Riario, Prince Caracciolo the
elder were arrested.   The whole political landscape
was overcast.   Next year was to be one of " public
mourning and prayer," of plague, famine, and
pestilence.   The ragged remnant of the squadron, forwarded with such royal elation to Toulon, returned in
shame for shelter; and with it the ship of Trogoff,
whom the French had branded as traitor.   Two hundred victims had been slaughtered, four hundred languished in French prisons.   These fresh disasters were

heightened and shadowed by the terrible earthquake of June 12-16, when the sun was blotted out; and while the Archbishop, grasping the gilt image of St. Januarius, groped his way in solemn procession to the cathedral, the darkened sky bombarded the interceding city with emblematic bolts of relentless artillery.

CHAPTER VI

" STATESWOMAN "

1794-1797

"**STATESWOMAN**" is Swift's term for Stella. It fits better the Trilby of the political studio. The muse as medium was already being transferred from attitude to affairs.

Since Nelson's brief sojourn and its keen impress, the Queen, under growing troubles, leaned more and more on the English. The King's pro-Spanish faction was now defied; even the pro-Austrian group lost ground and flagged. Acton, save for a brief interval, remained her right hand—*hic, hæc, et hoc et omnia*, as they now styled him. The Hamiltons' enthusiasm for the budding hero had communicated itself through Emma to her royal friend, who had hitherto cared little even for the English language. Maria Carolina clung more closely to a consoler not only responsive and diverting, but unversed enough in courts to be flattered by the intimacy and free in it. They were constantly together; by 1795 so often as every other day. It was "naturalness" and "sensibility" once more that prevailed. Doubtless, policy entered also into her motives. Notes to Emma would pass unsuspected where notes to Sir William might be watched. Verbal confidences to a frequenter of the palace would never excite the curiosity which Sir William's formal presence must arouse. But the bond of policy was mutual. Hamilton encouraged his wife to glean secret in-

formation for the British Government. What the
Queen did not at first realise, though afterwards she
recognised it to the full, was Lady Hamilton's " native
energy of mind " which Hayley, comforting her after
Nelson's death, recalled as one of her earliest char-
acteristics; and for the work of life, as has been truly
said, inborn vigour is apter than cultivated refinement.

Emma now definitely emerges as patriot and politician. Did she aspire thus early to help her country?
The field of controversy begins to open, and controversy is always irksome. It is necessary, however,
at this juncture, to consider this first of Emma's
" claims " in its context.

In her latest memorial for the recognition of her
" services "—her petition to the Prince Regent of 1813
—she claimed to have responded to the then Sir John
Jervis's appeals for help while employed upon the reduction of Corsica. In this statement, which is one of
several, she makes some confusion between two names
influential in two successive years. If such lapses as
these stood alone, without substantial evidence beneath
them, her censors might have been fairly justified in
pressing them to the utmost. But since (as will be
shown) there is strong corroboration of the substance
of her services in 1796, considerable proof of her *main*
service in 1798, with abundant new and historical evidence for her truthfulness in the account of the part
played by her in the royal escape just before Christmas
of the same year—they amount to little more than the
immaterial inaccuracies which recur in several of her
recitals. Her critics, in fixing on the memorial to the
Prince Regent—framed in her declining years and her
extremest need—have consistently ignored her other
applications for relief, and especially that to King
George III. in which she does not specify this claim

at all, but only implies it under "many inferior services."

In her "Prince Regent" memorial she urges that "In the year 1793, when Lord Hood had taken possession of Toulon, and Sir John Jervis was employ'd upon the reduction of Corsica, the latter kept writing to me for everything he wanted which I procured to be promptly provided him; and, as his letters to me prove, had considerably facilitated the reduction of that island. I had by this time induced the King through my influence with the Queen to become so zealous in the good cause, that both would often say I had de-Bourboniz'd them and made them English."

In the same "memorial" she mentions a side-circumstance which can now be fully substantiated. She there asserts that Sir William in his "latter moments, in deputing Mr. Greville to deliver the Order of the Bath to the King, desired that he would tell His Majesty that he died in the confident hope that his pension would be continued to me for my zeal and service." Greville's letter of 1803 more than bears out her veracity in this trifle. Greville himself, the precisest of officials, and just after his uncle's death by no means on the best of terms with Lady Hamilton, added that he *knew* that the public "records" confirmed "the testimony of their Sicilian Majesties by letter as well as by their ministers, *of circumstances peculiarly distinguished and honourable to her, and at the same time of high importance to the public service.*" Hamilton's own share in the many transactions which are to follow passed equally disregarded with his widow's. And with regard to the preliminary "service" which we must now discuss, she repeats her asseveration in almost the last letter that she ever wrote, adding that in this case, as in the others, she paid "often and often out of her own pocket at Naples."

As has been recounted, Hood took Toulon in August, 1793. It had to be evacuated on December 17th of that year; and it was Lord Hood, not the future Lord St. Vincent, who superintended the Corsican operations from the December of 1793 to their issue in Nelson's heroism at Calvi in July, 1794. Sir John Jervis, on the other hand, was in command of the West Indian expedition of 1794. He does not, it is true, figure as corresponding with the Hamiltons on naval affairs until 1798, when, in an interesting correspondence, he thanks her for services as " patroness of the navy," protests his " unfeigned affectionate regard," and signs himself her " faithful and devoted knight." But none the less he was (and this has eluded notice) in close correspondence with Acton throughout the early portion of 1796.

Such, then, in this instance, are the material discrepancies. In dwelling long afterwards on her first endeavours for her country, she transposed the sequence of two successive years, while she confounded Lord Hood and the future Lord St. Vincent together. Little sagacity, however, is needed to perceive that these very confusions point to her sincerity. Had she been forging claims, imperatively raised in the extremities of her fate, nothing would have been easier than to have verified these trifles, especially as many of Nelson's friends remained staunch to her till the close. Wilful liars do not concoct and elaborate evidence manifestly against themselves. For the truth of this, the least important and most general of her services, Acton's manuscript correspondence of these years with Hamilton supplies a new presumption. What England wanted during these two years from the Neapolitan premier was something outside and beyond what her treaty with Sicily enabled her, as a fact, to receive, and it was just these *extras* that Emma's rising ascendency with the Queen and her own ambition may have prompted her to procure. The real pretexts for refusal, as we shall find in their proper place, were not scepticism, but royal disfavour, technical precedent, lapse of time, private pique, and party interest. Canning thought her " richly entitled " to compensation. Grenville himself did not deny the performance of her services. Addington grounded his refusal mainly on the multiplicity of other claims on the Government.

The year 1794 at Naples was one of continuous calamity; while successive catastrophes were heightened by the undoubted tyrannies of the Queen. France, by fomenting the Neapolitan ferment, was deliberately inveigling the two Sicilies. No quarter would Maria Carolina give to the French assassins or to the Neapolitan republicans. Hitherto, in the main, her old clemency had found vent, and she had striven to be just. She still deemed justice her motive, but she deceived herself. While the King always remained optimist, her pessimism verged on madness. She treated affairs of State just as if they had been affairs of the heart. Her mistrust both of the conspiring nobles and the thankless students, now, from changed incentives, in attempted combination, showed signs of yielding to a paroxysm of revenge disguised by an inscrutable face. Robespierre was branded on her brain. Her word for every rebellious aristocrat was " We will not give him time to become a Robespierre." The close of the year witnessed Robespierre's doom, and a false lull brought with it a film of security. Yet the signal baseness now confronting her would have justified a moderate severity. Disaffection was not native but imported. The great mass of the people never wavered in allegiance to the King of the Lazzaroni, and agitation was bought and manipulated by France. The rest of Europe recognised the real significance of these insurrections. " God knows," wrote Nelson to the Hamiltons in 1796, " I only feel for the King of Naples, as I am confident the change in his Government would be subversive of the interest of all Europe." The English Government, the Russian, even the Prussian, felt the same. The Queen, who had really done so much in the teeth of sharp difficulties for the " Intellectuels," was beside herself. Jacobinism, at first narrowed to a faction, afterwards, at the worst, diffused as a leaven, was by this time hydra-headed. Its disorders had spread to Sicily, where their suppression had been signalised by the execution of the ringleaders and the imprisonment of three hundred. By the spring of 1795 the French had divulged their determination of attacking the British squadron in the Mediterranean. The receivers of her most generous bounty bit the hand of their benefactress. Luigi di Medici, the young cavalier on whom she had conferred absolute power, was denounced by a mathematical professor. As " Regente della Vicaria " he was tried by the last novelty in tribunals, an invention of Acton. Besides other old hands like the inevitable Prince Pignatelli, it consisted of three principal assessors—Guidobaldi, a judge; Prince Castelcicala, a prop always trusted; and lastly Vanni, a man of the people, a " professional " whom the Queen had actually made Marquis. This trio was nicknamed " Cerberus." It was the reverse of former experiments: for the first time two members of the disaffected " professionals " were admitted into the bureaucracy. Vanni, a miniature Marat, who well merited his subsequent downfall, dictated; and his dictatorship stank in the nostrils of all Italy as " the white terror of Naples." Di Medici had himself headed a fresh conspiracy—for the King's murder—

Lady Hamilton as Circe.

From the original painting by George Romney.

which for a long time simmered in the political caldron. He was imprisoned in the fortress of Gaeta, to reappear, however, a few years later as a pardoned protégé. Prince Caramanico, despatched after Sicigniano's sad suicide to the Embassy in London, died before starting, with the usual suspicion of poison. The execution in the " Mercato Vecchio " of the cultivated Tommaso Amato, who was deprived even of supreme unction, lent its first horror to the notorious death-chamber of the " Capella della Vicaria," and was soon followed by that of sixty more Jacobins. The cause of " order and religion " was publicly pitted against these damnable heresies. Even communications with the self-styled " Patriots " were to be punished. It was decreed treason for more than ten to assemble, save by license. The judges, it is true, were bidden to be " conscientious in equity and justice," but three witnesses sufficed for the death-sentence. Apart from capital sentences, the castles and prisons were crammed with suspects, so much so that those of Brindisi were requisitioned. Massacres desolated Sicily; blood ran in the Neapolitan streets. Ferdinand, who had been amusing himself by lengthened law-suits with the Prince of Tarsia over a silk monopoly, called on the clergy to expose the " French errors "; and at Naples devotion and disaster ever trod closely on each other's heels. Three days of solemn prayer were once more decreed in the Metropolitan Church of St. Januarius. Both King and Queen were perpetually seen in devout attendance at the principal shrines. The pulpits preached " death to the French," and war against Jacobinism was declared religious. To be a " patriot " (an innocent fault in palmier days) was now sacrilege. A fresh eve of St. Bartholomew was feared. In a word, the methods of crushing rebellion and opinion were eminently southern, but they were also a counterblast to equal barbarities in the north. Save for the sansculottes and their propaganda, Naples would have escaped the fever and remained a drowsy castle of contented indolence.

While, as queen, Maria Carolina cowed the city, as woman she was demented by Buonaparte's Italian victories. Naples, alone of all Italy, still defied him. The Neapolitan royalties—to their honour—sacrificed fortune and jewels to dare the new Alexander. At the same time, they called on both nobles and ecclesiastics to emulate their public spirit, and thereby unconsciously did much to hasten the " patriot " insurrection. One hundred and three thousand ducats were demanded from the town, one hundred and twenty thousand from the nobles; church property was alienated. Everything was seized for the common cause. The news of Nelson's heroism and the English triumph in Corsica was received with rapture. And the Neapolitan troops on *this* occasion shamed the general cowardice. By 1795 Prince Moliterno was acclaimed a national hero; the courage of General Cuto's three regiments in the Tyrol raised the Neapolitan name, while Mantua and Rome showed the white feather and necessitated the onerous peace of Brescia.

It may now be guessed what agitated the Queen's bosom as day by day she sat down to pen her French missives to Emma, and what were the feelings naturally instilled in Emma by Hamilton, Nelson's letters, and the Queen. The Jacobin cause was the prime pest of Europe, to be crushed at all costs; Napoleon, an impudent upstart and usurper; the Neapolitan rebels, monsters of ingratitude and treachery. All these convictions were as binding as articles of faith. Emma's own heart was tender to a fault. She detested bloodshed and liked to use her influence for mercy, as, to do her bare justice, was then the Queen's instinct, after the first spasm had passed.   In Emma's eyes the Queen herself, so kind and good at home, so sincere and friendly, was "adorable."   She could do no wrong. The past peccadilloes of this baffling woman, contrasting with her present domesticity, seemed to her, even if she believed them, merely a royal prerogative.   She was—as Emma assured Greville in a letter congratulating him on his new vice-chamberlainship, "Everything one can wish—the best mother, wife, and freind in the world.   I live constantly with her, and have done intimately so for 2 years, and I never have in all that time seen anything but goodness and sincerity in her, and if ever you hear any lyes about her, contradict them, and if you shou'd see a cursed book written by a vile French dog, with her character in it, don't believe one word."   Hours passed with her were "enchantment."   "No person can be so charming as the Queen.   If I was her daughter she could not be kinder to me, and I love her with my whole soul."   As she grew more influential on the stirring scene she caught and exaggerated her royal friend's effusiveness. "Oh that everyone," is her endorsement on a letter, "could know her as I do, they would esteem her as I do from my soul.   May every good attend her and hers."   Thus Ruth, of Naomi.   From such a friend impartiality was no more to be expected than from such enemies as the "vile French dogs."

The Queen's correspondence [1] with Emma opens earlier with a touching note about the fate of the poor Dauphin; a sweet little portrait still remains under its cover.   This innocent child, she wrote, implores a sig-

---

[1] Most of her letters of this and the next five years are transcribed from the various Egerton MS. by R. Palumbo in his *Maria Carolina and Emma Hamilton,* which to much valuable material adds some of the old rumours about her earlier and later life.

nal vengeance for the massacre of his parents before the Eternal Throne. His afflictions " have renewed wounds that will never heal." In January, 1794, a fête was given by the Hamiltons to Prince Augustus. It was a golden occasion for fanning the English fever, which by now had spread throughout the loyalist ranks. The Queen's letter of that afternoon begged the hostess to tell her company " God save great George our King," rejoiced over the Anglo-Sicilian alliance, and sent her compliments to all the English present. In the following June she exulted over George's speech to Parliament renewing the war. She longed for English news from Toulon. At his fête two years later, she was to protest that she loved the British prince as a son. She was perpetually anxious about Emma's health and prescribing remedies. As for her own " old health," it was not worth her young friend's disquietude. When Sir William lay at death's door she bade her " put confidence in God, who never forsakes those who trust in Him," and count on the " sincere friendship" of her " attached friend." Emma's performances she applauded to the skies, especially that of " Nina," which had been Romney's favourite.

In one of her constant billets she tenderly inquired after " *ce cher aimable bienfaisant évêque* "—the flippant but kindly worldling and " Right Reverend Father in God " (as Beckford terms him) Lord Bristol, Bishop of Derry. Of this odd wit, erratic vagrant and sentimental scapegrace, so typical of a century that included both Horace Walpole and Laurence Sterne—a veritable Gallio-in-gaiters, with his whimsical projects for endless improvements, his connoisseurship, his restlessness, his real pluck and independence, we have already caught glimpses in eccentric attire at Caserta. One of his queerest features was the blended care

and carelessness both of money and family.   Attached
to his devoted and economical daughter Louisa, he
quarrelled with his son for not marrying an heiress.
His bitterest reproach against his old wife was that
she disbelieved " in the current coin of the realm."
Lady Hamilton thus at this time described him to
Greville : " He is very fond of me, and very kind.
He is very entertaining and dashes at everything.   Nor
does he mind King and Queen when he is inclined to
shew his talents."   The French victories were soon
to be fatal to the *esprit moqueur,* and to cool his volatile
impatience for some eighteen months within the
clammy walls of a Milanese fortress.   Besides his
autographs in the Morrison Collection, and two now
belonging to the writer, a few letters from him to
Emma exist in that surreptitious edition of the pilfered
Nelson Letters which, in 1814, were to add one more
drop to her cup of bitterness.   They all show that he
purveyed information, both serious and scandalous,
through Emma to the Queen.   They stamp the in-
triguer, the patriot, and the friend.   The first seems
written among the embroilments of 1793.

The sale and purchase of antiquities absorbed him
like Sir William; unlike the Ambassador, he never
shirked labour, but rather meddled officiously with the
departments over which his leisurely friend had been
up to now so disposed to loiter.   In 1793 he is to be
found spying on the spies who misled " the dear, dear
Queen."   At the opening, too, of 1794, he forwards
Venetian secrets to be communicated *" à la première
des femmes, cette maîtresse femme."*   " I have been
in bed," he adds, " these four weeks with what is called
a flying gout, but were it such it would be gone long
ago, and it hovers round me like a ghost round its
sepulchre."   In 1795 again the nomad was at Berlin
routing out State-secrets.   The date of the following

must be that of the shameful Austrian treaties in
1797 which succeeded the galling peace of Brescia.

"MY EVER DEAREST LADY HAMILTON,—I should
certainly have made this Sunday an holy day to me, and
have taken a Sabbath day's journey to Caserta, had not
poor Mr. Lovel been confined to his bed above three
days with a fever.   To-day it is departed; to-morrow
Dr. Nudi has secured us from its resurrection; and
after to-morrow, I hope, virtue will be its own reward.
. . . All public and private accounts agree in the immediate prospect of a general peace.   It will make a
delicious foreground in the picture of the new year;
many of which I wish, from the top, bottom, and
centre of my heart, to the incomparable Emma—*quella
senza paragone."*   The next snatch is worth quoting
for its humour :—" I went down to your opera-box
two minutes after you left; and should have seen you
on the morning of your departure—but was detained in
the arms of Murphy, as Lady Eden expresses it, and
was too late.   You say nothing of the adorable Queen;
I hope she has not forgot me. . . . I veritably deem
her the very best edition of a woman I ever saw—I
mean of such as are not in *folio.* . . . My duties ob-
struct my pleasure. . . . You see, I am but the second letter of your alphabet, though you are the first of
mine."

A last extract, penned a few months after his liberation, must complete this vignette :—" I know not, dearest Emma, whether friend Sir William has been able
to obtain my passport or not; but this I know—that
if they have refused it, they are damned fools for their
pains: for never was a Malta orange better worth
squeezing or sucking; and if they leave me to die, without a tombstone over me to tell the contents—*tant pis
pour eux.*   In the meantime, I will frankly confess
to you that my health most seriously and urgently re-

quires the balmy air of dear Naples, and the more
balmy atmosphere of those I love, and who love me;
and that I shall forego my garret with more regret
than most people of my silly rank in society forego
a palace or a drawing-room." He then sketched his
tour on horseback to "that unexplored region Dal-
matia"; he described Spalato as "a modern city built
within the precincts of an ancient palace." Spalato
reminded him of Diocletian, the "wise sovereign who
quitted the sceptre of an architect's rule," and the two
together, of a new project for a "packet-boat in these
perilous times between Spalato and Manfredonia."

The serious *début* of Emma as "Stateswoman" (in
the sense of England's spokeswoman at Naples) chimes
with the episode of the King of Spain's secret letters
heralding and announcing his rupture with the anti-
French alliance during 1795 and 1796. But before
dealing with that crisis, I may be pardoned for glanc-
ing at one more picturesque figure among Emma's surroundings—that of Wilhelmina, Countess of Lich-
tenau.

She was nobly born and bred; but in girlhood, under
a broken promise, it would seem, of morganatic marriage, had become mistress and intellectual companion
of Frederick, King of Prussia—a tie countenanced by
her mother. Political intrigue drove her from Berlin
to Italy, as it afterwards involved her in despair and
ruin. She was cultivated, artistic, sensitive, and unhappy. She became the honoured correspondent of
many distinguished statesmen and authors. Lavater
and Arthur Paget were her firm friends, as also the
luckless Alexandre Sauveur, already noticed in his
"hermitage" on Mount Vesuvius. Lord Bristol,
naturally, knelt at her shrine. In her *Mémoires* she
frankly admits that she (like Emma) was vain; but
maintains that all women are so by birthright. Lovel,

the parson friend of the Bishop of Derry, used to sign himself her "brother by adoption," and address her as "a very dear sister"; Paget corresponded with her as "dear Wilhelmina." Throughout 1795 she was at Naples, where her cicisbeo was the handsome Chevalier de Saxe, afterwards killed in a duel with the Russian M. Saboff. A letter from him towards the close of this year of Neapolitan enthusiasm for the English, when the Elliots among others were praising and applauding Emma to the skies, describes the great ball given by Lady Plymouth in celebration of Prince Augustus's birthday. The supper was one of enthusiasm and "God save the King." "They drank," he chronicles, "*à l'Anglaise:* the toasts were noisy, and the healths of others were so flattered as to derange our own." Sir William was constantly begging of her to forward the sale of his collections at the Russian capital; nor was tea, now fashionable at court, the least agent for English interests. Emma herself had become the "fair tea-maker" of the Chiaja instead of, as once, of Edgware Row, and Mrs. Cadogan too held her own tea-parties. Emma often corresponded with the beautiful Countess, and one of her letters of this period, not here transcribed, supplies evidence of what kind of French she had learned to write by a period when she had mastered not only Neapolitan *patois* but Spanish and Italian. At the troublous outset of 1796 Wilhelmina quitted Italy never to return.

These characters are scarcely edifying. The scoffing Bishop, the frail Countess, however, were a typical outcome of sincere reaction against hollow and hypocritical observance. There was nothing diabolical about them. The virtues that they professed, they practised; their faults, those of free thinkers and free livers, do not differentiate them from their contemporaries. It is surely remarkable that these, and such as these, paved the way for Nelson's vindication of Great Britain in the Mediterranean, far more than the train of decent frivolity and formal virtue that did nothing without distinction. High Bohemia has always wielded some power in the world. Far more was it a force when the French Revolution threatened the very foundations of society, and opened up avenues to every sort of adventure and adventurer.

Emma has already been found twice acquainting Greville of her new *métier* as politician. Her present circumstances and influence over the Queen may be gauged independently by a letter from her husband to his nephew from Caserta of November, which has only recently passed into the national collection :—

". . . Here we are as usual for the winter hunting and shooting season, and Emma is not at all displeased to retire with me at times from the great world, altho' no one is better received when she chuses to go into it. The Queen of Naples seems to have great pleasure in her society. She sends for her generally three or four times a week. . . . In fact, all goes well *chez nous.* [He is taking more exercise.] . . . *I have not neglected of my duty,* and flatter myself that I must be approved of at home *for some real services* which my particular situation at this court has enabled me to render to our Ministry. I have at least the satisfaction of feeling that I have done all in my power, *altho' at the expense of my own health and fortune."* This last sentence points to the political situation, and Emma's assistance in the episode of the King of Spain's letters; for not one, but a whole series were involved.

These letters, from 1795 to 1796, were the secret channels by which Ferdinand was made aware first of his brother's intention to desert the Alliance, and, in the next year, to join the enemy.

In touching the effects and causes of an event so critical, Emma's pretensions to a part in its discovery must be discussed also. Their consideration, interrupting the sequence of our narrative, will not affect its movement. It is no dry recital, for it concerns events and character.

From 1795 to the opening of 1797 the league against Napoleon, as thrones and principalities one by one tottered before him, was faced by rising republics and defecting allies. In vain were Wurmser and the Neapolitan troops to rally the Romagna. In vain did Nelson recount to the Hamiltons Hood's and Hotham's successes along the Italian coast. Acton's own letters of about this period complain of the Austrian delays and suspicions. Prussia estranged herself from the banded powers. England herself was, for a moment, ready to throw up the sponge. In 1795, so great was the popular fear of conflict, that prints in every London shop window represented the blessings of peace and the horrors of war. Even in the October of 1796 Nelson told the Hamiltons, with a wrathful sigh, " We have a narrow-minded party to work against, but I feel above it." And writing from Bastia in December, 1796, he was again indignant at the orders for the evacuation of the Mediterranean, which plunged the Queen in despair. " Till this time," commented the true patriot, " it has been usual for the allies of England to fall from her, but till now she never was known to desert her friends whilst she had the power of supporting them."

The home explosion had been arrested; Neapolitan discontent had been appeased; but the frauds of the corn-contractor, Mackinnon, added knavery to increasing fiscal embarrassments. And Naples was soon to become involved in a mesh of degrading treaties. The Peace of Brescia, enforcing her neutrality and mulcting

her of eight million francs, sounded the first note of
Austrian retreat.   It culminated by 1797 in the shameful treaties of Campoformio and Tolentino, which
eventually bound Austria to cry off.   By the close of
1796 the distraught Queen raved over a separate and
partly secret compact exacted by France—the most
galling condition of which excluded more than four
vessels of the allies *at one time* from any Neapolitan
or Sicilian port—a proviso critical in 1798.   By 1797
Naples was forced to acknowledge the French Cisalpine
Republic, and France had gained the natural frontiers
of the Alps and the Rhine.   Buonaparte returned to
Paris covered with glory.   In a single campaign he
had defeated five armies, and won eighteen pitched battles and sixty-seven smaller combats.   He had made
one hundred and fifty thousand prisoners.   He had
freed eighteen states.   He had rifled Italy of her
statues, pictures, and manuscripts.   For his adopted
country's arsenals he had pillaged eleven hundred and
eighty pieces of artillery, and fifty-one muniments for
her harbours; while no less than two hundred million
francs were secured for her treasuries.

But a worse defection than Prussia's or Austria's
was that of Spain, which fell like a bomb on the coalition against France, and which, as Emma alleged, first
brought her on the political stage to the knowledge of
the English Ministry.

Her claim, and Nelson's for her, differing in dates,
since there were several transactions, was that her
friendship with the Queen obtained the loan of a secret
document addressed by the Spanish monarch to the
King of Naples, and forewarning him of his intention
to ally himself with France, a copy of which she got
forwarded to London.

This service has been more questioned by Professor
Laughton than by Mr. Jeaffreson, who, however,

doubts some particulars in her account of this obscure matter, and her direct initiative in it. Whatever its subsequent embroidery, Emma's contention, certified by Nelson, nor ever denied by the truthful Hamilton, is favoured by its likelihood. At the very outset, any subsidiary objection raised as to the improbability that an important despatch in cipher would have been entrusted to her keeping, falls at once to the ground, since there exists such a document in her own handwriting among the Morrison autographs;[1] while in the Queen's correspondence occurs more than one mention of a cipher transmitted to her. But, indeed, neither in her memorial of 1813 to the Prince of Wales, nor in that other to the King, nor in Nelson's last codicil, is a "*ciphered* letter" mentioned. The first document styles it only a "private letter." The last two agree in calling it the King of Spain's letter "expressive of" or "acquainting him with" his "intention of declaring war against England." Such pains perhaps need hardly have been bestowed to identify the document meant, with the celebrated cipher of Galatone, which the Queen handed to Emma in the spring of 1795. Some circumstantial evidence may favour the view that the substance of her claim relates to information sent home in autumn 1796, the year specified by Nelson's last codicil, by his conversation at Dresden in 1800, and on many other occasions.

Roughly speaking, the facts are these.

From the opening of the year 1795 to the autumn of 1796 the Neapolitan Ambassador at Madrid (in 1795 "Galatone," Prince Belmonte) was in constant communication, both open and secret, with the King, Queen, and Gallo, then foreign minister; and in such

---

[1] Morrison MS. 259. Transcript (in Italian) in Lady Hamilton's handwriting of a letter (in cipher) to the Foreign Minister of Naples. Dated Aranjuez, March 31, 1796.

cases official letters, which are naturally guarded, should be carefully distinguished from private information surreptitiously conveyed. From the moment that the French Directory replaced the Reign of Terror in Thermidor, 1794, and represented itself under the dazzling triumphs of Napoleon as a stable, if *épicier,* Government, Spain had been steadily smoothing the way for wriggling out of the Anti-Gallic Coalition, the more so as she longed to try conclusions with Great Britain in partnership with France, whom she had hitherto been bound to attack. For this purpose— as Acton's manuscript letters attest—she sought to bully Naples, first out of the Anti-Gallic league, and subsequently, in 1797, out of enforced neutrality. She still considered her navy powerful, although throughout 1795 Nelson derided it as worse than useless. Her Florentine envoy wrote insolently in the autumn of 1795 that it was of no consequence that the English flag was flaunted in Mediterranean waters; the real Spanish objective ought to be Cuba, Porto Rico, St. Domingo. Tradition, national pride, and inclination all united in her effort gradually and insidiously to prepare a breach with the allied powers and a *rapprochement* with France.

During these long negotiations both Acton and Hamilton were kept in designed ignorance by the King, who, under his inherited bias for Spanish influence, rejoiced to think that he was now at last his own minister, outwitting and emancipated from his thwarted Queen. Maria Carolina, however, had provided her own channels of information also. All that she could ferret out was carefully communicated to Lady Hamilton, and forwarded, under strict pledges not to compromise by naming her, to Lord Grenville in London.

There are two distinct sets of the correspondence between Hamilton and Acton and Acton and Hamilton—

that of spring and early summer, 1795, relative to the
Spanish *peace* with France achieved in July, the project
for which, however, had leaked out long before; and
that of late summer and autumn, 1796, regarding
Spain's much more secret and momentous decision to
strike a definite *alliance,* offensive as well as defensive,
with the enemy of Europe.

It was in connection with the latter that Nelson's last
codicil claimed Emma's assistance in divulging it to
the ministers, while he regretted the opportunities
missed by their failure to improve the occasion.   Lady
Hamilton's last memorial assigns no specific date,
though her brief narrative there confuses (as usual)
the peace and the alliance together.   The evidence
points to a possibility of her having been *twice* instrumental in procuring documents weighty for both
these emergencies; but her main exertion, as Nelson
averred, was bound up with the last.   Professor
Laughton's acumen bears most strongly upon the letters of 1795, though at the same time he supplies and
discusses the data for 1796.   To his article the student is referred.   Both he and Mr. Jeaffreson fasten
upon her statement in the " Prince Regent " memorial
alone,[1] and have not considered her undecorated and

[1] These are its words:—" By unceasing application of that
influence "—*i. e.* with the Queen—" and no less watchfulness to
turn it to my country's good, it happened that I discovered a
courier had brought the King of Naples a private letter from
the King of Spain.   I prevailed on the Queen to take it from
his pocket unseen.   We found it to contain the King of Spain's
intention to withdraw from the Coalition, and join the French
against England.   My husband at that time lay dangerously ill.
I prevailed on the Queen to allow my taking a copy, with which
I immediately despatched a messenger to Lord Grenville, taking
all the necessary precautions; for his safe arrival then became
very difficult, and altogether cost me about £400 paid out of my
privy purse."—Cf. Morrison MS. 1046, where the date con-
jectured " March, 1813 " tallies with her letter in the Rose diaries
inclosing it.
Her memorial to the King contains a simpler statement.

simple account tallying with Nelson's in her memorial
to the King. I beg the reader's patient attention to
the wording of both of these, below cited.

It is clear from the first that Emma in treating of
two years mixes up the documents which she admit-
tedly obtained from the Queen and delivered to Hamilton for transmission both in April and June, 1795,
with one of several that she obtained in 1796. No
single "letter" could have comprised both the rupture
with the alliance and the compact with France, belonging respectively to two successive years. On April
28, 1795, the Queen sent her a ciphered letter from
Galatone, demanding its return "before midnight."
Next day she sent her "the promised cipher," "too
glad in being able to render a service." Emma recorded on her copy of the first that her husband forwarded it with the cipher to England.

It is open, however, to argument that Emma's chief
aid in unravelling a long and tangled skein of matur-
ing crisis may have been rendered about September,
1796. Its history will resume our thread; and, since
the next chapter's evidence is to support not only her
crowning service with regard to the Mediterranean

"That it was the good fortune of your Majesty's memorialist to
acquire the confidential friendship of that great and august
Princess, the Queen of Naples, your Majesty's most faithful and
ardently attached Ally, at a period of peculiar peril, and when
her august Consort . . . was unhappily constrained to profess
a neutrality, but little in accordance with the feelings of his
own excellent heart. By which means your Majesty's memorialist, among many inferior services, *had an opportunity of obtaining, and actually did obtain, the King of Spain's letter to the
King of Naples expressive of his intention to declare war against
England. This important document, your Majesty's memorialist
delivered to her husband, Sir William Hamilton, who immediately transmitted it to your Majesty's Ministers.*" This as-
sertion tallies with Nelson's. There is no proof of the date of
this paper, which in the Morrison MS. (1045) is guessed to be
identical with that of the "Prince Regent" memorial above
transcribed.

fleet, but the substantial accuracy of her two statements of it, it is worth while in this matter also to inquire somewhat closely whether Emma was a liar, and Nelson a dupe.

Two Acton manuscripts towards the end of August, 1796, cast a sidelight on the numerous letters of that year from the Spanish court, culminating in some kind of announcement by the Spanish King to his brother of Naples of his final decision to join the French.

Acton vied amicably with Hamilton in obtaining the first advices for transmission to London; and indeed to Acton's *penchant* (like our own Harley's under Queen Anne) for engrossing business and favour Nelson afterwards referred in a letter to Lady Hamilton, where he declares that he will no longer " get everything done " through Acton, as was his " old way." Both Acton and Wyndham, England's envoy at Leghorn, were already aware of Spain's tentatives with France; but neither they nor the English Ambassador at Madrid could have discovered till later the precise terms of a coming alliance, vital to Europe. It would press the more on Naples, in view of that undignified and stringent accommodation with the French Directory, into which the Franco-Hispanian conspiracy, after a brief armistice, was fast driving her reluctant councils. For months Prince Belmonte (transferred from Madrid to Paris) had been dangling his heels as negotiator in the French capital, subjected to insolent demands and mortifying delays and chicanes. From the spring of 1796 onwards a series of threatening letters had been received by Ferdinand from Charles; and all the time the pro-Spanish party, designing a dethronement of the Neapolitan Bourbons, kept even pace with Maria Carolina's hatred of a sister-in-law caballing for her son. Ferdinand himself still clung to the Spanish raft; Charles of Spain was his brother, and blood is thicker than water. While England grew more and more faint-hearted, and Grenville forwarded despatch after despatch advising Naples to give up the game and make the best terms available with the Directory; while Napoleon's victories swelled the republicanisation of Italy, the Spanish plot also for sapping Great Britain's Mediterranean power, and overthrowing the dynasty of the Two Sicilies, increased in strength. Yet the King of Naples still temporised. For a space even Acton veered; he listened to Gallo and the King, the more readily because his own post was endangered in 1795, when there had been actual rumours of his replacement by Gallo. In 1796 he saw no way out but the sorry compromise with France, which he half desired, and the enforced neutrality which disgusted Naples in December. Milan had fallen. Piedmont had been Buonaparte's latest democratic experiment. The Austrians, led by Wurmser, were failing in combat, as their court by the first month of the next year was to fail in faith. Naples was fast being isolated both from Italy and Britain; small wonder then that through Acton's earlier letters of 1796 there peers a sour smile of cynical desperation. But directly he realised the full force of the Franco-Hispanian complot, and the stress of reverses to the allied arms, he changed his ply. He avowed himself ready " to break the peace "; he rejoined and rejoiced the Queen; he again looked to England. As Grenville waxed colder, the more warmly did Acton compete with Hamilton in egging on the British Government by disclosing the hard facts detected. Hamilton, however, forestalled him. He, Emma, and the Queen had throughout been in frequent confabulation, while the Hamiltons were also in close correspondence with Nelson. But it was Emma, not her husband, that was daily closeted with Carolina, whose letters to the ambassadress prove how well she was informed of Spain's machinations. . So early as June, 1793, we have seen Emma already politicising. In April, 1795, she reports once more to Greville: "Against my will, *owing to my situation here,* I am got into politics, and I wish to have news for my dear, much loved Queen whom I adore." She had already transcribed a ciphered communication from Spain as to King Charles's probable defection from the alliance. She now definitely advances towards the political footlights.

The preceding year had settled the habit by which the Queen conveyed secret documents to the friend who as regularly copied or translated them for her husband.[1] So far the chief of these had been the " Chiffre de Galatone " transmitted to England at the close of April, 1795.[2] All of them, however, principally related to the Spanish *peace* with France then brewing in Madrid, of which the British Government had gained other advices from their representative at the Spanish court. That even this, however, was not quite a

[1] On April 21, 1795, for example, the Queen sends three papers " confidentially," " which may be useful to your husband." Cf. Professor Laughton's article in Colburn's *United Service Magazine*, April, 1889, and for the famous letter of April 28, cf. also Eg. MS. 1615, f. 22, containing another example. It is needless to multiply instances. One citation only will illustrate Emma's initiative. In Hamilton's despatch of April 30, 1795, he says, "However, Lady Hamilton having had the honour of seeing the Queen yesterday morning, H.M. was pleased to promise me one, etc." In another of the following year he speaks of documents being " communicated " to him " as usual."

[2] Cf. Emma's copy of the Queen's note forwarding it to her, Eg. MS. 1615, f. 22, and Emma's reference to the courier and her having " got into politicks," April 19. Morrison MS. 263. On June 9 she copied another despatch from presumably Galatone (Prince Belmonte), *ibid.* 265. Later in the year the Queen communicated information about Spain and, in another letter, rumours about Hood having got out of Toulon, Eg. MS. 1617, ff. 3, 4.

secret de Polichinelle, is likely from the scarcity of references to it in the Acton correspondence with Hamilton about this time. Nor is it any answer to Emma's activities, even in this and less material years, that she voiced the Queen's urgent interest, because it is abundantly manifest that the Queen, in her need, did for Emma what she would never have done for Hamilton apart, while in return Emma doubtless communicated also Nelson's Mediterranean information to Maria Carolina. She had suddenly become a safe and trusted go-between, and none other at this juncture could have performed her office. The supine Sir William had at last been pricked into action. He had now every incentive to earn the King of England's gratitude. In a private missive to Lord Grenville of April 30, 1795, alluding to the communication of this very " cipher of Galatone," he himself asserts, " Your Lordship will have seen by my despatch of 21st April the unbounded confidence which the Queen of Naples has placed in me *and my wife."* Emma could now advantage not only herself and her country, but her royal friend and her own husband—*Tria juncta in uno.*

But the position in the later summer of 1796 was far more serious both for Naples and England than it had ever been before. Acton had been dallying. During the interval Ferdinand seems to have been pelted with letters from Charles, menacing, cajoling, persuading him. Already in August Hamilton had communicated secrets respecting the movements of the French and Spanish squadrons. Every one knew that Spanish retirement from the European Coalition was soon to be succeeded by some sort of league; but nobody, either at Naples or in England, could ascertain its exact conditions revealed to Ferdinand alone. If it was to be (as it was) an alliance of offence, the issues must prove momentous for Great Britain. All was kept a profound secret.

About September, 1796, apparently, Charles the Fourth's final letter reached the hands of his Neapolitan brother. But his coming alliance with France had already been notified by Acton to Hamilton. The murder was out. The compact between the two courts was fixed as one of war to the knife against the allied powers, among whom England was wavering and Austria on the verge of concluding a scandalous peace. Ferdinand, who alone knew what was impending, must have chuckled as he thought how he had worsted his masterful spouse. If Emma could only clear up the mystery and the uncertainty, England might be forearmed against the veiled sequel of that long train of hidden *pourparlers* which she had been able to discover and announce during the previous year; and in such a case she counted with assurance on her country's gratitude towards her and her husband.

How the Queen or Emma, or both, obtained the loan of this document, whether out of the King's pocket, as Emma avers in her Prince Regent's memorial, and Pettigrew, with embellishments, in his *Life of Nelson;* or whether, according to the posthumous *Memoirs of Lady Hamilton,* through a bribed page, does not concern us. Such strokes of the theatre are, at any rate, quite consonant with the atmosphere of the court. The sole question is: Did she manage to receive and transmit it?

The letter to which I apply her pretensions was in Spanish—a " private letter " or a " letter," as Emma and Nelson respectively describe it, and not a " letter in cipher " like the one received from Galatone in the year preceding. The problem's intricacy defies a real solution. In the main, habit and motive only can be urged for Emma's use of the Queen's friendship in this instance also. What she had done in the one year, she may well have done in the other. On the other hand, there is no definite document that she can be proved to have procured.

Is there any distinct circumstance in her favour to counterweigh the hypotheses against her? One such exists of some weight. It relates to her statement that a messenger of her own was despatched with the document to London.

Sir William Hamilton gave wind of the critical news in a " secret " despatch to Lord Grenville. It is dated September 21, 1796; and the bearer of it seems to have started on the 23rd. It should be observed that this official missive appears exceptional in only transmitting the *purport* of the letter, and not, as repeatedly before and afterwards, either copies of hazardous documents, or, in earlier cases, the originals themselves.

On this very September 21st the Queen of Naples wrote to thank Emma for putting at her service the unexpected medium of " the poor Count of Munster's courier," available through his employer's misfortune. She says that she and the General will profit by the opportunity, and that Emma shall receive " our packet " the day after to-morrow (mid-day, Friday). Acton, once more addressing Hamilton on September 22, and before this special courier had started, begged him to include both his and the Queen's despatches to Circello, Ambassador at St. James's, " by the courier which goes to-morrow for London."

On this identical September 21, 1796, once again Lady Hamilton herself sat down for a hurried chat with Greville. " We have not time," she says, " to write to you, as we have been 3 days and nights writing to send by *this courier* letters of *consequence* for our Government. They ought to be gratefull to Sir William and *myself in particular,* as my situation in this Court is very *extraordinary,* and what no person [h]as yet arrived at." She adds, " He is *our* Courrier."

The coincidence of these combined statements of two successive days suggests the " poor Count of Munster's " courier as the possible bearer both of official despatches and of any copy of the King of Spain's most crucial declaration, that Emma may have made.

It is only fair to state that another contingency presents itself. Emma's service may really have amounted to little more than having been the means of procuring a prompt courier for this urgent despatch. If, however, she also got the original document, or even a copy, forwarded, Hamilton's omission to include it in his despatch is explained. In any case it is material. He may have feared to do so, or she may not have been allowed to retain it long enough, in which case Emma could truthfully describe his brief summary of its pith as the King of Spain's letter.

Professor Laughton has urged with force that no Treasury minute relating to Emma's service is to be found. But must it be assumed that the bare absence of such record is fatal to her case? It might further be urged that no copy of this particular King of Spain's letter exists in our archives. But has every important document mentioned in the despatches of this period invariably come to light?

That the Spanish letter may have arrived about a month earlier than the date of the despatch, and that Acton also may have gleaned its contents, appears from the close similarity between Acton's two letters to Hamilton of August 18 and 21, and the spirit of Hamilton's short summary in his communication of September 21 to Lord Grenville. Hamilton wrote that the King of Naples was " bitterly reproached for acting constantly in opposition to his brother's advice," and was warned that Charles would " soon be obliged to take another course with him." Acton wrote of the King's " odd and open threatenings to his brother," and in his first letter that Spain had " certainly signed a treaty of alliance with the French," and was to " join with them even against us. We are assured of this by threatenings even not equivocal."

Mr. Jeaffreson has further dwelt on the unlikelihood of such a sum as Emma names being spent on retaining the messenger out of her private purse, when her allowance was limited to £200 a year. But this allowance seems to have been only nominal. From the Morrison Collection it would appear that for some time she had been authorised by her husband to overdraw her account in view of increasing requirements. Then there are the minutiæ about their health in 1795 and 1796 to show that the former year better fits her claim. These would seem indecisive, considering his constant ailments. But a strange confirmation of her story remains in the fact of a locket given by Nelson to Emma in 1796, and recording the date. Such a present from one who had never seen her since 1793 may well betoken a real service. Everything, it must be conceded, remains inconclusive. All rests on circumstantial evidence merely, but apart from the problems of 1796, it will be owned that she succeeded in serving England during 1795.

During the following month of October, Emma is still to be found transcribing documents and endorsing effusive gratitude on one of the Queen's letters. She had exerted herself, even if she exaggerates her exertions. It is perfectly possible, of course, that her memory, in confusing the events of these two years, may have also confused the date of her husband's illness. But that her story, stripped of accidentals, is a myth, I cannot bring myself to believe. Even Lord

Grenville, thirteen years later, did not apparently specify fabrication as his reason for rejecting her claims. That during her future she proved often and otherwise blameworthy, that her distant past had been soiled, are scarcely reasons for discrediting the substance of her story, though her efforts passed unheeded by the Government; nor should Greville's repeated acknowledgments of her natural candour be forgotten. To every motive for political exertion had now been added immense opportunity. There is ample reason why she should have used it for her country's advantage. She was no dabbler. She had wished to play a big part, and she was playing it. She had every qualification for acquitting herself well in the arena where she longed to shine, and promptitude alone could ensure success.

Gloom deepened with the opening of the year 1797, but it riveted the Neapolitan House faster to England. The many French immigrants exulted. The pro-Spanish party and all the Anglophobes became confident. Austria had ignobly desisted, and her ministers were rewarded by diamonds from the Pope. Great Britain —hesitating though she seemed—remained the sole champion against Buonaparte. Lord St. Vincent's name and Nelson's rang throughout Europe on the " glorious Valentine's day," and Emma infused fresh hope in the downcast Queen. She delighted to vaunt England's sinew and backbone. She prevented Hamilton from relaxing his efforts, and kept him at his post of honour. She was already ambitious for Nelson. Maria Carolina at last divined that Buonaparte's objective was the Mediterranean. But Nelson had divined the aims of France earlier, when he wrote in October, 1796, " We are all preparing to leave the Mediterranean, a measure which I cannot approve.

They at home do not know what this fleet is capable
of performing; anything and everything." But
Downing Street, in the person of the narrow-sighted
Lord Grenville, still closed its eyes, shut its ears,
and hardened its heart. At Rome the French republicans organised an uprising, and were driven for shelter into Joseph Buonaparte's Palazzo Corsini. He
himself was threatened, and Duphot was killed, by the
Papal guard. Eugène Beauharnais made a sortie of
vengeance. Napoleon utilised the manœuvre to
despatch General Berthier against the Pope's dominions. By the February of the ensuing year the Castle
of St. Angelo was taken. On Ascension Day the Pope
himself, in the Forum, heard the shouts of " Viva la
Republica; abasso il Papa!" He did what other weak
pontiffs have done before and since. He protested his
" divine right," took his stand on it—and fled. Ousted
from Sienna by earthquake, he retired to the Florentine
Certosa, where his rooms fronting that beautiful prospect may still be viewed. Hounded out once more, he
was harried from pillar to post—from Tortona to
Turin, from Briançon to Valence—in the citadel of
which, old and distressed, he breathed his last.

At home Maria Carolina now reversed her policy of
the knout. Vanni, the brutal Inquisitor of State, was
deposed and banished, the diplomatic Castelcicala was
given a free hand. All the captives were released.
The Lazzaroni cheered till they were hoarse over the
magnanimity of their rulers.

And Acton, relieved from the burdens of bureaucracy,
at last pressed Great Britain for a Mediterranean
squadron. He and the Queen had both determined
that their forced neutrality should be of short duration.

If we would appreciate Emma's influence for England at Naples, the tone of his correspondence at this
date should be compared with his indifference during

the earlier portion of the preceding year. The Mediterranean expedition which Nelson was to lead to such decisive triumph was far more the fruit of Neapolitan importunities than of English foresight.

Buonaparte had boasted that he would republicanise the Two Sicilies also. No sooner was Acton apprised of the fact than he immediately invited Sir Gilbert Elliot, who happened to be visiting Naples, to meet him and the Hamiltons. He again murmured against Lord Grenville's finesse. He assured Sir Gilbert that his country had strained every sinew " to move and engage seventeen million Italians to defend themselves, their property, and their honour "; all had been vain for lack of extraneous assistance; even their fleet had laboured to no purpose; in his quaint English, their " head-shipman had lost his head, if ever he had any." The case was now desperate. All hinged on a sufficient Mediterranean squadron. " Any English man-of-war, to the number of *four* at a time," could still be provisioned in Sicilian or Neapolitan ports. Their compelled compact with France allowed no more. And at a moment when the French were disquieting Naples by insurgent fugitives from the Romagna and elsewhere, Napoleon's smooth speeches were, said Acton, mere dissimulation. A " change of masters " might soon ensue. By the April of 1798 Acton was still more explicit in his correspondence with Hamilton. A fresh incursion was now definitely menaced. Naples was being blackmailed. The Parisian Directors offered her immunity, but only if she would pay them an exorbitant sum; otherwise she must be absorbed in the constellation of republics, while her monarch must join the *débris* of falling stars. Viennese support was little more than a forlorn hope for ravaged Italy. In the King's name he implored Hamilton to forward an English privateer to announce their desperate plight

and urgent necessities to Lord St. Vincent.—"Their
Majesties observe the critical moment for all Europe,
and the *threatens* of an invasion even in England.
They are perfectly convinced of the generous and extensive exertions of the British nation at this moment,
but a diversion in these points might operate advantage for the common war. Will England see all
Italy, and even the two Sicilies, in the French hands
with indifference?" The half-hearted Emperor had
at last consented to think of assisting his relations,
though only should Naples be assailed; this perhaps
might "hurry England." Seventeen ships of the line
would soon be ready; there were seventy in Genoa,
thirty at Civita Vecchia. These could carry "perhaps
8000 men." But the French at Toulon could convey
18,000. "With the English expedition we shall be
saved. This is my communication from their
Majesties."

Hamilton's reply must have been bitterly cautious,
for Acton in his answer observes, "We cannot avoid
to expose that His Sicilian Majesty *confides too much*
in His Britannic Majesty's Ministry's help."

And all this time Emma is never from Maria Carolina's side; writing to her, urging, praising, heartening,
caressing the English. The Queen is all gratitude to
her humble friend, whose enthusiasm is an asset of her
hopes:—"Vous en êtes le maître de mon cœur, ma
chère miledy," she writes in her bad and disjointed
French; "ni pour mes amis, comme vous, ni pour mes
opinions [je] ne change jamais." She is "impatient
for news of the English squadron." But she is still
a wretched woman, disquieted by doubts and worn with
care, as she may be viewed in the portraits of this
period. She had deemed herself a pattern of duty,
but had now woke up to the consciousness of being
execrated by her victims; while the loyal Lazzaroni, al-

ways her mislikers, visited each national calamity on
her head. Gallo, Acton, Belmonte, Castelcicala, Di
Medici—all had been tried, and except Acton, who
himself had wavered, all had been found wanting. It
is the Nemesis of despots, even if enlightened, to rely
successively on false supports, to fly by turns from
betrayed trust to treachery once more trusted. Emma
at all events would not fail her, and never did. " You
may read," says Thackeray, " Pompeii in some folks'
faces." Such a Pompeii-countenance must have been
the Queen's.

The English squadron was at last a fact. On
March 29, 1798, Nelson hoisted his flag as Rear-
Admiral of the Blue on board the *Vanguard*. On
April 10 he sailed on one of the most eventful voyages
in history.

. And meanwhile Maria Carolina, with Emma under
her wing, might be seen pacing the palace garden, and
eagerly scanning the horizon from sunny Caserta for
a glimpse of one white sail.

Sister Anne stands and waits on her watch-tower,
feverish for Selim's arrival, while anguished Fatima
peers into Bluebeard's cupboard, horror-stricken at its
gruesome medley of dismembered sovereigns—martyrs
or tyrants—which you please.

CHAPTER VII

TRIUMPH

1798

NELSON was in chase of Buonaparte's fleet.
Napoleon's Egyptian expedition was, per-
haps, the greatest wonder in a course rife with
them. He was not yet thirty; he had been victorious
by land, and had dictated terms at the gates of Vienna.
In Italy, like Tarquin, he had knocked off the tallest
heads first. Debt and jealousy hampered him at home.
It was the gambler's *first* throw, that rarest audacity.
For years his far-sightedness had fastened on the
Mediterranean; and now that Spain was friends with
France, he divined the moment for crushing Britain.
But even then his schemes were far vaster than his
contemporaries could comprehend. His plan was to
obtain Eastern Empire, to reduce Syria, and, after re-
casting sheikhdoms in the dominion of the Pharaohs,
possibly after subduing India, to dash back and conquer England. Italy was honeycombed with his republics. To Egypt France should be suzerain, a democracy
with vassals; as for Great Britain, if she kept her King,
it must be on worse terms than even Louis the Bourbon had once dared to prescribe to the Stuarts. This,
too, was the first and only time when he, an unskilled
mariner, was for a space in chief naval command.
Most characteristic was it also of him—the encyclo-
pædist in action—to have remembered science in this
enterprise against science's home of origin. That vast

Armada of ships and frigates, that huge *L'Orient,* whose very name was augury, those forty thousand men in transports, did not suffice. An array of savants, with all their apparatus, swelling the muster on board their vessel to no less than two thousand, accompanied the new man who was to make all things new. It was nigh a month after Nelson started when Napoleon sailed. Sudden as a flash of lightning, yet impenetrable as the cloud from which it darts, he veiled his movements and doubled in his course.

It was on Saturday, June 16, that Hamilton first sighted Nelson's approach. The van of the small squadron of fourteen sail was visible as it neared Ischia from the westward and made for Capri. He at once took up his pen to send him the latest tidings of the armament which, eluding his pursuit, had now passed the Sicilian seaboard. The glad news of Nelson's arrival spread like wildfire. The French residents mocked and scowled. The people cheered. The solemn ministers smiled. The royal family, in the depths of dejection, plucked up heart; the Queen was in ecstasy. But Gallo and the anti-English group were suspicious and perplexed. They and the King still waited on Austria. On Spain they could no longer fawn.

Nelson's instructions were to water and provide his fleet in any Mediterranean port, except in Sardinia, if necessary by arms. It was not that for the moment he needed refreshment for those scanty frigates, the want of which, he wrote afterwards, would be found graven on his heart. But he had a long and intricate enterprise before him. He was hunting a fox that would profit by every bend and crevice, so to speak, of the country. He could not track him without the certainty that, apart from the delays that force must entail, all his requirements, perhaps for two months,

would be granted on mere demand. Even so early as
June 12 he had requested definite answers from Hamilton as to what precise aid he could count upon from
a pseudo-neutral power trifling over diplomatic
pedantries with the slippery chancelleries of Vienna;
while some days before, Hamilton received from Eden
at Vienna a despatch from Grenville emphasising the
"*necessity*," as it was now regarded at home, for ensuring the "free and *unlimited*" admission of British
ships into Sicilian harbours, and "every species of
provisions and supplies usually afforded by an ally."
Hamilton had tried in vain to surmount an obstacle important alike to France, to the King, and to Austria.
Nelson also knew too well the barrier set against compliance by the terms of the fatal Franco-Neapolitan
pact of 1796. Not more than four frigates at once
might be received into any harbour of Ferdinand's
coasts. He knew that the Queen and her friends were
in the slough of despond. He knew too—for the
Hamiltons had been in continual correspondence—that
Austria was once more shilly-shallying. While Naples
was longing to break her neutrality, Austria, for the
moment satisfied with shame, was now secretly nego-
tiating, with all the long and tedious array of etiquette,
preliminaries to a half-hearted arrangement. Even in
deliberation she would, as we have seen, only succour
Naples if Naples were attacked. Against this Napoleon had guarded: so far as concerned him and the
present, Naples should be left in perilous peace. He
was content with the seeds of revolution that he had
stealthily sown. Even as he passed Trapani on his
way to Malta, which already by the 10th of June he
had invested (and whose plunder he had promised to
his troops), he pacified the Sicilians with unlimited re-
assurances of good-will. And Nelson knew well also
that Maria Carolina and Emma chafed under the fet-

ters of diplomacy and of treaty that shackled action.
If only he could obtain some royal mandate for his
purpose, either through them—for the Queen had
rights in Council—or from Acton, rather than the
King still swayed by Gallo, he felt convinced of success.
Otherwise, should emergencies arise within the next
few weeks, as arise they must, he would perforce hark
back to Gibraltar; and in such a water-hunt of views
and checks as he now contemplated, delay might spell
failure, and failure his country's ruin.

About six o'clock by Neapolitan time, on a lovely
June morning, Captains Troubridge and Hardy landed
from the *Mutine,* which, together with the *Monarch,*
on which was Captain T. Carrol, lay anchored in the
bay, leaving Nelson in the *Vanguard* with his fleet off
Capri.   Troubridge, charged with important requests
by Nelson, at once proceeded to the Embassy.

Lady Hamilton's after-allegations have been much
criticised, and, step by step, stubbornly disputed, while
even these, as will be urged, have perhaps been mis-
read; nor has her simpler account in her " King's
Memorial " been taken, still less Nelson's repeated assurances about her " exclusive interposition " to Rose,
Pitt's favourable consideration, Canning's own acknowledgment, the neutrality at any rate of Grenville,
and a statement by Lord Melville, afterwards to be
mentioned.

Emma and her husband were awakened by their
early visitors, who included Hardy and, perhaps,
Bowen.   Hamilton arose hurriedly, and took the officers off to Acton's neighbouring house.   Some kind
of council was held, probably at the palace.   In that
case Gallo, as foreign minister, may well have been
present.   Troubridge, as Nelson's mouthpiece, stated
his requirements.   Gallo, we know, was hesitating and
hostile.   The whole arrangement with the court of

Vienna now lagging under his procrastination, would be spoiled if Naples were prematurely to break with France, and an open breach must be certain if succour for the whole of Nelson's fleet were afforded at the Sicilian ports in contravention of the burdensome engagement with the French Directory; while it would further be implied that the British fleet was at the Neapolitan service. Recourse to the King would not only be dangerous, but probably futile; the more so, since the French minister at Naples was now citizen Garat, a pedant, pamphleteer, and lecturer of the straitest sect among busybodying theorists. Such a man, Gallo would urge, must be the loudest in umbrage at even the appearance of pro-British zeal. Acton could have rebutted these objections by observing that the " order " need not be signed by Ferdinand, but merely informally by himself " in the King's name "; as, in fact, a sort of roving " credential "; that it could be so worded as to imply no breach of treaty, but only the refreshment of four ships at a time; that the governors of the ports might be separately instructed to offer a show of resistance if more were demanded of them; that Garat need never know what had transpired till the moment came when Austria had signed her pact with Naples, and France might be dared in the face of day; Troubridge's reception could be (and was) represented as no more than a common civility which Acton paid not only to English visitors, but even to French officers. All must be " under the rose," and thus far only could Nelson be obliged. To Nelson's further requisition for frigates a polite *non possumus* could be the only answer. Pending these delicate Austrian negotiations, and until an open rupture with France was possible with safety, Naples was in urgent need of a permanent fleet in the Mediterranean, and this, *quid pro quo,* Nelson naturally would not bind himself to concede, though, so far as his instructions and the situation warranted, he was ready, even eager, to do so.

This half-formal but scarcely effectual " order " was obtained.

There exists an original draft of Hamilton's *official* recital of what passed to Lord Grenville. One of its interlineations is perhaps significant. He first omitted, and afterwards added that the order was in Acton's handwriting as well as in the King's name. Nelson had wanted a quick royal mandate. He received a ministerial order involving further instructions and diplomatic delays. Moreover, five days after Troubridge's visit, Acton thanked Hamilton for his " delicate and kind part " " under all the circumstances." It may not have been quite such a plain-sailing affair as it has seemed.

" We did more business in half an hour," wrote Hamilton in a final despatch to the same minister, " than we should have done in a week in the usual official way. Captain Troubridge went straight to the point. . . . I prevailed upon General Acton to write himself an order in the name of His Sicilian Majesty, directed to the governors of every port in Sicily, to supply the King's ships with all sorts of provisions, and in case of an action to permit the British seamen, sick or wounded, to be landed and taken proper care of in their ports." The draft, however, contains a telling supplement. " He expressed only a wish to get sight of Buonaparte and his army, ' for,' said he, *'By God, we shall lick them.'* " Before Nelson's officers departed, they received also from Hamilton's hands Gallo's fatuous replies to their Admiral's questions of five days before.

Troubridge was " perfectly satisfied," he could even be called perfectly happy. But meanwhile that may

have passed which Emma afterwards maintained. Fate
was at stake. She may have rushed to the Queen, for
they both knew how little such a conclave would probably achieve; and Gallo's attitude might well deter
Acton from straightforward compliance. Nelson
might fancy this council's " order " a quick passport to
his desires. But *they* knew its formal flourishes to be
doubtful. In the result, it would hardly seem to have
acted with speed or unaided. Emma's own after-
story is that she besought Maria Carolina, with tears
and on bended knees, to exercise her prerogative and
supplement the mandate by the promise of direct instructions. From after events and from inveterate
habit the dramatic scene is probable. According to
Emma (and Pettigrew), Hamilton wrote forthwith to
Nelson, " You will receive from Emma herself what
will do the business and procure all your wants." One
can see this impulsive woman clapping her hands for
joy, and singing aloud with exultation. In some two
hours Troubridge and Hardy had rowed back to the
Mutine and set sail towards Capri.

Within a few hours at any rate Emma, throbbing
with excitement, penned two hasty notes to Nelson himself, both included in her newly found correspondence
of this year. Each—and they are brief—must be repeated here, for the second of them disposes of the
version, hitherto accepted, that Nelson never received
that from the Queen which his famous letter to Lady
Hamilton represents him as " kissing "; while the first
suggests a likelihood that this thrilling day did not
close before Emma had managed to see Nelson himself
at Capri. Both these letters are scrawled in evident
haste.

[*17th June,* 1798.]

" My dear Admiral,—I write in a hurry as Captain

T. Carrol stays on *Monarch*. God bless you, and send
you victorious, and that I may see you bring back
Buonaparte with you. Pray send Captain Hardy out
to us, for I shall have a fever with anxiety. The
Queen desires me to say everything that's kind, and
bids me say with her whole heart and soul she wishes
you victory. God bless you, my dear Sir. I will not
say how glad I shall be to see you. Indeed I cannot
describe to you my feelings on your being so near
us.—Ever, Ever, dear Sir, Your affte. and gratefull

" EMMA HAMILTON."

But now comes a decisive epistle, the missing link,
bearing in mind Nelson's disputed answer to it, the date
of which has been most ingeniously transferred to the
following May—a date not perhaps wholly appropriate.
Theory, however, must here yield to this piece of reality
on a scrap of notepaper.

The letter, written very hurriedly, is on similar paper
and presumably of the same date as its predecessor :—

" DEAR SIR,—I send you a letter I have received this
moment from the Queen. *Kiss it,* and send it back by
Bowen, as I am bound not to give any of her letters.—
Ever your

" EMMA."

Captain Bowen of the *Transfer* had brought Hamilton despatches from Lord St. Vincent just a week
before, and was his guest until the 2nd of August subsequent.

The fact that Emma begs for the letter's return in-
dicates that it was one of importance, and might compromise the Queen. After the battle of the Nile Emma
sent Nelson *two* of the Queen's ordinary letters about

him, as a token of gratitude, and without any request for their redelivery.

This missive from the Queen seems to have been one promising Nelson some further document of direct instructions to the governors of ports in event of future urgency. It is right, however, to state that during revision I have lit on a Queen's letter of about this date telling Emma that "circumstances . . . do not permit of opening our ports and arms entirely to our brave defenders"; "our gratitude is none the less"; she hopes for victory, and wanted to have seen Troubridge had prudence allowed. The Queen's anxiety, however, to aid is again manifest from this new letter, which shows, too, how keenly she realised the diplomatic situation on which such stress has been laid. In the absence of other evidence it need not be unduly pressed against my theory about her letter of mere promise to Nelson on June 17.

The immediate reply and pendant to that cheering communication was Nelson's familiar and much-debated letter written an hour before he weighed anchor:—

"MY DEAR LADY HAMILTON,—*I have kissed* the Queen's letter. Pray say I hope for the honor of kissing her hand when no fears will intervene, assure her Majesty that no person has her felicity more than myself at heart and that the sufferings of her family will be a Tower of Strength on the day of Battle, fear not the event, God is with us, God bless you and Sir William, pray say I cannot stay to answer his letter.— Ever Yours faithfully,

"HORATIO NELSON." [1]

[1] This letter is misdated in the hurry (as was sometimes the way with Nelson), 17th *May,* 6 P.M. It is admitted, of course, that on that day he was off Cape Sicie, so that if applicable to 1798, it must be a slip of the pen for *June* 17. With regard to

On this (still visible in the British Museum) Emma's
after-indorsement runs, " This letter I received after
I had sent the Queen's letter for receiving our ships
into their ports, for the Queen had decided to act in
opposition to the King, who would not then break with
France, and our Fleet must have gone down to Gibraltar to have watered, and the battle of the Nile would
not have been fought, for the French fleet would have
got back to Toulon." She is reviewing the whole
length of the transaction, the critical issues at Syracuse
of next month on Nelson's first return from Egypt, the
ultimate victory. She does the same in other parts of
her two long memorials. Her statements have been
construed as post-dating Nelson's momentous visit
to the time when he returned from pursuit for supplies
to Sicily and resailed equipped to Aboukir Bay.
Emma's words, " this awful period," tally with the
general impression given by some of Acton's letters and

"my dear," etc., cf. Morrison MS. 317, where on the *preceding*
day Hamilton mentions her as " Emma " to his " dear Nelson "
and " brave friend," and says she wishes him victory "heart
and soul." In her " Addington " memorial of 1803 she puts the
matter quite clearly :—" The fleet itself, I can truly say, could not
have got into *Sicily,* but for what I was happily able to do with
the Queen of Naples, and through her *secret* instructions so obtained."

The material wording of the familiar " Prince Regent's "
memorial runs : " It was at this awful period in June 1798, about
three days after the French fleet passed by for Malta, Sir
William and myself were awakened at six o'clock in the morning by Captain Trowbridge with a letter from Sir Horatio
Nelson, then with his fleet off the bay near to Caprea, request-
ing that the Ambassador would procure him permission to enter
with his fleet into Naples or any of the Sicilian ports, to provision, water, etc., as otherwise he must run for Gibraltar,
being in urgent want, and that, consequently, he would be
obliged to give over all further pursuit of the French fleet,
which he missed at Egypt, on account of their having put in to
Malta."

The wording of her King's memorial, which seems never to
have been presented, is more clearly expressed and more explicit :—" That Your Majesty's Memorialist on a subsequent oc-

the Queen's as to the present crisis. Hamilton himself in a draft for his known despatch of this date to Grenville adds the significant postscript—" This Court, as you may perceive, is in great distiess." A note has already sought to show that Nelson must surely have been aware of the court's suffering condition. There seems, therefore, nothing improbable in his use of the phrase, " the sufferings of her family."

I hope now to have proved that this long-questioned Nelson letter was, undoubtedly, the instant answer to Emma's own communication, for the first time here brought to light. The twin letters are at length reunited, and at least a new complexion is placed on the received account. Emma assuredly sent Nelson a letter covering one from the Queen, and so far her claim is supported. In this respect, therefore, modern scepticism has proved mistaken. I cannot but hope that such as have doubted may now find reason to modify their verdict, and will honour Nelson, whose love for Emma has been begrudged as debasement, by admit-

casion, by means of the same confidential communication with that great and good woman, the Queen of Naples, had the unspeakable felicity of procuring a secret order for victualling and watering, at the port of Syracuse, the fleet of Your Most Gracious Majesty under the command of Admiral Nelson; by which means that heroic man, the pride and glory of his King and country, was enabled to proceed the *second* time to Egypt with a promptitude and celerity which certainly hastened the glorious battle of the Nile, and occasioned his good and grateful heart to admit your humble Memorialist as well as the Queen of Naples to a participation in that important victory." Her words speak for themselves to every unprejudiced mind.

The wording of Nelson's codicil is:—" Secondly, the British fleet under my command could never have returned a second time to Egypt had not Lady Hamilton's influence with the Queen of Naples caused letters to be wrote to the Governor of Syracuse, that he was to encourage the fleet to be supplied with every thing, should they put into any port in Sicily. We put into Syracuse, and received every supply; went to Egypt and destroyed the French fleet. Could I have rewarded these services, I would not now call upon my country."

ting that what he claimed in his last codicil for the woman of his heart was neither "infatuation" nor falsehood, and that without her it would hardly have happened.

Scarcely had Nelson put to sea when he at once resumed communication with the Hamiltons. He wishes the Neapolitans to depend upon him. If only supplies are forthcoming when his need presses, his fleet shall be their mainstay. He laments his lack of frigates, but "thank God," he adds, "I am not apt to feel difficulties." He confides to Lady Hamilton his hope to be "presented" to her "crowned with laurels or cypress." He presses them to exert themselves in procuring for him masts and stores. He deprecates the diplomatic quibbles about "co-operation," while lagging Austria manœuvres, and after he himself has come in crisis to their assistance. He points out the peril from Napoleon at Malta, he repeats, "Malta is the direct road to Sicily." The Two Sicilies are the key of the position.

And, indeed, the catastrophe of Malta formed the dirge of all this summer. The Queen was distracted at the royal and ministerial delays and punctilios. La Valette was in French hands "without a blow," the Maltese knights were dastards, and she could not pity them. "*Ces coquins de Français*" pretended to have grenades to burn the fleet of her hopes. She disparages Garat. She sends her "dear, faithful" Emma the Austrian ciphers to copy under vows of secrecy: Emma will see how little sincerity exists in Vienna. Emma is indispensable. Emma has infused her whole being with Nelson. The Queen bids her shout and sing once more before the assembled throng, "Hip, hip, hip!" "God save the King!" and "God save Nelson!" She harps on Malta, "an irreparable loss," and "gallant Nelson, with his British fleet," which she strained her mind's eye to follow past Cape Passaro. She owns Emma's initiative. In some matter seemingly relative to British ships, she writes that Emma's wishes are assured by a reputation (was it Maltese?) ; the " brave English " are now assured of the national sympathy.

Nor was Hamilton behindhand.   He furnished Nelson with advices.   He informed him how Napoleon had quitted Malta; how Garat's insolent demand that the French should usurp the Maltese privilege of buying Sicilian corn had eventually succeeded; "shocking," he comments, that neither King nor Emperor will " abandon half measures."   He sent him Captain Hope with Irish intelligence.   He looked hourly for news of the French Armada's overthrow.

Lady Hamilton also continued her correspondence. She thanks him for his letter through Captain Bowen, which she has translated for the Queen, who " prays for " his " honour and safety—victory, she is sure, you will have "; she " sees and feels " all Nelson's grounds for complaint,—so does Emma, who calls Garat " an impudent, insolent dog."   " I see plainly," she adds with emphasis, *" The Court of Naples must declare war,* if they mean to save their country.   But alas! their First Minister Gallo is a frivolous, ignorant, self-conceited coxcomb, that thinks of nothing but his fine embroidered coat, ring and snuff-box; and half Naples thinks him half a Frenchman; and God knows, if one may judge of what he did in making the peace for the Emperor, he must either be very ignorant, or not attached to his masters or the *Cause Commune.*   The Queen and Acton cannot bear him, and consequently he cannot have much power; but still a First Minister, although he may be a minister of smoke, yet he has always something, at least enough to do mischief.   The Jacobins have all been lately declared innocent, after suffering four years' imprisonment; and I know, they all deserved to be hanged long ago; and since Garat has been here, and through his insolent letters to Gallo, these pretty gentlemen, *that had planned the death of their Majesties,* are to be let out in society again. In short, I am afraid, all is lost here; and I am grieved to the heart for our dear, charming Queen, who deserves a better fate. . . . I hope you will not quit the Mediterranean without taking *us.* . . . But yet, I trust in God and you, that we shall destroy those monsters before we go from hence. God bless you, my dear, dear sir."

And meanwhile Nelson, in hot pursuit, scoured the Mediterranean—Malta, Candia, Alexandria, Syria—in vain. The commander of both fleet and army, with genius, youth, and Corsican strategy to back him, still baffled the daring " sea-wolf," as he always called him. Nelson lived " in hopes," he never rested. But " the Devil's children have the Devil's luck," as he and Hamilton both assured each other.

The 19th of July saw him back at Syracuse in recoil for his last spring, and in the very need against which his foresight had forearmed him. He lacked both stores and water. He seemed as far from his goal as when he started.

Let him speak for himself. Writing from Syracuse and in retrospect, he told Hamilton: ". . . I stretched over to the coast of Caramania; where not speaking a vessel who could give me information, I became distressed for the kingdom of the Two Sicilies; and having gone a round of six hundred leagues, at this season of the year (with a single ship, with an expedition incredible), here I am, as *ignorant* of the situation of the enemy as I was twenty-seven days ago!"

Now was the time for the Queen's " open sesame," if both Acton's " order " and her own " letter " of promise failed to operate with expedition. That such a letter was probably in Nelson's pocket may be inferred from the subsequent narrative.

While Nelson nears the Syracusan harbour bar, modern criticism once more intercepts our view, and must for a moment delay our story. It will not do so long, because one of the documents on which its controversy relies will enable us to resume our thread. But three preliminaries must first be mentioned.

It is important to distinguish between the *official* and the *private* letters of Nelson and Hamilton—the former meant to be shown to others, the latter written for the recipient alone; and, more especially, beween these two distinct classes of correspondence, and those other half-private letters intended for Hamilton to show Acton in confidence, and yet hinting or suggesting more than the General was meant to gather from them.

It has also escaped full notice that for some time past a private correspondence had regularly passed between Nelson and the Hamiltons. This is clear from a letter (soon to be quoted) of July 22 from Nelson to Lady Hamilton in the Morrison Collection, where he inquires after her *plans* for " coming down the Mediterranean " with her husband, presumably to help him. Thirdly, so late as the first week in August, after Nelson's battle had been won, Acton was still ignorant that his ships had been adequately provisioned, and was arranging further measures for the purpose; aware on August 15 of the Sicilian provisions, he planned more.

Let us glance at a little farce enacted with exquisite gravity by the Governor of Syracuse.

It emerges from a document addressed by him to General Sir John Acton. A key to this is supplied by the fact that General Acton, days after handing the informal " order," had expressly cautioned Hamilton that, pending the as yet unsigned articles with Austria, all the governors of all Sicilian ports had been specially directed to make an *"ostensible opposition,"* lest the French might be incensed into attack by any open breach of the stipulated Neapolitan neutrality. Above all, it should be noted that this Governor's letter at Naples seems to distinguish between a *royal despatch* signed by Acton, and a *royal letter* in Nelson's possession. On the other hand, the other construction is open. When the "Vice-Admiral" declared that the *letter* entitled the whole fleet to be watered, he may only have been making the best of the *despatch*.

The whole scene rises vividly before us. On the morning of Thursday the 19th "several ships" were seen sailing in slow procession from the east. Gradually fourteen emerged from "the distance." As they became more distinct in the freshening east wind, the Governor ordered the castle flag to be hoisted, and the British flag was instantly flown in reply.

The Governor next sent out his boat with the "Captain of the Port" and the "Adjutant of the Town," civilians charged with compliments and offers. Nelson, however, regardless of these ceremonies, profited by the wind to steer "straight into the harbour." The pompous Governor, shocked at such haste, forwarded a second boat with two military functionaries to repeat his compliments, and to acquaint the Admiral with what he had known and resented for weeks—the impediment of "not more than four ships of war at a time." But Nelson had anticipated these formal courtesies. A shore-boat promptly met the Governor's with "a royal *letter*" purporting to contain royal instructions for the admission of the *whole* squadron. This I take to have been the Queen's private letter, forwarded in pursuance of her promise to Emma, and holding the Governor harmless in disobeying the strict letter of the law. While, therefore, in

pursuance of certainty, the entire squadron advanced
to cross the bar, the British " Vice-Admiral " proceeded
with the officers, and was received by the Governor
at his house.   There he delivered a further (and separate?) missive, " a royal *despatch* " written in the
King's name, and signed by Acton—in fact, the ir-
regular " order " obtained on that memorable morning
of June 17, and by no means expressly empowering the
reception of the whole fleet.   The Governor, conform-
ing to the prescribed comedy, feigned hesitation; thereupon a letter from Nelson himself was shown—" difficult to read," and justifying the *entire* squadron's en-
trance.   Hereupon the Governor, " struck " by what
he must have known, and also by *other reflections* [The
Queen's private order?], reminds one of Byron's " and
whispering I will ne'er consent, consented."   He affected to raise " friendly protests," while he enforced
the King's directions to save appearances by spreading
the ships over different regions and at various distances.
He even hinted in confidence the " propriety " of quitting the port as soon as possible, and of landing none
but unarmed sailors, and even these under a promise to
return so soon as the city gates were closed at sunset.
On the following afternoon Nelson and his " staff "
paid their respects.   The Governor grasped him
warmly by the hand, but still maintained his outward
show of resistance.   There were, he said, royal orders,
under present circumstances, forbidding him to return
the call on shipboard.   And the last sentence of his
record perhaps best illustrates the whole comedy by
solemnly informing Sir John that the recital was only
addressed to him for the official purpose of being
shown to his Sicilian Majesty.   Ferdinand was to be
kept in the dark.   He was ignorant of anything that
the Queen might have dared through Emma's request.
He was to believe that the stretch of international ci-

vility had been empowered by Acton's document alone, the document signed in his name.

So much for outward semblance. Nelson's inner feelings at this most critical juncture supplement the story.

We have reached July the 21st. The fleet was not completely stocked and watered till the 23rd. Before that date the whole town rejoiced and fraternised with the British sailors: of sympathy at least there was no concealment, and—a real Sicilian trait—all the country-folk immediately raised the price of their provisions.

On July 22nd Nelson forwarded two private letters, one to Sir William, the other to Lady Hamilton.

They are both indignant and irritable at delay aggravated by intense disappointment. It was not only that he was still without news of the French. He had counted on the instant virtue of Acton's order, without the need of recourse to a secret charm. For Hamilton had been told only three weeks before by the General that, in pursuance of it, " every proper order " for the British squadron " had been already given in Sicily," and " in the *way* mentioned here with the brave Captain Troubridge." Nelson had therefore good reason to hope for prepared co-operation. He had been met by farcical routine; and red-tape, even when most expected, always repelled and ruffled him. Nor so far had the Queen's letter of indemnity to the Governors been followed by the actual " open sesame " which she had promised as a last resort. For disappointment concerning Acton's order he was prepared, but not for the failure of his hidden talisman. So far the charm had not worked; a fresh letter from the Queen might still be required.

" I have heard so much said," runs Nelson's first outburst—which he entrusted to the Governor himself for transit—" about the *King* of Naples' orders only to admit three or four of the ships . . . that I am astonished. I understood that *private* orders at least would have been given for our free admission. . . . Our treatment is scandalous for a great nation to put up with and the King's flag is insulted at every friendly port we look at."

The second—to Lady Hamilton—is almost cool in ironical displeasure, a coolness betokening how unexpectedly his cherished hopes had been belied:—

" My DEAR MADAM,—I am so hurt at the treatment we received from the power we came to assist and fight for, that I am hardly in a situation to write a letter to an elegant body: therefore you must on this occasion forgive my want of those attentions which I am ever anxious to shew you. *I wish to know your and Sir William's plans for coming down the Mediterranean,* for if we are to be kicked at every port of the Sicilian dominions, the sooner we are gone, the better. Good God! how sensibly I feel our treatment. I have only to pray that I may find the French and throw all my vengeance on them."

The omission in these lines of any specific mention either of the Queen or her letter, so far from being singular, is exactly what was to be expected. She always stipulated in such matters that her name should never be breathed, nor her position jeopardised with the King, and in this instance Acton also had to be kept in the dark. It will be remembered also that Emma's letter inclosing the Queen's promise to Nelson expressly stated that she was " bound not to give any of her letters," and, indeed, claimed its instant return.

But meanwhile, on this very 22nd of July, a sudden change came over Nelson's tone; still more so, on the following day before he weighed anchor. Melancholy

and annoyance gave way to delight. *Something* must
have intervened to alter the face of affairs, something
with which Nelson's temper accorded, and that something was certainly not any sight of the French fleet.
Delay had been removed.

Shortly after these two epistles to the Hamiltons
Nelson further penned his short but memorable
" Arethusa " letter to them.   Both Sir Harris Nicolas,
and Professor Laughton following him, have denied
the authenticity of this letter on the internal evidence of
its style.   They say that Nelson could never have used
such a classical or poetical phrase as " surely watering
by the fountain of Arethusa."   But in the first place
it is not, in Syracuse, poetical or classical, as every
traveller is aware.   Each Syracusan street-boy to this
day calls the spring by the sea, with its rim of Egyptian
cotton-plants, " the fountain of Arethusa."   And in
the second, if it were, it would be in accordance with
many of Nelson's phrases caught from the Hamiltons.
Professor Laughton has, I believe, gone so far as even
to doubt that Hamilton about this period could address
his friend as " My dear Nelson."   He is mistaken.
Writing to Nelson a month previously, Sir William
ends with " All our present dependance is in you, *my
dear Nelson,* and I am convinced that what is in the
power of mortal man, you will do."

The " Arethusa " letter springs, it is true, from the
suspected source of the *Life* of Nelson by the hireling
Harrison—that same Harrison who, perhaps, was one
of those to embitter the darkening days and fortunes of
Lady Hamilton, his benefactress.   But it is sanctioned
by Pettigrew, who, as a collector *par excellence* of Nelson autographs, was, on questions of style, an expert
of tried judgment; and it will be noticed with interest
that " the laurel or cypress " passage (itself both
poetical and classical) forms a feature also of his in-

disputable " private " letter to Hamilton already noticed, and following immediately on his authentic answer to Lady Hamilton's newly found note of June
17:—

" My dear Friends,—Thanks to your exertions, we
have victualled and watered: and surely watering at
the Fountain of Arethusa we must have victory.   We
shall sail with the first breeze and be assured I will return either crowned with laurel, or covered with
cypress."

The " first breeze " did not apparently rise until the
day following; and even if the " Arethusa " letter
were a fabrication, which I can see no valid reason for
supposing, we are able to dispense with its witness to
Nelson's sudden relief of mood.   He was now enabled
to start about two days earlier than he had hoped, and
on the 23rd, before departing, he wrote yet again to
his dear friends in joyful gratitude, and in phrases im-
plying that the long-deferred " private orders " had
arrived, though the evidently guarded wording provides, as so often, against its being shown to General
Acton.   This letter's authenticity can hardly be
doubted.
" The fleet is unmoored, and the moment the wind
comes off the land shall go out of this delightful harbour, where our present wants have been amply supplied, and where every attention has been paid to us;
but I *have been* tormented by no *private orders* being
given to the Governor for our admission.   I have only
to hope that I shall still find the French fleet, and be
able to get at them. . . . *No frigates!*"   Even a fortnight later Acton still excuses himself to Hamilton.
Assuredly throughout these quick transitions the un-
dertone of Emma and the Queen is audible.   Nelson

knew what had really happened; his commentators are
left to guess the truth from disputed shreds of correspondence.

Refitted and reheartened, Nelson, who, as ever, had
long been rehearsing his plans to his officers, hastened
with his fleet to Aboukir Bay. There is no need to recount that memorable struggle of the 1st of August,
which lasted over twenty-four hours—the daring
strategy of a master-pilot, the giant *L'Orient* blazing
with colours already struck, and exploded under a sullen sky torn with livid lightning, the terrific thunder-
storm interrupting the death-throes of the battle, the
complete triumph of an encounter which delivered
England from France, and nerved a revived Europe
against her. Villeneuve had been outwitted; Brueys
was dead; so was Ducheyla. Even Napoleon's papers
had been captured. Nelson stands out after the turmoil, once more battered, once again far more zealous
for the fame of his officers than his own, yet furious
at the escape of the only two French frigates that
avoided practical annihilation. Never was there a
supreme naval encounter that exercised such a moral
effect, and so defeated both the foe and anticipation.
He was acclaimed the " saviour " both of Britain and
the Continent.

And his trust in the Hamiltons, his unshakable belief in Emma, were at once evinced by his giving them
the earliest intelligence of what set all Europe tingling.
Emma's ears and her husband's were the very first to
hear it.

The French had vaunted that Buonaparte would
erase Britain from the map. In their desperation they
still vowed to burn her fleet. Their insolence on
Garat's lips had resounded in the streets and on the
very house-tops of Naples. It was not long before that
same Garat was to be curtly dismissed, before not a

" French dog " dared " show his face," before at the
opera " not a French cockade was to be seen "; before
the Queen, half-mad for joy, addressed an English
letter to the British sailors, doubtless with her Emma's
aid, sent them casks of wine *incognita,* and presented
Hoste with a diamond ring, before Britain and Naples
had struck up a close alliance against the common foe.

The world was a changed world from that of a
week before.   History had been made and was making.
On Nelson's life, to quote Lord St. Vincent's words,
hung the fate of the remaining Governments in Europe,
" whose system has not been deranged by these devils."
But for him Britain might have been France, and the
Mediterranean a French lake.   To the end of time the
Nile would rank with Marathon, with Actium, with
Blenheim.   Nelson had entered the Pantheon of fame,
he had embodied his country, he *was* Great Britain.
He belonged to Time no longer.   Emma's heart
leaped, as she flew exulting with the first breath of victory to the Queen.   So early as September the 1st
she had heard the triumph of which ministers and
potentates were ignorant; she, the poor Cheshire girl,
the " Lancashire Witch," whose dawn of life had been
smirched and sullied; she, the *élève* of lecturing and
hectoring Greville, the wife of an ambassador whose
lethargy she had stirred to purpose; she, the admired
of artists, the Queen's comrade.   Was anything impossible to youth and beauty, and energy and charm?
It had proved the same of old with those classical
freed women—Epicharis, staunch amid false knights
and senators; and Panthea, perhaps Emma's own pro-
totype, whose giftedness and " chiselled " beauty Lu-
cian has extolled.   Had she not from the first fed her
inordinate fancy with grandiose reveries of achievement?   Had she not burst her leading-strings?   More
than all, had not Nelson, already in August, asked her

to welcome " the remains of Horatio "?   And now, in this universal moment, she had both part and lot. Was it wonderful that, throbbing in every vein, she swooned to the ground and bruised her side with Nelson's letter in her hand? We have only to read the series of her correspondence at this date with Nelson, to realise her intoxication of rapture.

But there was more than this. It often happens that when glowing and inflammable natures, such as hers and Nelson's, have dreamed united visions, the mere fulfilment links them irrevocably together. Mutual hope and mutual faith refuse to be sundered. The hero creates his heroine, the heroine worships her maker, who has transformed her in her own eyes as well as his. It is the old romance of Pygmalion and Galatea. He places her on a pedestal and in a shrine. Henceforth for Nelson, however misguided in outward " fact," Emma stands out adorable as Britannia. " She and the French fleet " are his all in all. His ecstasies in her honour spring from his firm conviction that but for her that mighty blow might never have been struck, nor Buonaparte crushed. Emma, for him, is England. He returns to her crowned not with " cypress," but laurels ever green. And she has plucked some of them for his wreath. He acknowledges that *his* was the *first* approach. As he wrote to her not three years later in a passage now first brought to light, " I want not to conquer any heart, if that which I have conquered is happy in its lot: I am confident, *for the Conqueror is become the Conquered.*"

And once more, with regard to Emma herself. She had never yet been free in her affections. Her devotion to Greville, her attachment to her husband, had grown up out of loyal gratitude, not from spontaneous choice, and the contrast first presented itself to her, not as an untutored girl, but as a skilled woman of the

world.   Sir William was now sixty-eight, Nelson just
on forty—"*l'âge critique*," as the French term it.
She firmly believed that she had helped his heroism to
triumph; he as firmly, that his battle had been half won
through her aid. Both were susceptible. Both
despised the crowd from which in character and circumstances they stood apart.   Emma's morality had
been largely one of discretion.   Nelson's was one of
religion.   If Nelson came to persuade himself that she
was born to be his wife in the sight of God—and all
his after expressions to her prove it—it would not be
strange if such a woman, still beautiful, in a sybarite
atmosphere where she was held up as a paragon, should
throw discretion to the winds of chance.   It was after
some such manner that these problems of heart and
temperament were already shaping themselves.

Consult the first among those jubilant letters, a few
excerpts from which have been quoted in the second
chapter.   They eclipse the very transports of the
Queen, "mad with joy," and hysterically embracing
all around her, whose own letter of that memorable
Monday evening fully bears out Emma's account in
these outpourings.   She would rather have been a
"powder-monkey in that great *Victory* than an Emperor out of it."   Her self-elation is all for Nelson.
Posterity ought to worship the deliverer in every form
and under every title.   His statue should be "of pure
gold."   Her song is "See the Conquering Hero
Comes," her strain is "Rule Britannia."   Her gifts of
voice and rhapsody are dedicated to these.   For these
she hymns the general joy, while the illuminations of
her windows reflect the glow of her bosom.   Nelson,
Britain *in excelsis,* down with the execrable Jacobins, a
fig for foreign dictation—these are her refrains.   Even
her "shawl is in blue with gold anchors all over"; her
"earrings all Nelson anchors"; she wears a bandeau

round her forehead with the words " Nelson and Victory." Her " head will not permit " her to tell " half
of the rejoicing." " The Neapolitans are mad, and
if he was here now he would be killed with kindness."
How can she " begin " to her " dear, dear Sir " ? Since
the Monday when the tidings had been specially conveyed to her, she has been " delirious with joy " and
has " a fever caused by agitation and pleasure." She
fell fainting and hurt herself at the news. " God, what
a Victory! Never, never has there been anything half
so glorious, so complete." She would " feel it a
glory to die in such a cause." " No, I would not like
to die till I see and embrace the Victor of the Nile."
The care of the navy now engrosses her. There is
nothing she will not do for any fellow-worker with
the prince of men. Captain Hoste, her guest from
September 1, never forgot her tender kindness. She
begged and procured from Lord St. Vincent Captain
Bowen's promotion to the command of *L'Aquilon*.
Directly Nelson had cut short his brief stay of con-
valescence almost before the plaudits had died away,
she sat down to write to the hero's wife, as she was to
do again later in December. She tells her how Nelson
is adored by King and Queen and people, " as if he
had been their brother "; how delighted they are with
the stepson. She sends her Miss Knight's " ode."
She enumerates with pride the royal presents; the sultan's aigrette and pelisse, which she " tastes " and
" touches." She resents the inadequacy of his Government's acknowledgment—" Hang them, *I* say ! "

Both she and Hamilton were soon, in Nelson's words
to his wife, " seriously ill, first from anxiety and
then from joy."

But now she is " preparing his apartments against
he comes." On September 22 the *Vanguard* anchored
in the bay, and he came.

The King and Queen had prepared a gorgeous ovation. It was midsummer weather, and a cloudless sky.
No sooner was Nelson's small contingent descried off
the rock of Tiberius at Capri, than the royal yacht,
commanded by Caracciolo, draped with emblems and
covered with spangled awnings, advanced three leagues
out to meet him. On deck the music of Paisiello and
of Cimarosa—at last pardoned for composing a republican ode—resounded over the glassy waters, while a
whole "serenata" of smaller craft followed in its
wake and swelled the chorus. All the flower of the
court, including the Hamiltons, was on board, where
stood the King and the melancholy bride of the heir-
apparent, Princess Clementina. The Queen, herself
unwell, stayed at home and sent her grateful homage
through Emma. As the procession started from the
quay, citizen Garat, foiled and sullen, mewed in his
palace with drawn blinds, caught from afar the strains
of triumph, and vowed revenge.

As the cortège neared the *Vanguard,* both the Hamiltons, worn with fatigue and excitement, and the royal
party, greeted him. The picture of their meeting is
familiar. It has been painted in Nelson's own words to
his wife:—" Alongside came my honoured friends:
the scene in the boat was terribly affecting. Up flew
her Ladyship, and exclaiming, ' O God! Is it possible?'
she fell into my *arm* more dead than alive. Tears,
however, soon set matters to rights; when alongside
came the King. The scene was in its way as interesting. He took me by the hand, calling me his ' Deliverer and Preserver,' with every other expression of
kindness. In short, all Naples calls me ' *Nostro
Liberatore.*" My greeting from the lower classes was
truly affecting. I hope some day to have the pleasure
of introducing you to Lady Hamilton; she is one of
the very best women in this world, she is an honour

to her sex. Her kindness, with Sir William's to me, is more than I can express. I am in their house, and I may now tell you it required all the kindness of my friends to set me up. Lady Hamilton intends writing to you. God bless you!"

Little did Nelson yet reck of the ironies of the future. In this very letter he uses the warmest expressions about his wife that had as yet appeared in any of his letters. Had he pursued his first intention of proceeding from Egypt to Syracuse, how much, besides Naples, might have been avoided! Was he even now face to face with a passionate conflict?

During the twenty-three days that Nelson remained ashore, much happened besides rejoicing, and much had to be done. Not only did Nelson's wound (like his battered ships) require instant attention, but, as constantly happened with him, the protracted strain of nervous effort was followed by a severe fever. Lady Hamilton and her mother tended him; a brief visit with the Hamiltons to Castellamare, where Troubridge was refitting the maimed vessels, and a diet of " asses' milk " did much to mend his general health. Nor was it to him alone that Emma, herself ailing, ministered. Sir William was exhausted. The Queen was ill and miserable under the troubles gathering both at Malta and in the council-chamber; Captain Ball also needed her care, which he requited with an enthusiastic letter of thanks to " the best friend and patroness of the British Navy "; Troubridge, too, was far from well at Castellamare; many were in hospital. But Lady Hamilton owned the strength of highly-strung natures—the strength of spurts; and she found time and energy for all her tasks.

These good offices are here mentioned, among many more remaining for subsequent mention, because, in the future, after the fatal dividing line of her triumphal progress to Vienna with the Queen, her husband, and Nelson, they were all forgotten. She was to estrange some of her old admirers, who inveighed against her behind her back not only as ill-bred, but as artful. Beckford, for instance, who had hitherto praised her highly, became unkindly critical on her second visit to Fonthill in 1801; Miss Knight, her firm ally at this moment, turned the reverse of friendly. Troubridge (the baker's son, beloved and promoted by Nelson), who throughout had supported her, grew obstinate in antagonism both to her and him; while the seemly Elliots were shocked at her loudness and scorn of *convenances*. Even the Queen's ardour cooled; and the English official world began to look askance at the trio, and to make merry over Samson and Delilah.

Nelson's birthday gave full scope for a colossal demonstration at the English Embassy. Emma's huge assembly, where royalty and all the cream of society presided, was hardly an enjoyment for the worn conqueror. A "rostral column" of the classical pattern, with inscriptions celebrating his achievements, had been erected in the gay garden festooned with lamps, and alive with music. The artistic Miss Cornelia Knight (with her mother, a refugee from the terrors of war at Rome) added one more ode to the foreign thousands, and made a sketch of the scene. The festivity was chequered by Josiah Nisbet, Nelson's scapegrace but petted stepson, who brawled with him in his cups, until Troubridge parted them, and ended the indecent scuffle. That this arose from his habits, and not of design, is shown by Emma's affectionate references to him in her letter to his mother only four days afterwards.

Nelson was dispirited, and disgusted not only with the "fiddlers" and loose dames of the court, but with

its finicking *petit maître*, Gallo, the foreign minister, all
airs and pouncet; so afraid lest the wind should step
between him and his nobility, that, solemn over trifles,
he persistently dallied with the grave issues now at
stake. The halting Acton himself proved energetic
mainly in professions, though by the end of October
Emma had won him also to their side. Not only had
the " Grand Knights " of Malta, Hompesch the master,
and Wittig, shown the white feather at Valetta, and
left the French practically masters of the field, but in
the Romagna and in Tuscany the enemy was daily gaining ground. Moreover, while the Queen was reassured
as to the goodwill of the middle class and the Lazzaroni, she now realised, as may be gathered from her
letters, that the various factions of the nobles were
—from separate motives—a nest of perfidy. Her husband trounced her as the cause of his woes, and despite
his enthusiasm for the " hero," he remained in the
Anglophobe party's clutches. The delaying Gallo was
averse to open hostilities until Austria had engaged in
offensive alliance, for the compact (which had been
signed in July) only promised Austrian aid in the
event of Naples itself being attacked. Russia had declared, the Porte was on the verge of declaring, war
against the French Republic. The preceding May had
seen yet another treaty between both these powers and
Naples, binding the latter to furnish twelve ships and
four hundred men for the coalition. Yet the Emperor,
son-in-law to the Neapolitan Bourbons, still waited,
and on him the King of Naples waited also, much more
concerned with the impending birth of a grandchild
who might inherit the throne, than with the portents of
affairs. His disposition shunned reality, notwithstand-
ing the fact, however, that he had sanctioned the summons of General Mack from Vienna to command his
forces. And, added to all these manifold preoccupa-

tions, Lady Spencer, who had acclaimed Nelson's triumph with " Hurrah, hurrah, hurrah," the wife of the first Lord of the British Admiralty, was now at Naples, and constantly with the Hamiltons and Nelson.

From late September to early October Nelson and Emma were in frequent conference. The French had been attempting in Ireland what they had succeeded in doing at Naples: their complots with rebellion threatened all that was established.

He divined the situation in its European bearings at a glance. *She* knew every twist and turn of the Neapolitan road, with all its buffoons, adventurers, and highwaymen; the tact of quick experience was hers. He, the masculine genius, created. She, the feminine, was receptive, interpretative. And, whatever may be urged or moralised, the human fact remains that she was a woman after his own heart, and he a man after hers. He was the first unselfish man who had as yet been closely drawn towards her. However unlike in upbringing, in environment, in standing—above all, in things of the spirit, in passionate energy, in courage, in romance, in " sensibility " and enthusiasm they were affinities.

The result of these consultations is shown by the long draft of a letter outlining a policy, which Nelson drew up as a lever for Emma herself to force the court into decision, and which formed the basis of a shorter letter that has been published. He emphasised " the anxiety which you and Sir William have always had for the happiness and welfare of their Sicilian Majesties." He pointed out that the mass of the Neapolitans were loyally eager to try conclusions with France; that Naples was her natural " plunder," but that the ministers were " lulled into a false security," and a prey " to the worst of all policies, that of procrastination." He dwelt on Garat's insolence. and the readiness of the Neapolitan army to march into the Romagna " ready to receive them." He hoped that Mack's imminent arrival would brace ministers into resolution. He welcomed with admiring respect a " dignified " letter from the Queen, according with his own favourite quotation from Chatham, " the boldest measures are the safest." He presented his manifesto as a " preparitive " and as " the unalterable opinion of a British Admiral anxious to approve himself a faithful servant to his sovereign by doing everything in his power for the happiness and dignity of their Sicilian Majesties." To Sir William he would write separately. He recognised the signs of revolution, and already he sounded the note of warning. He recommended that their " persons and property " should be ready in case of need for embarkation at the shortest notice. If " the present ruinous system of procrastination " persevered, it would be his " duty " to provide for the safety not only of the Hamiltons, but of " the amiable Queen of these kingdoms and her family."

The address of this paper to Emma, the emphasis of the Queen's letter, the promise of a separate one to Hamilton, show that the document was intended for the Queen's eye alone, and point to the suggestion of it by Emma herself. We shall see that while Sir William was pushing affairs with the English Government, Emma, during Nelson's absence in the Adriatic and the Mediterranean, was practically to be Ambassador at Naples.

Next day Nelson ordered Ball to Malta with the expressed objects not only of intercepting French communications with Egypt, of the island's blockade, and of co-operation with the Turkish and Russian fleets in the Archipelago, but specially of protecting the Sicilian and Neapolitan coasts. So annoyed was he at the

King's inaction, that he even told Lord Spencer that
" Naples sees this squadron no more, except the King,"
who is losing " the glorious moments," " calls for our
help." By mid-October Nelson himself had set out
first for Malta, and, after a brief interval of return, for
the deliverance of Leghorn. Before the month's close
the King and General Mack had started on their ill-
starred campaign; before the year's end a definitive
Anglo-Sicilian alliance had been signed, and Grenville's former attitude reversed.

The very day of Nelson's departure drew from him
the tribute to Lady Hamilton which was in Pettigrew's
possession, and a facsimile of which accompanied the
first volume of his *Memoirs of Lord Nelson*.

" I honour and respect you," it ran, " and my dear
friend Sir William Hamilton, and believe me ever your
faithful and affectionate Nelson "—the first letter, as
" his true friend " Emma recorded on it, written to
her " after his dignity to the peerage."

The girl who, after the bartering Greville trampled
upon her affections, had been gained into grateful attachment by Hamilton, with the covert resolve of becoming his wife and winning her spurs in the political
tournament, had at length carved a career. Greville's
neglect of her self-sacrifice had not hardened her, but
her tender care of Sir William was fast assuming a
new complexion. She had twice saved his life; she
had perpetually urged his activities; she still watched
over him. But, under her standards of instinct and
experience, she was half gravitating towards the per-
suasion that they might warrant her in taking her fate
into her own hands. She hated " half measures ";
neck or nothing, she would realise herself. Her chief
cravings remained as yet unsatisfied. Womanlike, she
had yearned for true sympathy. Here was one willing
and eager to listen. She had long been in love with

glory. Here was a hero who personified it. She had sighed for adventures in the grand style. Here was opportunity. She wavered on the verge of a new temptation. She felt as though her wandering soul had at last found its way. Yet, in reality, she still groped in a maze of contending emotions, nor would she stop to inquire by what clue her quick steps were hurrying her: the moment was all in all. She still identified her intense friendship with her husband's. Disloyalty still revolted her in its masked approaches; and yet she struggled, half-consciously, with a " faith unfaithful " that was to keep her " falsely true."

Omitting further historical detail, we may turn at once to the part played by Emma with the Queen at Caserta as her hero's vice-gerent during his nine weeks' absence. Her heart was with the ships, and she pined to quit the *villeggiatura* for Naples.

It was, in her own words, with Nelson's " spirit " that Emma inflamed the Queen, from whom she was now inseparable. The King still looked to Austria, and thought of little else but his daughter-in-law's coming confinement. The Queen, who had hesitated, at last caught the promptness of Nelson's policy. General Mack had arrived, but a thousand official obstacles impeded his preparations. " He does not go to visit the frontiers," wrote Emma to Nelson, " but is now working night and day, and then goes for good, and I tell her Majesty, for God's sake, for the country's sake, and for your own sake, send him off as soon as possible, no time to be lost, and I believe he goes after to-morrow." The suppression of the Irish rebellion had removed yet another spoke from the Republican wheel. " I translate from our papers," said Emma, " to inspire her or *them*, I should say, with some of your spirit and energy. How delighted we both were to speak of you. She loves, respects, and admires you. For myself, I will leave you to guess my feelings. Poor dear Troubridge stayed that night with us to comfort us. What a good dear soul he is. . . . He is to come down soon, and I am to present him. She sees she could not feel happy if she had not an English ship here to send off. . . . How we abused Gallo yesterday. How *she* hates him. He won't reign long— so much the better. . . . You are *wanted at Caserta*. All their noddles are not worth yours." There were affectionate mentions of Tyson and Hardy, with the hope that the " Italian spoil-stomach sauce of a dirty Neapolitan " might not hurt the invalid, but that perhaps Nelson's steward provided him " with John Bull's Roast and Boil." Then followed her enthusiasm over Nelson's honours, and her wrath at the stint of home recognition, which have been echoed already. In the same long letter, containing, as was her wont, the diary of a week, she resumes her political story. She and her Queen had been ecstatic over the Sultan's lavish acknowledgments of Nelson's victory.

" The Queen says that, after the English she loves the Turks, and she has reason, for, as to Vienna, the ministers deserve to be hanged, and if Naples is saved, no thanks to the Emperor. For he is kindly leaving his father in the lurch. We have been two days desperate on account of the weak and cool acting of the Cabinet of Vienna. Thugut must be gained; but the Emperor—oh, but he is a poor sop, a machine in the hands of his corrupted ministers. The Queen is in a rage. . . . Sunday last, two couriers, one from London, one from Vienna; the first with the lovely news of a fleet to remain in the Mediterranean, and a treaty made of the most flattering kind for Naples. In short, everything amicable . . . and most truly honourable. T'other from their dear son and daughter, cold, un-

friendly, mistrustful, Frenchified; and saying plainly,
help yourselves. How the dear Maria Carolina cried
for joy at the one and rage at the other. But Mack
is gone to the army to prepare all to march immediately." And here, too, is the place of that dramatic
outburst, cited in the Prelude, where Emma extended
her *left* arm, like Nelson, and " painted the drooping
situation," stimulating the Queen's decision in face of
those hampering obstacles on the part of Gallo and the
King, which proved so unconscionable a time in dying.
" In short, there was a council, and it was decided to
march out and help themselves; and, sure, their poor
fool of a son will not, cannot but come out. He must
bring 150,000 men in the Venetian State. The French
could be shut in between the two armies, Italy cleared,
and peace restored. I saw a person from Milan yesterday, who says that a small army would do, for the
Milanese have had enough of liberty." She depicts the
horrid state of that capital, the starvation side by side
with the rampant licentiousness of the Jacobins " putting Virtue out of countenance by their . . . libertin-
age. . . . So, you see, a little would do. *Now is the
moment,* and, indeed, everything is going on as we
could wish." Emma has been hitherto and often
painted as the Queen's mouthpiece. She was really
Nelson's, and her intuition had grasped his mastership
of the political prospect. Was she not right in declaring that she had " spurred them on "? The Queen
had been actually heartened into resolving on a
regency, a new fact which reveals the political di-
vergences between the royal pair at this period. " The
King is to go in a few days, never to return. The
regency is to be in the name of the Prince Royal, but
the Queen will direct all. Her head is worth a thousand. I have a pain in my head, . . . and must go
take an airing. . . . May you live long, long, long

for the sake of your country, your King, your family, all Europe, Asia, Africa, and America [Emma is on her stilts once more], and for the scourge of France, but particularly for the happiness of Sir William and self, who love you, admire you, and glory in your friendship." Sir William's new name for Nelson was now "the friend of our hearts." And these hearts were certainly stamped with his image:—" Your statue ought to be made of pure gold and placed in the middle of London. Never, never was there such a battle, and if you are not regarded as you ought and I wish, I will renounce my country and become either a Mameluke or a Turk. The Queen yesterday said to me, the more I think on it, the greater I find it, and I feel such gratitude to the warrior, . . . my respect is such, that I could fall at his honoured feet and kiss them. You that know us both, and how alike we are in many things, that is, I as Emma Hamilton, she as Queen of Naples, imagine us both speaking of you. . . . I would not be a lukewarm friend for the world. I . . . cannot make friendships with all, but the few friends I have, I would die for them. . . . I told her Majesty we only wanted Lady Nelson to be the female *Tria juncta in uno,* for we all love you, and yet all three differently, and yet all equally, if you can make that out." . . . And Lady Nelson, accordingly, she congratulated twice, both on the Queen's behalf and her own.

Nelson returned for a fortnight in the earlier days of November, more than ever dissatisfied with the Neapolitan succours and the Portuguese co-operation at Malta. There, with strong significance in view of next year's crisis at Naples, he had notified the French, who rejected his overtures, that he would certainly disregard any capitulation into which the Maltese General might afterwards be forced to enter. He learned the decision for definite war, and the King's reluctant consent at length to accompany the army to Rome. No sooner had Garat been dismissed, than the French declared war also. Force, then, must repel force, for the Ligurian Republic meant nothing but France in Italy. Throughout, moreover, Nelson's guiding aim was the destruction of Jacobinism, which, indeed, he regarded as anti-Christ. He collected his forces and set out for Leghorn, which soon surrendered (although Buonaparte's brother Louis escaped the blockade), landing once more at Naples in the first week of December. At first Mack and the Neapolitan troops prevailed, and Prince Moliterno's valour covered the cowardice of his troops. The King entered Rome; the Queen's mercurial hopes ran high. But her exultation was short-lived. Before the end of the first week in December Carolina wrote to her confidante that she now pitied the King intensely, and " would be with him." " God only knows what evils are in reserve. I am deeply affected by it, and expect every day something more terrible. The good only will be the victims. . . . Mack is in despair, and has reason to be so." The French Berthier proved an abler, though not a braver, general than the Austrian, but Mack had raw and wretched levies under his command; his officers were bribed and their men deserted. Rome was retaken; a retreat became unavoidable, and by the second week in December that retreat had already become a rout. From the close of November onwards the Queen grew more and more despondent, though Duckworth's naval success at Minorca, the promise by the Czar Paul of his fleet, and the retirement of the Republicans from Frosinone had cheered her. She was very ill, and fresh home conspiracies were in course of discovery.

Emma still lingered in her neighbourhood at Caserta.

Beseeching Nelson not to go ashore at Leghorn, and rejoicing at the unfounded rumour that his " dear, venerable father " had been made a bishop, she informed him that the King had at length issued a clear manifesto. The army had marched, the Queen had just gone to pray for them in the cathedral. She announced the King's triumphal entry into Rome from Frascati; she hoped the best from the battle of Velletri, fought even as she writes. " Everybody here," she assured Nelson, " prays for you. Even the Neapolitans say mass for you, but Sir William and I are so anxious that we neither eat, drink, nor sleep; and till you are safely landed and come back we shall feel mad." The secret of Nelson's movements and preparations she will never betray, nor would red-hot torture wrest it from her. " We send you one of your midshipmen, left here by accident; . . . pray don't punish him. Oh! I had forgot I would never ask favours, but you are so good I cannot help it." And then follows a telltale passage: " We have got Josiah. How glad I was to see him. Lady Knight, Miss Knight, Carrol, and Josiah dined to-day with us, but alas! your place at table was occupied by Lady K. I could have cried, I felt so low-spirited."

Is it a wonder that Nelson was moved? One can hear how her confidence impressed him. Shortly after his return he frankly avowed, " My situation in this country has had, doubtless, one rose, but it has been plucked from a bed of thorns." This, then, was no waxen camellia, but a rose whose fresh scent contrasted with the hot atmosphere of the court and the prickles of perpetual vexation.

The reader must judge whether such efforts and appeals, this developing energy and tenderness, were the manœuvres of craft. It is patent from the correspondence that Emma's interjectional letters, which

think aloud, answer epistles from Nelson of even
tenor. A comparison, moreover, with her girlish
epistles to Greville shows a sameness of quality that
will stand the same test. She remains "the same
Emma."

Nelson rejoined the Hamiltons at a critical moment.
His wise forecast that unless Ferdinand and Maria
coveted the fate of Louis XVI. and Marie Antoinette,
flight alone could save them, was fast being justified.
The nobles, jealous of English influence, were now
thoroughly disaffected. Gathering reverses incensed
a populace that was only too likely to be frenzied
should their King prefer escape Sicilyward to trust in
their tried loyalty. As yet Naples had been free from
the French, but the likelihood of invasion grew daily;
and even in June Neapolitan neutrality had been known
to be merely nominal. The proud Queen, as we shall
find when the dreaded moment arrived, would rather
have welcomed death than retreat. But Acton, at
present in Rome, had slowly come to concur with the
trio of the Embassy.

The melodrama of the actual escape, on which new
manuscripts cast fresh lights, must be reserved for a
separate chapter. "The devil take most Kings and
Queens, I say, for they are shabbier than their subjects!" had been Sir Joseph Banks's exclamation to Sir
William Hamilton in 1795. At this present end of
1798 the devil (or Buonaparte) proved especially busy
in this particular branch of his business.

CHAPTER VIII

FLIGHT

December, 1798—January, 1799

IT is clear all along that Emma chafed against
vegetation. Tameness and sameness wearied her,
and she longed for historical adventures. She
had now lit on a thrilling one indeed. To aid in plan-
ning, preparing, deciding, and executing a royal escape
in the midst of revolution, on the brink of invasion,
and at the risk of life, was a task the romance and
the danger of which allured her dramatic fancy. That
it did not repeat the blunders of Varennes was largely
owing to Nelson's foresight and her own indefatigable
energy. And omens—for they each believed in them—
must have appeared to both. Before the battle of the
Nile a white bird had perched in his cabin. He and
Emma marked the same white bird when the King was
restored in the following July; and Nelson always declared that he saw it again before Copenhagen, though
it was missed at Trafalgar. It was his herald of victory. Nor under the auspices of triumph was death
also ever absent from the thoughts of the man, who
accepted, as a welcome present from a favoured Captain, the coffin made from a mast of the ruined
L'Orient.

For flight Emma had not influenced her friend: it
was Nelson's project. " If things take an unfortunate
turn here," she had written to Nelson two months be-

fore, "and the Queen dies at her post, I will remain
with her. If she goes, I follow her."

The second week of December proved to the Queen
that events were inexorable, and her selfish son-in-law
cold and unmoved: he shifted with the political
barometer. She had despatched her courier, Rosen-
heim, to Vienna, but he only returned with ill tidings.
Vienna would "give no orders." In vain she supplicated her daughter, "may your dear husband be our
saviour." The Emperor flatly refused his aid. His
subjects now desired peace, and the Neapolitans must
"help themselves." If Naples were assailed, the
Austrian treaty, it is true, would entitle reinforcements
from Vienna. But even so, the poorness of their
troops, and the grudging inclination of their ruler,
left the issue but little mended. The Queen was in
despair. The French excuse for war had been the alleged breach of their treaty by the watering of the
British fleet. A threatening army of invaders was already known to be on its way; yet still she hoped
against hope, and hesitated over the final plunge. She
despatched Gallo to Vienna to beseech her son-in-law
once more. She cursed the treaty of Campoformio,
to which she attributed the whole sad sequel of disaster. She vowed that her own kinsfolk were leagued
together in spite against "the daughter" and the
grandchildren "of the great Maria Theresa." When
the news fell like a thunderbolt that Mack's case was
desperate, the French troops in occupation of Castel
St. Angelo, and her husband about to scurry out of
Rome, those children could only "weep and pray."
The fact that the Jacobins—the "right-minded," as
they already styled themselves—welcomed each crowning blow as a help to their cause, heightened the humil-
iation. The Queen, slighted and indignant, betook
herself to Nelson and to Emma. They both pressed

anew the urgent necessity of flight; she disdained it.
It was a " fresh blow to her soul and spirit "; her original plan had been to have gone with her children elsewhere. Its bare possibility was difficult to realise;
and, after her husband's ashamed return, the popular
ferment seemed to bar its very execution. She dreaded
a repetition of Varennes. In the midst of brawl and
tumult the King returned, and, faltering, showed himself on his balcony. Lusty shouts of " You will not
go! *We* will deal with the Jacobins!" burst from the
surging crowd. A spy was knifed in the open streets,
and the false nobles cast the blame on the Queen. She
should be held blood-guilty. In bitter agony she apprised her daughter that death was preferable to such
dishonour. She would die every inch a Queen. " I
have renounced this world," wrote Maria Theresa's
true offspring, " I have renounced my reputation as
wife and mother. I am preparing to die, and making
ready for an eternity for which I long. This is all
that is left to me." Even when she had been brought
to the last gasp of obeying her kind friends and her
hard fate, her letters to Vienna sound the tone of one
stepping to the scaffold. While the furious mob
growled and groaned outside, her last requests to her
daughter were for her husband and children. On the
very edge of her secret start, the advices that General
Burchardt had marched his thousand men, if not
with flying colours, at least in fighting trim, so far as
Isoletta, may have once more made her rue her forced
surrender.

But meanwhile the Hamiltons, Nelson, and Acton
were in determined and close consultation, with Emma
for Nelson's interpreter. The establishment of the
Ligurian Republic had for some time boded the certainty of Buonaparte's designs against the Two Sicilies.
The General had at first written to Sir William with

some *sang-froid* of the "troublesome and dangerous circumstances" of the "crisis," but within a few days he was a zealous co-operator. Nelson, above all men, would never have counselled a base desertion. But he knew the real circumstances, the general perfidy, the Austrian weakness, both playing into the hands of the French. Already, to his knowledge, the aggressor's footfall was audible, and, after General Mack's fiasco, no resources were left at home. His firm resolve was to await the moment when he might deal a fresh death-blow to Buonaparte, and meanwhile to seize the first opportunity for crushing the Neapolitan Jacobins and reinstating the Neapolitan King. For him the cause symbolised not despotism against freedom, not the progress from law to liberty, but discipline and patriotism against license and anarchy. He had summoned ships to protect the *Vanguard:* the *Culloden* with Troubridge from the north and west coasts of Italy, the *Goliath* from off Malta, the *Alcmene* under Captain Hope from Egypt. After ordering the blockade of Genoa, he had ironically asked if the King was at war with its flag. He had foreseen that "within six months the Neapolitan Republic would be armed, organised, and called forth," that malingering Austria was herself *in extremis.*

They urged the Queen to prepare for the worst; and from December 17 onwards, while their measures were being concerted, Emma superintended the gradual transport from the palace of valuables both private and public. The process occupied her night and day for nearly a week, and required the strictest secrecy and caution. Some she may have fetched, some she received, many she stowed.

Criticism, biassed, may be, by anxiety to impugn Emma's latest memorial, makes much of evidence in a few isolated letters, indicating that the Queen forwarded some of her effects by trusted messengers, and omitting that Emma caused any herself to be carried from the palace to the Embassy. The detail is not very material, since her assistance is evident, even if her memory enlarged it. The very bulk of the many chests and boxes to be removed was to cause a dangerous delay in the eventual voyage. They were conveyed in different ways, some on shipboard (among them the public treasure), others, including jewels and linen, by the hands of the servant Saverio; others again to be transported by Emma herself. The Queen, in one of her almost hourly notes, expressly hoped that she was not " indiscreet in *sending* these," thereby suggesting that various means of conveyance had been used for some of the rest. In another, too, she excused herself for her " abuse of *your kindnesses* and that of our brave Admiral." Nelson's official account to Lord St. Vincent stated that " Lady Hamilton " from December 14 to 21 " received the jewels, etc." Emma's own recital to Greville, less than a fortnight after the terrors of the journey were past, included as the least of her long fatigues that " for six nights before the embarkation " she " sat up " at her own house " receiving all the jewels, money and effects of the royal family, and from thence conveying them on board the *Vanguard,* living in fear of being torn to pieces by the tumultuous mob, who suspected our departure," but " Sir William and I being beloved in the Country saved us." Sir William himself informed Greville that " Emma has had a very principal part in this delicate business, as she is, and has been for several years the real and only confidential friend of the Queen of Naples."

In the pathos of the Queen's letters to Emma resides their true interest. Maria Carolina's anguish increased as the plot for her preservation thickened; she clung piteously to the strong arms of Emma and Nelson, who really managed the whole business. Sobs and tears, paroxysms of scorn and sighs of rage more and more pervade them, as one by one the strongholds of her country yield or are captured. She is "the most unfortunate of Queens, mothers, women, but Emma's sincerest friend." It is to her "habitually" that she "opens her heart." Emma's indorsements may serve as an index :—"My adorable, unfortunate Queen. God bless and protect her and her august family." "Dear, dear Queen" — "Unfortunate Queen." More than a month earlier she had protested to Nelson her readiness, if need be, to accompany her to the block. One of these *billets tristes* of the Queen to her friend encloses a little blue-printed picture. It is an elegiac. A wreathed Amorino pipes mournfully beside a cypress-shadowed tomb, behind which two Cupids are carelessly dancing : on the tomb is inscribed "Embarque je vous en prie. M. C."—Emma's melancholy refrain to the would-be martyr.

Prince Belmonte, now chamberlain, acted as the King's agent with Caracciolo in effecting a scheme full of difficulty, owing to the great number of the refugees, the ridiculous etiquette of precedences, insisted on even at such an hour, the vast quantity of their united baggage, the avowed designs of the French Directory, the covert conspiracies of false courtiers in which the War Minister himself was implicated, the fierceness of popular tumult, and the Jacobin spies who kept a sharp lookout on Nelson, but were foiled by Emma's and the Queen's adroitness.

The plan originally concerted was as follows. The escape was to happen on the night of the 20th. After the last instalments of treasure and detachments of foreigners had been safely and ceremoniously deposited on board their several vessels, Count Thurn (an

Austrian admiral of the Neapolitan navy) would attend outside the secret passage leading from the royal
rooms to the "Molesiglio," or little quay, to receive
Nelson or his nominees.   It is said that Brigadier Caracciolo had begged to convoy the royal party and
float the royal standard on his frigate, but had been
dryly denied; and this, perhaps, was the first prick to
that treacherous revenge which six months later he was
to expiate by his death.

But on a sudden, at the eleventh hour, the whole was
put off till the next evening.   The chests in which some
of the treasure had been bestowed on the *Alcmene*
were rotten; at least this was one of the pretexts
which Nelson, who had already signed orders for safe
conduct, one possibly referring to the royalties, evidently mistrusted.   On this eventful day at least six
communications passed between Hamilton and Acton
(if the inclosures from the palace are included), and
Nelson, prompt and impatient, was acutely irritated.
In vain Acton expressed his acquiescence.   He was " in
hopes that these few hours will not exasperate more
than at present our position."   Nelson remained polite, but decided.   The fact was that both King and
Queen waited on Providence at the last gasp.   The
former dreaded to desert his people at the moment of
defeat; the latter feared a step which, if futile, might
irreparably alienate her husband, and must render her
execrable to the faithful Lazzaroni.

By means of the old manuscripts the scene rises
vividly before us.   Within the precincts of the palace,
flurry, dissension, wavering perplexity, confusion, a
spectral misery.   In its purlieus, treason.   Outside, a
seditious loyalty withholding the King from the Queen.
In the council-chamber, Belmonte, serene and punctilious; Gallo, dainty in danger; Caracciolo, jealous
and sullen; Acton, slow, doubtful, and stolid.   At the

English Embassy alone reigned vigilance, resolve, and resourcefulness. Every English merchant (and there were many both here and at Leghorn) looked to Nelson and Hamilton and Emma. Among phantoms these were realities. On them alone counted those poor "old demoiselles of France" who had sought asylum in the Neapolitan palace. On them alone hung the destinies of a dynasty threatened at home, forsaken abroad, and faced with the certainty of invasion. They stood for the British fleet, and the British fleet for the salvation of Europe.

The ominous morning dawned of the 21st.

All that day General Acton pelted Nelson and Hamilton with contradictory announcements, of which no fewer than seven remain. At first he agrees that the moment has come when " no time should be lost," but the inevitable proviso follows—"If the wind does not blow too hard." He next writes that, in such a case, all had best be deferred afresh. The *Alcmene, too,* with the bullion on board—as much as two million and a half sterling—was off Posilippo, and its signals might alarm the angry crowds, clamouring for their King at Santa Lucia, and on the Chiaja. Another billet promises the "King's desire" as soon forthcoming. In another, once more, grave consideration is devoted to the usual retiring hour of the young princes, and to the "feeding-time" of the King's grandchild, the babe in arms of the heir-apparent and Princess Clementina, which had been so anxiously awaited in October; "a sucking child," says Acton in a crowning instance of unconscious humour, "makes a most dreadful spectacle to the eyes of the servant women and in the rest of the family." Nelson, pressing for expedition, must have been beside himself over the precious moments thus being squandered. What Acton remarks in one of these letters, once more in his peculiar English, applies also to his own communications, " Heavings from every side . . . contradictions from every corner."

Nelson, however, would brook no more trifling. Everything should be settled by about seven. Count Thurn should be at the appointed *rendezvous,* the Molesiglio. His password, unless some unexpected force intervened, was to be the English, *" All goes right and well "*; otherwise, *" All is wrong, you may go back."*

One can imagine the unfortunate Count rehearsing his provoking part that afternoon with an Austrian accent: *" Al goes raight "*—*" Al ees vrong."*

Acton and Caracciolo drew up the order of embarkation. By half-past eight the royal contingent, convoyed by Nelson and his friends through the secret passage to the little quay, were to have been rowed on board the *Vanguard.* It comprised besides the King, Queen, the Hereditary Prince with his wife and infant (whose " zafatta," or nurse, was no less a personage than the Duchess of Gravina), the little Prince Albert, to whom Emma was devoted (with his " zafatta " also), Prince Leopold, the three remaining princesses, Acton, Princes Castelcicala and Belmonte, Thurn, and the court physician Vincenzo Ruzzi. The second embarkation was to follow two hours later with a great retinue, including, it is interesting for Mendelssohn-admirers to notice, the name of " Bartoldi." The rest were to proceed in three several detachments, amounting to nearly four hundred souls, noble and otherwise, among whom Joseph Acton's family are specified. The two royal spinsters of France were to be conducted with every precaution by land to Portici, whence they might find their way over the border. All friendly Ambassadors were to be notified. Such was the routine. It should be especially noticed that from these exact lists, detailing the names of every passenger, the Hamiltons are absent. They were under Nelson's care, and of his party—a point most material to the future narrative substantiating Lady Hamilton's own subsequent story. And it must further be emphasised that these Acton letters, as well as a reference in one of the Queen's, go far to establish the plan of the secret passage as an historical fact, instead of as any figment or after-inlay of Emma's imagination.

As night drew on Maria Carolina sat down to indite two letters, the one to her daughter at Vienna, the other to Emma, who would rejoin her so soon in this crisis of her fate. She wrote them amid horrors and in wretchedness. The army could no more be trusted. Even the navy was in revolt. Orders had been given that, after the royal departure, the remaining ships were to be burned lest they should fall into French or revolutionary hands. As she wrote, the tidings came that the miserable Vanni—the creature of her inquisition—had shot himself dead, and she loads herself with reproaches. Massacre continued; the very French émigrés were not spared by the Italian Jacobins. Everywhere tumult, disgrace, bloodshed. The crowd, calmed for a moment, still howled at intervals for their King, whose departure they now suspected. The "cruel determination" had been foisted on her. Once on board, the Queen tells the empress, "God help us, . . . saved, but ruined and dishonoured." To Lady Hamilton she repeats the same distracted burden. Discipline has vanished. "Unbridled" license grows hourly. Their "concert with their liberator" is their mainstay. Her last thoughts are for the safety of friends and dependants, whom she confides by name to Emma's charge. Her torn heart bleeds. Mack despairs also, for Aquila is taken, "to the eternal shame of our country." She trembles for the horrors that a cowardly people may commit.

The sky was clouded. There was a lull in the strong wind off the shore, but a heavy ground-swell prevailed as the appointed hour approached. The royal party anxiously waited in their apartments—the Queen's room with its dark exit, so familiar to the romantic Emma,—for the signal which should summon them through the tunnel to the water-side. On the Mole-siglio, and at his station near the Arsenal, stood Thurn, muffled and ill at ease. It was the night of a reception given in Nelson's honour by Kelim Effendi, the bearer from the Sultan of his " plume of triumph."

The exact sequence of what now occurred is difficult, but possible, to collect from the three contemporary and, at first sight, conflicting documents that survive. There is the Queen's own brief recital to her daughter. There is Nelson's dry official despatch to Lord St. Vincent, accentuating, however, Emma's conspicuous services. There are Emma's own hurried lines to Greville, thirteen days after that awful voyage, which, for three days and nights, deprived her of sleep and strained every faculty of mind and body.

Let us try to ascertain the truth by collation. Nelson's account is brief and doubtless accurate :—

" On the 21st, at 8.30 P.M., three barges with myself and Captain Hope landed at a corner of the Arsenal. I went into the palace and brought out the whole royal family, put them into the boats, and at 9.30 they were all safely on board."

It is an official statement, which naturally omits the Count in waiting, the password, the mysteries of the secret corridor, which Acton in his letters, confirming Emma's after account, had arranged with Nelson.

The Queen's short notice to the Empress of Austria (hitherto unmarked) makes no mention of Emma's name—the Queen *never* does in any of her letters to her daughter—but further corroborates the melodrama of the secret staircase winding down to the little quay :—

"We *descended*—all our family, ten in number, with the utmost secrecy, in the dark, without our women or any one, and in two boats. Nelson was our guide."

Now let us listen carefully to Emma's own graphic narrative. The hours named in it do not tally with Nelson's, and after the long strain of the tragic occurrences, culminating in the death of the little Prince Albert, she may well have been confused. They are really irrelevant. The point is the real sequence and substance of events, which, more or less, must have stayed in her immediate remembrance. It will be found that her vivid words bear a construction different from that which might appear at the first blush, and it should be borne in mind that no possible motive for distorting the facts can be alleged in this friendly communication to her old friend :—

"On the 21st at ten at night, Lord Nelson, Sir Wm., Mother and self went out to pay a visit, sent all our servants .away, and ordered them in 2 hours to come with the coach, and ordered supper at home. When they were gone, we sett off, walked to our boat, and after two hours got to the *Vanguard*. Lord N. *then* went with armed boats to a secret passage adjoining to the pallace, got up the dark staircase that goes into the Queen's room, and with a dark lantern, cutlasses, pistols, etc., brought off every soul, ten in number, to the *Vanguard* at twelve o'clock. If we had remained to the next day, we shou'd have all been imprisoned."

Reading this account loosely, it might be imagined that Emma transposed the true order; that Nelson, stealing with the Hamiltons away from the reception, first brought them on board, and afterwards returned for the royal fugitives. But the reverse of this admits of proof from her own statement. She, with her family and Nelson, quitted the party at (as she here puts it) *ten*. It took them *two* hours to reach the *Vanguard*. Nelson saved the royalties, who were not on board till *" twelve."* It is obvious, therefore, that (whatever the precise hour) the Hamiltons and Mrs. Cadogan arrived on the *Vanguard* at *the selfsame moment* as the King, the Queen, their children, and grandchild. The misimpression arises from the phrasing " Lord Nelson *then* went with armed boats," etc., following the previous statement of their being at their destination " after two hours." But this *" then,"* as so often in Emma's thinking-aloud letters, seems an enclitic merely carrying on disjointed sentences. It may be no mark of time at all, but a mere reference to what happened after they hastened from the entertainment, having ordered everything as if they intended to remain until its close. Otherwise they must have " got to " the *Vanguard* long before the King and Queen, which, by her own recollection in this letter, they do not. It will be noted from Nelson's recital that the *Vanguard* could be reached in an hour.

What happened, then, seems to be this. After their hurried exit, the Hamiltons accompanied Nelson on foot. The Acton correspondence shows that, as has appeared from the pre-arrangements, the Hamiltons must have been of Nelson's private and unspecified party. Together they went to *their* boat where, before their start, they awaited the separate escape of the royalties. Eventually the two contingents stepped on to the deck of the *Vanguard* at the same moment and together. But, in the interval, something must have necessitated and occupied their attendance.

What was it?

Here Emma's own account in her " Prince Regent's

Memorial," more than fourteen years afterwards, perhaps comes to our aid.   It has been discredited even as
regards the "secret passage" incident which Acton's
letters reveal by distinct allusion.   This is what Emma
says :—

"To shew the caution and secrecy that was necessarily used in thus getting away, I had on the night of
our embarkation to attend the party given by the Kilim
Effendi, who was sent by the grand seignior to Naples
to present Nelson with the Shahlerih or Plume of Triumph.   I had to steal from the party, leaving our carriages and equipages waiting at his house, and in about
fifteen minutes to be at my post, where it was my task
to conduct the Royal Family through the subterranean
passage to *Nelson's boats,* by that moment waiting for
us on the shore.   The season for this voyage was extremely hazardous, and our miraculous preservation is
recorded by the Admiral upon our arrival at Palermo."

I venture, therefore, to suggest the following probability.   Count Thurn is keeping watch, in accordance
with the preconcerted plan.   Captain Hope and Nelson arrive at about 7.30 by Neapolitan time at the
Molesiglio.   Leaving Captain Hope in charge, Nelson
hurries to the reception, as if nothing were in process,
and, as designed, meets the Hamiltons and Mrs. Cadogan.   Within a quarter of an hour they all sally forth,
walk to the shore, and proceed in Sir William's private
boat to the *rendezvous.*   Emma, quitting her mother
and husband, hastens by the palace postern to the side
of her "adored Queen."   The signal for the flight
has already been made by Count Thurn.   Emma ac-
companies the royal family to the winding and underground staircase, up which Nelson climbs with pistols
and lanterns to conduct them.   They all emerge from
the inner to the outer darkness.   The royal family are
bestowed by Hope and Nelson in their barges.   The

Hamiltons re-enter their own private boat. In another hour they again meet on board the *Vanguard*.

Emma's temperament alike and circumstances forbid us to suppose that, at such an hour, she would allow herself to stay apart from the Queen. She lived, and had for weeks been living, on tension. The melodrama of the moment, the danger, the descent down the cavernous passage, the lanterns, pistols, and cutlasses, the armed boats, the safe conduct of her hero, would all appeal to her. It was an experience unlikely to be repeated, and one that she would be most unlikely to forgo. Affection and excitement would both unite in prompting her to persuade Nelson into permitting her to assist in this thrilling scene. And it would be equally unlikely that either she or Nelson would report this episode to England. In any case, the incident was one more of personal adventure than of necessary help. What Nelson does single out for the highest commendation in his despatches, what *was* published both at home and abroad, and universally acknowledged, what Lord St. Vincent praised with gratitude, was her signal service before the voyage and under that awful storm which arose during it, in which, by every authentic account, she enacted the true heroine, exerting her energies for every one except herself, caring for and comforting all, till she was called their "guardian angel." "What a scene," wrote Sir John Macpherson to Hamilton, "you, your Sicilian King, his Queen, Lady Hamilton, and our noble Nelson have lately gone through! . . . Lady Hamilton has shown, with honour to you and herself, the merit of your predilection and selection of so good a heart and so fine a mind. She is admired here from the court to the cottage. The King and Prince of Wales often speak of her."

It was not till seven o'clock on the morning of the

23rd that the *Vanguard* could weigh anchor. Fresh consignments of things left behind were awaited. It was still hoped that riot might be pacified and disaffection subdued. Prince Francesco Pignatelli had been commissioned to reign at Naples during the King's absence, and was nominated Deputy-Captain-General—of anarchy. During this interval of suspense, a deputation of the magistrates came on board and implored the King to remain among his people. He was inflexible, and every effort to move him proved unavailing. On the one hand, the Lazzaroni, incensed against the Jacobins despoiling them of their King; on the other, the French Ambassador, smarting under his formal dismissal procured by Emma's influence, were each precipitating an upheaval itself engineered by French arms and agitators and used by traitorous nobles, whom both mob and bourgeoisie had grown to detest. While Maria Carolina's name was now execrated at Naples by loyalist and disloyalist alike, her misfortunes called forth sympathy from England, alarmed by the French excesses, and regarding the Jacobin mercilessness as fastening on faith, allegiance, and freedom.

Not a murmur escaped the lips of the pig-headed King or the hysterical Queen, though inwardly both repined. From the *Vanguard,* ere it set sail, Maria Carolina wrote her sad letter to her daughter. The " cruel resolution had to be taken." Her " one consolation " was that all faithful to their house had been saved.

After two days' anxious inaction the *Vanguard* and *Sannite,* with about twenty sail of vessels, at last left the bay in disturbed weather and under a lowering sky. Among the last visitors was General Mack, at the end of his hopes, his wits, and his health: " my heart bled for him," wrote Nelson, " worn to a shadow." The next morning witnessed the worst storm in Nelson's long recollection.

And here Emma approved herself worthy of her hero's ideal. A splendid sailor, intrepid and energetic, she owned a physique which, like her muscular arms, she perhaps inherited from her blacksmith father. So quick had proved the eventual decision to fly, such had been the precautions against attracting notice by any show of preparation, so many public provisions had been hurried, that the private had been perforce neglected. Nelson himself thus paints her conduct on this "trying occasion." "They necessarily came on board without a bed. . . . Lady Hamilton provided her own beds, linen, etc., and became their slave; for except one man, no person belonging to royalty assisted the royal family, nor did her Ladyship enter a bed the whole time they were on board." Emma's Palermo letter to Greville, which is very characteristic, will best resume the narrative:—

"We arrived on Christmas day at night, after having been near lost, a tempest that Lord Nelson had never seen for thirty years he has been at sea, the like; all our sails torn to pieces, and all the men ready with their axes to cut away the masts. And poor I to attend and keep up the spirits of the Queen, the Princess Royall, three young princesses, a baby six weeks old, and 2 young princes Leopold and Albert; the last, six years old, my favourite, taken with convulsion in the midst of the storm, and, at seven in the evening of Christmas day, expired in my arms, not a soul to help me, as the few women her Majesty brought on board were incapable of helping her or the poor royal children. The King and Prince were below in the ward room with Castelcicala, Belmonte, Gravina, Acton, and Sir William, my mother there assisting them, all their attendants being so frighten'd, and on their knees

praying.   The King says my mother is an angel.   I
have been for 12 nights without once closing my eyes.
. . . The gallant Mack is now at Capua, fighting it out
to the last, and, I believe, coming with the remains of
his vile army into Calabria to protect Sicily, but thank
God we have got our brave Lord Nelson.   The King
and Queen and the Sicilians adore, next to worship
him, and so they ought; for we shou'd not have had
this Island but for his glorious victory.   He is called
here *Nostro Liberatore, nostro Salvatore*.   We have
left everything at Naples but the vases and best pictures.   3 houses elegantly furnished, all our horses
and our 6 or 7 carriages, I think is enough for the vile
French.   For we cou'd not get our things off, not to
betray the royal family.   And, as we were in council,
we were sworn to secrecy.   So we are the worst off.
All the other ministers have saved all by staying some
days after us.   Nothing can equal the manner we have
been received here; but *dear, dear* Naples, we now dare
not show our love for that place; for this country is
je[a]lous of the other.   We cannot at present proffit
of our leave of absence, for we cannot leave the royal
family in their distress.   Sir William, however, says
that in the Spring we shall leave this, as Lord St. Vincent has ordered a ship to carry us down to Gibraltar.
God only knows what yet is to become of us.   We are
worn out.   I am with anxiety and fatigue.   Sir William [h]as had 3 days a bilious attack, but is now well.
. . . The Queen, whom I love better than any person
in the world, is very unwell.   We weep together, and
now that is our onely comfort.   Sir William and
the King are philosophers; nothing affects them, thank
God, and *we* are scolded even for shewing proper sensibility.   God bless you, my dear Sir.   Excuse this
scrawl."

At three in the afternoon of that sad Christmas Day,

the royal standard was hoisted at the head of the *Vanguard* in face of Palermo. The tempest-tossed Queen, prostrate with grief at the death of her little son, refused to go on shore. The King entered his barge and was received with loyal acclamations. The *Vanguard* did not anchor till two o'clock of the following morning. To spare the feelings of the bereaved Queen, Nelson accompanied her and the Princesses privately to the land. Even then she was surrounded by half-enemies. Caracciolo had not yet evinced his Jacobin sympathies and was already sailing under dubious colours. The Neapolitan Captain Bausan, whose skill contributed to the safety of the ships, and who was again to pilot the King next year into port, became, in that very year, himself a suspect and an exile.

Among the furniture abandoned at the English Embassy may have been a beautiful table and cabinet which the grateful Nelson had ordered from England as mementos for Emma, and whose classical designs of muses and hovering cupids are said to have been painted by Angelica Kauffmann. These still exist, and are in the present possession of Mr. Sanderson, the eminent Edinburgh collector, to whose kindness the writer is indebted for a photograph. Was it to these, perhaps, that Nelson alluded when he mentioned the " Amorins " to Emma in 1804?

The Queen secluded herself in the old palace of Colli. It seemed ages, she soon wrote, since she had seen one to whom she repeated her eternal gratitude and perpetual concern. Her throat, head, and chest were affected; the physicians were summoned, but her malady lay beyond their cure. Not only had she been sorely bereaved, disgraced by defeats, and stung by treacheries, but her husband now began to make her a scapegoat. This, forsooth, was the fruit of her Anglo-

mania—a revolted kingdom, a maddened though ador-
ing populace, an advancing and arrogant enemy.
Every day the Queen frequented the churches for
prayer and the convents for meditation. Each evening she poured out her heart to the helpful friend of
her choice, whose sympathy lightened a load else insupportable.

With some difficulty the Hamiltons, whose permanent guest Nelson now first became, found a suitable
abode not too distant from the palace, and, as they
hoped, healthier in situation than most of a then
malarious city. But they all suffered from the bad
air, the more so in the reaction of the change from their
Neapolitan home. On Emma now devolved half the
duties of the transferred Embassy. Sir William
waxed peevish and querulous. He bemoaned the
wreck of the *Colossus,* which had carried his art treasures home. Homeward he himself yearned to retire,
leaving the Consul Lock as his *chargé d'affaires.* " I
have been driven," he told Greville, " from my comfortable house at Naples to a house here without chim-
neys, and calculated only for summer. . . . As I wax
old, it has been hard upon me, having had both bilious
and rheumatic complaints. I am still most desirous of
returning home by the first ship that Lord Nelson
sends down to Gibraltar, as I am worn out and want
repose." But he shared his wife's enthusiasm for
Nelson, which acted like a tonic on his nerves. " I love
Lord Nelson more and more," he adds ; " his activity is
wonderful, and he loves us sincerely." He consoled
himself with the thought that he had done his duty.

By January 24 the " Parthenopean Republic " had
been proclaimed in a town betrayed, against the will
of its populace, to a French General. The Tree of
Liberty had been planted ; the wooden image of the
giant, crowned with the red cap of Revolution, had

been set up in full sight of the palace. Every loiterer on the Chiaja wore the *tricolor;* the Toledo itself rang with the Marseillaise. For a time the enemies of Naples played the part of its deliverers. For the Royalists Naples seemed lost to the Neapolitans; for the Jacobins she appeared the trophy of freedom.

The successive episodes both before and after this terrible transformation scene are a " witches' Sabbath." All of worst and wildest in every class of the population was set loose.

And the royal flight had been a Pandora's box which had let forth the whole brood of winged mischiefs. If the Queen scathed the rebels as parricide poltroons, they, in their turn, branded her as villain, and the King as coward and selfish deserter, at the very moment when the French had crossed the boundary. But with that invading host most of them were already in collusion; it was the Lazzaroni alone who had the real right of denouncement. No sooner had Pignatelli published the absconded King's proclamation, and placarded the edict appointing him as temporary viceroy, than " chaos was come again." Their rough-and-tumble macaroni-monarch had vanished; their loathed French Revolution was in the air. The French troops were on their insolent march cityward. If the Neapolitan Bourbons were indeed Baal, as the Jacobins averred, there were now few but Lazzaroni to bow the knee; if, the Tree of Liberty, as the loyalists declared it, its votaries might be counted by thousands. But on both sides there was no Elijah—no seer to call down fire from heaven. The flames, so soon to enwrap the stricken city, were those of Mephistopheles.

CHAPTER IX

To August, 1799

"CONSPIRACIES are for aristocrats, not for nations," is a pregnant apophthegm of Disraeli. Viewed at its full length and from its inner side, the great Jacobin outburst at Naples was more a conspiracy than a revolution, or even an insurrection.

To appreciate Nelson's part, and Emma's help, in the much-criticised suppression of the Neapolitan Jacobins during June, it behoves us to track, however briefly, the course of that most interesting and singular movement. This is not the occasion for a minute inquiry; but four preliminary considerations must be kept in mind. In the first place, this revolt differs from all others in that it was one of the noblesse and bourgeoisie against the whole mass of the people. In the second, its chief leaders, both men and women (and it is doubly engrossing from the fact that women played a great part in it), confessedly took their lives into their hands. They were quite ready to annihilate the objects of their loathing, and, therefore, they had small right to complain when opportunity transferred to themselves the doom that they had planned for others. They proved fully as much tyrants and tormentors as their sovereign; and the whole conflict was really one between two absolutisms, democratic and bureaucratic—a struggle between extreme systems

exhibiting equal symptoms of the same evil. The
" Civic Guard," to be erected by the " Deputies," persecuted just as Maria Carolina's secret police had persecuted before. Acton's exactions were to be out-
done by the French Commissary Faypoult's pillage,
and the French General Championnet's " indemnities."
As for brutality, it was tripled by the new reign of
terror, and when Championnet compassed the conciliation of the brave populace, he contrived even to
" brutalise miracles." Again, the Neapolitan Jacobins
were not only oppressors of all authority, but traitors
to the people as well as to the King; while at last they
openly confederated with the invaders of their father-
land and of Europe. It was thus that the force and
guile of Napoleon trafficked in the reveries of
Rousseau.

It is true, nevertheless, that many of them were inspired by noble motives and proved conscientious victims. Such children of light as these redeem the
movement as a real step in the progress of law to liberty. Some were lofty idealists, while others, however, dreamed of realising theories impossible even in
Cloud-Cuckoo-land. Savants and ignoramuses, phi-
lanthropists and cosmopolitans abounded. But the
majority were actuated by very personal motives, and
inspired by overweening ambitions. None of them,
not the noblest, were orginative. All were under the
spell of France; the worst, under that of French gold;
the best, under that of French sentiment. And, before the close, there were very few even among the
least practical who did not rue the day when they invited self-interest masquerading as friendship, and
opened their gates and their hearts to the busybodying
emissaries of the Directory. The very name of Faypoult soon became more odious than the fact of Ferdinand.

Once more, just as the contemporary Jacobins confounded license with freedom, and ascribed to paper
constitutions the virtues of native patriotism, so the
more modern Italians have always, and naturally,
viewed in the blood of these martyrs the seed of United
Italy. It is a legend ineradicable from history; and,
after the same manner, William Tell is made by Schiller the prophet of United Germany. Yet, in the main,
a legend it remains. The " Parthenopean Republic "
was a venture purely local, unillumined by any vision
of broadened or strengthened nationality. What was
not French in its fantasies, was derived from the models of ancient Rome. Nothing was farther from the
aspirations of the Neapolitan Jacobins from December,
1798, up to June, 1799, than the ideal of one confederated commonwealth. Like the Ligurian Republic,
the Neapolitan was the creature of France. Through
France it rose; through France it fell. And it is not
a little curious that, some sixty years later, it was to
the third Napoleon once more that many in Italy looked
up for regeneration.

> " Il merto oppresso,—il nazional mendico,
> Carco d'onor e gloria ogni straniero "

had been Eleonora de Fonseca Pimentel's lament to
the King in 1792. By the revival alone of national
institutions, expressing national character, could a
natural elasticity be restored. A theoretic and antinational uprising actually deprived Naples of those enlightened schemes by which in her prime Maria Carolina had sought to renovate her people. She had cut
the claws of the enraged nobles by abolishing their
feudal prerogatives. She had sought to improve the
superstitious Lazzaroni by projects of industry and
education. She had exalted the applauding students
into an aristocracy of talent. But it was as puppets

dancing on her own wires that she had benefited them all. And the result showed that their real resentment was against any dependence whatever and any pauperisation. Whether by democracy or by bureaucracy, they refused to be transformed. From the feudal baron to the pagan beggar, each class wished to keep its distinctive flavour, and to live by its instincts. The " intellectuals "—a small remnant—were the sole cosmopolitans. They tried to transfigure Naples into Utopia, and for that purpose invited a foe that forsook them. Denationalism (or a-nationalism) failed; Naples remained Naples still. But the miserable alternative proved the grinding sway of an avenging tyrant, bereft by rebellion of his old jollity, and untempered by the earlier intellectualism of his now fanatical wife.

The Revolution presents the spectacle of characteristic class-instincts in orgy. It was a protest far more against Acton's bureaucratic routine than against monarchy. Its eruptions were those of its physical surroundings. It was a Vesuvius, with all its attendants of whirlwind, earthquake, and waterspout. The light of heaven was blotted out from the firmament, molten lava seared the whole social landscape, and the deeps of unbridled instinct shook in the tornado.

Prince Pignatelli proved himself little but driftwood on the deluge. After conceding the Jacobin demands, he proceeded to gratify the Lazzaroni's. He ended by pleasing none; the " Eletti " nullified his office, of which the King said they deprived him. He opened with the usual paper-constitution. A " civic guard " was formed, the military and civil functions were divided, a chamber of " deputies " was constituted. Nominally, the elective system had been restored. But the first act of the new body was to abolish their viceroy's own provisions. They decreed that henceforward royal power should devolve on two authorities alone—a chamber of nobles, and themselves, the "Patriots"; the really popular element was thus excluded, and the real power became vested in a "Venetian Oligarchy." Pignatelli was rendered a cipher, and the Lazzaroni, who, strange to relate, proved themselves the sole realities in a limbo of phantoms, were furious at their own incapacitation. Pignatelli at once burned one hundred and twenty bombardier boats—a work of needless destruction completed by Commodore Campbell, to Nelson's disgust, some few months later; Count Thurn—our watchman of a fortnight ago—blew up two vessels and three frigates. Amid this flare and detonation were born the calamity and carnage that succeeded. Alarm was the prelude to violence, and violence to panic. Ere long, the powerless Pignatelli offered the French a truce in his alarm, and fled to Sicily, where he was imprisoned, but soon released. Save for the Lazzaroni, Naples was without authority or governance, and lay exposed a helpless prey to the common enemy.

Two striking scenes happened within three weeks, and in that short but crowded period formed the *dénouements* of two separate acts in the drama. Both of them passed under the patronage of St. Januarius, whose sanction, as declared by the Archbishop Zurlo, was always law to the Lazzaroni. They may serve as landmarks before a miniature of what led to them is attempted. The recital (though there are many Italian authorities for the whole history) is most vividly given by a contemporary who cannot be accused of partiality to the Lazzaroni. The future General Pepé was then a stripling of revolutionary enthusiasm, and one of the first recruits in the new and transitory " civic guard."

On the night of January 15 a strange sight might

have been viewed in the cathedral. The proud and brave Prince Moliterno, among the few distinguished in the late humiliating campaign, and just chosen by the Lazzaroni as their chief, wended his way, barefooted, with bowed head and in penitential tatters, towards the glimmering altar, and on his knees besought leave of the venerable archbishop to harangue the people. In that procession of St. Januarius this grandee was the humblest and perhaps the saddest. The French general was already encamped before Capua. Moliterno rallied the Lazzaroni and assured them that he would lead them victorious against the foe. Four days afterwards they were betrayed to the patriots.

Only a week later, and yet another and even stranger tableau happened in the same spot, for St. Januarius haunts the Neapolitan Revolution. A second solemn procession was formed, but by this time Championnet and his French troops had advanced to Naples. During the morning he had addressed the assembled people in the stately hall of San Lorenzo. His speech had been a string of fair-weather promises, not one of which was kept. In the evening he steps cathedralward on one side of the archbishop, the clever general Macdonald and the mocking French commissary Abrial, on the other. The prelate holds aloft the sacred relics and the miraculous ewer. Priests, nobles, " patriots," and a vast throng of Lazzaroni march in his wake. Suddenly a halt is called. The fate of Naples trembles in the balance. All depends on whether the blood of the saint shall announce by its liquefaction to his believers that Heaven favours the French Republic. Archbishop Zurlo raises the crystal basin. The saint's blood is obdurate, and still monarchical. Macdonald holds a concealed but significant pistol. Championnet whispers, your miracle or your life! The terrorised ecclesiastic announces the prodigy to the crowd. St.

Januarius, then, *is* a democrat.   The Lazzaroni shout
in their thousands, " Long live St. Januarius! long live
his republic! "   The trick is palmed off successfully
on the credulous populace, and Championnet with Macdonald returns chuckling to St. Elmo.   But miracle or
no miracle, the end of this coarse jugglery was civil
war.

The two intervals must now be briefly supplied.

On January 12 Pignatelli, from the first hampered
by the Deputies, negotiated secretly and in panic with
the enemy, by this time possessed of the chief provincial fortresses, as the " patriots " were of the Neapolitan.   The Lazzaroni, however, were staunch, so that
the French commissaries despatched next day by Championnet to receive their first payment were forced to
return.   The whole first episode is the triumph of the
Lazzaroni.   Reinforcements, under General Naselli,
reached them from Palermo, and they attacked the
quailing " civic guard," composed mainly of " intellectuals " and professionals.   They seized the " patriots' " arms, the troops and the castles surrendered to
them; they opened the prisons and the galleys.   They
dismayed the " patriots," while the town shuddered
under the license of their patrols.   On the whole, however, their moderation at first was extraordinary.   Pepé,
himself their captive, bears it especial witness in re-
counting how they disdained the money offered by his
relations and released him unharmed.   The Lazzaroni
adored Prince Moliterno and his colleague in leader-
ship, the Duke of Roccaromana.   They would gladly
have died for these, as for the Duke della Torre and
Clemente Filomarino, their associate.   But when they
discovered that the leading magnates were already
treating with the national foe and combining to yield
General Championnet and his French troops admittance, their wrath knew no bounds.   It was fanned by

the priests, who vociferated against the Neapolitan foes of Naples from their pulpits. Even Moliterno and Roccaromana were now suspected by their mob-followers of Jacobinism. In an access o'f mad resentment the Lazzaroni fired the Duke della Torre's palace, piled and burned its treasures, and dragged forth both him and the luckless Clemente Filomarino, to be roasted alive on the pyre. These atrocities culminated in the first scene that has just been described.

The Lazzaroni's suspicions were well founded. On January 19, their hitherto trusted Roccaromana himself betrayed them. By complot with the "patriots" he entered the fort of St. Elmo, and won over its commandant to his stratagem. The Lazzaroni garrison were sent out of their quarters, ostensibly to buy provisions for the approaching siege. On their return they were suddenly disarmed. The *tricolor* standard was hoisted as a signal to Championnet, encamped with his legions in the "Largo della Pigna." By Pepé's own confession, the Lazzaroni, deserted and defrauded, evinced a "marvellous intrepidity." Against desperate odds they stood their ground. Only a fortnight before, they had seen of what poor stuff the "civic guard" had been made. But sturdier "patriots" than weak-kneed students now garrisoned St. Elmo. Overwhelming numbers soon closed the conflict.

Meanwhile Championnet had waved his flag of truce in response to the three-coloured ensign, and while the Lazzaroni hung back tricked and abashed, he entered the city. He at once made "an affectionate discourse." Everybody was promised everything: he had come for all their *goods*. The "patriots" loved the people, and to himself both they and the Lazzaroni were brothers more in hearts than in arms. He was there to emancipate them all; a golden age was at hand. His army was not French but Neapolitan.

The Lazzaroni, gullible and volatile, believed him
and cheered; mob fury was allayed. "God save San
Gennaro!" burst from every lip. "God save San
Gennaro!" reiterated Championnet and Macdonald.
Before a day had passed they should see a sign from
their saint. And then followed the solemn juggle of
our second act. Relics were very helpful to the Directory, and for a moment those who had panted to exterminate the French welcomed them as brothers under
the celestial portent. The "Parthenopean Republic"
was proclaimed. The poets burst into song, the pam-
phleteers into doctrine, the journalists into execration
of monarchy and eulogies of Reason and the Millen-
nium. The printing-presses could hardly cope with the
demand, and their muse—the tenth muse "Ephemera"
—was the fair Eleonora Fonseca di Pimentel, who had
been allowed to republicanise unmolested, and was now
editress of the new and ebullient *Monitore*. Its amen-
ities did not compliment the self-exiled court at
Palermo. Of Nelson and the Hamiltons as yet there
was no abuse. But Ferdinand was called a "debased
despot," a "caitiff fugitive," a "dense imbecile," and
a "stupid tyrant," while, so far, Carolina fared better
as "that Amazon, his wife." It was not long before
the middle-class phase of the movement retaliated on
the notables even more violently than on the sovereign. "Duke" was derived from coachman ("a
ducendo"), "Count" from lackey ("a comitando");
epithets were actually changing the nature of
things.

But Championnet's deeds were to refute his words.
A few days of paper systems were the parenthesis between a spurious peace and a civil war.

A bad harvest served Championnet as excuse for dis-
persing the Lazzaroni to their homesteads; a bare
treasury soon caused him to levy toll. A general in-

surrection ensued in the provinces, repressed by a fresh
"National Guard" wearing the cockade and commanded by the once loyalist Count Ruvo. The cloven
hoof of French "emancipation" soon discovered itself.
The Directory acquainted Championnet that, since
"right of conquest" had prevailed, the vanquished
must pay for the luxury of defeat. Commissary-Gen-
eral Faypoult was already on his road from Paris as
collector of taxes by special appointment. His orders
were to expropriate even the palaces and museums, to
loot the very treasures of Pompeii. The General himself kicked at such exactions. He protested—and was
recalled to Paris. General Macdonald, who, as creature
of the Directory, had perhaps anticipated his own advantage, promptly stepped into his shoes. The Directory forwarded more "commissaries," with orders
from the "patriotic associations" to pillage the provinces and to "dictate Republican laws." The French
troops dared not linger too long at Naples, and eventually their whole garrison only amounted to two thousand five hundred. But their brief sojourn was long
enough to denude the city. They were billeted in Sir
William's houses, among the rest, and did infinite dam-
age to his treasures. Emma—his "Grecian," as her
husband delighted to call her—rued the vandalism
which now terrorised the town.

The lack of the Parthenopean Republic was an organised army with a capable leader. Calabria and
Apulia were at this very moment overrun by Corsican
adventurers, one of whom assumed the title of Prince
Francis, and pretended that he was the lawful heir to
the throne.

It was at this juncture that the King designated
Cardinal Ruffo his Vicar-General in place of Pignatelli, the absconder, and invested him with supreme
military command, although, at the same time, he em-

phatically bound him not to do more than suppress the rising, without previous consultation with his master; nor was he on any account at any time to treat with the rebels.

It should be noted at this his first introduction on to our scene, that so early as June 17, Hamilton and Nelson seem to have lost all confidence in him; and his behaviour a week later was to justify their discernment.

This singular priest-militant, whose rugged hardihood concealed astute subtlety, and who was at once Legate and Lazzarone, landed on the Calabrian coast to proclaim " a holy cause." He was the royal Robin Hood, while his Friar Tuck was the Sicilian brigand, Fra Diavolo. His cardinalate alienated from the " patriot " cause many of the priests, who by this time had joined hands with the insurgents; for they could never forget how the Queen had once withstood the Pope. The raising of his standard, and the co-operation of the Russian and Turkish frigates from Corfu, soon forced the French into an active provincial campaign. The Bourbonites had secured the fastness of Andia. The French stormed and took it. Their maltreatment of young girls had rendered them abominable even in the eyes of their better " patriot " allies, one of whom on this occasion, Prince Carafa, heading the " Neapolitan legion," chivalrously rescued a girl victim from their brutality. A long sequel of sickening butcheries on both sides followed. The French and the " patriots " shot down even old women. Ruffo and his savage bandits gave no quarter; yet they were welcomed as deliverers from rapine and murder. One by one the hill-strongholds, that France had taken, were seized by Ruffo for the King. By June the Republic had become limited afresh to Naples, and " patriot " Naples itself smarted under the greedy despotism of "commissary" Abrial, who now reigned in Macdonald's shoes, and chastised them with scorpions where the others had chastised them with whips.

The Royalist counter-stroke of April, with Ruffo for instrument, and subsequently a new "extraordinary" tribunal as executive, was long kept a secret, but it was divulged to the Jacobins through a remarkable woman —Luisa Molines Sanfelice. She and her cousin-husband had long before been banished for extravagance, but they had both been able to return in safety when the Revolution began. Her passion for a loyalist member of an Italianised Swiss family, Baccher, involved the wife in sedition. To her Baccher confided the King's commission, and the secret thus became disclosed to Vincenzo Coco, the Jacobin historian and renegade, who afterwards attached himself to the Bourbons. "*Cherchez la femme,*" indeed, is an adage exemplified throughout a rebellion abounding in "the rage of the vulture, the love of the turtle"—

"Oh wild as the accents of lovers' farewell,
Are the hearts which they bear, and the tales which they tell."

In September, 1800, this Luisa, well surnamed "the hapless," was to be respited by the Queen's compassion on the eve of her death-sentence. The King, however, in defiance both of his wife and of the amnesty which he had then solemnly proclaimed, refused to commute the sentence.

Except for Ruffo's commission, we have been too long absent from Palermo.

Nelson's thoughts were for the hard-beset Malta, the Neapolitan succours for which continued most unsatisfactory. Now, as a few months later, his endeavour was "so to *divide*" his "forces, that *all*" might "have security." To Ball, with characteristic generosity, he entrusted the Maltese opportunities of distinction. He

was still uneasy and unwell; and he was deeply dispirited, after his recent strain, at the home-slight offered him by the appointment of Sidney Smith to a
superior command, with Lord Grenville's orders for
his obedience, though on this point Lord Spencer soon
reassured him.   His stepson's ill-behaviour, though he
excused it to his wife, proved a fresh source of annoyance.   His Fanny, too, began to wonder at his neglect
of home affairs.   " If I have the happiness," he answered, " of seeing their Sicilian Majesties safe on the
throne again, it is probable I shall still be home in the
summer.   Good Sir William, Lady Hamilton and myself are the mainsprings of the machine which manages
what is going on in this country.   We are all bound to
England, when we can quit our posts with propriety."
The " we " and the " all " must have set her wondering the more.

The freedom of Palermo, among other honours, was
conferred on him in March, but the unfolding tragedy
of Naples added to his general discouragement.   He
was preoccupied in many directions.   The establishment of (in his own phrase) " the Vesuvian Republic,"
Pignatelli's armistice with the French, " in which the
name of the King was not mentioned," the surrender of
Leghorn to the French, boding a Tuscan revolution, incensed him as much as it did the royal family.   Sicily,
he thought, would soon be endangered.   The French
successes at Capua, their installation at Naples, so affected him, that he inclined to vindicate the royal
honour himself.   " I am ready," he wrote in mid-
March, " to assist in the enterprise.   I only wish to
die in the cause."   Jacobinism, he repeated, was ter-
rorism.   The agreeable surprise of General Sir Charles
Stuart's arrival in Sicily with a thousand troops, that
secured Messina against invasion, relieved and elated
both him and the court.   He even believed—for his

wishes ever fathered his thoughts—that these might expel the French from Naples.

France, indeed, was on his nerves and brain. So soon as he learned that the hero of Acre had given passports freeing the remnant of the French fleet off Syria and Egypt, he was beside himself: at any moment a new squadron might effect a junction with the Spanish frigates and bear down on the two Sicilies. By the close of March he had already despatched the truculent and sometimes ferocious Troubridge to Procida for the blockade of Naples. Much was hoped, too, from the co-operation of the Russian and Turkish fleets. It was quite possible, even now, that Britain might restore the Neapolitan monarch to his people. And in the meantime, with eyes alert to ensure preparedness in every direction, he mediated with the Bey of Tunis and freed Mohammedan slaves.

Nor below this tide of varying emotions is an undercurrent lacking of inward conflict. In his own heart a miniature revolution was also in process. The spell of Lady Hamilton was over him, and he struggled against the devious promptings of his heart. To protect Naples and Sicily against France had been the declared policy of his Government; to exterminate French predominance was his own chief ambition; he chafed against the survival of a single ship. " I *know*," he was soon to write, " it is His Majesty's pleasure that I should pay such attention to the safety of His Sicilian Majesty and his kingdom that *nothing shall induce* me to risk those objects of my special care." Every public motive riveted him to the spot where fascination lured and tempted. It is a mistake to imagine that Emma held him from duty; all his duties were performed, and to her last moment she protested to those most in his confidence, and best able to refute her if she erred, that her influence never tried to detain him. It was duty that actuated him—a duty, it is true, that jumped with inclination, and fatally fastened him to her side. Such was his health, that he had desired to quit the Mediterranean altogether. Away from the Mediterranean coasts, he could have steeled himself at any rate to absence, if not to forgetfulness. In the very centre of the seaboard that embodied the true interests of his country, and to which his instructions tied him, he was in hourly neighbourhood of his idol. She interpreted, translated, cheered, and companioned him. She contrasted with the soullessness of his wife. She was often his as well as her husband's amanuensis. She drank in every word of patriotic fervour, and redoubled it. Her courage spoke to his; so did her compassion and energy. Together they received the Maltese deputies. Together they listened, in disguise, to the talk of Sicilian taverns. Together they also went on errands of mercy. From the Queen she carried him perpetual information and praise. Through her and her husband he was able to work on Acton. Every British officer that landed with advices or despatches, every friendly though foreign crew, was welcomed at the table over which Emma presided. No veriest trifle that could assist them ever escaped her. Indeed, her lavish hospitality and the noisy heartiness of the coming and going guests oppressed the Ambassador, who sighed on the eve of superannuation for home and quiet, for the excitements of Christie's, and the fisherman's tranquil diplomacy. It was not the toils of the huntress that ensnared Nelson. It was Britain that demanded his vigilance and enchained him here; while for him, more and more, Britain's " guardian angel " was becoming Emma.

Imploring Sir Alexander Ball in February to return from Malta, she had avowed a foreboding that " Fate " might " carry " her " down."

A great shock had been followed by a great fear. The main body of the French army had gone, but the Neapolitan rebellion, if the French fleet managed to reach and rally it, might still engulf them all. Gallo was again playing the King off against the Queen. Who knew what might happen in this conspiracy of gods and men? And when she presaged some fatality, may she not also have pondered whither she herself was now drifting? The doom of Paolo and Francesca may well have been within the range of her Italian reading. To the complexity of her feelings I shall revert when I come to the events of a month afterwards. Only two years later she and Nelson were thus to poeticise the affection that was now ripening:—

LORD NELSON TO HIS GUARDIAN ANGEL.

"From my best cable tho' I'm forced to part,
I leave my anchor in my Angel's heart.
Love, like a pilot, shall the pledge defend,
And for a prong his happiest quiver lend."

ANSWER OF LORD NELSON'S GUARDIAN ANGEL.

"Go where you list, each thought of Emma's soul
Shall follow you from Indus to the Pole:
East, West, North, South, our minds shall never part;
Your Angel's loadstone shall be Nelson's heart.

Farewell! and o'er the wide, wide sea
    Bright glory's course pursue,
And adverse winds to love and me
    Prove fair to fame and you.
And when the dreaded hour of battle's nigh,
Your Angel's heart, which trembles at a sigh,
By your superior danger bolder grown,
Shall dauntless place itself before your own.
Happy, thrice happy, should her fond heart prove—
A shield to Valour, Constancy, and Love."

But a fresh influence was also, may be, about to steal into her being. To the pinch of adversity and her misgivings for the Queen she loved, was now being added the stress of a passion half realised but hard to resist. She would not have been the emotional woman that she was, if in some shape, however dimly, religion as consoler had not whispered in the recesses of her heart. Hitherto among her immediate surroundings only Nelson could have been called really religious. He was a strong Protestant. But as she beheld the Queen comforted by an older ritual and a communion less severe, it may have crossed her mind that the cere- monies which she had mocked as superstitions held in them some rare power of healing. Southern religion thrives on its adopted and hybrid forms, as to this day is attested by Sicilian peasants hugging the image of their swarthy saint; Sicilian reapers chanting their weird litany to the sinking sun; Sicilian farmers meting out their harvested grain by their image of the rosaried Madonna. There was at this time at Palermo an Abbé Campbell, who had followed the fugitives thither- ward. Twelve years before, he had been chaplain to the Neapolitan Embassy in London, and is said to have been the priest who secretly united the future George IV. to Mrs. Fitzherbert. He was a genial soul, in the world but not wholly of it, musical and romantic. He remained constant to Emma throughout her chequered fortunes, and in future years he often crosses her path again and Nelson's. One may guess that through him first arose those promptings that eventually made Emma a proselyte to the faith that, perhaps above others, openly welcomes the strayed and the fallen.

Troubridge girded to his work as Jacobin-killer in grim earnest. The Governor of Procida, its peasants and Ischia's, were loyal to the core. The English sailor was acclaimed by the people as a deliverer from a faction; and he was not over-squeamish in his task of quelling what Lord Bristol termed to Hamilton " that gang of thieves, pickpockets, highwaymen, cut-throats and cut-purses called the French Republic." " Oh! " wrote Troubridge to Nelson, " how I long to have a dash at the thieves." And again, " The villainy we must combat is great indeed. I have just flogged a rascal for loading bread with sand. The loaf was hung round his neck in sight of the people." The " trials " of rebels he admits to be " curious," as the culprits were frequently " not present." He actually apologised to Nelson, on the score of hot weather, for not sending him a Jacobin's head; with charming pleasantry he calls the donor " a jolly fellow." The " rascally nobles, tired of standing as common sentinels," confessed that sheer discomfort had loyalised them. Even here Lady Hamilton's energy was conspicuous. She exerted herself for the Queen in communicating with the island, while Troubridge in his turn forwarded documents to her. She had got conveyed to him a letter from the Queen intended for Pignatelli. The bearer, Troubridge's servant, was loaded by the noble with irons. " I trust before long," Troubridge exclaimed, " I shall have a pull at his nose for it. I have two or three to settle with if we get in." He was " mad " at the infamous conduct of the officers despatched to him by the King. They had violated discipline, and a promise was given that they should be court-martialled. But the most important statement of his despatches to Nelson relates to Caracciolo, who must have been trusted, or he would not have been suffered to return home whether his errand was his own or his master's. " I am now satisfied," declares Troubridge, " that he is a Jacobin. He came in the gunboat to Castellamare himself and spirited up the Jacobins." By April 7 Troubridge had reduced the Neapolitan islands.

Prospects at last looked brighter. Ruffo had nearly

subdued the provinces, and the Austrians at length, in
formal alliance with Naples, Russia, and the Porte, had
rejoiced the Queen by their victory at Padua. It was
commemorated by a salute from the British fleet. The
Bishop of Derry—now at Augsburg—communicated
the news to Emma in an amusing letter, which opens
with her own favourite " Hip, hip, hip, huzza, huzza,
huzza ! " Ball was now pushing forward the Maltese
operations, while Duckworth had been active near the
Balearic islands. On every point of the Mediterranean compass Nelson kept his watchful eye. But
for him the Mediterranean was mainly a theatre for
the as yet invisible French frigates. The spectre of
that squadron haunted him by night and day; he han-
kered after the moment when he could re-attack it. It
was for him what Godolphin was for Charles the Second—never in and never out of the way.

Early in May, the brig *L'Espoir* brought Nelson the
glad tidings that the French fleet had quitted Brest,
and had been seen off Oporto. He at once concerted
plans with Lord St. Vincent, Troubridge, and Duckworth. It was said to consist at most of nineteen
ships and ten frigates or sloops. Its destination was
unknown. By May its junction with the ships of
Spain had been notified.

Nelson made sure that the Two Sicilies were intended, and that France still hoped by one decisive
stroke to end at once monarchy and independence. He
pressed Lord St. Vincent on no account to remove him
from the impending action, wherever it might take
place. He feared that St. Vincent's failing health,
which necessitated his resignation, might help the
French to elude the commander's vigilance. In the
end, elude it they did.

He resolved to cruise off Maritimo as the likeliest
point of sight, and on May 13 he was on board the

Vanguard. But contrary winds intervened, and kept him waiting for Duckworth's vessels till the 20th, to his keen vexation. His absence heightened the attachment with which he had inspired the Hamiltons. " I can assure you," wrote Hamilton amid the festivities that even at such a moment celebrated the birth of a son to the Imperial House of Austria, " I can assure you that neither Emma nor I knew how much we loved you until this separation, and we are convinced your Lordship feels the same as we do." And on other occasions Sir William writes to Nelson most intimately and admiringly, dating one of his letters " near winding-up-watch hour." Two of his three remaining letters to Emma, before he started, open a little window both on to the interior of the Hamiltons' *ménage* and of his own heart. On the 12th he writes :—

" MY DEAR LADY HAMILTON,—Accept my sincere thanks for your kind letter. Nobody writes so well: therefore pray say not you write ill; for if you do, I will say what your goodness sometimes told me—' You lie!' I can read and perfectly understand every word you write. We drank your and Sir William's health. Troubridge, Louis, Hallowell and the new Portuguese captain dined here. I shall soon be at Palermo, for this business must very soon be settled. . . . I am pleased with little Mary: kiss her for me. I thank all the house for their regard. God bless you all! I shall send on shore if fine to-morrow; for the feluccas are going to leave us, and I am sea-sick. I have got the piece of wood for the tea-chest: it shall soon be sent. Pray, present my humble duty and gratitude to the Queen."

On the 19th—

" To tell you how dreary and uncomfortable the *Vanguard* appears, is only telling you what it is to go from the pleasantest society to a solitary cell, or from the dearest friends to no friends.   I am now perfectly the *great man*—not a creature near me.   From my heart I wish myself the little man again!   You and good Sir William have spoiled me for any place but with you.   I love Mrs. Cadogan.   You cannot conceive what I feel when I call you all to my remembrance, even to Mira, do not forget your faithful and affectionate, Nelson."

Indeed, all these days he was in constant correspondence with the Hamiltons.   On May 25, so great was his admiration for them, that he drew up his first codicil—a precursor of many to come—in their favour.   To Emma he bequeathed "the nearly round box" set with diamonds, the gift of the Sultan's mother; to her husband fifty guineas for a memorial ring.   For his risks were now great; he carried his life in his hands.   The French contingent should still be found: his efforts were bent on more ships, that success might be assured when the clash of arms must recur.

Up to May 28, when he again landed at Palermo, he was still without sight, without result, though not wholly without effect.   He resolved to withdraw some ships from Malta and concentrate his whole forces.   On June 8, as Rear-Admiral of the *Red,* he had shifted from the *Vanguard* to the *Foudroyant.*   By June 12 he heard of Lord St. Vincent's intention to return home, and his replacement by Lord Keith, with genuine distress.   "If you are sick," he wrote to him, " I will fag for you, and our dear Lady Hamilton will nurse you with the most affectionate attention.   Good Sir William will make you laugh with his wit and inexhaustible pleasantry. . . . Come then to your sincere friends."

Still not a glimpse of the French fleet.   But large

issues were pending. The very day before the date
of this invitation to his commander, the Queen herself
addressed to him a pleading letter. The state of
Naples, the uncertainty as to the enemy's movements,
had decided her on a definite plan. An expedition,
forestalling the arrival of the Gallic squadron, might
strike a bloodless blow. The bloodshed even of her
enemies was far, she urged, from her thoughts. The
heir-apparent, as representative of his family, would
accompany him and chafe the embers of Neapolitan
loyalty into a blaze. "Other duties" obliged her to
remain at Palermo. He would earn the "sincere and
profound gratitude" of his "devoted friend." At the
same time—and this is the key to after events—Ferdinand himself conferred on him the fullest powers.
In every sense of the word he was to be his plenipotentiary. Already a month before, Nelson had
despatched Foote with a commission to reduce the
mainland, as Troubridge had reduced the islands.
Foote, Thurn, and Governor Curtis had already issued
their proclamation of a Neapolitan blockade, and had
bidden the insurgents take advantage of clemency
while there was yet time. Had they only complied, a
chapter of misery would have been avoided; but, divided as they were, they still trusted to the invisible
French fleet. Short shrift was to be granted to rebels
and traitors. Only the misguided and the innocent
were to be spared. Already Foote reported that thirteen Jacobins had been hung. The Queen poured out
her renewed hopes and prayers to Lady Hamilton.

Emma was all devotion and excitement, yet misgivings blent with her hopes. Who could foretell the
issues? After all, the moment must decide. And
who could foresee her own part in this great struggle?
Out of a narrow room she had been lifted into the
spheres. Even as she pondered, Greville—Greville

of the suburban " retreat "—was writing to her husband that the eyes of Europe were now fixed on Italy.
He had already been trumpeting her own achievements
to the Prince of Wales: " Many and all " admired
her much; she had been " instrumental in good."
" Tell Lady Hamilton," was his message, " with my
kindest remembrances, that all her friends love her
more than ever, and those who did not know her admire her." Greville, then, had at length learned to
know her worth. His " crystals " would hardly have
weighed in the scale if, thirteen years ago, his ap-
praisement had been one of insight.

Nelson responded to the Queen with all his heart.
His zeal quickened with uncertainty. Lady Hamilton was the Queen's friend, and Lady Hamilton's
friends were his. Maria Carolina was " a great
woman," and greatness was his affinity. He thought
in dominants—the predominance of his country; and
Naples loyalised would signify France quelled. Ruffo
was fast advancing from the provinces against the forsworn city. The Neapolitan Jacobins were on tenter-
hooks for even an inkling of the French squadron,
their deliverer. What Nelson dreaded was that the
Franco-Hispanian force might be joined by ships from
Toulon. In that event he would be fighting against
heavy odds; and his " principle," as he afterwards assured Lord Spencer, " was to assist in driving the
French to the devil, and in restoring peace and happiness to mankind."

And still of that veiled flotilla not a token.

It was reported as bearing on the Italian coast. Nelson had been eager to set off within about a week of
the Queen's appeal. That appeal decided him to wait
one week longer. Maria Carolina was impatient for a
second Aboukir, and for such a stroke reinforcements
were needed. On June 12 he and Sir William were

still concerting their plans.   The Queen now used the
Hamiltons for her purposes and urged them to fasten
her champion's resolve by accompanying him.   Emma
was ill, worn with inward struggle and suspense; her
patroness was perpetually and anxiously inquiring
after her health, Sir William was almost prostrate with
indisposition.   He wrote that Emma " was unwell and
low-spirited with phantoms in her fertile brain that
torment her . . . too much Sensibility "; he hoped
Nelson was not " fretting " his " guts to fiddle-
strings."   Emma shrank from the turbid scenes that
she would be called upon to interpret and to encounter;
she also dimly dreaded the results of constant association with her hero.   But her knowledge of men, circumstances, and language would be indispensable on
this fateful errand, and already on June 12 she thus, as
Queen's advocate, besought Nelson :—

" Thursday evening, June 12.

" I have been with the Queen this evening.   She is
very miserable, and says, that although the people of
Naples are for them in general, yet things will not be
brought to that state of quietness and subordination
till the Fleet of Lord Nelson appears *off Naples*.   She
therefore begs, intreats, and conjures you, my dear
Lord, if it is possible, to arrange matters so as to
be able to go to Naples.   Sir William is writing for
General Acton's *answer*.   For God's sake consider it,
and do !   We will go with you if you will come and
fetch us.

" Sir William is ill; I am ill : it will do us good.
God bless you !   Ever, ever, yours sincerely."

The Queen's insistence, Emma's mediation, per-
meate every line.   Just after this manner, some thirteen years earlier, the mimic Muse had echoed Greville

in her answer to the invitation that first lured her to Naples.

Her heart was heavy with forebodings. She would have much to do and perhaps to suffer. She was charged with a triple task: to rehabilitate the Queen, to single out the traitors from the true amongst the notables, to assist Nelson in his "campaign." She knew that the risk would be great and the nervous strain severe. Privately, as well as publicly, she feared the uncertain upshot. Her phases of mind and mood and memory all joined in bodying forth the future. For thirteen years not a breath of scandal had sullied her name. She had long, indeed, been held up as a pattern of conjugal virtue. Yet Josiah Nisbet, the boy whom both she and his stepfather had generously helped and forgiven, far more and oftener indeed than his own mother, was already tattling to that mother of the Calypso who was detaining Ulysses. Hitherto she could honestly acquit herself of the imputation. So much that was glorious had happened in so few months, that her tender friendship had been absorbed by memories and reveries of glory. And for *her*, glory meant honour. This is the clue to her nature. To honour she fancied that she, like Nelson, was dedicating existence. And now, even while she justi-fied to herself the chances in relation to her own hus-band by the thought of a past debt amply repaid, she paused on the threshold of the irreparable, as the pale face of Nelson's unknown wife rose up before her. She had been only stiff and condescending to Emma's warm-hearted advances immediately after the battle of the Nile. Was this cold partner jealous then, and spiteful without an overt cause? Let her covert sus-picions dare their worst; Emma would brave them out. And another and higher feeling mixed with her agitations. She was quitting her much-loved mother, by whom she had always stood loyally, even when most to her disadvantage; by whom she was always to stand; whom, if that French navy fell in with them, she might possibly never see again. "My mother," she wrote when all was over, "is at Palermo, longing to see her Emma. You can't think how she is loved and respected by all. She has adopted a mode of living that is charming. She has good apartments in our house, always lives with us, dines, etc. etc. Only when she does not like it (for example at great dinners) she herself refuses, and has always a friend to dine with her; and the Signora Madre dell' Ambasciatrice is known all over Palermo, the same as she was at Naples. The Queen has been very kind to her in my absence, and went to see her, and told her she ought to be proud of her glorious and energick daughter, that has done so much in these last suffering months." Other chords in her being might be snapped asunder and replaced, but at least this pure note of daughterly devotion would never fail.

And if Emma was at once happy and tormented, so now was Nelson. He was racked alike by hopes and fears. His love for her was gradually vanquishing his allegiance to his wife, and his heart was fast triumphing over his conscience. He had not yet persuaded himself that his love accorded with the scheme divine, that his formal marriage was no longer consecrated, and that to profane it was not to profane a sacrament. It was barely a year since Captain Hallowell had presented him with the coffin framed out of his Egyptian spoils—a *memento mori* indeed. Every one remembers the strain of dejection about this date in his home letters, which have been constantly cited from Southey. "There is," he wrote, "no true happiness in this life, and in my present state I could quit it with a smile." He protested the same to his

old friend Davison, adding that his sole wish was to
" sink with honour into the grave." On the one side
beckoned the French enemy and Emma, on the other
the offended Fanny, his pious father, and the call of
God.

While, however, both the cause of his heart and the
voice that it loved were thus pleading with its doubts
and anxieties, vexation also spurred him into irretrievable decision. Lord Keith's interfering summons to Minorca had reached him. These orders he
resented and disobeyed, as he had so often disobeyed
unwarrantable orders before. Minorca was a bagatelle compared with the big issues now at stake, and
Minorca, moreover, was by this time comparatively
safe. " I will take care," he was soon to write, " that
no superior fleet shall annoy it, but many other countries are entrusted to my care." Jacobinism, the
French fleet—these were the dangers for Britain and
for Europe. His reply was that the " best defence "
was to " place himself alongside the French." He appealed from Lord St. Vincent's meddlesome successor
to Lord St. Vincent. " I cannot think myself justified in exposing the world—I may almost say—to be
plundered by these miscreants . . . I trust your lordship will not think me wrong . . . for agonised indeed was the mind of your lordship's faithful and affectionate servant." These were no sophistries, and
" wrong " St. Vincent certainly never held him. It
was not long before he learned that Lord Keith himself had sailed in search of the fleet which unluckily he
never found. Nelson still believed Naples to be that
fleet's objective, and in this conviction many private
advices supported him. But more than all, his resolve
to vindicate royalty against Jacobinism was strengthened by the fact that at this very moment his own,
and Emma's, grave suspicions concerning Cardinal

Ruffo's misuse of his powers were being strikingly confirmed by new and startling reports; while at the same time another Austrian success at Spezzia had fortified afresh the cause of loyalty. He discerned the moment for reclaiming the hotbed of Jacobinism. His mind was fixed. He would go.

On June 13, then, he embarked the young Crown Prince in the *Foudroyant* and hastened off once again, while the Hamiltons remained behind. The King had apparently forbidden the Queen to revisit the scene of disgrace, and reserved his own appearance for the necessity which Ruffo's double-dealing, that he still half-discredited, might entail. But on learning definite news near Maritimo that the French fleet in full force had at length got out of Toulon, and was now actually bound for the south coast, Nelson at once tacked, and once more returned to Palermo to gain time for Ball's and Duckworth's further reinforcements. He arrived the next day, and, to the Queen's infinite surprise, landed her son, who was at once taken by her to his father at Colli. Though Nelson still feared for Sicily, he had hoped to have re-departed immediately, but calms and obstacles intervened. Now that he was certain of his mission, he welcomed the company and invaluable aid of the Hamiltons, whose entreaties had overborne his consideration for their health and safety. Yet even now he would not receive them until he had made a fourth cruise of hurried survey and final preparation to the islands of Maritimo and Ustica. He started, therefore, on June 16, but five mornings afterwards he again heard from Hamilton the momentous certainty that Ruffo had dared to conclude a definite armistice with the Neapolitan rebels; while he also learned that the Jacobins were bragging that his return to Palermo was due to fear of the French fleet. The policy of the Cardinal and the insolence of the

rebels allowed not a moment to be lost.   Forthwith
he left his squadron once more and reached Palermo in
the afternoon.   A council was immediately held.
Ruffo, who, despite the despatches heralding Nelson's
voyage, had probably counted on his many false starts,
received warning of his imminent approach; the Hamiltons, in the full flush of excitement, were conveyed on
board the *Foudroyant;* Nelson, still longing for that
unconscionable fleet and reinvested by the King with
unlimited powers, started at once to cancel the infamous compact.   That same evening he had rejoined
his command off Ustica.   By noon on the 22nd the
united squadron weighed anchor for Naples—" stealing
on," wrote Hamilton to Acton, " with light winds,"
and " I believe the business will soon be done."

These dates and details have been minutely followed,
as tending to establish that what really decided Nelson's movements was the dearest wish of his heart—
the honour and interest of Great Britain.   After suppressing the enemies of all authority and order, he
still hoped to fall in with the long-hunted French fleet,
and to deal a death-blow to the universal enemy.   All
along, his convictions and motives must be taken into
account before the tribunal of history.   It would never
have been insinuated that he was a renegade to duty in
making Palermo the base of his many operations, and
the Neapolitan dynasty the touchstone of his country's
cause, if Lady Hamilton had not been in Sicily; in
Sicily he neither tarried nor dallied.   To estimate his
conduct, one should inquire if his policy could have
been called dereliction supposing her to have been
eliminated from its scene.   And what applies to him in
these matters henceforward applies to Emma, whose
whole soul is fast becoming coloured by his.   For a
space she must now act a minor, though by no means,
as will soon appear, a supernumerary part, as his col-

league in the real tragedy that now opens before us.

Thus at last he, with the Hamiltons, set sail on an errand which has constantly been described as tarnishing his fame.

Mr. Gutteridge's scholarlike and impartial review of all the intricate facts and documents has proved that Nelson neither exceeded his powers nor violated his conscience. In championing the royal house of Naples he was as entirely consistent with the declared policy of his country as with his own convictions. His error, if any, was one of judgment. In rebellions clemency is often the best policy, and proscription is always the worst. Happy indeed would it have been for Naples, and for Nelson, if during the next two months the King had not intervened as director, inquisitor, and hangman, if Cardinal Ruffo had not favoured the nobles and wished to restore the feudal system.

Before the *Foudroyant* proceeds further, let us glance at the intervening events in Naples.

In that citadel of turbulence much had again happened, and was happening to the court's knowledge, ere Nelson weighed anchor at Palermo. Before May even, the successful blockade of Corfu by the Russians and Turks had largely cleared · Ruffo's conquering course. The Austrians and Russians had prepared to drive the French from Upper Italy. In May, General Macdonald had already beaten a skilful retreat to the Po, leaving only a small detachment behind him to garrison the Neapolitan and Capuan castles. Benvenuto had welcomed the loyalists. By early June the Cardinal, close to the city, had succeeded in intercepting all communications by land. Schipani, a royalist officer of distinction, had disembarked his troops at Torre Annunziata. The Republican fleet, commanded by Caracciolo, now a rebel against his sovereign, had avoided close quarters; while that traitor, by compulsion as he pleaded, who two months ago had quitted Sicily in favour with his master, had even fired on the flag of the frigate *Minerva*.

· By the 13th of June—amid the solemn rites of the Lazzaroni's other patron, St. Antonio—Ruffo, with his miscellaneous forty thousand, gave battle on the side of Ponte Della Maddalena, and won. Duke Roccaromana, the people's old favourite, was now one of his generals, and the populace, tired of bloodshed and the " patriots," rejoiced at the hope of a royal restoration. The young Pepé, a boy-prisoner, has left an account of the terrible scenes that he witnessed. He saw the wretched captives, stripped and streaming with blood, being dragged along to confinement in the public granary by the bridge. He heard the Lazzaroni, " who used to look so honest, and to melt as their mountebanks recited the woes of ' Rinaldo,' shrieking and howling." He watched the clergy whipping the rabble with their words, till they threw stones at the miserable prisoners. Some of them Ruffo had to protect from brutal assaults. These were thrown into hospitals, all filth and disorder; while others feigned insanity to gain even this doubtful privilege. He beheld Vincenzo Ruvo, the " Cato " of the " patriots," and Jerocades, their " Father," bruised and bound; and he marked, huddled and draggled among their comrades, the " four poets," feebly striving to animate their starved spirits by snatches of broken song. He learned that the Castellamare garrison had also succumbed, but, above all, that Ruffo and Micheroux, a most intriguing agent for his Russian allies, were at last ready to grant a demand expressed by some of the " patriots " for a " truce " so as to end this pandemonium, and to arrange some terms of " capitulation " for the castles still in rebel occupation.

Terms of any kind the Lazzaroni, on their side, vehemently resisted; Ruffo was even accused of caballing to place his own brother on the throne. Nelson's own views of such unsanctioned capitulation had already been strikingly exemplified by his manifesto at Malta in the previous October—a point to which special attention should be drawn. Capitulation the French still stoutly rejected. Méjean, commandant of the French garrison in St. Elmo, still defended the dominating fortress, from which Ruffo would now have to dislodge him at the risk of the town's destruction. Their single hope was for a glimpse of the French fleet, which was as much the object of their yearning as Nelson's. Counting on this, in their sore straits they had refused every conciliatory overture. Counting on this again, Méjean's aim was to gain time by the threat that he would fire on the town unless Ruffo forbore to attack him. When on June 24 the first sight of Nelson's ships was descried in the distance, the "patriots" cheered to the echo. They deemed it was St. Louis to the rescue. To their dismay it proved St. George.

Micheroux's name, Ruffo's truce, and Nelson's arrival must recall us to what Captain Foote of the *Seahorse* had been doing in the interval. He appears as no diplomatist, but a most humane and honourable seaman. His powers had been strictly limited. He, like Troubridge, was a suppressor of rebellion. He was to co-operate with the Russians in the Neapolitan blockade. He does not seem to have been told by Ruffo—who had already received the second of several warnings—that since the insurgents had rejected initial offers, no armistice whatever could be entertained. In the event, Ruffo and the Russians overbore him.

Already, on June 13 and 14, Foote had been assisting Ruffo and his generals in a series of battles on the

coast, all of which had proved decisive discomfitures
for the rebels. Throughout, Ruffo trembled not only
for the town, but lest the Franco-Hispanian fleet should
be on them like a thief in the night. In disorder both
of troops and plans, amid Jacobin advisers, he temporised, and pressed on Foote the need of terms. He
also dreaded the results of the mob-violence displayed
in those awful scenes on the Ponte Maddalena. " The
duty," he informed Acton on June 21, just before the
capitulations were signed, " of controlling a score of
uneducated and subordinate chiefs, all intent on plunder, murder, and violence, is so terrible and complicated, that it is absolutely beyond my powers. . . .
If the surrender of the two castles is obtained, I hope
to restore complete quiet." He may have used the
imminence of the French fleet as a bogey to frighten
his coadjutors, and the imminence of his own attack
on St. Elmo as a lever for persuading the French commandant into assent. Fear for the city, for the situation, possessed him. St. Elmo was his object, but he
dreaded the danger from its guns. He deemed his
unauthorised compact warranted. Two days before it
was in train Foote had offered asylum on board the
Seahorse to the Dell' Uovo garrison, then about to be
stormed. Its answer was an indignant repulse : " We
want the indivisible Republic; for the Republic we will
die ! *Eloignez-vous, citoyen, vite, vite, vite!* " The
same day Ruffo himself told Foote that St. Elmo must
be assailed; it was useless now to think of capitulation.
He had previously hoped that both French and rebels
might surrender to the sailor, though they disdained
an ecclesiastic. And yet within the next few days he
was in close if unwilling league with Micheroux (the
King's minister attached to the Russian forces), whom
he feared to disoblige, and had sanctioned his arrangement with the rebels, which was subject to Méjean's

approval.   On June 21 he told Foote that the terms
were settled, yet he then wrote to Acton that he did
not know them.   He kept the court in long ignorance
of his manœuvres.   The strain of difficulty told on
his nerves.   Whatever his motives—and they were
suspected—his action, though far less than Micheroux's, was plainly equivocal, and while he mys-
tified Foote, he failed to give any clear lead to the
loyalists.

There is not much material to explain the tortuous
negotiations of this period.   The clue to them may perhaps be found in a desire to accord the patriots the
same honourable terms as would be due to the French.
If the rebels could secure these they would be more
than satisfied, while Méjean trusted to time and the
chance of the French squadron's arrival.   Another
motive was supplied by the hostages (including
Micheroux's brother and cousin) and the refugees in
the castles, among whom was Caracciolo, who, however, fled.   Some amount of underhand collusion
seems to have taken place now as afterwards.   Foote
was perplexed both by Ruffo's contradictory letters,
and by Micheroux, whose authority he refused to
recognise.   On June 19, by invitation, Micheroux attended a conference at St. Elmo, with Méjean, Massa
(commanding the Nuovo Castle), and Ruffo.   A draft
capitulation was signed with an armistice—afterwards
extended to the French—which was to last till the arrival of the boats at Toulon, conveying such rebels as
elected to go there, was notified.   The whole affair
was probably engineered by Micheroux in close touch
with Méjean.   Ruffo's compliance may be attributed
to the necessities of his position and the importance of
the Russian troops.   He and Micheroux alternately
laid the blame on each other's shoulders.   By the 23rd
the capitulation itself reached Foote, who was the last

to sign, and did so under a protest as to anything which might prejudice his king and country.

The document itself was most peculiar, considering the conditions of hostile and insurgent garrisons in the face of a successful conqueror. While it was conditional on Méjean's approval, it contained no mention of St. Elmo, and it was attended by a concurrent armistice, unspecified in it but very material to two of its main provisions. The truce's tenor may be gathered both from allusions in letters and from Nelson's emphatic memorandum, written before he had seen it, but read to and rejected by Ruffo. One must feel for the " patriots " in the mass, since they seem to have been ultimately deceived, and many of them were noble. One must detest the vindictiveness with which the royal house pursued its triumph, though all that Jacobinism meant at the time should be recalled. One must condemn the violence of the mob, for it was general and indiscriminate. But both the duplicity and the brutality were the outcome of the two despotisms which had so long been pitted against each other. Nor should it be forgotten that, as already noticed, Ferdinand himself had no objection to treat with the French, if only they would hand over St. Elmo to the loyalists. What he had strictly and constantly forbidden was any sort of capitulation for the *rebels*. And lastly it should be emphasised that, since on a previous occasion the rebels had broken a concluded truce, they might well repeat that perfidy. The city's horrors had been swelled by the reprisals of the Jacobins. They were now, in Hamilton's words, " reduced to a shabby condition," and it was this that led them to listen to the persuasions of Micheroux and the dictation of Méjean.

The terms of the armistice, according to Nelson's version of it, seem to have been as follows:—

It provided for a truce of twenty-one days, by the expiry of which the French and the patriot garrisons, *if unrelieved,* were to evacuate Naples. From Sacchinelli's account of the preliminaries, their transport was to be free, *i.e.* at the King's expense. No wonder that Foote found the terms of capitulation " very favourable to the Republicans," though he based his consent on the express grounds that Ruffo was Viceroy, and that St. Elmo could not " with propriety be attacked " till advices were received that the Republicans had reached Toulon.

Nelson, however, took a much stronger view of this transaction. All armistices were *reciprocal;* if *either* party were " relieved " or succoured within a given time, a *status quo* must result. This armistice, however, provided, and on the most monstrous conditions, for the interruption of hostilities pending the mere chance of the enemy being relieved. If the French fleet had appeared instead of his, no one could suppose that the rebels would keep their word. If, on the other hand, the King's army were, as it was now being, " relieved " by the British squadron, the truce was *ipso facto* determined. The very presence of Nelson's ships, therefore, annulled this armistice.

So much for the truce. Now for the capitulation.

The troops composing the garrisons were to keep possession of the forts till the boats for their safe-conduct to Toulon were ready to sail. They were then to march out *with all the honours of war.* Should they prefer it, they were granted the option of remaining " unmolested " at Naples instead of proceeding by sea. These terms were to comprise all prisoners of war. All hostages were to be freed, but Micheroux's brother and cousin, the Bishop of Avellino, and the Archbishop of Salerno, were to remain in St. Elmo and in Méjean's hands, until the arrival of those sent to Toulon should be ascertained. Every condition was subject to the French Méjean's approval. "They demand," wrote the raging Queen in her indignant comments, not "the approval of their sovereign, but the approval of a small number of Frenchmen. . . . What an absurdity to give hostages as though *we* were the conquered!"

This luckless treaty it was that intensified the morbid paroxysms of royal vengeance, for it converted the rebels of Naples into a *foreign* enemy. By insisting on amnesty as a right, by leaguing with the common foe, by rejecting more than one previous offer of clemency, by demanding their very utmost, they forfeited the least right to a grace which, however, it would have been far better in equity to have accorded. Ruffo, by owning himself unable to govern, by his helplessness to stem the riotous anarchy of vanquishers maddened by the suspicion of a second betrayal to the French, by his oblique manœuvres, by his open breach of the royal trust, endangered not only himself but the countrymen whom he had so bravely led, and whom even now he desired to benefit.

Such was the state of affairs when Nelson, rounding the Posilippo point with his nineteen ships, sailed into the bay, drew up his fleet facing the harbour, and eyed the white flags flying from the castle towers. The *Foudroyant* was hailed as an ark after the deluge. The quay was thronged with cheering loyalists. Ruffo, however, at his post by the bridge, must have been ill at ease. Nor could the Russians have been pleased, as they had reckoned on reaping the sole credit of a clever pacification. The poor patriots skulked and trembled in their fortresses. By night the whole city was all joy and illuminations, for Naples during the last few years had proved a kaleidoscope of massacre and merry-making. Not a minute was wasted by Nelson. He instantly signalled that the truce was ended. To Ruffo, through Hamilton, he communicated his fixed resolve " on no account to remain neutral." In accord with the Queen's advice, first to require a voluntary surrender, he further proposed to him that within two hours the French should be summoned to surrender, in which case they should receive a safe-conduct to France, but " as for the rebels and traitors, no power on earth" should " stand between their gracious King and them." He sent Ball and Troubridge with both these missives to the Cardinal, who flatly refused assent or concert. Next morning he sent them again, with no better result. He therefore himself notified to Méjean his curt summons to surrender, and to the rebels in the two castles that they must yield, and were forbidden " to embark or quit those places." The supple Cardinal, in his haste, had not only exceeded his commission, he had violated his express directions. Next evening Ruffo and Micheroux (who was not admitted) visited the *Foudroyant* to confer with Nelson. During the whole of this stormy interview the Hamiltons were present, Emma acting as interpretess. Nelson flatly repudiated all the subtleties of one called by Hamilton the pink of Italian finesse. He stood by the law that kings do not capitulate to rebels, and he dismissed Ruffo with his written opinion that the treaty needed to be ratified by his master. An Admiral, he added, was no match in such matters for a Cardinal.

All that day of June 25, letters, conferences, intrigues, confusion proceeded. From Palermo Acton wrote thrice. The foreign signatories entered a formal protest, probably arranged, and certainly carried by Micheroux to Nelson, who refused to recognise either it or him. Ruffo threatened to withdraw his riotous troops, and advised the rebels to profit by his treaty and retire by land—a course fatal for them. By night a trumpeter had even announced that this move had the sanction of Méjean, who had told Micheroux that if war was resumed he would not be answerable for consequences. Massa, who asked for a conference, however, repulsed all Ruffo's overtures as coercion. The whole of Naples lay between two suspended fires; and yet Ruffo, afraid of St. Elmo, now besought Nelson to land the troops, the offer of which he had put off that very morning. By the next evening the two castles had *unconditionally* surrendered. The royal colours streamed from their turrets. The loyalist nobles of the " Eletti " had started to implore the King's presence, and Ruffo, leagued with the feudal barons, must have trembled. *Feux de joie* blazed in all the streets, and from every window, side by side, waved the British and Neapolitan flags.

In the meantime neither had Emma's energy been dormant; she did more than copy, and interpret, and translate the *patois*. She was a woman of action. Her enthusiasm spread among the common people, who adored her. She conjured with the Queen's name :— " I had privily seen all the Loyal party, and having the head of the Lazzaronys an old friend, he came in the night of our arrival, and told me he had 90 thousand Lazeronis [*sic*] ready, at the holding up of his finger, but only twenty with arms. Lord Nelson, to whom I enterpreted, got a large supply of arms for the rest, and they were deposited with this man. In the mean time the Calabreas [*sic*] were comiting murders; the bombs we sent . . . were returned, and the city in confusion. I sent for this Pali, the *head of the Lazeroni,* and told him, in great confidence, that the King wou'd be soon at Naples, and that all that we required of him was to keep the city quiet for ten days from that moment. We gave him only one hundred of our marine

Lady Hamilton at the spinning wheel.

From the original painting by George Romney.

troops. He with these brave men kept all the town in order . . . and he is to *have promotion*. I have thro' him made 'the Queen's party,' and the people have prayed for her to come back, and she is now very popular. I send her every night a messenger to Palermo, with all the news and letters, and she gives me the orders the same [way]. I have given audiences to those of her party, and settled matters between the nobility and Her Majesty. She is not to see on her arrival any of her former evil counsellors, nor the women of fashion, alltho' Ladys of the Bedchamber, formerly her friends and companions, who did her dishonour by their desolute life. *All, all* is changed. She has been very *unfortunate;* but she is a good woman, and has sense enough to profit by her *past unhappiness,* and will make for the future *amende honorable* for the past. In short, if I can judge, it may turn out fortunate that the Neapolitans have had a dose of Republicanism. . . . *P.S.*—It wou'd be a charity to send me some things; for in saving all for my dear and royal friend, I lost my little all. Never mind."

Bravo! Emma, rash organiser and populariser of the Queen's party, bold equipper and encourager of Pali the Lazzaroni, who, when the King at last came to his own again, brought all his ninety thousand men to welcome him at sea. We shall hearken to Emma again ere long. For the present, the recital of sterner events must be resumed.

The plot, then, to place Naples at the mercy of the French had been foiled. The question that was to convulse the city on the following day was, *On what terms had the castles surrendered?*

In trying to disentangle the difficulties of the next few days, a distinction should be borne in mind between the *armistice* made by the Cardinal with the rebels (and afterwards with the French), and the

capitulation itself, which it was designed to further.
It would almost seem as if some of the rebels had already contrived to escape from the convent of St.
Martino, though not under the capitulatory clauses.
Nelson would be most unlikely to reconsider any of
these clauses, which he had peremptorily cancelled.
But it might be thought possible that he would respect
the *armistice,* which he had equally annulled. He
might forbear to attack the rebel castles and even St.
Elmo, with a view to their surrender. In exacting the
unconditional surrender of the rebels, of which he had
already given notice, and which he was again to notify,
he never wavered. But it will be found that for the
sake of the town's quietude, and pending some author-
itative announcement of the King's pleasure (possibly
recalling Ruffo), he did now temporarily desist from
a siege, and so far obliged Ruffo. Mr. Gutteridge has
shown by comparing and contrasting the documents,
that when Nelson suddenly informed the Cardinal on
June 26 that he would respect the armistice, he had no
thought of respecting the capitulation, and that in the
sequel he did not go back on his promise. It seems
likely that the two cases of armistice and capitulation
were so involved together by Micheroux and Ruffo as
to persuade the patriots that they were free to escape
under the terms of their convention, without submit-
ting themselves to the sovereign whom they had defied,
or abjuring the national foe.

From the confusions of many documents the situation can be clearly discerned. Méjean's main
thought was for his own garrison. Capua still held
out, and till it fell he disdained to surrender. His
threats to bombard the town embarrassed Nelson alike
and Ruffo; and, indeed, they were more than threats
for an intermittent fire from St. Elmo nightly terrified
Naples. Though Méjean had dictated the patriots'

capitulation, he had restricted himself to a precarious armistice. Micheroux praised his nobility and moderation, but he was not above the possibility of a bribe, and he was perhaps indifferent to the fate of the rebels so long as he could stave off his own surrender. They on their side were willing to sacrifice the lives of the hostages for the security of their compact. One is driven to suspect that it was through Micheroux and Ruffo that they came to believe that Nelson had suddenly and entirely changed his mind. On June 25, Ruffo even in offering them the choice of departure had warned them that Nelson refused to recognise their compact, and was master of the sea. That the next day they were misled by somebody into thinking that the treaty would be respected appears from a letter in July of ex-Commandant Aurora to Nelson, where he states his belief " in common with the garrison " of being " taken to Toulon." But their misleader was not Nelson. If they could be persuaded that in yielding they were free to go, the odium of consequences would be cast on the British Admiral.

Early on June 26 Hamilton informed Ruffo that Nelson had " resolved to do nothing that might break the *armistice* "; and this Nelson confirmed with his own hand.

Awaiting the King's mandate, he now humoured the Cardinal and forebore to attack the rebels, even while concerting measures against the French. His letter to Ruffo of June 26 breathes not a word about the capitulation, and a day earlier, Ruffo had handed Nelson's ultimatum to the castles. Nelson, it was afterwards alleged, signified in writing to Micheroux that he would carry out the *treaty*. But Micheroux owns that these declarations were unused, averring that his agent took over Castel Uovo, and the rebels marched out with honours of war. Troubridge, an eye-witness, is silent on these points, all of which Mr. Gutteridge traverses. Ruffo's own construction, however, of Nelson's promise was evidenced by a service of thanksgiving. That evening, Troubridge and Ball with 500 marines occupied the castles. Next day they made short work of the Jacobin insignia. They hewed down the Tree of Liberty and the red-capped giant. Rejoicing pervaded the town. The castle flags were expected on board the *Foudroyant*.

Ruffo, safe as he now felt from the King's certain anger, expressed his gratitude to Emma and her husband. Hamilton answered civilly, and his wife, who had been slaving at correspondence, must have rejoiced. Nelson was bound by no conditions whatever. If, as seems doubtful, he authorised the notice (attributed by Sacchinelli to Troubridge) that he would not oppose the embarkation, he went no further. A small quota of polaccas awaited the refugees. For the present, Nelson pledged his word that he would not molest them. But he promised no more. The day before, Acton was informing Hamilton that the King might very soon come in person, and that the Cardinal was probably at the end of his tether; while on the next he wrote rejoicing that the "infamous capitulation" had been rescinded. If Ruffo persisted, he must be arrested and deposed, and a direct communication from the King must by this time have reached Nelson. It reached him on June 28. Nelson at once ordered the *Seahorse* off to Palermo for the King's service, and he *now* distinctly warned the rebels that they "must submit to the King's clemency" under "pain of death."

It was this letter that decided the doom of the miserable patriots who, under these circumstances, had been caught in a death-trap. Had the King's directions been deferred Nelson would have stayed his hand.

As it was, the rebels instead of seeing the capitulations executed, were executed themselves. His warnings of June 25 and 28 had been disregarded by those who were somehow misled by his action next morning, which was designed to keep Ruffo quiet. Years afterwards, Nelson affirmed in a document dictated to Lady Hamilton: " I put aside the dishonourable treaty, and sent the rebels notice of it. Therefore, when the rebels surrendered, they came out of the castles as they ought, without any honours of war, and trusting to the judgment of their sovereign." And the British Government in October, 1799, fully endorsed Nelson's policy.

The King's good nature had hitherto been proverbial; it was the Queen and Acton who had hitherto shared the odium of repression. But Ferdinand was now at length his own master, and his latent cruelty emerged the more savage because it had been long in abeyance, and he had now heavy scores to settle with fawning courtiers and spurious loyalists. No quarter was to be given to these false prophets; not a man of them was to escape. In the ensuing hecatomb of slaughter the Queen acted from policy rather than revenge, while Emma was so compassionate that she thought it necessary to reason with her.

In Hamilton's missive to Acton of the following day—June 27—occurred a significant sentence :—

" Captain Troubridge is gone to execute the business, and the rebels on board of the polaccas cannot stir without a passport from Lord Nelson."

The heartrending scenes that shortly ensued may be inferred from the numerous documents transcribed in Mr. Gutteridge's masterly volume. The few appeals to Emma's intercession given in the Morrison papers and by Pettigrew must stand for many more. It is not a creditable contrast, that of the misery of Naples with the triumphal salvos and Te Deum at Palermo. *Væ Victoribus!*

That very night thirteen chained rebels were brought on board. The next day, the passengers awaiting deliverance in fourteen polaccas found themselves bondsmen in Nelson's ships. Nelson certainly did not underdo his part of avenging angel—the part of what the Queen styled his " heroic firmness." He was St. Michael against the seven devils of Jacobinism, and the whole iron vials of retribution were poured forth. He represented a King who had wronged before in his turn he had been wronged, and who had hoarded his injuries.

While the crowd on the quays vociferated with joy, it was not long before the dungeons of the fleet re-echoed to the groans and curses of ensnared and intercepted patriots. Emma must have shuddered as she kept to her cabin and tried to write to her Queen.

The thirteenth of the thirteen confined in the *Foudroyant* on that 27th of June, was Caracciolo. He had not been included in any amnesty. On the cession of the castles he had fled to the mountains, but had been dragged from his lair by a dastardly spy. Pale, ashamed, and trembling, unwashen and unkempt, he stood silent before the stern Nelson and Troubridge. Who could recognise in this quailing figure the proud son of a feudal prince, the commodore who had learned seamanship in England, the trusted adherent who had gone to Naples such a short time since apparently loyal, only to become Admiral of the rebel navy?

He had fired on his King's colours.

That was the sole thought in the breasts of the grim sailors who confronted him.

Such a catastrophe inspires horror, but of all the victims that were soon to glut the scaffold, Caracciolo had least the excuse of oppression. Many had been forced by the French into tempting posts on the provisional administration. Such, for example, was the errant but charming Domenico Cirillo, for whom Emma was to plead so warmly. Others, again, had been heroic. Such was Eleonora de Pimentel.

But Caracciolo, though he set up the plea of duress, had purposely left Sicily. He was powerful, he was trusted, and he had proved disloyal. He has figured as an old man bowed with years and care. He was still in the prime of life. He has been pictured as a veteran Casabianca. To Nelson he was a rat who left what he supposed was a sinking ship. It might be pleaded as a further extenuation that his estates had been ravaged, and that his hapless family was large. But every one's property had been plundered by the French, and not every one had turned rebel. And yet despair should always command pity, and the despair of treachery, perhaps, most of all, for it is the torment of a lost soul. Had Caracciolo lived under Nero, he might have died by himself opening a vein, like Vestinus. But, on the other hand, the great evil of unconstitutional monarchy lies in its proneness to visit crime with crime; as Tacitus has put it : " Scelera sceleribus tuenda."

The imagination of cherishing Italy and of free England has long enshrined him as the type of Liberty sacrificed in cold blood to Despotism, as innocent and murdered.

In England this idea mainly originated in the generous eloquence of Charles James Fox, who loved freedom, it is true, but loved politics also; that Fox, be it remembered, who, when in power, once politely told his Catholic supporters, in opposition, to go to the devil. More than sixty years later, the attitude of a section towards the case of Governor Eyre and the negroes presents a close analogy to the attitude of the same section towards the case of Nelson and Caracciolo.

Caracciolo had fired on his King's colours. From the yard-arm of that frigate he must hang. So thought his captors; so, perchance, thought Caracciolo as his ashy lips refused the relief of words. Nelson had himself requested Ruffo to deliver Caracciolo into his hands instead of sending him to be tried at Procida. He was not rhadamanthine, but he was an English Admiral; and the English had killed even Admiral Byng, whose crime—if crime it was—was a trifle compared with Caracciolo's. " To encourage the others," said Voltaire; " as an example," said Nelson.

The next day Caracciolo was " tried." Emma never beheld him. The process was short and sharp. He was condemned. Caracciolo was guilty before trial, but this summary trial was a farce. It would have been far juster—though the issue was undoubted—if Caracciolo had passed the ordeal of impartial judges. His Neapolitan inquisitors refused him the death of a gentleman, or even a day's reprieve for his poor soul's comfort. In vain the Hamiltons supplicated Nelson for these fitting mercies. Naturally humane, he was here relentless. He was neither lawyer nor priest. *He* had not been his judge. Caracciolo's own peers had pronounced him guilty of death, and Nelson sentenced him.

Caracciolo had fired at the *Minerva,* now commanded by our old friend Count Thurn, the sentinel of last December.

On June the 28th, at about five of the afternoon, the scarecrow of sedition swung, lashed to the *Minerva's* gallows. Though imprisonment, as was first suggested, would have been far humaner and wiser, Nelson might have echoed Homer's line:

" So perish all who do the like again."

The bay was alive with hundreds of boats crowded with thousands of loyalists. For two full hours he dangled in sight of a gloating mob, before the rope was cut, and its grisly burden dropped into the sea. As the big southern sun dipped suddenly below the waves which had once witnessed the revel by which Nero had enticed his own mother to destruction, one by one the little lights of boats and quays began to glimmer, the scent of flowers was wafted, the bells of church towers tolled over the ghostly waters. The shore was thronged with eager spectators, gesticulating, applauding, pointing at the mast where Caracciolo had expiated his treason.

Méjean had himself broken the truce by assailing the city with his fusillade. Nelson now attacked St. Elmo, while Troubridge, with his troops, invested it by land. Its fall was timed to greet the King's arrival.

The *Seahorse* brought him, together with Acton and Castelcicala, on the night of the 9th to the channel of Procida, where they awaited Nelson. Next morning they stepped together on to the deck of the *Foudroyant*. As the Admiral and his guests sailed into the gulf before the last shot had reduced the stronghold on the hill, the sea bristled with the barques, the two banks of the Chiaja with the dense array of his welcomers. At ten o'clock he anchored. The boom of cannon, the noise of batteries, the " shouts of Generals " acclaimed the restoration of the King amid the salutes of victory. The King had at last come to his own again. But, as Emma wrote, " Il est bon[ne] d'être chez le roi, mais mieux d'être chez soi[t]." She had toiled like a Trojan. " Our dear Lady," wrote Nelson a week later to her mother, "La Signora Madre," " has her time so much taken up with excuses from rebels, Jacobins, and fools, that she is every day most heartily tired. . . . I hope we shall very soon return to see you. Till then, recollect that we are restoring happiness to the Kingdom of Naples and doing good to millions." "The King," wrote Emma gravely, pouring out, two days afterwards, her triumphs to Greville, who must have opened wide his eyes as he read, "has bought his experience most dearly, but at last he knows his friends from his enemies, and also knows the defects of his former government, and is determined to remedy them; . . . his misfortunes have made him steady, and [to] look into himself. The Queen is not yet come. She sent me as her Deputy; for I am very popular, speak the Neapolitan language, and [am] considered, with Sir William, the friend of the people. The Queen is waiting at Palermo, and she has determined, as there has been a great outcry against her, not to risk coming with the King; for if he had not succeeded [on] his arrival, and not been well received, she wou'd not bear the blame or be in the way." "But"—and here we catch the true beat of Emma's heart—"But what a glory to our good King, to our Country, that *we*—our brave fleet, our great Nelson—have had the happiness of restoring the King to his throne, to the Neapolitans their much-loved King, and been the instrument of giving a future good and just government to the Neapolitans! . . . The guilty are punished and the faithful rewarded. I have not been on shore but once. The King gave us leave to go as far as St. Elmo's, to see the effect of the bombs! I saw at a distance our despoiled house in town, and Villa Emma, that have been plundered. Sir William's new apartment—a bomb burst in it! It made me so low-spirited, I don't desire to go again.

"We shall, as soon as the Government is fixed,

return to Palermo, and bring back the royal family; for I foresee not any permanent government till that event takes place. Nor wou'd it be politick, after all the hospitality the King and Queen received at Palermo, to carry them off in a hurry. So you see there is great management required. I am quite worn out. For I am interpreter to Lord Nelson, the King and Queen; and altogether feil quite shattered; but as things go well, that keeps me up. We dine now every day with the King at 12 o'clock. Dinner is over by one. His Majesty goes to sleep, and we sit down to write in this heat; and on board you may guess what we suffer. My mother is at Palermo, but I have an English lady [1] with me, who is of use to me, in writing, and helping to keep papers and things in order. We have given the King all the upper cabin, all but one room that we write in and receive the ladies who come to the King. Sir William and I have an apartment below in the ward-room, and as to Lord Nelson, he is here and there and everywhere. I never saw such zeal and activity in any one as in this wonderful man. My dearest Sir William, thank God, is well and of the greatest use now to the King. We hope Capua will fall in a few days, and then we will be able to return to Palermo. On Sunday last we had prayers on board. The King assisted, and was much pleased with the order, decency, and good behaviour of the men, the officers, etc."

The self-consciousness, the strenuousness, the devotion, the enthusiasm, the egotism, and yet the sympathy —all the old elements are here. She had thirsted for the blood and thunder of her girlhood's romances; she now beheld blood and thunder in reality. The "much-loved" King had a summary way of finishing off his enemies, and bribery as well as butchery reigned in

[1] Miss Cornelia Knight.

Naples. The Morrison Collection gives but three of the appeals to Lady Hamilton's kind heart. Of one the ring is tragic. A snatch of humour is welcome. A certain Englishman, Matthew Wade, was a loyalist in Naples. He it was who had begged Ruffo to grant him troops for the occupation of the castles. Troubles, in these troublous times, had fallen on his household, and I cannot refrain from subjoining a passage in a letter of his about them to Emma.

" I beg leave to remind your Ladyship that the Governour's finances is become very low, and I suppose in a short time I will lose my credit, as my house was plundered when I was in prison, under a pretext of finding papers and being a Royalist; and after, by the Calabrace before my return here, for being a Jacobine. The last was a dirty business, as they robbed my mother-in-law of her shift. She said six, tho' I never knew her and her daughter to have but three, as I well remember they usually disputed who was to put on the clean shift of a Sunday morning. However, I was obliged to buy six shifts in order to live quiet. Pray assure her Majesty and General Acton that I can't hold out much longer. Besides, my family is increased. I have got a cat and a horse which has been robbed from me by the Jacobines. I met him with a prince, and took emediately possession of him as my real proprity. . . . I am told a conspiracy has been discovered and a sum of money found, in order to let seventeen of the principal Jacobines escape, now confined (and they are marked for execution) in the Castell-Nuovo; they say the Governor (from whom they have taken the command) is deeply conserned in the business. I am sorry for him, tho' I have no acquaintance with the man, but I am told he is a brave man and a soldier. But there is something in the air of the climate that softens the nerve so much, that I never knew a man—nay, nor a woman of the country—that cou'd resist the temptation of gold." Thus Matthew Wade, humourist and philosopher.

The Vicariate of Naples was now reposed in the Duke of Salandra, who had always been loyal. Nelson appointed Troubridge Commodore of the Naples squadron, and presented him with the broad, red pennant. Nelson himself was soon to be elevated for a time to the chief Mediterranean command. The 1st of August was celebrated with as much rejoicing as the situation allowed. Nelson relates to his wife, not in " vanity " but in " gratitude," the King's toast, the royal salute from the Sicilian ships of war, the vessel turned into a Roman galley in the midst of which, among the " fixed lamps," stood a repetition of last year's " rostral column," the illuminations, the magnificent orchestra, the proud cantata—Nelson came, the invincible Nelson, and they were preserved and again made happy. Indeed, Leghorn and Capua had both surrendered, as well as Naples. By the 9th of August the *Foudroyant* with its jubilant inmates had returned to Palermo.

Emma had again triumphed. But at what a cost to her peace of mind ! A royal reign of terror had unnerved her. She was never to see " dear, dear Naples " again. Her husband leaned upon her daily more and more ; and yet the active association of nearly two months, which seemed like two years, had brought her and Nelson closer than ever together as affinities. All along it was the force and vigour of her character far more than her charms and accomplishments that appealed to him, and her unflagging strength of spirit had never displayed itself to greater advantage than during these trials of the last few months. She tended faster and faster towards some irrevocable step, the

very shadow of which perturbed while it allured her.
A note of discord jars on the whole tune of her
triumph.

On one of the short sea expeditions, so rumour goes,
that time had allowed them to join in making, a phantom had startled them.   Out of the depths the livid
body of Caracciolo, long immersed but still buoyant,
had risen from nothingness and fixed them with its
sightless gaze.

CHAPTER X

To December, 1800

THERE is an almost imperceptible turning-point in career, as in age, when the slope of the hill verges downwards. Emma had now reached her summit. Henceforward, in gradual curves, her path descends.

The royal *fête champêtre* at Palermo in Nelson's honour eclipsed each previous pageant. No splendour seemed adequate to the national gratitude. The Temple of Fame in the palace gardens, its exquisitely modelled group of Nelson led by Sir William to receive his wreath from the hands of Emma as Victory; the royal reception and embrace of the trio at its portals, and the laurel-wreaths with which Ferdinand crowned them; the Egyptian pyramids with their heroic inscriptions; the Turkish Admiral and his suite in their gorgeous trappings, grave and contemptuous of the homage paid to the fair sex; the young Prince Leopold in his midshipman's uniform, who, mounting the steps at the pedestal of Nelson's statue, crowned it with a diamond laurel-wreath to the strains of " See the Conquering Hero "; the whole court blazing with jewels emblematic of the allied conquests; the mimic battle of the Nile in fireworks; the new cantata of the " Happy Concord," and the whole Opera band, with the younger Senesino at their head, bursting at the close into " Rule

Britannia" and "God save the King"; the weather-beaten Nelson himself moved to tears—all these formed picturesque features of a memorable night. Lieutenant Parsons, an eye-witness, thus alludes to it and the tutelary goddess both of the royal house and its two defenders, by sword and pen:—

"A fairy scene . . . presided over by the Genius of Taste, whose attitudes were never equalled, and with a suavity of manner and a generous openness of mind and heart, where selfishness, with its unamiable concomitants, pride, envy, and jealousy, would never dwell —I mean Emma, Lady Hamilton. . . . The scene [of the young Prince crowning Nelson] was deeply affecting, and many a countenance that had looked with unconcern on the battle . . . now turned aside, ashamed of their . . . weakness." *Viva Nelson! Viva Miledi! Viva Hamilton!* rent the air.

Emma divided the honours with Nelson. A torrent of stanzas gushed from the Sicilian improvisatori; even surgeons burst into song.

But there were more substantial favours. Nelson received not only a magnificent sword of honour and caskets of remembrance, together with, a few months later, the newly founded order of merit, but, partly by means of Emma's advocacy, the title and estates of the Duchy of Bronte. These, however, through the mismanagement first of Gräfer and afterwards of Gibbs, yielded a poor and most precarious revenue for him, and, as will be seen hereafter, a fluctuating one for Emma, whose annuity was to be charged upon it. The title "Bronte," with its Greek derivation of thunder, so curiously according with the name of his vessel, caused Nelson afterwards to be continually styled by Emma and his sisters "Jove" the thunderer. Presents poured in upon him: the Crescent from the Grand Signior, the sword and cane from Zante, commemorating the deliverance of Greece, the grants from English companies. Nor was Emma without royal recognition. A queenly trousseau awaited her on her arrival, and she received regal jewels, valued, it was said, at six thousand pounds, but which she sold two years afterwards, to Nelson's admiration, for her husband's benefit. " Nestor," indeed, was becoming more and more involved in debt, and about this period he borrowed over two thousand pounds from Nelson. He was not only worried, but worn. He took offence at trifles, and had quarrelled even with Acton.

Nelson did not dally, though Downing Street pained him by its insinuations. From all these festivities his alertness at once returned to vigilance and service. Not a fortnight passed before—occupied as he was with every sort of multifarious correspondence—he sent Duckworth to protect the British trade, on the maintenance of which he laid infinite stress, at Lisbon and Oporto, to watch Cadiz, and to keep the Straits open. He minutely directed Ball's operations at Malta, still hampered by every vexatious delay on the Italian side, and by the follies of Nizza, the Portuguese Admiral. Early in September he charged Troubridge and Louis with their mission to Civita Vecchia, which within a month freed Rome from the French. Directly he received this most cheering intelligence, he himself started in the *Foudroyant* for Port Mahon, with the one object of concentrating every available force by land and sea on the complete reduction of Malta, which remained ever in his " thoughts, sleeping or waking." He did not land at Palermo till October, when he was able to announce to Sidney Smith (uniformly and magnanimously helped, praised, and counselled by him throughout) that Buonaparte had passed Corsica in a bombard steering for France. No crusader ever returned with more humility—contrast his going in *L'Orient*. All

the same this was ill news, and Nelson was furious also
at not receiving troops from Minorca, and at the frauds
of the victualling department.   He kept a sharp lookout on the Barbary States and pirates.   He deplored
the inactivity of the Russian squadron at La Valetta,
and he resented the Austrian demand for their presence elsewhere; his representations caused a " cool reception " to the Archduke's suite when they visited
Palermo.   By Christmas he cursed the stupidity which
had allowed Napoleon, hasting back for his strokes at
Paris, to elude the allies.   But above all, both he and
Emma strained every nerve to extort grain for starv-
ing Malta from the King and Queen of Naples chican-
ing with Acton to retain every bushel for their own
necessities.   Until, after " infamous " delays and falsi-
fied promises, the dole was granted which saved thirty
thousand of the Maltese loyalists from death, he
" cursed the day " he " ever served the King of Naples."   " Such," he wrote to Troubridge, " is the fever
of my brain this minute, that I assure you, on my honour, if the Palermo traitors were here, I would shoot
them first and myself afterwards."   Troubridge was
equally emphatic.   The Maltese deputies lodged under
Emma's roof.   She was their " Ambassadress."   It
was not long before Emma's services in this matter
were publicly recognised by the Czar, as Grand Master
of the Maltese Knights.   When he bestowed the Grand
Cross on Nelson and on Ball, he also bestowed it on
Lady Hamilton, with a special request to the King of
England for his licence to wear it there, the only occasion, as she was ever proud to relate, that it had ever
been conferred upon an Englishwoman.[1]   This order

---

[1] Cf. *Nelson Letters*, vol. 1. p. 271.   The vexed question of
whether she spent as much as £5000 on this matter scarcely re-
pays investigation.   The fact remains that her services were
sufficient for imperial recognition, and that the King of England

she wore next year at Vienna, and it still figures in a portrait of her taken there, as well as in a drawing of her in 1803 by Sir Thomas Lawrence.   She was styled "Dame Chevaliere of the Order of St. John of Jerusalem," and from this time forward Ball always addressed her as "sister."

But the Maltese embroilments were by no means the sole annoyances that distracted Nelson's sensitive nature.   He was stung to the quick by the Admiralty's complaints and suspicions.   "As a junior Flag officer, . . . without secretaries, etc.," he wrote home, "I have been thrown into a more extensive correspondence than ever perhaps fell to the lot of any Admiral, and into a political situation, I own, out of my sphere. . . . It is a fact that I have never but three times put my feet on the ground since December, 1798, and except to the court, that till after 8 o'clock at night I never relax from my business."   "Do not," he breaks out to Lord Spencer, "let the Admiralty write harshly to me—my generous soul cannot bear it, being conscious that it is entirely unmerited"; and, once more, to Commissioner Inglefield, "You must make allowances for a worn-out, blind, left-handed man."

Nor was he least tormented by the growing passion

allowed her to wear the order on her return. Her own account in a letter to Greville, hitherto uncited, is this: "I have rendered some service to the poor Maltese. I *got them* ten thousand pounds, and sent corn when they were in distress."—*Nelson Letters,* vol. i. p. 277. Her Prince Regent's Memorial alleges details: "I received the deputies, open'd their despatches, and without hesitation I went down to the port to try what could be done. I found lying there several vessels loaded with corn for Ragusa. I immediately purchased the cargoes: . . . this service Sir Alexander Ball in his letters to me, as well as to Lord Nelson, plainly states to be the means whereby he was enabled to preserve that important island. I had to borrow a considerable sum on this occasion, which I since repaid, and *with* my own private money this expended was nothing short of £5000."—Morrison MS. 1046.

of his heart. His utterances are despondent. The
East India Company had voted ten thousand pounds in
token of their gratitude. Two thousand pounds of it
he bestowed on his relations; the whole was placed at
his wife's disposal. " I that never yet had any money
to think about, should be surprised if I troubled my
head about it," he told his old intimate and business
manager, Davison (the rich contractor of St. James's
Square), whom, after the Nile battle, he had appointed
agent for his scanty prize-money. "In my state of
health, of what consequence is all the wealth of this
world? I took for granted that the East India Company would pay their noble gift to Lady Nelson; and
whether she lays it out in house or land, is, I assure
you, a matter of perfect indifference to me. . . . Oh!
my dear friend, if I have a morsel of bread and cheese
in comfort it is all I ask of kind Heaven, until I reach
the estate of six foot by two which I am fast approaching." It was not long before Maltese successes had
quite restored his spirits, and Ball could write to say
how happy it made him to think that " His Grace "
could enjoy exercise in company with the Hamiltons.
All this is characteristic of a tense organisation by turns
on the rack and on the rebound, yet with an evenness
of patriotism and purpose immovable beneath its
elasticity.

Emma's fever of enthusiasm showed no abatement.
She immediately gave Nelson the pine-appled teapot
which has this year been generously presented with
other relics to the Greenwich Painted Chamber. His
letters to her breathed an affectionate respect. " May
God almighty bless you," one of them closes, " and all
my friends about you, and believe me amongst the most
faithful and affectionate of your friends." Was she
not the " Victory " who had crowned him with honour?
He reposed such confidence in the Hamiltons that dur-

ing his absences he empowered them to open all his letters.

But already there appeared a seamier side to Emma's heroic gloss. The unreinstated Queen still ailed in health and spirits. She had set her heart on accompanying the King to Naples in his projected visit this November, yet he had flatly refused. She seems to have turned from the pious devotions which after her darling boy's death had engrossed her to the delirium of play. The King loved his quiet rubber, but he was no gambler. The Queen gambled furiously—all her moods were extreme; she was a medley of passions. She had been Emma's lucky star, but all along her evil genius. Emma for the first time was bitten by the mania. Sir William's fortunes were crippled; she might sometimes be seen nightly with piles of gold beside her on the green baize. Troubridge bluntly remonstrated. His remonstrance, however, he added, did not arise from any " impertinent interference, but from a wish to warn you of the ideas that are going about," and to " the construction put on things which may appear to your Ladyship innocent, and I make no doubt done with the best intention. Still, your enemies will, and do, give things a different colouring." To his delight, she promised him to play no more. That promise was shortlived; it was not likely to last. Women of Emma's buoyancy and volatile salt are not easily weaned from the false flutter of such a game. All along her vein had been one of thrill under uncertainty, and her whole course a cast for high stakes. " I wish not to trust to Dame Fortune too long," wrote Nelson to her in possible allusion; " she is a fickle dame, and I am no courtier." And reports—some of them untrue and most, exaggerated—were beginning to filter into England and affront the regularities of red-tape. Nelson was depicted as Rinaldo in Armida's bower.

He is not shown to have himself gambled, but it was rumoured that he assisted, half asleep, at these revels, till the small hours of the morning, and this though his father appears to have been unwell at the time. That she played with Nelson's money to the tune of £500 a night—a rumour hardly confirmed by his bankbook. That Sir William and he had nearly settled differences by duel—a preposterous idea. That the royal bounty to her amounted to a value some five times greater than it seemingly was. That the singers whom Emma was constantly befriending and recommending were a byword for their scandalous behaviour. It never crossed her mind that anybody wished her ill. Both the Hamiltons and Nelson had been living in an isolated fool's paradise of popularity, remote from the canons or the realities of England. They hugged the illusion of home popularity. Unpopularity, whether deserved or due to envy or ill-nature, usually comes as a shock and a surprise to those who have provoked it far less than Lady Hamilton. She had long passed the patronage of that English society which only condones in a *parvenue* what it can patronise. It now resented her intrusion, while it resented more, and with better reason, her perpetual association with Nelson, who owned himself happy with the Hamiltons alone, and suspicious of letters being opened. The Government too had now decided to recall Hamilton. "You may not know," Troubridge told her, "that you have many enemies. I therefore risk your displeasure by telling you. I am much gratified you have taken it, as *I meant it—purely good*. You tell me I must write you all my wants. The Queen is the only person who *pushes things; you must excuse me;* I trust nothing there," he continues with personal soreness, "nor do I, or ever shall ask from the court of Naples anything but for their service, and the *just demands* I have on them."

His motives leak out in the concluding sentences about Lord Keith: ". . . I should have been a very rich man if I had served George III. *instead of the King of Naples.* . . . The new Admiral, I suppose, will send us home—the new hands will *serve* them better, as they will soon be all from the *north, full of liberality and generosity, as all Scots are with some exceptions."* Emma's own account deserves to be cited also. It occurs in a letter to Greville, hitherto unnoticed, is perfectly truthful, and seeks to protect not herself, but her husband and Nelson:—" We are more united and comfortable than ever, in spite of the infamous Jacobin papers jealous of Lord Nelson's glory and Sir William's and mine. But we do not mind them. Lord N. is a truly vertuous and great man; and because we have been fagging, and ruining our health, and sacrificing every comfort in the cause of loyalty, our private characters are to be stabbed in the dark. First it was said Sir W. and Lord N. fought; then that we played and lost. First Sir W. and Lord N. live like brothers; next Lord N. never plays: and this I give you my word of honour. So I beg you will contradict any of these vile reports. Not that Sir W. and Lord N. mind it; and I get scolded by the Queen and all of them for having suffered one day's uneasiness." [1]

Yet she was by no means the slave of her new excitement. She tried to heal old wounds, she corresponded with diplomatists; she could not relinquish her part of female politician, the less so as Hamilton had now settled to return home on the first opportunity, and the Queen was desolated at the mere thought of separation.[2] The Duchess of Sorrentino besought her good

[1] *Nelson Letters,* vol. i. p. 269, Lady Hamilton to Greville, February 25, 1800.
[2] Morrison MS. 444, 484. In the first Hamilton tells Greville "the Queen is really so fond of Emma that the parting will be

offices from Vienna, and in urging her suit Emma
abused the King so roundly, that in his umbrage he
turned violently both on her and the Queen. A heated
scene ensued—so heated, indeed, that the monarch demanded Emma's death and threatened to throw her out
of the window for her contempt of court.[1]

Nelson's acting chief command expired on January
6, 1800. Ill, and with a fresh murmur of "unkind-
ness," he put himself under Lord Keith's directions at
Leghorn. The blockade of Malta, which had lasted
over a year, the as yet uncaptured remnant of the
French squadron from the Nile, the resolve that the
French army should not be suffered to quit Egypt—
these were the objects, now shared with Emma, of his
thoughts and of his dreams. He determined to run
the risk of independent action. To Malta he proceeded instantly, and he was transported with joy when
he captured *Le Généreux,* though he had yet to wait
for the eventual surrender of the single remaining
frigate to his officers. "I feel anxious," he wrote in
February to Emma, during his constant correspondence with the Hamiltons, "to get up with these ships,
and shall be unhappy not to take them myself, for first
my greatest happiness is to serve my gracious King
and Country, and I am envious only of glory; for if it
be a sin to covet glory, I am the most offending soul
alive. But *here I am* in a heavy sea and thick fog!—
Oh God! the wind subsided—but I trust to Providence
I shall have them. Eighteenth, in the evening, I have
got her—*Le Généreux*—thank God! twelve out of

a serious business." In the second, "Emma is in despair at the
thought of parting from the Queen." Emma herself says,
" . . . I am miserable to leave my dearest friend. She cannot
be consoled."—*Nelson Letters,* vol. i. p. 272.

[1] He became excellent friends, however, with her afterwards,
and joined in pleasant messages to her so late as 1803.

thirteen, only the *Guillaume Telle* remaining; I am after the others. I have not suffered the French Admiral to contaminate the *Foudroyant* by setting his foot in her." By the end of March the end of the Maltese blockade was in sight, and Nelson was back again in Palermo. His health was so "precarious," that he "dropped with a pain in his heart," and was "always in a fever." Troubridge was deputed to finish the Maltese operations. When Nelson heard of the capture of the *Guillaume Telle* through Long and Blackwood, his cup of thankfulness ran over, and his despatch to Nepean is a *Nunc dimittis*.

"Pray let me know," wrote Ball from Malta in March, "what Sir William Hamilton is determined on; he is the most amiable and accomplished man I know, and his heart is certainly one of the best in the world. I wish he and her Ladyship would pay me a visit; they are an irreparable loss to me. . . . I long to know Lord Nelson's determination." Ball had not long to wait. Nelson was anxious to settle affairs finally for Great Britain at Malta,—a settlement that eventually transferred it to Britain and greatly exasperated Maria Carolina. Sir William had now been definitely superseded by his unwelcome successor Paget, although he allowed himself the fond hope of a future return. He resolved to sail on the *Foudroyant,* accompanied by his friends and the indispensable poetess, Miss Knight. On April 23 they proceeded from Palermo to Syracuse— the scene of Emma's triumph by the waters of Arethusa. Her birthday was celebrated on board by toasts and songs. On May 3 they again set sail and anchored in St. Paul's Bay before the next evening.

Hitherto only rumour had been busy with Nelson's philanderings. Lord St. Vincent persisted to the last in saying that he and Emma were only a simpering edition of Romeo and Juliet—just a silly pair of sentimental fools.   And at this time Sir William seems to have thought the same; it was all Emma's " Sensibility," all Nelson's loyal devotion.   He was the idol of them both.   But this voyage southward under the large Sicilian stars marks the climax of that fence of passion, the first approaches, the feints, parries, and thrusts of which I have sought to depict.   The " three joined in one," as they called themselves, had long been unsevered.   From the date of the Malta visit, as events prove, the *liaison* between the two of the trio ceases to be one of hearts merely.   The Mediterranean has been the cradle of religion, of commerce, and of empire.   On the Mediterranean Nelson had won his spurs and ventured his greatest exploit; on it had happened the rise of Emma's passion and his own, and it was now to be the theatre of their fall.[1]

It has been well said that apologies only try to excuse what they fail to explain, and any apology for the bond which ever afterwards united them would be idle.   Yet a few reflections should be borne seriously in mind.   The firm tie that bound them, they themselves felt eternally binding; no passing whim had fastened it, nor any madness of a moment.   They had plighted a real troth which neither of them ever either broke or repented.   Both found and lost themselves in each other.   Their love was no sacrifice to lower instincts; it was a true link of hearts.   Nelson would have adored Emma had she not been so beautiful.   She worshipped him the more for never basking in court or official sunshine.   And their passion was lasting as well as deep.   Not even calumny has whispered that

[1] From a passage, however, in a letter from Nelson of February 17, 1801, it would seem to have happened earlier. Cf. Morrison MS. 516: "Ah! my dear friend, I did remember well the 12th February, and also the two months afterwards. I never shall forget them, and never be sorry for the consequences."

Emma was ever unfaithful even to Nelson's memory; and Nelson held their union, though unconsecrated, as wholly sacred and unalterable. If the light of their torch was not from heaven, at least its intensity was undimmed.

Their worst wrong, however, was to the defied and wounded wife. Cold letters had already reached Nelson, and rankling words may already have been exchanged; Lady Nelson's jealousy was justified, although as yet Nelson never meditated repudiation. Emma had no scruple in hardening his heart and her own towards one whom she had offended unseen and unprovoked; she would suffer none to dispute her dominion. Under her spell, Nelson perverted the whole scale of duty and of circumstance. In his enchanted eyes wedlock became sacrilege, and passion a sacrament; his insulted Fanny seemed the insulter; his Emma's dishonour, honour. The woman who had failed to nerve or share his genius, turned into an unworthy persecutress and termagant; she who had succeeded, into the pattern of womankind. The mistress of his home was confronted by the mistress of his heart, Vesta by Venus; nor did he for one moment doubt which was the interloper. Unregenerateness appeared grace to his warped vision. Nothing but sincerity can extenuate, nothing but sheer human nature can explain these deplorable transposals. The *reality* for him of this marriage of the spirit without the letter, blinded both of them to all other realities outside it. Emma's few surviving letters to him are those of an idolising wife. One unfamiliar sentence from one of his, written within a year of this period, speaks volumes: " I worship, nay, adore you, and if you was single, and I found you under a hedge, I would instantly marry you." [1]

[1] Morrison MS. 539, Nelson to Lady H., March 6, 1801.

But the part of Sir William in this strange alliance formed, perhaps, its strangest element. Throughout, even after Greville and the caricatures in the shop windows must have opened his eyes, he deliberately shut them. He never ceased his attachment to Emma or abated his chivalrous fealty to Nelson. Those feelings, incredible as it may sound, were genuinely reciprocated by both of them. He seems almost to have more than accepted that veil of mystification with which the next year was to shroud their intimacy. Indeed, it was Emma's care for Nelson's career, and Nelson's for her good name, that constrained the fiction. That a woman should join a daughter's devotion to an old husband with a wife's devotion to the lover of her choice, is a phenomenon in female psychology. Swift towards Stella and Vanessa, Goethe towards Mina and Bettina, are not the only men who have cherished a dual constancy; but, as a rule, the woman inconstant to one will prove inconstant to many others.

Miss Knight noticed how low-spirited Emma seemed on the return passage to Palermo. Indeed, the familiar stanzas of her composing, " Come, cheer up, fair Emma "—a line often repeated in Nelson's later letters—were prompted by this unaccountable melancholy.[1] Such dispiritment hardly betokens the mood of an adventuress intriguing to secure a successor to the fading Hamilton. Yet such was Lord Minto's conviction two years later. It is curious that the imputers of craft always deny her a spark of cleverness, and they must certainly have thought Nelson much

[1] Nelson, writing to Lady Hamilton in the following year (only three days before Horatia's birth), says: " When I consider that this day nine months was your birthday, and that although we had a gale of wind, yet I was happy and sang ' Come, cheer up, fair Emma,' etc., even the thoughts compared with this day make me melancholy."—Morrison MS. 503, January 26, 1801.

stupider than themselves.   Worldlings do not always know the world, still less the world of such a complex heart as Emma's.   Her feelings may perhaps be best imagined by her little poem sent to Nelson at the opening of his last year on earth.

"I think I have not lost my heart,
    Since I with truth can swear,
At every moment of my life,
    I feel my Nelson there.

If from thine Emma's breast her heart
    Were stolen or thrown away,
Where, where should she my Nelson's love
    Record, each happy day?

If from thine Emma's breast her heart
    Were stolen or flown away,
Where, where should she engrave, my Love,
    Each tender word you say?

Where, where should Emma treasure up
    Her Nelson's smiles and sighs,
Where mark with joy each secret look
    Of love from Nelson's eyes?

Then do not rob me of my heart,
    Unless you first forsake it;
And then so wretched it would be,
    Despair alone will take it." [1]

In these lines, surely, there is a ring of "*les larmes dans la voix.*"

In sixteen days the Maltese episode was over, but Palermo was not reached for eleven days more.   Nelson had pleaded complete exhaustion as his reason for being unable to continue at present in his subordinate command.   Lord Spencer sent him a dry and suspicious answer.   Nelson desired to recruit his health at home.   He bemoaned the supineness of those who

---

[1] *Nelson Letters,* vol. ii. p. 127.

might have prevented the fresh invasion of Italy. Already he had bidden his friend Davison to announce his impending return to Lady Nelson: " I fancy," the mutual friend wrote to her, " that your anxious mind will be relieved by receiving all that you hold sacred and valuable." She " alternated between a menace and a sigh." But she was not to behold him so soon as had been expected, or to test the truth of what had been darkly hinted. The Hamiltons were to be his companions, and the Queen had for the last three months been preparing a plan for their joint convenience. Now wholly bereft of her power over and the affection of her husband, vainly exerting herself to induce Lord Grenville to retain Hamilton at his post, dreading that England would withdraw her fleet, suspicious, too, that Britain might rob the Sicilies of Malta, she resolved, in her isolation, to visit her relatives at Vienna, after a private and political visit to Leghorn. The three princesses and Prince Leopold were to go with her, and Prince Castelcicala, bound on a special mission to the Court of St. James, was to head the train of a numerous suite. The French were now once more beginning to defeat the Austrians, and she longed to set off before it might be too late. What so natural as that the *Tria juncta in uno* should accompany her till the inevitable wrench of parting?

One of her letters to Emma three months previously reveals at once the state of her own perplexed and perplexing mind, her reliance on Emma's counsel, and the cause of Castelcicala's mission. So much depends on the point of view. Throughout, hers had been utterly alien to the average Englishwoman's:—

" MY DEAR LADY,—I have been compelled by a painful affair to delay my reply, and I write this, my dear friend, in great pain. . . . Do you remember that on Tuesday evening I asked you if you had received any letter; you told me no: my eyes filling with tears, I was obliged to leave you. I wrote that I was dreadfully depressed. . . . I send you the substance of my letter from Circello. The official one seems to contain no more, but as this fatal packet from Paget appears to hinge upon our not being left here without a minister during your husband's absence, I think it may yet be remedied. I am in despair. I am excessively angry with Circello for not having more strongly opposed it, and if you, my good, honest, true friends, quit us, let them leave Keith in the Mediterranean. We begin by losing you, our good friends, then our hero Nelson, and finally, the friendship and alliance of England; for a young man [Paget?] liable to misbehave himself through the temptations of wrong-headed men who will induce him to abuse his power, will not be tolerated, and troubles will arise from it. I grieve to cause you uneasiness; my own is concealed, but bitterly felt. I send you, my good friend, the original letter from Circello. Do not let Campbell see it, or know that you have seen it, and return it to-morrow morning. . . . Suggest to me what should be done to prevent this misfortune . . . both for the State and for my feelings. . . . *I will do whatever you counsel me.* . . . Do not afflict yourself. Tell the Chevalier I have never felt till now how much I am attached to him, how much I owe him. My eyes swim with tears, and I must finish by begging you to suggest to me what to do, and believe that all my life happy or wretched, wherever it may be, I shall be always your sincere, attached, tender, grateful, devoted, sorrowful friend."

None the less, the anniversary of King George's birthday was celebrated with undiminished fervour at Palermo. Every member of the royal family addressed separate letters of compliment to Lady Hamilton. Their Anglomania still prevailed.

Among these valedictions is a letter of less formal interest. Lady Betty Foster had commended a protégée—Miss Ashburner—to Emma's protection. She had married a Neapolitan, and, as Eliza Perconte, was now governess to one of the princesses. "With me," she says, "the old English proverb, 'out of sight, out of mind,' will never find a place." Emma had conciliated all but the Jacobins. Her unceremonious kindness had endeared her to many loving friends among the lowest as well as the highest. The sailors and the common people would have died for her. Her absence made a real void. Lord Bristol was now once more at Naples—it is a pity that the farewell of one so unaccountable is missing. Prince Belmonte's, however, is not, though it was addressed from Petersburg to Vienna. "I am so indebted to you," he writes in English, "and you deserve so much to be loved, that my gratitude and sincere friendship will last till my tomb. God bless you in your long travels."

Farewell was now said not only to Palermo, but to Italy. Nevermore did Emma behold "the land of the cypress and myrtle," the land of her hero's laurels, of her husband's adoption, of her own zenith. It must often hereafter have haunted her dreams.

She, with her husband, mother, and Miss Knight, accompanied the Queen and Nelson to Leghorn. They sailed on June 10, and anchored five days later, though Nelson's usual tempest prevented a landing for two days more. This marks the last of the *Foudroyant* for the chief actors in the memorable scenes of this and the previous year. It had proved a ship of history and of romance. Nelson had pressed the Government to put it at the Queen's disposal as far as Trieste, but it was promptly requisitioned for repairs; Mrs.

Grundy, in the person of Queen Charlotte, may have intervened. Bitterly disappointed, its barge's crew at once petitioned to be allowed to serve in any ship which their great Admiral might still choose for his homeward journey. The news that on July 11 Nelson had struck his flag spread consternation at Palermo.

For three weeks more they all tarried at Leghorn. Nelson and his party met with a royal welcome, and were conducted in state to the Cathedral with the Queen. All received ·splendid memorials from Maria Carolina. Emma's was a diamond necklace with ciphers of the royal children's names intertwined with locks of their hair. The Queen, in presenting it, assured her that it was she who had been their means of safety. Nor were they safe at present. The French army was gradually advancing towards Lucca in their immediate neighbourhood. Nelson sent a line of assurance to Acton that till safety was secured and plans were settled, he would not desert the Queen. Emma was still paramount; nor was it long before, and for the last time, she displayed that ready presence of mind, and power of popularity with crowds that had often astonished Maria Carolina, and contributed so much to Nelson's admiration. She had armed the Lazzaroni at Naples, she harangued and pacified the insurgents during their stay at Leghorn.

On July 17 they started together for Vienna by way of Florence, Ancona, and Trieste.

This journey, with its after stages of fresh pomp and pageant at Prague, at Dresden, and at Hamburg, was the most ill-advised step that Nelson and the Hamiltons could have taken. Had they proceeded, according to their original plan, by sea, they would never have so irritated the motherland which, after long absence, they were all revisiting. They were, indeed, quite ignorant of the prejudices which they would be called upon to combat. They deemed themselves children of the world by virtue of their association with great events, great persons, and a great career; but of our island-world they had grown curiously forgetful. Well, indeed, would it have been for them if they had remembered. They had lived in a hot-house; they were going into the fog. They had long been closely isolated in an inner, as well as an outer, world of their own. Every one, except the detestable Jacobins, had hymned their praises. Nelson's supreme renown had coloured every word and every action. For them the Neapolitan and Sicilian court stood for every court elsewhere. As it had been with the allies of Britain, so would it prove in Britain itself. They hugged their illusions. They were aware, of course, of whispers and comments and suspicions, but these they derided as the makeshifts of envious busybodies.[1] Even now Sir William gave out that he would shortly return, a more youthful Ambassador than ever, though he was even more worn out than Nelson. He and Emma were under the wing of the greatest hero on earth, who had only to sound the trumpet of his fame for the ramparts of official Jericho to fall. Emma herself was

[1] Lord Minto, writing from Vienna in March, 1800, and hoping that Nelson, who was worn to a shadow, would take Malta before returning home, says: "He does not seem at all conscious of the sort of discredit he has fallen into, or the cause of it, for he writes still not wisely about Lady Hamilton and all that   But it is hard to condemn and use ill a hero, as he is in his own element, for being foolish about a woman who has art enough to make fools of many wiser than an Admiral. . .   Sir William sends home to Lord Grenville the Emperor of Russia's letter . . . [about the Maltese decoration for the Maltese service].   All this is against them, but *they do not seem conscious.*"—*Minto Life and Letters*, vol. ii. p. 114.   On p. 139 Lady Minto writes, "His zeal for the public service seems entirely lost in his love and vanity, and they sit and flatter each other all day long."

in her most aggressive mood; " Nature " certainly now outweighed " Sensibility " : she would be an Ishmaelite in face of icy English officialism discrediting each of her words and suspecting her every step. She was at length conscious of what, in its very concealment, was about to rivet her for ever to her lover. She would brave it out with nerves of iron and front of brass, for that which other women were incapable of enduring, her strength and courage could achieve. At Vienna the Empress loaded Maria Carolina's intimate with attentions; with the Esterhazys she was the observed of all observers. The bitter parting with her Queen but nerved her to greater and louder demonstrations. When hushed diplomacy sneered and sniggered in pointedly remote corners, she raised her fine voice higher than ever to teach John Bull on the Continent a lesson of robustness. At the mere hint that English influence was hoping to dissuade the Saxon Elector from receiving one who was the friend of a Queen and an Empress, she protested, with a laugh, that she would knock him down. In the Saxon capital she braced herself to perform her Attitudes to perfection; nobody should guess her real condition. She was ill at ease, and to mask it she was all retaliation and defiance. The finical got upon her nerves, and she on theirs.

And, added to this, the tour itself combined the features of a royal progress and of a travelling show. At Vienna no attentions sufficed to prove the gratitude to Nelson, ay, and to Emma, of the Austrian house. Lady Minto herself, an old ally, but the wife of an Ambassador, who soon made up his mind never to " countenance " her, stood her sponsor at the drawing-room. The Bathyanis vied with the Esterhazys. Emma was constantly with Maria Carolina at Schönbrunn as the tearful hour of separation approached.

The Queen's parting letter, which begins " My dear
Lady and tender friend," contains one notable passage :
" May I soon have the consolation of seeing you again
at Naples. I repeat what I have already said, that at
all times and places, and under all circumstances,
Emma, dear Emma, shall be my friend and sister, and
this sentiment will remain unchanged. Receive my
thanks once more for all you have done, and for the
sincere friendship you have shown me. Let me hear
from you; I will manage to let you hear from me."
We shall see how Maria Carolina kept her word. It
was said that Emma refused from her the offer of a
large annuity. It has, of course, been denied that
Emma was ever endued with the grace of refusal.
But, quite apart from the natural pride of independence, which characterised her from her girlhood to
her grave, it is improbable that either Hamilton or
Nelson would have permitted her to be the pensioner
of a foreign court.

Banquets and functions abounded, and they were not
restricted to the court. Banker Arnstein—" the Goldsmid," as Lady Hamilton afterwards called him, " of
Germany "—showered his splendours upon them.
There were endless concerts, operas, entertainments,
excursions, visits of ceremony and of pleasure, shooting parties, water parties, and, it must be owned,
parties of cards. One of their fellow-guests at St.
Veit, a castle of the Esterhazys', has recorded his
hostile impressions. He was Lord Fitzharris, naturally annoyed to see her with Nelson, and he may have
lost his money in this encounter, and, possibly, his
temper.

" Sunday, grand fireworks. Monday (the *jour de
fête*), a very good ball. And yesterday, the *chasse*.
Nelson and the Hamiltons were there. We never sat
down to supper or dinner less than sixty or seventy

persons, in a fine hall superbly illuminated; in short, the whole in a most princely style. Nelson's health was drunk with flourish of trumpets and firing of cannon. Lady Hamilton is, without exception, the most coarse, ill-mannered, disagreeable woman we met with. The Princess with great kindness had got a number of musicians, and the famous Haydn, who is in their service, to play, knowing Lady H. was fond of music. Instead of attending to them, she sat down to the faro table, played Nelson's cards for him, and won between £300 and £400. . . ." Haydn, it must be thought, was hardly a suitable accompaniment to cards.

When, after Dresden with its fussy state and so-lemnity, they embarked on the Elbe for Hamburg, a stock passage in the diaries of a charming woman re-lates how that other Elliot, who was minister here (there was always an Elliot), was pained to the quick of his refinement by the noise of Emma and her party; how undignified Nelson's excitability appeared to all; how Sir William, to prove his nimbleness, " hopped " on " his backbone," his legs, star and ribbon " all flying about in the air "; how he and his friends withdrew shuddering at the shock of such breaches of taste; how relieved they were when bated breath was restored, and they were quit of these oddities and vulgarities; how, when the Nelsonians at last got on board, they looked like a troupe of strolling players; how Mrs. Cadogan immediately began to cook the Irish stew for which her daughter clamoured, while Emma's French maid bawled out coarse abuse about forgotten provi-sions. Most of this is probably true, but here again the point of view needs adjusting. Fastidiousness is as movable, and sometimes as unbearable, a term as vulgarity, and no doubt the stiff Elliot would have been equally troubled at a violent sneeze, at any undue

emphasis whatever, or infringement of etiquette. He
had, it must be owned, good reason for being shocked
at Emma's want of manners. But over-nicety has its
own pitfalls also. There have been people who eat
dry toast with a knife and fork. There are others
who shiver at the stir of an unconventional footfall on
the pile carpets of " culture." At any rate, till now
nobody had ever reproached Sir William, a paragon of
" taste," with violating the semblances of decorum.
However we may regret Emma's unpolished " coarse-
ness," at least this is true : blatant and self-assertive
or not, she had certainly carried her own life and the
lives of others in her hand. The daughter of the
servants' hall had braved crisis without blenching.
The son of the Foreign Office had of necessity performed its function of words, and had naturally sacrificed himself to the *comme il faut*.

But if Emma, at bay, thus misbehaved, whither were
her inmost thoughts wandering?

She was thinking of how she could carry matters
through, of what would become of her poor Sir William. She was thinking of Greville's reception, of
Romney and Hayley and Flaxman, and her old friends.
And of those new friends which Nelson had promised
and described to her ; of his pious and revered father,
whose heart must be broken if ever he guessed the
truth ; of his favourite brother Maurice, whose poor,
blind " wife," beloved and befriended by Nelson till
she died, was no more his wedded partner than she was
Nelson's ; of his eldest brother—the pompous and
bishopric-hunting " Reverend," a schemer and a gour-
mand, who added the sentimental selfishness of Har-
old Skimpole to the mock humility of Mr. Pecksniff ;
of that brother's cheery, bustling little wife ; of their
pet daughter Charlotte, whom the father always styled
his " jewel " ; of the son already destined for the

navy, and long afterwards designated by Nelson to marry Horatia; of his two plain-speaking, plain-living sisters—sickly Mrs. Matcham with her brood of eight, and a husband always absent, ever changing plans and abodes; of Mrs. Bolton, more prosperous and more ambitious, with the two rather quarrelsome daughters for whom she coveted an entry into the world of " deportment " and fashion; of Davison, the hero's fickle factotum, whom Nelson had already requested to find inexpensive lodgings in London. Beckford, the magnificent, had put his house in Grosvenor Square at the disposal of the Hamiltons. It was an offer of self-interest, for he was already manœuvring to rehabilitate himself by bribing his embarrassed kinsman into procuring him a peerage, and the astute Greville suspected his generosity from the first.   Indeed he wrote to Sir Joseph Banks that he had warned his uncle of " consequences," and that he " hoped to put him out of the line of ridicule," even if he could not " help him to the comfort and credit to which his character and good qualities entitle him."

At Vienna Emma had found Nelson yet another factotum in the person of the interpreter Oliver, who during the next five years was so often to be the depositary of their secret correspondence.

From Dresden the Nelsonians repaired to Altona, from Altona to Hamburg. Their sojourn there was the most interesting of all, though it only lasted ten days, before the three embarked in the *St. George* packet-boat for London.   There Emma, who had met the young poet Goethe, now met, and was appreciated by, the aged poet Klopstock.   There Nelson met, and afterwards munificently befriended, the unfortunate General Dumouriez.   There the Lutheran pastor hastened many miles to implore the signature of the great man for the flyleaf of his Bible.   Hamburg was en-

raptured over Emma's "Attitudes" and her personality, which called forth an interesting book by a well-
known author. It was the more enraptured when the
whole party witnessed a performance at the "German
Theatre." Both Emma and Nelson exhibited their
usual generosity towards the "poor devils" who applied to them. Another and a different experience may
be also mentioned as indicating how really artless they
were. A wine merchant of the city hastened to beg
the hero's acceptance of his offering—six bottles of
the rarest hock, dating from the vintage of 1625.
Emma was warmly grateful, and urged Nelson to receive the present. Nelson took it with the thankful
compliment that he would drink a bottle of it after
each future victory, in "honour of the donor." This
"respectable" wine merchant cannot have been so
simple a benefactor as he appeared. Hock one hundred and eighty years old must have been quite un-
drinkable, and only fit for a museum.

And Nelson was wondering whether and how his
wife would greet his arrival. When, on November
6, they reached Yarmouth, after such a storm that
only he could force the pilot to land, that wife was
absent from his enthusiastic welcomers. Amid the
music, the bunting, the deputations that seized his one
hand, the offended Fanny was missing. The carriage
was dragged by the cheerers to the Wrestlers' Inn, before which the troops paraded. The whole party
marched in state churchward to a service of thanksgiving; the town was illuminated, his departure was
escorted by cavalry; but the wife, no longer of his
bosom, stayed in London with the dear old rector,
who had hurried up to greet him from Burnham-
Thorpe. The two days before the capital huzza'd him,
his route was one triumphal procession. His own
Ipswich rivalled Yarmouth, and Colchester, Ips-

wich. But as the acclamations of the countryside rang
in their ears, a single thought must have possessed the
minds of Nelson and of Emma—the thought of Fanny.
Nelson entered London in full uniform, with the three
stars and the two golden medals on his breast.[1] It was
Sunday—a day which witnessed many of the crises in
his career. They all drove together to Nerot's Hotel
in King Street, where Greville had already called to
welcome his uncle, ailing and anxious about his pension. While Lady Hamilton disguised her tremor,
Nelson was left alone with his proud father and the indignant wife, who had believed, and brooded over,
every whisper against him—even the malicious slan-
ders of the Jacobins. Joy could not be expected of
her, but a word of pride in the achievements that had
immortalised him, and won her the very title which she
immoderately prized, she might surely have shown.
Not a soft answer escaped her pinched lips. That
night must have been one of hot entreaty on the one
side, and cold recrimination on the other. Her mind
was thoroughly poisoned against him. He at once
presented himself at the Admiralty, just as Hamilton,
under Greville's tutelage, at once repaired to my Lord
Grenville in Cleveland Row. Together the three attended the Lord Mayor's banquet the following night,
when the sword of honour was presented, after the citi-
zens of London, like those of Yarmouth, had un-
horsed the car of triumph and themselves drawn it
along the streets lined with applauding crowds, to the
Mansion House. There also Lady Nelson was absent.
Whether business or ovation detained him, the spectre
abode in its cupboard. For a time their open breach

[1] Medals were struck to commemorate his return. On one
side is the medallion; on the reverse Britannia crowning his
vessel with laurels. The legend round runs: "Hail, virtuous
hero! Thy victories we acknowledge, and thy God." And
underneath, "Return to England, November 5, 1800."

was patched up, but nevertheless the distance between them widened. Nelson was to aggravate it by harping on Emma's virtues and graces till Fanny sickened at her very name. Nor could Emma's early and friendly approaches, in which Sir William joined, have been expected to bridge it over.[1]

Emma soon resumed her post as his amanuensis, his companion, his almoner, his *vade mecum*. Nelson again accompanied the Hamiltons on their speedy visit to Fonthill, whose bizarre master desired to compound for a peerage with Sir William. Prints exist of the postchaise with postilions, flambeaux in hand, driving the Nelsonians into the Gothic archway of that fantastic demesne. Nelson may well have thought, " Que diable allait-il faire dans cette galère ! " Beckford had addressed his invitation to Emma in terms of extravagant flattery, to his " Madonna della Gloria." He singled out, too, her performance as Cleopatra for critical and special admiration. Yet so insincere was he, that some forty years afterwards he not only belittled her beauty to Cyrus Redding, but claimed the entire brunt of service to Britain for Hamilton, while his ignorance of facts is shown by the egregious errors in his account.

Nelson and Emma were always in evidence together. He ordered his wife to appear in public with himself and the Hamiltons at the theatre. Emma's sudden faintness, and Lady Nelson's withdrawal from their

[1] Cf. a remarkable letter from Lady Hamilton to Lady Nelson. It bears no date, but must refer to a time shortly after their return.—" I would have done myself the honour of calling on you and Lord Nelson this day, but I am not well nor in spirits. Sir William and myself feel the loss of our good friend, the good Lord Nelson. Permit me in the morning to have the pleasure of seeing you, and hoping, my dear Lady Nelson, the continuance of your friendship, which will be in Sir William and myself for ever lasting to you and your family." And she closes by Sir William's proffer of any service possible.

box with her, gave the wife the first inkling of a secret worse even than she had suspected. A violent scene is said to have occurred between the two women, and Lady Hamilton used to assert that Nelson wandered about all night in his misery, and presented himself early next morning to implore the comfort and the companionship of his friends. Emma and Nelson continued all injured innocence. The circumstances of Horatia's birth in the January following were to be carefully veiled even from Horatia herself; nor were they ever proved till some fifty years afterwards, and even then generally disbelieved. Henceforward Nelson and his wife were strangers; further efforts at reconciliation failed. By the March of 1801 he had provided for and repudiated her. " I have done," he was to write, " all in my power for you, and if I died, you will find I have done the same. Therefore, my only wish is to be left to myself, and wishing you every happiness, believe that I am your affectionate Nelson and Bronte." On this " letter of dismissal " she endorsed her " astonishment." That astonishment must surely have been strained.

Without question, sympathy is her due. Without question she had been grievously wronged. But her bearing, both before she had reason to be convinced of the fact and afterwards, was such perhaps as to decrease her deserts. She seems to have been more aggrieved than heart-stricken. From this time forth she withdrew completely from every member of his family except Maurice and the good old father. At Bath, or in London, she sulked and hugged her grievance, her virtue, her money, and her rank. She proceeded —naturally—to babble of the woman who had injured her, and the husband of whom she had been despoiled. Nelson's brother and sisters, who accepted Emma, always entitled her " Tom Tit," nor would they concede a grain of true love to her disposition. That she was not the helpmeet for a hero was not her fault; it was her drawback and misfortune. She failed in the temperament that understands temperament, and the spirit that answers and applauds. Her piety never sought to win back the wanderer. She incensed him by desiring even now to rent Shelburne House. She caused him to feel " an outcast on shore." While she could have avenged her cause by suing for a divorce, she preferred to avenge herself on the culprits by their punishment in being barred from wedlock. After Nelson's death she litigated with his successor.

This was Emma's doing, and Nelson's. They were both pitiless, while the other was implacable. Emma could be far tenderer than gentle. She was never a gentlewoman, nor was over-delicacy her foible. Her " Sensibility " did not extend to her discarded rival, whose very wardrobe she could handle, at Nelson's bidding, and return. She rode rough-shod over poor Lady Nelson's discomfiture. " Tom Tit," she told Mrs. William Nelson in the next February, " does not come to town. She offered to go down, but was refused. She only wanted to go to do mischief to all the great Jove's relations. 'Tis now shown, all her ill treatment and bad *heart*. Jove has found it out."

It is a sorry, but hardly a sordid spectacle. Rather it is, in a sense, volcanic.[1] Here is no barter, no balance of interests or convenience. It is a passionate convulsion, which uprooted the wife. I can but vary the apophthegm already quoted: " Apologies only try to explain what they cannot undo."

[1] On January 25 following Nelson wrote to her: " Where friendship is of so strong a cast as ours, it is no easy matter to shake it. Mine is as fixed as Mount Etna, and as warm in the inside as that mountain."—Morrison MS. 502.

CHAPTER XI

IT was not long before the Hamiltons were installed in a new abode, No. 23 Piccadilly, one of the smaller houses fronting the Green Park. Sir William had been querulous over the loss of so many treasures in the *Colossus*—among them the second version of Romney's " Bacchante," which has never to this day reappeared. Most of their furniture had been rifled by French Jacobins. Emma promptly sold enough of her jewels to buy furniture for the new mansion, and these purchases were afterwards legally assigned to her by her husband.

Among the first visitors to their new home were Hayley and Flaxman, whom Emma had eagerly invited. A letter from the latter to the former commemorates an interesting little scene. As they entered, Nelson was just leaving the room. " Pray stop a little, my Lord," exclaimed Sir William; " I desire you to·shake hands with Mr. Flaxman, for he is a man as extraordinary, in his way, as you are in yours. Believe me, he is the sculptor who ought to make your monument." " Is he? " replied Nelson, seizing his hand with alacrity; " then I heartily wish he may." And eventually he did.

This year was to link her and Nelson for ever. It was the year of Horatia's birth, of the Copenhagen victory, of the preliminaries to the acquirement of Merton.

> "Sooner shall Britain's sons resign
>   The empire of the sea;
> Than Henry shall renounce his faith
>   *And plighted vows to thee!*
>
> And waves on waves shall cease to roll,
>   And tides forget to flow,
> Ere thy true Henry's constant love
>   Or ebb or change shall know."[1]

"I want but one true heart; there can be but one love, although many real well-wishers," is his prose version in a hitherto unpublished letter.

These were the refrains of all this year, and, indeed, of the little span allotted to Nelson before he was no more seen.

Emma had an ordeal to pass through with a light step and a bright face. She had forfeited the comfort of that sense of innocence which she had welcomed ten years before. She awaited Nelson's child, and none but her mother and Nelson were to know it. She was to seem as if nothing chequered her dance of gaiety. Old friends flocked around her. Greville was a constant caller, curious about her, vigilant over his uncle. Her old supporter, Louis Dutens, was also in attendance. The stricken Romney, who pined for the sight of her, was now in the north, but Hayley and Flaxman we have seen in her company. There was Mrs. Denis, too, her singing friend at Naples, and the hardly used Mrs. Billington. And—for she was always loyal to them—she delighted in beholding or hearing from her humble kindred again: the Connors, the Reynoldses, the Moores of Liverpool; and that

[1] Nelson's verses enclosed in his letter to Emma of February 11, 1801; *Nelson Letters,* vol. 1. p. 30.

daughter, long ago parted from her by Greville, Emma
"Carew." And there were Bohemian refugees from
Naples, the Banti among their number, who in after
days were less than grateful to their impetuous
patroness. New friends also pressed for her acquaintance. There was Nelson's "smart" relative Mrs.
Walpole, a fribble of fashion in the Prince of Wales's
set, Mrs. Udney and a Mrs. Nisbet, with their frivolous
on-hangers. But, more acceptable than these, were
Nelson's country sisters and sister-in-law, who loved
her at first sight and never relinquished their friendship. With her soul of attitudes, she must have felt
herself in a double mood—heroic under strain, and
laughtersome at care. The artistic and musical world
raved of her afresh; they might well now have celebrated her both as "La Penserosa" and "L'Allegra."
It was about this time that Walter Savage Landor
sang of her—

> "Gone are the Sirens from their sunny shore,
> The Muses afterwards were heard no more,
> But of the Graces there remains but one—
> Gods name her Emma, mortals, Hamilton."

And perhaps too he remembered her when he wrote
of Dido—

> "Ill-starred Elisa, hence arose
> Thy faithless joys, thy steadfast woes."

Of old she had been praised for her tarantella.
Nothing more beautiful could be imagined, was Lady
Malmesbury's verdict more than five years earlier.
How was Emma now to trip it through heavy trial,
and hide an aching heart with smiles and songs? Misguided love lent her strength, and its misguidance
found out the way. She was ready to sacrifice everything, and to forsake all for one whose absence must
mean her own and her country's glory. Sir William,

out of the saddle, was practically in hospital; Nelson, practically in hospital, longed for the saddle once more. The Northern Coalition threatened a now isolated Britain with a stroke more formidable than the Southern had done formerly. Napoleon was exultant. Sir William, who really worshipped Nelson, and for whom Emma cared to the last, found himself none the less rather thankful that Nelson was off in search of fresh triumphs, and, with him, the disturbing clamour of hero-worship. He longed for his little fishing expeditions and picture hunts; he was anxious about his pension,[1] his late wife's property as well as the tatters of his own. So, committing with a sigh the racket of life to his demonstrative Emma, he resigned himself to the worldly wisdom of his calculating and still bachelor nephew, Greville, whose ruling motive had always been interest. Zeal was not in Greville's nature, but something like it coloured his coldness whenever chattels were concerned. He was studiously respectful to Nelson. He was amiably attentive to his " aunt." All the same, he was already tincturing Hamilton's mind with an alien cynicism; he and Sir William were gradually forming a little northern coalition of their own. While he exerted himself in assiduously forwarding Sir William's claim on the generosity of the Government, he took good care to discourage any expenditure that might anticipate a chance so doubtful.

Nelson was in a fever of impatience and suspense, for Emma, for his country—his two obsessions—for all but himself. He was ever a creaking door, but his health, though in his eagerness for action he protested it restored, was now beyond measure miserable. His eye grew inflamed, his heart constantly palpitated, his cough seemed the premonitor of consumption. And

---

[1] He wanted a real, not a nominal, £2000 a year from Lord Grenville, and £8000 compensation.

vexations, public as well as private, troubled him. The authorities, whether in the guise of Cato, or of Paul Pry, or of Tartuffe, hampered his every step, while the curs of office snapped about his heels. Added to this, he had been forced into a lawsuit—an " amicable squabble " he terms it—with his admired and admiring Lord St. Vincent, who laid claim to the prize-money of victories won during his absence.   St. Vincent had retired into civil service, and was now the mainspring of the Admiralty, in which the new Sir Thomas Troubridge, who owed his rise entirely to Nelson, had also found the snuggest of berths.   Both the men who had taught Nelson, and the men that he had taught, were setting up as his critics and often his spies.   His coming expedition was to be a thirteenth labour of Hercules.   Yet the tribe of cavillers could only insinuate (for aloud they dared not speak) of his dalliance with Omphale.   At least they might have re-membered that Nelson had saved them and his coun-try, and that if his impulsiveness gave himself away to their self-satisfied ingratitude, he was at this moment called to give himself up on the altar of duty.   On Hardy, and Louis, and the two Parkers, and Berry and Carrol, he could still count; like all chivalrous leaders, he had his round table, and this was his pride and consolation.   But it was also his solace to remain mag-nanimous, and even now he sent the most generous congratulations on his adversary's birthday, which were warmly and honourably reciprocated.   He had hoped for supreme command, but Sir Hyde Parker was preferred: Nelson was only Vice-Admiral of the Blue.   Scarcely had he been in London a fortnight when, with his brother William, he repaired to his flagship at Portsmouth, to superintend the equipment of the fleet.   He had already taken his seat in the House of Lords, though he had still to complain that his honours had not yet been gazetted. He had accompanied the Hamiltons on their Wiltshire excursion. He had nominated Hardy his captain. On January 13 he quitted Emma, it might be for the last time, and with Emma he left both his new hopes and old ties. His wife, who had beaten her retreat to Brighton, he had now irrevocably renounced; his mind was " as fixed as fate," and of none does the adage *" Vestigia nulla retrorsum "* hold good more than of Nelson; it was not long before he wrote significantly, alluding to her West Indian extraction, " Buonaparte's wife is of Martinique." Lady Nelson had made no advance, not the slightest attempt to provide him for the voyage. " Anxiety for friends left," he informed his " wife before heaven " the day after he set out, " and various workings of my imagination, gave me one of those severe pains of the heart that all the windows were obliged to be put down, the carriage stopped, and the perspiration was so strong that I never was wetter, and yet dead with cold." And some days afterwards: " Keep up your spirits, all will end well. The dearest of friends must part, and we only part, I trust, to meet again."

By mid-January he had hoisted his flag on the *San Josef.* In March he was commanding the *St. George,* the vessel which, he wrote with exaltation, " will stamp an additional ray of glory on England's fame, if Nelson survives; and that Almighty Providence, who has hitherto protected me in all dangers, and covered my head in the day of battle, will still, if it be His pleasure, support and assist me."

Emma had earned her lover's fresh admiration by steeling herself to undergo a test that would have prostrated even those who would most have recoiled from it. She and Nelson had resolved to hide from Sir William what was shortly to happen. But Emma would take no refuge in absence from home; sne would stand firm and face guilt and danger under her own roof-tree. Though this trial might cost her life, she would be up and doing directly it was over. If for a few days she kept to her room with one of those attacks which had been habitual at Naples, who but her mother and herself need be the worse or the wiser?

The sudden blow of their parting under such circumstances had been exceptionally severe. It recalls the famous line of Fénelon:

"Calypso ne pouvait se consoler du départ d'Ulysse."

In their mutual anxiety they framed a plan of correspondence, in which Emma and Nelson were to masquerade as the befrienders of a Mr. Thomson, one of his officers, distracted with anxiety about the impending confinement of his wife, who was bidden to entrust herself and the child to the loving guardianship and "kind heart" of Lady Hamilton. These secret letters were all addressed to "Mrs. Thomson," while Nelson's ordinary letters were addressed as usual to Lady Hamilton. Without some such dissimulation they could have very rarely corresponded, for their communications were constantly opened; and, even so, Hamilton's curiosity must have been often piqued by his wife's receipt of so many communications in Nelson's hand to this unknown friend. But they did manage to exchange fragments even more intimate than the interpolations in the body of these extraordinary "Thomson" letters. Not all these, nor all of such as he possessed, were given by Pettigrew in his convincing proof of Horatia's real origin. The Morrison Collection presents many of Pettigrew's documents in their entirety, and adds others confirming them; so also do the less ample *Nelson Letters,* and others from private sources.

Emma's agitated feelings must be guessed from Nelson's answers, for, as he assured her afterwards, he deliberately burned all her own "kind, dear letters," read and fingered over and over again; any day his life might be laid down, and he feared lest they might pass into hostile hands. From one of hers, however, written at Merton a year later in commemoration of the victory he was now about to win, something of their tenor may be gathered :—

"Our dear glorious friend, immortal and great Nelson, what shall I say to you on this day? My heart and feeling are so overpowered that I cannot give vent to my full soul to tell you, as an Englishwoman gratefull to her country's saviour, what I feel towards you. And as a much loved friend that has the happiness of being beloved, esteemed, and admired by the good and virtuos Nelson, what must be my pride, my glory, to say this day have I the happiness of being with him, one of his select, and how gratefull to God Almighty do I feel in having preserved you through such glorious dangers that never man before got through them with such Honner and Success. Nelson, I want Eloquence to tell you what I feil, to avow the sentiments of respect and adoration with which you have inspired me. Admiration and delight you must ever raise in all who behold you, looking on you only as the guardian of England. But how far short are those sensations to what I as a much loved friend feil! And I confess to you the predominant sentiments of my heart will ever be, till it ceases to beat, the most unfeigned anxiety for your happiness, and the sincerest and most disinterested determination to promote your felicity even at the hasard of my life. Excuse this scrawl, my dearest friend, but next to talking with you is writing to you. I wish this day I . . . could be near for your sake. . . . God bless you, my ever dear Nelson. Long may you live to be the admiration of Europe, the delight of your country, and the idol of your constant, attached Emma."

She is "still the same Emma." A rhapsody of " None but the brave deserve the fair " rings in every line. It is melodrama, but genuine melodrama; and melodrama of the heart, Nelson loved. It was what all along he had missed in his wife, who had lived aloof from his career; whereas Emma and he had lived through its thrilling scenes together. It was what he himself felt, and that to which Emma answered with every pulse. At no time was she in the least awe of her hero, whose strong will and gentle heart marked him off from those she had best known. With Nelson she was always perfectly natural, using none but her own voice and gestures. Had she been really the conventional " serpent of old Nile " (and it is odd what an historical affinity the " Nile " has had to " serpents "), that part would thoroughly have clashed with her unchanging outspokenness of tone. Nelson was always emphatic and picturesque; he possessed to an eminent degree, both in warfare and otherwise, the intuition of temperament for temperament. Admitting idealisation, I cannot think that he was absolutely mistaken in Emma's.

" I shall write to Troubridge this day " is Nelson's communication to Lady Hamilton, in the earliest letter extant of the " Thomson " series, penned on the passage to Torbay only four days before the child was born, " to send me your letter, which I look for as constantly and with more anxiety than my dinner. Let her [Lady Nelson] go to Briton, or where she pleases, I care not; she is a great fool, and, thank God! you are not the least bit like her. I delivered poor Mrs. Thomson's note; her friend is truly thankful for her kindness and your goodness. Who does not admire your benevolent heart? Poor man, he is very anxious, and begs you will, if she is not able, write a line just to comfort him. He appears to feel very much her situation. He is so agitated, and will be so for 2 or 3 days, that he says he cannot write, and that I must send his kind love and affectionate regards. . . . I hate Plymouth." Yet Plymouth had just conferred on him the freedom of the city. Nelson's whole soul was with Emma; in the suspense of fatherhood he shrank into himself and recoiled from publicity. He had no compunctions about Lady Nelson. On the very evening of the Plymouth honours he had despatched a remarkable epistle, published by its owner last year. Nelson was never rich, and his allowance of £2000 a year to his wife had been handsome in the extreme. Nelson had already heard with incredulity " nonsensical reports " that Lady Nelson was instructing the agent to buy a " fine house for him." From his wife, he now acquaints Emma, he had received but half one side of a slip of paper to tell him of her cold and her withdrawal from London. He alludes to a rumour that she was about to take Shelburne House. He treats it with scornful ridicule. He had just met Troubridge's sister who lived at Exeter, " pitted with small-pox and deafer far than Sir Thomas." Emma need never be jealous. " Pray tell Mrs. Thomson her kind friend is very uneasy about her, and prays most fervently for her safety—and he says he can only depend on your goodness. . . . May the Heavens bless and preserve my dearest friend and give her every comfort this world can afford, is the sincerest prayer of your faithful and affectionate Nelson and Bronte."

Nelson is all prayer and piety for Emma. It is one of the most singular features of his erratic greatness that he lays her, the coming child, and himself as humble and acceptable offerings before God's throne. His sincerity resembles in another plane that of Carlyle, who, in some of his epistles to his mother, translated his own earnest free-thought into terms of the Scotch Covenanter. But at the same time the reader is often tempted to echo what the same Carlyle objected to in French eighteenth-century sentimentalism: " So much talk about *Virtue*. In the devil and his grandmother's name, *be* Virtuous then! "

Every night Nelson withdrew after the day's fatigues, and amid incessant occupations, to hint (when he feared to pour forth) his torture of anxiety and passionate fulness of unbounded affection. He bade her be of good cheer. He assured " Mr. Thomson " of her " innate worth and affectionate disposition." But during these weary days of waiting, a full month before Oliver had been chosen to convey his famous and self-convicting letter, he must have disclosed his inmost soul to its idol through him, or perhaps through Davison, who at this very time had travelled over two hundred miles to pay him a visit. Another letter of far less reserve, and one never, so far as I know, cited, exists in relation to the coming birth of the *second* child—the little Emma who died so soon—in the earlier months of 1804. It is so remarkable, and probably so identical with others which he must have written on this earlier occasion, that I subjoin a portion of it here, venturing to fill in some of the excisions:—

" MY DEAREST BELOVED,—. . . To say that I think of you by day, night, and all day, and all night, but too faintly expresses my feelings of love and affection towards you. [Mine is indeed an] unbounded affection. Our dear, excellent, good [Mrs. Cadogan] is the only one who knows anything of the matter; and she has promised me when you [are well] again to take every possible care of you, as a proof of her never-failing regard to your own dear Nelson. Believe me that I am incapable of wronging you in thought, word, or deed. No; not all the wealth of Peru could buy me for one moment; it is all yours and reserved wholly for you. And . . . certainly . . . from the first moment of our happy, dear, enchanting, blessed meeting. . . . The call of our country is a duty which you would deservedly, in the cool moments of reflection, reprobate, was I to abandon: and I should feel so disgraced by seeing you ashamed of me! No longer saying, ' This is the man who has saved his country! This is he, who is the first to go forth to fight our battles, and the last to return!' . . . ' Ah!' they will think, ' What a man! What sacrifices has he not made to secure our homes and property; even the society and happy union with the finest and most accomplished woman in the world.' As you love, how must you feel! My heart is with you, cherish it. I shall, my best beloved, return—if it pleases God—a victor; and it shall be my study to transmit an unsullied name. There is no desire of wealth, no ambition that could keep me from all my soul holds dear. No; it is to save my country, my wife in the eye of God. . . . Only think of our happy meeting. Ever, for ever I am your's, only your's, even beyond this world. . . . For ever, for ever, your own Nelson." [1]

Emma certainly inspired the Nelson who delivered England; and for all time this surely ought to outweigh the carping diatribes of half-moralists who narrow the whole of virtue to a part. It cannot be too much emphasised that Nelson loved *her* and not merely

[1] *Nelson Letters*, vol. i. p. 175, "August 26 [1803]."

her enhancements. " Thank God," he wrote at the beginning of February, " you want not the society of princes or dukes. If you happened to fall down and break your nose or knock out your eyes, you might go to the devil for what they care, but it is your good heart that attaches to you, your faithful and affectionate Nelson." [1]

About January 29, in a week of storm, Horatia was born. Within the week Emma, unattended, had taken the baby by night in a hackney coach to the nurse, Mrs. Gibson, of Little Titchfield Street. Within a fortnight, " thinner . . . but handsomer than ever," she could play hostess at her husband's table; in three weeks she was importuned by, though she refused to entertain, royalty. From first to last, she wrote daily to Nelson, and she was active in concealment. Her force of will and endurance at this juncture pass comprehension. She behaved as if nothing had happened, though she must seriously have deranged her health.

" I believe," wrote the transported father so soon as her glad tidings reached him, " I believe dear Mrs. Thomson's friend will go mad with joy. He cries, prays, and performs all tricks, yet dares not show all or any of his feelings, but he has only me to consult with. He swears he will drink your health this day in a bumper, and damn me if I don't join him in spite of all the doctors in Europe, for none regard you with truer affection than myself. You are a dear good creature, and your kindness and attention to poor Mrs. T. stamps you higher than ever in my mind. I cannot write, I am so agitated by this young man at my elbow. I believe he is foolish, he does nothing but rave about you and her. I own I participate in his joy and cannot write anything."

It is noteworthy that the eccentric demeanour of

[1] Letter of February 1, 1801.

" dear Mrs. Thomson's friend " accords with what was
evidently a trait in the Nelson family; for Sir William, describing to Nelson the joy of his brother " the
reverend doctor," on hearing the first intelligence of
Copenhagen while dining with him in Piccadilly, says:
" Your brother was more extraordinary than ever. He
would get up suddenly and cut a caper; rubbing his
hands every time that the thought of your fresh
laurels came into his head."

The day after the " young man " at Nelson's elbow had been thus disporting himself, Nelson again
addressed Lady Hamilton. He had cut out two lines
from her letter with which, he declares, he will never
part. He had exceeded his promise of the day before,
and had drained two bumpers to the health of Mrs.
Thomson and her child in the company of Troubridge,
Hardy, Parker, and his brother, till the latter said he
would " hurt " himself: " that friend of our dear Mrs.
T. is a good soul and full of feeling," he wrote; " he
wishes much to see her and her little one. If possible
I will get him leave for two or three days when I go
to Portsmouth, and you will see his gratitude to you."
Next morning he communicates with her indirectly as
" Mrs. Thomson." Her " good and dear friend does
not think it proper at present to write with his own
hand," but he " hopes the day may not be far distant
when he may be united for ever to the object of his
wishes, his only, *only* love. He swears before heaven
that he will marry her as soon as possible, which he
fervently prays may be soon. Nelson is charged " to
say how dear you are to him, and that you must [at]
every opportunity kiss and bless for him his dear little
girl, which he wishes to be called Emma, out of gratitude to our dear, good Lady Hamilton, but in either
[case?] its [name?], [whether?] from Lord N., he
says, or Lady H., he leaves to your judgment and

choice." He has "given poor Thomson a hundred
pounds this morning for which he will give Lady H.
an order on his agents"; and he begs her to "dis-
tribute it amongst those who have been useful to you on
the late occasion; and your friend, my dear Mrs.
Thomson," he adds, "may be sure of my care of him
and his interest, which I consider as dearly as my
own. . . ."

But perhaps the least guarded of this long series is
a fragment to be found in the old volume of *Nelson
Letters,* though Pettigrew's transcripts and the Morrison original do not comprise it. It bears date February 16. "I sit down, my dear Mrs. T.," it runs, "by
desire of poor Thomson, to write you a line: not to
assure you of his eternal love and affection for you
and his dear child, but only to say that he is well and
as happy as he can be, separated from all which he
holds dear in this world. He has no thoughts separated from your love and your interest. They are
united with his; one fate, one destiny, he assures me,
awaits you both. What can I say more? Only to
kiss his child for him: and love him as truly, sincerely,
and faithfully as he does you; which is from the bottom of his soul. He desires that you will more and
more attach yourself to dear Lady Hamilton." Only
a week earlier he had addressed to her that stirring
passage which told her that it was she who urged him
forth to glory, that he had been the whole world
round, and had never yet seen "her equal, or even one
who could be put in comparison."

Every night he and his "band of brothers" continue to raise the glass to the toast of Emma. Letter
succeeds to letter, affection to impatience, and impatience to ecstasy. He makes a new will, bequeathing
her, besides other jewelled presentations, the portrait
which Maria Carolina had given him of herself at part-

ing; charging, too, in her favour the rental of Bronte, but on this occasion only in the case of the failure of its male heirs; creating, above all, a trust for the child, of whom " Emma Hamilton alone knows the parents," of whom too she is besought to act as guardian, and by her honour and integrity to " shield it from want and disgrace." He would " steal white bread rather than that the child should want." He and she are to be and be known as godparents of an infant in whom they take a " very particular interest," and he especially requests that it may be brought up as " the child of her dear friend Nelson and Bronte." He discusses the name; Emma had evidently begged that it might be *his,* nor hers as originally proposed. Let it be christened " Horatia " and be registered, anagramatically, as " daughter of Johem and Morata Etnorb."[1] As for the date of baptism, he leaves it entirely to his Emma's discretion, but, on the whole, after some hesitation he favours its postponement, since a clergyman might ask inconvenient questions. He rejoices to hear that the baby is handsome, for then it must be like his dear " Lady Hamilton," between whom and Mrs. Thomson there is said to be a striking resemblance. After all, there is no immediate hurry to settle these trifles. He *must* soon rejoin her, if only for a day. Till March he would still be kept off the English coasts, near and yet far from Emma; he chafes at a division uncaused by duty or by distance. He will run up so soon as " Mr. Thomson " can get leave, and propitiate that watch-dragon, Troubridge.

Emma's correspondence with Mrs. William Nelson from the latter end of February shows how and when he appeared in London. But before he hastened to her side, a curious and undetailed episode, mixing a drop of bitter disquiet with his draught of rapture, will

---

[1] *i. e.* Horatio and Emma Bronte.

be followed with interest.   It exhibits Emma's constancy and fortitude under a temptation which surprised her, and anguished her fretting lover.   Her
firmness in overcoming it and, with it, his jealousy,
riveted him, if possible, more closely than ever.   It
pervades every one of Nelson's letters, from the February of this year to the end of March, and many long
afterwards.

While, strained and nervous beyond measure, she
now awaited Horatia's birth, she was annoyed and
alarmed, though probably flattered also, by a message
from the Prince of Wales—eager to bridge over the
dull interval till Parliament might pronounce his father
imbecile and himself Regent.   He politely commanded
Sir William to invite him to dinner on a Sunday evening.   It was his desire to hear Lady Hamilton sing,
together with La Banti, who was now in London,
and whose son Nelson actually placed in the navy
together with Emma's cousin, Charles Connor.   Sir
William was anxious to obtain from the Government
not only his full pension, but also a liberal reward
for the heavy losses which Jacobinism had inflicted on
his property.   Moreover, he hoped, though in vain, for
a new appointment—the governorship of Malta.   The
Prince's aid was all-important for the ex-Ambassador.
He had been more than civil during the short visit of
1791, when he had commissioned portraits of the fair
Ambassadress; and, though an ill-natured world might
put the worst construction on his presence in Piccadilly, Sir William trusted to Emma's prudence and his
own interest.[1]   The fiery Nelson, however, infuriated,

[1] Cf. his letter to Nelson of Feb. 11, *Nelson Letters,* vol. ii.
p. 200.   " . . . She has got one of her terrible sick headaches.
Among other things that vex her is—that we have been drawn
in to be under the *absolute necessity* of giving a dinner to the
P. of Wales on Sunday next.   He asked it himself, having
expressed a strong desire of hearing Banti's and Emma's voices

even demented, at the bare suspicion, ascribed the whole manœuvre to the bad offices and influence of Lady Abercorn, Mrs. Walpole, and a " Mrs. Nisbet," who had been heard publicly to assert that Lady Hamilton had " hit " the Prince's " fancy." Sir William, however, was now once more under Greville's thumb, and it is likely that the mild Mephistopheles of King's Mews had his finger in this pie. At a moment so awkward, Emma certainly disbelieved that her husband ever did more than countenance the affair. She was proud of her talent, and pleased at the sensation it created in the Duke of Queensberry's circle. But the attentions of such a charmer as the First Gentleman in Europe were doubtless of design; and she was on her guard at the outset, though in after years she cultivated the new friendship of the Prince, together with the long-standing one of his admiring brothers. Her child had half-hallowed in her eyes the sin that sacrifice had endeared, and she resented the buzz of the scandalmongers. She welcomed, indeed invited, Nelson's plan of bringing up his sister-in-law to the rescue.

Sir William's intention that the royal visit should be *en famille,* and its projected secrecy, worked up Nelson's feelings to their highest pitch : better by far, if it had to be, a big reception. In the end, however, no party took place, still less was there any *éclat.* The Prince was baffled, despite Sir William. Emma

together. I am well aware of the dangers, etc. . . . As this dinner must be, or he would be offended, I shall keep strictly to the musical part, invite only Banti, her husband, and Taylor; and as I wish to show a civility to Davison, I have sent him an invitation. In short, we will get rid of it as well as we can, and guard against its producing more meetings of the same sort. *Emma would really have gone any lengths to have avoided Sunday's dinner. But I thought it would not be prudent* to break with the P. of Wales, etc. . . . I have been thus explicit as I know well your Lordship's way of thinking, and your very kind attachment to us and to everything that concerns us."

showed that she could renounce vanity for love, and that she dared to rebuff importunity in high places. Nelson's mountain brought forth a mouse, nor did he ever cease to commemorate his appreciation of Emma's firmness—" firm as a rock," he said of his trust in her afterwards.

Nelson was really on the rack. His distracted letters of more than a fortnight—until his apprehensions of the main danger had been calmed—present a striking self-revelation, and are doubly interesting because Emma's own letters to Mrs. William Nelson supplement them. It is only through his own words that we can realise his feelings. His overwrought nature magnified every shadow, and overbore his strong common sense. He was morbid, and conjured up suspicions and anticipations alike unworthy of him. Throughout his life his geese were too often swans, and his *bêtes noires,* even oftener, demons. His Jeremiads sound a monotone. He tears his passion to tatters in a crescendo of self-torture. The man whose bracing and unblenching nerves were iron in action, who was shortly to urge " these are not times for nervous systems," grew unstrung and abased when his immense love lost its foothold for a moment. At first he could scarcely believe that " Sir William should have a wish for the Prince of Wales to come under your roof "; no good could come from it, but every harm. " You are too beautiful not to have enemies, and even one visit will stamp you. . . . We know that he is without one spark of honour in these respects and would leave you to bewail your folly. But, my dear friend, I know you too well not to be convinced you cannot be seduced by any prince in Europe. You are, in my opinion, the pattern of perfection." " Sir William should say to the Prince that, situated as you are, it would be highly improper for you to admit H.R.H.

That the Prince should wish it, I am not surprised at.
. . . Sir William should speak out, and if the Prince
is a man of honour, he will quit the pursuit of you.
. . . The thought so agitates me that I cannot write.
I had wrote a few lines last night but I am in tears, I
cannot bear it." " I own I sometimes fear that you
will not be so true to me as I am to you, yet I cannot,
will not believe, you can be false. No! I judge you
by myself. I hope to be dead before that should happen, but it will not. Forgive me, Emma, oh, forgive
your own dear, disinterested Nelson. Tell Davison
how sensible I am of his goodness. He knows my attachment to you. . . . May God send . . . happiness!
I have a letter from Sir William; he speaks of the
Regency as certain; and then probably he thinks
you will sell better—horrid thought!" " Your dear
friend, my dear and truly beloved Mr. T., is almost
distracted; he wishes there was peace, or if your uncle
would die, he would instantly then come and marry
you, for he doats on nothing but you and his child.
. . . He has implicit faith in your fidelity, even in conversation with those he dislikes, and that you will be
faithful in greater things he has no doubt." When
Emma scolded, and sought to pique him by a piece of
jesting jealousy into reason, he reassured both her [1]
and himself for a few days; but on February 11, addressing her as " My dear Lady," he tells her that " *it
is very easy to find a stick to beat your Dog,*" and to
find a pretext for blaming one " who will never forget you, but to the last moment of his existence, pray
to God to give you happiness and to remove from this
ungrateful world your old friend." Three days later,

[1] " Suppose I did say that the West Country women wore
black stockings, what is it more than if you was to say what
puppies all the present young men are? You cannot help your
eyes, and God knows I cannot see much." Morrison MS. 514.

however, he again changes his note; he trusts his " dear Lady " to " do him full justice, and to make her dear mind at ease for ever, for ever and ever." But on February 17 he burst out afresh: " I am so agitated that I can write nothing. I knew it would be so, and you can't help it. Do not sit long at table. Good God! He will be next you, and telling you soft things. If he does, tell it out at table, and turn him out of the house. . . . Oh, God! that I was dead! But I do not, my dearest Emma, blame you, nor do I fear your constancy. . . . I am gone almost mad, but you cannot help it. It will be in all the newspapers with hints. . . . I could not write another line if I was to be made King. If I was in town, nothing should make me dine with you that damned day, but, my dear Emma, I do not blame you, only remember your poor miserable friend. That you must be singing and appear gay! . . . I have read . . . your resolution never to go where the fellow is, but you must have him at home. Oh, God! but you cannot, I suppose, help it, and you cannot turn him out of your own house. . . . I see your determination to be on your guard, and as fixed as fate. . . . I am more dead than alive . . . to the last breath your's. If you cannot get rid of this, I hope you will tell Sir William never to bring the fellow again." " 'Tis not that I believe you will do anything that injures me, but I cannot help saying a few words on that fellow's dining with you, for you do not believe it to be out of love for Sir William. . . . You have been taken in. You that are such a woman of good sense, put so often on your guard by myself [against] Mrs. Udney, Mrs. Spilsbury, Mrs. Dent, and Mrs. Nisbet. . . . I knew that he would visit you, and you could not help coming downstairs when the Prince was there. . . . But his words are so charming that, I am told, no person can withstand them. If I

had been worth ten millions I would have betted
every farthing that you would not have gone into the
house knowing that he was there, and if you did,
which I would not have believed, that you would have
sent him a proper message by Sir William, and sent
him to hell. And knowing your determined courage
when you had got down, I would have laid my head
upon the block with the axe uplifted, and said ' strike,'
if Emma does not say to Sir William before the fellow, ' my character cannot, shall not suffer by permitting him to visit.' . . . Hush, hush, my poor heart,
keep in my breast, be calm, Emma is true. . . . But
no one, not even Emma, could resist the serpent's flattering tongue. . . . What will they all say and think,
that Emma is like other women, when I would have
killed anybody who had said so. . . . Forgive me. I
know I am almost distracted, but I have still sense
enough left to burn every word of yours. . . . All
your pictures are before me. What will Mrs. Denis
say, and what will she sing—*Be Calm, be Gentle, the
Wind has Changed?* Do you go to the opera to-
night? They say he sings well. I have eat nothing
but a little rice and drank water. But forgive me. I
know my Emma, and don't forget that you had once
a Nelson, a friend, a dear friend, but alas! he has his
misfortunes. He has lost the best, his only friend, his
only love. Don't forget him, poor fellow! He is
honest. Oh! I could thunder and strike dead with
my lightning. I dreamt it last night, my Emma. I
am calmer. . . . Tears have relieved me; you never
will again receive the villain to rob me. . . . May the
heavens bless you! I am better. Only tell me you
forgive me; don't scold me, indeed I am not worth it,
and am to my last breath your's, and if not your's, no
one's in the world. . . . You cannot now help the villain's dining with you. Get rid of it as well as you

can. Do not let him come downstairs with you or hand you up. *If you do,* tell me, and then——!" "Forgive my letter wrote and sent last night, perhaps my head was a little affected. No wonder, it was such an unexpected, such a knock-down blow; such a death. But I will not go on, for I shall get out of my senses again. Will you sing for the fellow *The Prince, unable to conceal his Pain,* etc.? No, you will not."

And here follows, like a lull in the storm, his joy at hearing from Emma herself that Sir William, "who asks all parties to dinner," was not to have his way; she had resolved to evade the Prince. He cursed the would-be intruder. Even now he implored her not to risk being at home that next Sunday evening, but to dine with Mrs. Denis. If the Prince still insisted on coming, Emma must be away. But till he had certainty he would continue to starve himself. He thanked her "ten thousand times." She was never to say that her letters bored him; they were "the only real comfort of his life." If ever he proved false to her, might "God's vengeance" light upon him. Parker knew his love for her—"who does not?" He was "all astonishment at her uncle's conduct"; as for his "aunt," he did not care "a fig for her." He would buy Madame Le Brun's portrait of her as well as Romney's. Still, the yellow demon had not yet quite deserted him. He still brooded on imaginary fears and scenes. "Did you sit alone with the villain? No! I will not believe it. Oh, God! Oh, God! keep my sences. Do not let the rascal in. Tell the Duke [1] that you will never go to his house. Mr. G. [2] must be a scoundrel. He treated you once ill enough [3] and cannot love you, or he would sooner die. . . . I have this

[1] Of Queensberry.   [2] Greville.
[3] This is proof positive that Nelson was aware of Emma's past.

moment got my orders to put myself under Sir Hyde Parker's orders, and suppose I shall be ordered to Portsmouth to-morrow or next day, and then I will try to get to London for 3 days. May Heaven bless us, but don't let that fellow dine with you. . . . *Forget every cross word: I now live."* That very night he received the assurance of Emma's staunch determination, however Sir William and Greville might remonstrate, and his answer breathes a profound and rapturous calm:—" Your good sense, judgment, and proper firmness must endear you to all your friends, and to none more than your old and firm friend Nelson. You have shown that you are above all temptation, and not to be drawn into the paths of dishonour for to gratify any prince, or to gain any riches. How Sir William can associate with a person of a character so diametrically opposed to his own—but I do not choose, as this letter goes through any hands, to enter more at large on this subject. I glory in your conduct and in your inestimable friendship. . . . I wish you were my sister that I might instantly give you half my fortune for your glorious conduct. Be firm! Your cause is that of honour against infamy. . . . You know that I would not, in Sir William's case, have gone to Court without my wife, and such a wife, never to be matched. It is true you would grace a Court better as a Queen than a visitor." " Good Sir William," he added, must, on reflection, " admire your virtuous and proper conduct."

Nelson never forgot or ceased to praise Emma's conduct in this ticklish transaction. William Nelson shared his brother's admiration. But the lover holds her aloft as a matchless example in letters compatible with the most platonic affection. She is incomparable. The more he reads, the more he admires her " whole conduct." The thought of it inspired that " Santa

Emma " letter written in the May of this very year on the *St. George* off Rostock, one excerpt from which, canonising her as a saint, has been already quoted. It inspired another uncited passage addressed to Emma a few weeks later. " I now know he never can dine with you; for you would go out of the house sooner than suffer it: and as to letting him hear you sing, I only hope he will be struck deaf and you dumb, sooner than such a thing should happen! But I know it never now can. You cannot think how my feelings are alive towards you: probably more than ever: and they never can be diminished."

In strength of will, in picturesqueness, in emphasis, in courage, it must be acknowledged that Nelson and Emma were affinities.

The fresh correspondence between Emma and Mrs. William Nelson is interesting in relation to this episode, for through it we are enabled to hear Emma's own voice. It rings out true and clear, confirming every word that Nelson uttered. There is also here and there a touch in it of Emma as " stateswoman " once more. She never relaxed her interest in politics, and she was still in correspondence with Maria Carolina.

Emma had welcomed Nelson's wish that his sister-in-law should be with her at such a trying moment. Unfortunately, " Reverend Doctor " and his wife had ended their stay in town just before the Sunday of the party which haunted Nelson came round. At Nelson's request, however, the little woman, whose " tongue," he said, " never lay still," returned in the nick of time to fill the blank caused by his departure. On the very Friday of Nelson's two letters to Emma, she also took up her own tale to Mrs. Nelson. She was still in bed with a headache: ". . . It is such a pain to part with dear friends, and you and I liked each other from the moment we met: our souls were congenial. Not so with Tom Tit,[1] for *there* was an antipathy not to be described. . . . I received yesterday letters from that *great adored* being that we all so love, esteem, and admire. The more one knows him, the more one wonders at his greatness, his heart, his head booth so perfect. He says he is coming down to Spithead soon, he hopes. Troubridge comes to town to-day as one of the Lords, so he is settled for the present, but depend on it, my dear friend, this poor *patched-up* party can never hold long. A new coat will bear many a lag and tag as the vulgar phrase is, but an old patched mended one must tear. . . . I am so unwell that I don't think we can have his Royal Highness to dinner on Sunday, which will not vex *me*. Addio, *mia Cara amica*. You know as you are learning Italian, I must say a word or so. How dull my *bedroom looks* without you. I miss our little friendly confidential chats. But in this world nothing is compleat." And here Emma's philosophy follows:—" If all went on smoothly, one shou'd regret quitting it, but 'tis the many little vexations and crosses, separations from one's dear friends that make one not regret leaving it. . . ."

On February the 24th Nelson hurried to London before he finally set out for the Baltic in the second week of the next month. A note from Emma in this new series describes his arrival to Mrs. Nelson. The letter is franked by Nelson himself to " Hillborough, Brandon, Suffolk ":—

" MY DEAREST FRIEND,—Your dear Brother arrived this morning by seven o'clock. He stays only 3 days, so by the time you wou'd be here, he will be gone. How unlucky you went so soon. I am in health *so so,*

[1] Lady Nelson.

but *spirits* to-day excellent. Oh, what real pleasure Sir William and I have in seeing this our great, good, virtuous Nelson. His eye is better. . . . Apropos Lady Nelson is at Brighton yet. The King, God bless him, is ill, and there are many speculations. Some say it is his old disorder. . . ."

And on the next day, February 25 :—

". . . Your good, dear Brother has just left me to go to pay a visit to Mr. Nepean, but is coming back to dinner with Morice, his brother, whom he brings *with him,* and Troubridge also. We shall be comfortable, but more so if you had been here. Oh, I wish you *was,* and how happy would Milord have been to have had that happiness, to have walked out with Mrs. Nelson. . . . Our dear Nelson is very well in health. Poor fellow, he travelled allmost all night, but you that know his great, good heart will not be surprised at any act of friendship *of his.* I shall send for Charlotte to see him before he goes, and he has given 2 guineas for her. . . ."

On the following morning again :—

" Yesterday I cou'd not, my dearest friend, write much, and Milord was not yet returned from the Admiralty time enough to frank your letters, and sorry I was you shou'd pay for such trash that I sent you, but I thought you wou'd be uneasy. We had a pleasant evening [" and night "—erased]. I often thought on you, but now the subject of the King's illness gives such a gloom to everything. . . . Mr. Addington is not minister, for his commission was not signed before the King was taken so ill, so Mr. Pitt is yet first Lord. . . . Our good Lord Nelson is lodged at

Lothian's; Tom Tit, at the same place [*Brighton*]. The Cub [1] is to have a frigate, the *Thalia.* I suppose HE will be up in a day or so. I only hope he does not come near me. If he does, *not at home* shall be the answer. I am glad he is going. . . . Milord has only Allen with him. We supped and talked politics till 2. Mr. East [Este?] who is a pleasant man, was with us. . . . Oh, my dearest friend, our dear Lord is just come in. He goes off to-night and sails imediately. My heart is fit to Burst quite with greef. Oh, what pain, God only knows. I can only say may the All-mighty God bless, prosper, and protect him! I shall go mad with grief. Oh, God only knows what it is to part with such a *friend, such a one.* We were truly called the Tria juncta in uno, for Sir W., he, and I have but one *heart in three bodies.* . . . He, our great Nelson, sends his love to you. . . . My greif will not let me say more. Heavens bless you, answer your af-flicted E. H."

From Yarmouth, after a brief spell of final prepara-tion, Nelson sailed for the double feat of annihilating the Northern Confederation single-handed, and nego-tiating with a mastery both of men and management the truce that preceded the Peace of Amiens. Copen-hagen was now the key of the situation, as it was to prove six years later, when Canning saved Europe from the ruin of Austerlitz and the ignominy of Tilsit by that secret expedition which would have glad-dened Nelson, had he been alive. As victor and peace-maker he was now to stand forth supreme. "Time is our best ally," he wrote to Lord St. Vincent a few days later, when the wind caused a week's delay in the start of the refitted ships. "I hope we shall not give her up, as all our allies have given us up. Our

---

[1] Nelson's stepson Josiah Nisbet.

friend here is a little nervous about dark nights and
fields of ice, but we must brace up; these are not times
for nervous systems.   I want peace, which is only to be
had through, I trust, our still invincible navy "; and,
just before sailing, he made a declaration to Berry
that no Briton should ever forget:—". . . As to the
plan for pointing a gun truer than we do at present, if
the person comes, I shall of course look at it, and be
happy, if necessary, to use it.   But I hope that we
shall be able, as usual, to get so close to our enemies,
that our shots cannot miss their object, and that we
shall again give our northern enemies that hailstorm
of bullets which is so emphatically described in the
Naval Chronicle, and which gives our dear country the
dominion of the seas.   *We have it, and all the devils
in hell cannot take it from us, if our wooden walls have
fair play."*   On the verge of battle he indited three
lines meant for Emma's eyes alone: " He has no fear
of death but parting from you."

Emma resumed her disconsolate epistles both to
him and, until her return, to Mrs. William Nelson.
The first can only be inferred from his most vehement answers, while of the second a few scraps may
find appropriate place.

With a single exception she had withheld nothing
from Nelson; their communion was unreserved.   But
of " Emma Carew," that " orphan," now a girl of
nineteen, for whom she was still caring, who was soon
to be put under the alternate charge of Mrs. Denis and
of Mrs. Connor, and who was frequently to see her
undisclosed mother at Merton, she seems to have kept
silence.   On the first day of March Nelson addressed
to the " friend of his bosom " that most remarkable
letter opening " Now, my own dear wife," which has
become so hackneyed.   He at last found a full vent
for his feelings, for Oliver was the bearer of the paper.

There was nothing, he said, that he would not do for them to live together, and to have *their* dear little child with them. He firmly believed that the imminent campaign would ensure peace, and then—who knew?—they might cross the water and live in avowed partnership at Bronte. He wanted to see his wife no more, but until he could quit the country with Emma (and before that possibility England must be safeguarded), there could be no open union. After ensuring a " glorious issue," he would return with " a little more fame " for his Emma, proud of him and their country. " I never did love any one else," he continues; " I never had a dear pledge of love till you gave me one, and you, thank my God, never gave one to anybody else. . . . You, my beloved Emma, and my country are the two dearest objects of my fond heart, a heart susceptible and true. Only place confidence in me and you never shall be disappointed." He is now convinced of his dominion over her. He protests in the most passionate phrases his longing and his constancy. He is hers all, only, and always. " My heart, body, and mind [1] is in perfect union of love towards my own dear beloved "—his matchless, his flawless Emma.

Yet a living proof of flaw lurked in oblivion. We have heard Emma in 1798 sighing over her married childlessness. Horatia, Nelson's Horatia, was at length hers. Horatia's name and influence tinge his every tone; he even writes to the babe-in-arms, the child of his own heart. As Horatia's mother, Emma seems holy in his eyes. Every letter that he kisses before he sends it, is sealed with her head; each of hers with " Nelson " and " The Nile," with his glori-

[1] It is worthy of notice that he omits "soul." In a much later letter to her he says that his being is hers entirely, but that his "soul" is his Creator's.

ous emblem—*"Honor est a Nilo."* Was it *now* possible, at this longed-for moment, to reveal the dark error of her day's clouded opening? She had been but seventeen when that other daughter, watched, befriended, but never acknowledged, had been born. The foundling's disavowal had been wholly the work and craft of Greville, once so " good," so " tender " to her and the offspring that he snatched away from her girl's embrace. Was this the moment, she might well plead with the Pharisees, for withdrawing the veil that hid Horatia's half-sister from Nelson? She remained a " Protestant of the flesh "—a born pagan. As pagan she would be true in trial. She would do her duty as she knew it, and act her double part of nurse and wife. She would be generous and warm-hearted. But such surrender!—Was it in human, in feminine nature? Had she been the born " saint " of Nelson's canonisation, she would have done so now. Pale and weeping, she would have humbled herself and placed that daughter by her side as some token of atonement. How the scribes of the long robe, like Greville, would have sneered, how Hamilton would have smiled! And Hamilton's name—poor, fading Hamilton's—must surely have struck some chord in her better self. Who was she, what manner of man was Nelson, to make or exact such sacrifice! Although Sir William's own recent weakness had endangered her, and belittled him before Nelson, they still esteemed him—formed together, indeed, his right hand. And yet, whether Greville and he had guessed the truth or not, to *him* they were half traitors—an ugly word for an ugly fact; for what had Caracciolo been but a traitor! This was a moment when self-illusions might have vanished, and Nelson's Roman virtue might have listened to the stern rebuke to David—" Thou art the man." Yet. contrasted with the lax crew of Carlton

House and many at St. James's, Nelson and she *were* all but virtuous, virtuous sinners. Would her sin, then, ever find her out? Was this the time to bare her conscience to the world?

And during that brief London visit they had surely both seen the child, as they must have often done in the two succeeding years. Their visits suggest a striking picture,—the spare, weather-beaten man in the plain black suit, with the firm yet morbid mouth; the beautiful woman longing to call aloud to her baby; the little, homely room; Nurse Gibson with her housekeeper air, furtively wondering why the great Lord Nelson and the Ambassador's lady were so much concerned in this work-a-day world, with the mysterious child of " Mr. and Mrs. Thomson."

The very day that Emma received Nelson's confession of faith in her, she took up her pen once more to his sister-in-law :—

" My dearest friend, anxiety and heart-bleedings for your dear brother's departure has made me so ill, I have not been able to write. I cannot eat or sleep. Oh, may God prosper and *bless him*. He has wrote to Lord Eldon for Mr. Nelson. You will have him at Yarmouth in two days. Oh, how I envy you! Oh God, how happy you are! . . . My spirits and health is bad endeed. . . . Tom Tit is at Brighton. She did not come, nor did he go. Jove, for such he is—quite a Jove—knows better than that. Morrice means to go to Yarmouth. The Cub dined with us, but I never asked how Tom Tit was. . . . How I long to see you; do try and come, for God's sake do." And a like burden pervades the notes of days following: she is " so very low-spirited and ill " since " the best and greatest man alive went away." She has " no spirit to do anything." She prays Mrs. Nelson of her charity to come. They can then " walk and talk, and be so happy together." She can hear "all the news of my *Hero.*" She has bought Charlotte presents, and will take them to her. The King is better, and Tom Tit is in the country. She sends every message to "little Horatio." She had been ill all night, and cannot even take the morning air. For the second time, "*Calypso ne pouvait se consoler du départ d'Ulysse.*"

Nelson had asked, Emma had hoped, that she and Sir William (for Nelson would never see her without her husband) might run down to Yarmouth, and bid him and the *St. George* farewell. But "his eternally obliged" Sir William (possibly warned by Greville) declined with civil thanks. He was dedicating every moment to art. Some of his choicest vases, to his great joy, had turned up from the wreck. Pending the dubious bounty of the Government, he was preparing to sell these and his pictures by auction. Among the latter were three portraits of his wife. Nelson was furious at Emma being thus for the second time "on sale." He bought the St. Cecilia, as has been re-counted earlier, for £300, and enshrined it as a true "saint" in his cabin: had it cost "300 drops of blood," he would "have given it with pleasure." And almost up to the date of departure, renewed uneasiness about the loose set that Sir William now encouraged harassed him. Should she ever find herself in extremities, she must summon him back, and he would fly to her deliverance. It was at this moment that in once more revising his will, he bequeathed to her a diamond star.

It is strange that the virtuously indignant Miss Knight's pen should have been employed in celebrating the loves of Nelson and Lady Hamilton; yet such had been the case. Nelson retained them until the great battle was over, when he enclosed them in a letter to Emma :—

"L'INFELICE EMMA AI VENTI."

"Blow, blow, thou winter wind,
  To Love and Emma kind!
Ah! come! more grateful far
  Than perfumed zephyrs are.
Blow, blow, and on thy welcome wing
My Life, my Love, my Hero bring.

.   .   .

Blest, blest the compass be
Which steers my love to me!
And blest the happy gale
Which fills his homeward sail;
And blest the boat, and blest each oar
Which rows my True Love back to shore."

And *"blest,"* one might add, this maudlin trash. Robuster, at any rate, than these, surely, is the mediocre set that Emma composed for her hero in the same month.

"Silent grief, and sad forebodings
    (Lest I ne'er should see him more),
  Fill my heart when gallant Nelson
    Hoists Blue Peter at the fore.

On his Pendant anxious gazing,
    Filled with tears mine eyes run o'er;
  At each change of wind I tremble
    While Blue Peter's at the fore.

All the livelong day I wander,
    Sighing on the sea-beat shore,
  But my sighs are all unheeded,
    When Blue Peter's at the fore.

Oh that I might with my Nelson
    Sail the whole world o'er and o'er,
  Never should I then with sorrow
    See Blue Peter at the fore.

But (ah me!) his ship's unmooring;
    Nelson's last boat rows from shore;
  Every sail is set and swelling,
    And Blue Peter's seen no more."

While Nelson reaped fresh laurels to lay at her feet,
Emma waited for the peace which should bring him
back, but which was indefinitely delayed.   Among the
frequenters of the Piccadilly household, " Old Q." and
Lord William Douglas, an indefatigable scribbler of
vers de société, remained real friends, as Nelson constantly acknowledged, but the Carlton House gang still
seems to have pestered her.   For a space she became
cross with herself, cross with Sir William and cross
even with Nelson, whose most unselfish devotion to her
never allowed the gall in her imperious nature to embitter its honey.   But, despite her own ailments and
her husband's, she soon resumed her energy.   Never
did she appear to better advantage, except in days of
danger, than in those of sickness.   She was always
trying to get promotions for Nelson's old Captains, and
caring for his protégés and dependants; she even acted
as Nelson's deputy in urging the authorities to supply
him with the requisite officers so often denied him,
that he would protest himself forgotten " by the great
folks at home."   To Nelson she wrote constantly,
pouring out her heart and soul.

From Kioge Bay Nelson sailed to Revel, from Revel
to Finland; and thence Russia-ward to complete his
work of peace by an interview with the new Czar, and
with that Count Pahlen who had headed the assassina-
tors of Paul in his bedroom.   The Russians fêted him
and found him the facsimile of their " young
Suwaroff."   Nelson's new triumph—one of naviga-
tion, of strategy, and of ubiquitous diplomacy as well
—which had again saved England and awoke the un-
measured gratitude of the people, met with the same
chill reception from the Government as of old.   Nelson had always been his own Admiral.   He habitually disobeyed orders: it was intolerable.   They suspected the armistice that he had made in the thick of

the battle; all along, the white flag seems to have pursued Nelson with misconstruction. He has himself recorded in two letters to Lady Hamilton a telling vindication, which does honour to his humanity and to his prudence. He did not conceal his vexation. " I know mankind well enough," he told Hamilton, " to be sure that there are those in England who wish me at the devil. If they only wish me out of England, they will soon be gratified, for to go to Bronte I am determined. So I have wrote the King of the Two Sicilies, whose situation I most sincerely pity." He comforts himself that he is " backed with a just cause and the prayers of all good people. No medals were struck for Copenhagen; even the City began to flag in its appreciation. He flew out against the Lord Mayor who had once said, " Do *you* find victories, and we will find rewards." It was not for himself but for his officers that he coveted the latter; and yet, as he was to write in the following year, " I have since that time found two complete victories. I have kept *my* word. They who exist by victories at sea have not." Nelson " could not obey the Scriptures and bless them." The victory itself he extolled as the most hard-earned and complete in the annals of the navy. He was a bold man, Addington told him, to disregard orders: he rejoined that in taking the risk he counted on Addington's support. And Nelson was further troubled not only by wretched health and disappointment at the frustration of an earlier return, but by the blow of his brother Maurice's death. Amid his own engrossing avocations, he hastened to assure the poor blind " widow " that she was to cease fretting over her prospects, remain at Laleham, and count on him as a brother. " I am sure you will comfort poor blind Mrs. Nelson," he writes to Emma.

Both Sir William and Emma cheered him under depresssion.   He had now done enough, wrote Sir William.   It was the *ne plus ultra*.   He quoted Virgil:—

"Hic victor caestus artemque reponam."

As for Emma, let Sir William's words depict her:—
" You would have laughed to have seen what I saw yesterday.   *Emma* did not know whether she was on her head or her heels—in such a hurry to tell your great news, that she could utter nothing but tears of joy and tenderness."   Once more she is "the same Emma "—the Emma after the battle of the Nile.

Nelson responded with avidity to his now " dearest, *amiable* friend."   As her birthday neared he reminded her of those happy times a year gone by, and contrasted them with the present—" How different, how forlorn."   His body and spirit, like his ships, required refitting.   His " dearest wife " alone could nurse him, and only her generous soul comfort the " forlorn outcast."   He half hoped that the Admiralty wanted to replace him.   He would willingly have re-commanded in the Baltic, should emergencies re-arise, if only they would concede him his needed interval of rest.   He " would return with his shield or upon it."

With his shield the Pacificator of the North at length landed at Yarmouth on the 1st of July.   He repaired first to Lothian's hotel, as usual, but he was soon ensconced with the Hamiltons.   He was not suffered to remain long.   While the King and Queen of Naples —still Emma's *amie sœur*—were besetting him with lines of sympathy in the hope that he might re-emancipate them from renewed distress in the Mediterranean, Nelson was ordered, at the end of July, to baffle Buonaparte once more in the Channel.   The meditated invasion of England terrified the nation.   Consols tumbled, panic prevailed; all eyes were fixed on the one man who could save his country.

But an unheroic interlude happened before his worn frame was again called upon to bear the strain. Emma it was who took him out of town. Their first ramble was to Box Hill; and thence they went to the Thames. Sir William, as angler, frequented the " Bush Inn " at Staines—" a delightful place," writes Emma, " well situated, and a good garden on the Thames." " We thought it right to let him change the air and often." She had been ill at ease, chafing at the doubtful predicament in which devotion to the lover and care for the husband increasingly placed her; this little trip might afford a breathing-space. " The party," relates Emma, " consisted of Sir William and Lady Hamilton, the Rev. Dr. and Mrs. Nelson, Miss Nelson and the brave little Parker, who afterwards lost his life in that bold, excellent and vigorous attack at Boulogne, where such unexampled bravery was shown by our brave Nelson's followers."

" Old Q." and Lord William Douglas, detained with a sigh in town, forwarded their apologies in verse :—

> " So kind a letter from fair Emma's hands,
> Our deep regret and warmest thanks commands,"

and so forth. It satirises the parson's gluttony and banters his chatterbox of a wife. It depicts " Cleopatra " rowing " Antony " in the boat. It dwells on the old " Cavaliere " and his " waterpranks," his " bites," his *virtu,* his memories of excavation, and his stock of endless anecdotes. It holds up to our view poor, fatuous Hamilton as a prosy *raconteur.*

> " Or, if it were my fancy to regale
> My ears with some long, subterraneous tale,
> Still would I listen, at the same time picking
> A little morsel of Staines ham and chicken;
> But should he boast of Herculaneum jugs,
> Damme, I'd beat him with White's pewter mugs ";

while little red-cheeked, sloe-eyed Charlotte, rod in hand, yet shuddering at the fisherman's cruelty towards "the guileless victims of a murderous meal," is adjured to

"Heave a young sigh, and shun the proffered dish."

Emma's life was now wholly Nelson's; it is a relief to pass to a worthier scene. The main toils of the Channel defence were over. So was Nelson's keen disappointment in the deferred arrival of the Hamiltons to visit him at Deal on the *Amazon*. Sir William had been with Greville to look after the Milford estate. It was mid-September, and that second "little Parker," the truest friend of the man who felt that "without friendship life is misery," lay dying. Nelson had styled himself Parker's father. The death of one so young, promising, and affectionate, desolated him, and he would not be comforted. It was Parker who had looked up to him with implicit belief and absolute self-forgetfulness; Parker who had addressed his letters and run his and Emma's errands; Parker who, he had recently told her, "Knows my love for you; and to serve you, I am sure he would run bare-footed to London"; he had been called her "aide-de-camp." Together Nelson and Emma sat in the hospital and smoothed the pillows of the death-bed. Together they listened to his last requests and bade him still be of good cheer: for a few days there was "a gleam of hope." On September 27 he expired, and Nelson could say with truth that he "was grieved almost to death." The solemnity of that moment can never quite have deserted Emma.

Sad, but not hopeless, Nelson was purposely kept hovering round the Kentish coast until his final release towards the close of October. Yet Emma spurred him to his duty. "How often have I heard you say," he wrote to her at this very time, "that you would not quit the deck if you came near a Frenchman?" He made use of his time to forward Hamilton's interests with Pitt, on whom he called at Walmer, but found " Billy " " fast asleep." As he walked back, a scene with Emma of the previous spring rose again before him: " The same road that we came when the carriage could not come with us that night; and all rushed into my mind and brought tears into my eyes. Ah! how different to walking with such a friend as you, and Sir William, and Mrs. Nelson." In her anxiety for his return, Emma actually upbraided him with being a " time-server." The Admiralty would not yield even " one day's leave for Piccadilly." It was the 14th before he could tell her with gusto " To-morrow week all is over—no thanks to Sir Thomas." Just before he struck his flag he wrote, in pain as usual, " I wish the Admiralty had *my* complaint; but they have no bowels, at least for me."

He was now at length to possess a homestead and haven of his own. " Whatever Sir Thomas Troubridge may say," he wrote to his " guardian angel " in August, " out of your house I have no home." Soon after the Copenhagen conquest, he and his " dearest friend," at this moment with poor Mrs. Maurice Nelson, the widow of Laleham, had been mooting to each other projects for such a nest. He would like, he wrote, " a good *lodging* in an airy situation." A house in Turnham Green and others had been rejected, but at last one suitable had been found. Like almost everything connected with them both, difficulties and a dramatic moment attended its acquisition. The preliminaries of the Peace of Amiens were yet a secret, but Nelson had informed himself of the coming truce, so acceptable to him. Before its ratification had been divulged, Merton Place was bought—in the general depression—for the low sum of about six thousand pounds. But even this amount of capital was not easy for Nelson to raise, and the enthusiastic Davison —one of the few friends to whom Nelson would ever lie under the slightest obligation—lent him the money. Sir William seems to have objected to Emma's town hospitality to her relations. Nelson found in this an additional reason for purchasing a roof-tree which he desired her to treat as her own. " I received your kind letters last evening," he wrote to her on this and other heads, " and in many parts they pleased and made me sad. So life is chequered, and if the good predominates, then we are called happy. I trust the farm will make you more so than a dull London life. Make what use you please of it. It is as much yours as if you bought it. Therefore, if your relative cannot stay in your house in town, surely Sir William can have no objection to your taking to the farm [her relation] : the pride of the Hamiltons surely cannot be hurt by settling down with any of your relations; you have surely as much right for your relations to come into the house as his could have."

The whole affair was left entirely to Emma's management. She beset Nelson's solicitor, Haslewood, with letters, begging him to hurry forward the arrangements, and pressing the proprietor, Mr. Graves, to oblige Lord Nelson's " anxiety." Builders and painters were in the house immediately, to fit it for the hero's reception. The indispensable Mrs. Cadogan, now in charge of Nelson's new " Peer's robe," bustled in and out, covered to the elbows with brickdust. Emma set to work with a will, organising, ordering, preparing : in rough housework she delighted. She and her mother set up pigstyes, arranged the farm, stocked with fish the streamlet, spanned by its pretty Italian bridge. She procured the boat in which Nel-

son had promised she should row him on that miniature " Nile," which was really the Wandle.   Day after
day they slaved—glad to be quit of the artificial life
in Piccadilly—so that all might be spick and span
within the few weeks before the 22nd of October, the
great day of Nelson's arrival.   The whole village was
eager to greet him.   All the neighbours, the musical
Goldsmids, the rustic Halfhides, the literary Perrys,
the Parratts, the Newtons, the Pattersons, and Lan-
casters, were proud of the newcomers.   Never had
Merton experienced such excitement since one of the
first Parliaments had there told Henry III. that the
" laws of England " could not be changed.   There,
too, the same sovereign had concluded his peace with
the Dauphin—a good augury for the present moment.
Nelson wanted to defray all the annual expenses, but
Sir William insisted on an equal division, and rigorous
accounts were kept which still remain.

" I have lived with our dear Emma several years,"
he jests in a letter to Nelson, " I know her merit, have
a great opinion of the head and heart God Almighty
has been pleased to give her, but a seaman alone could
have given a fine woman full power to choose and fit up
a residence for him, without seeing it himself.   You
are in luck, for on my conscience, I verily believe that
a place so suitable to your views could not have been
found and at so cheap a rate.   For, if you stay away
three days longer, I do not think you can have any
wish but you will find it compleated here.   And then
the bargain was fortunately struck three days before
an idea of peace got about.   *Now,* every estate in this
neighbourhood has increased in value, and you might
get a thousand pounds for your bargain. . . . I never
saw so many conveniences united in so small a compass.   You have nothing but to come and to enjoy immediately.   You have a good mile of pleasant dry

walk around your farm. It would make you laugh to see Emma and her mother fitting up pigstyes and hencoops, and already the Canal is enlivened with ducks, and the cock is strutting with his hen about the walks."

Hamilton still retained the house in Piccadilly; he was now living above his means; as fast as money came in, the "housekeeping draughts" drew it out. His grand entertainments had proved a bad investment. One cannot help smiling when Nelson tells Emma during her Merton preparations, "You will make us rich with your economies."

When Nelson at length drove down from London in his postchaise to this suburban land of promise, it was under a triumphal arch that he entered it, while at night the village was illuminated. Here at last, and in the "piping" times of peace, the strange *Tria juncta in uno* were re-united; what Nelson had longed for had come to pass. Here, too, the man who loved retirement and privacy might hope to enjoy them; "Oh! how I hate to be stared at!" had been his ejaculation but two months before. And, above all, here he hoped to have Horatia with them in their walks, and to see her christened.

One of the first visitors was his simple old father, who maintained a friendly correspondence with Emma. By the close of the year the William Nelsons also stayed at Merton to rejoin their "jewel" of a daughter.

How smoothly and pleasantly things proceeded at first may be gleaned from Emma's further new letters to Mrs. William Nelson (then staying in Stafford Street). Emma occasionally drives into London for "shopping parties" (shops she could never resist) with Nelson's sister-in-law.

No sooner had Nelson returned, than they all went

together to beg a half-holiday for Charlotte.—"All girls pale before Charlotte"; and her classmate, a Miss Fuss, is "more stupid than ever, I think."— Charlotte came for her Exeat and fished with Sir William in the "Nile": they caught three large pike. She helped him and Nelson on with their great-coats, *"so now I have nothing to do."* "Dear Horace," whose birthday Nelson always remembered, must soon come also. Nelson was proud of Charlotte and of her "improvement" under Emma's directions. Emma, too, was proud of her rôle as governess. Charlotte turned over the prayers for the great little man in church. They were *all* regular church-goers. (Had not Nelson sincerely written to her earlier that they would do nothing but good in their village, and set "an example of godly life"?) Nelson and Sir William were the "greatest friends in the world." (Did he ever, one wonders, call him "my uncle"?) The "share-and-share alike" arrangement answered admirably—"it comes easy to booth partys." They none of them cared to visit much, though all were most kind in inviting them. "Our next door neighbours, Mr. Halfhide and his family, wou'd give us half of all they have, very pleasant people, and Mr. and Mrs. Newton allso; but I like Mrs. Halfhide very much indeed. She sent Charlotte grapes." As for Nelson, he was "very happy":—"Indeed we all make it our constant business to make him *happy*. He is better now, but not well yet." "He has frequent sickness, and is Low, and he throws himself on the sofa *tired and says, 'I am worn out.'"* She hopes "we shall get him up"—a phrase reminiscent of the laundry.

Hamilton himself averred to Greville that he too was quite satisfied. The early hours and fresh air agreed with him: he could run into town easily for his hobbies; he was cataloguing his books; he still hoped against hope that Addington would help him.

Eden at length without a serpent—at least so Nelson and Emma imagined. Merton idyllicised them. "Dear, dear Merton!" If only baby Horatia could be there (and soon she was) it would be perfect. As she was to express it in the last letter she could ever forward to him, and which he was never able to read —" Paradise Merton; for when you are there it will be paradise."

CHAPTER XII

January, 1802—May, 1803

THE winding high-road on the right of Wimble-
don towards Epsom leads to what once was
the Merton that Nelson and Emma loved. A
sordid modern street is now its main approach, but
there are still traces of the quaint old inns and houses
that jutted in and out of lanes and hedgerows. The
house that many a pilgrim thinks a piece of the old
structure may well be the remains of Mr. Halfhide's
or Mr. Newton's. Through a side road is found the
sole relic of Merton Place that has braved the ravages
of time and steam. Opposite a small railway station,
and near a timber-yard, stands the ruin of an ivied and
castellated gate, through which the stream meanders
on which Emma would row her hero, around which
the small Horatia played, in which Charlotte and
Horatio fished; while on its banks Nelson planted a
mulberry-tree that Emma fondly vaunted would rival
Shakespeare's. Goldsmid's Georgian house still
stands; but Merton Place has vanished into the vista
of crumbled yet unforgotten things. The ancient
church, however, though enlarged and well restored,
is much the same. Its churchyard still shows familiar
names—Thomas Bowen, and the Smiths who were to
be poor Emma's last befrienders. In the south aisle
is a picture attributed to Luca Giordano whose name

must have recalled Naples to Hamilton. The very bench on which they sat is still kept in the vestry. The hatchment with Nelson's bearings, which Emma presented after Trafalgar, still hangs in the nave. The fine old house—" Church House "—which they must have passed so often, still fronts the church porch. Even when they were there, the famous Priory where the great Becket was educated, and round which Merton's feudal memories clustered, had been replaced by calico factories. How eagerly must Nelson have awaited a glimpse even of these, when he drove up along the Portsmouth road for his last brief sojourn in the home of his heart; how wistfully must he have passed them, when the door clicked to, and off he rattled to eternity!

The two snakes in the grass of " Paradise " Merton were lavishness and, as it would seem, its contrast, Greville.

Nelson's liberality was as unbounded as abused; even his skin-flint brother William begged him to refrain in his own favour. Applications rained from all quarters. A Yorkshireman wrote and said he would be pleased to receive £300. " Are these people mad? " sighed the hero, " or do they take me quite for a fool? " He was always bestowing handsome presents, while for his many regular benefactions he had sometimes to draw on Davison. And Emma's open-handedness was not far behindhand. She scattered broadcast to her relations, to the poor, deserving or the reverse. The Connors soon began to prey on her anticipated means. Money burned a hole in her pocket, and she never stopped to think of the future. Before the year closed she left a note from Coutts for her husband on her toilet-table to the effect that her ladyship's balance was now twelve shillings. Greville must have shuddered when his uncle forwarded it to him. "Sensibility" was always over-drawing its banking account, and "Nature" continu-ally forestalling expectations. Added to largesse was some extravagance, but not to the degree that has often been put forward: it was by no means enor-mous, and in these days might be considered normal for her husband's position. Emma was in a holiday mood. Hamilton would not brace himself to the real retrenchment of giving up the London house, nor would Emma forego superfluities. Merton, though with intervals of quiet, became open house. Nelson's sisters, with their families—the Boltons with six, the Matchams with eight, his brother, still hunting for preferment, with his "precious" Charlotte, and little Horatio, the heir; old naval friends, including "poor little fatherless Fady," whom, it will be remembered, Emma tended in 1798. Emma's kindred, Italian sing-ers, the theatrical and musical Mrs. Lind, Mrs. Billing-ton, and Mrs. Denis; "Old Q." from Richmond, Wol-cot the satirist, Hayley from Felpham, Dr. Fisher from Doctors' Commons; Admiralty big-wigs, disgusted of-ficials, noisy journalists, foreign bearers of Nelson's decorations, the Abbé Campbell, Prince Castelcicala the Neapolitan ambassador, the Marquis Schinato, Maria Carolina's own son, Prince Leopold—all were indiscriminately welcomed. It was a menagerie. The Tysons, too, were now at Woolwich, and to them, as Nelson's attached adherents, Emma was all atten-tion. She chaperoned their young people to balls. She healed their conjugal differences: Mrs. Tyson was never so happy as at Merton, when her dear husband was restored to her, and she could at last "take the sacrament with a *composed mind*," and "bless dear Lady Hamilton." Benevolence, hospitality, and racket each mingled in the miscellany, and all of them tended to outrun the constable. The cellar was stocked with wine, and perhaps included some of those large gifts from foreign potentates to which a reference is made in the *Life* of the Reverend Dr. Scott. However that may be, when Emma's affairs were liquidated seven years later, the valuation of the cellar amounted to no less than two thousand pounds.

Nelson, who had protested against large gatherings, affected to enjoy Liberty Hall; all that his Emma commanded was exemplary. And, indeed, as appears from the accounts preserved in the Morrison autographs, the profusion was far greater in London, allowing for the expenditure of *both* houses. The joint weekly expenses at Merton were often no higher than some £30. Hamilton, however, whose own extravagance contributed, though he justified it by hopes from Addington, soon began to murmur. Greville, the monitor, was at his elbow. The heir's prospects were being imperilled by that very Emma whose thrift he had first inculcated and extolled; it was too bad; he must protect his old uncle, who protested to him that only fear of an " explosion " which might destroy his best friend's comfort stopped his rebellion against the " nonsense " that invaded his quiet. Before the year was out he even meditated an amicable separation. He did not complain; he still loved her. But he could not but perceive that her whole time and attention were bestowed on Nelson and " his interest." Therefore (and here Greville's voice appears to recur), after his hard fag at Naples, at his waning age, and under the circumstances, *a wise and well-concerted* separation might be preferable to " nonsense " and silly altercations. He had not long to live, and " every moment was precious " to him. He only wanted to be left alone at Staines, or Christie's, the Tuesday Club, the Literary Society, and the British Museum. " Nestor " continued a philosopher. They might still get on well enough apart, or together, if Emma would but consult the comfort of a worn-out diplomatist and virtuoso: " I am arrived at the age when some repose is really necessary, and I promised myself a quiet home, and although I was sensible, and I said so when I married, that I should be superannuated when my wife would be in her full beauty and vigour of youth; that time is ar-rived, and we must make the best of it for the comfort of both parties." He " well knew " the " purity of Lord Nelson's friendship " for them both. Nelson was their best friend, and it would pain him deeply to disturb his life or hurt his feelings. " There is no time for nonsense or trifling. I know and admire your talents and many excellent qualities, but I am not blind to your defects, and confess having many myself; therefore, let us bear and forbear, for God's sake."

The voice of this last appeal is that of the kindly old epicurean, and not of the calculating cynic. Emma, erring Emma, responded to it, and peace was restored for the few months remaining. So far, our entire sympathy must be with the worried and injured Ham-ilton. But ere this his necessities, and the cunning use to which his nephew seems to have put them, had prompted a plan which must lower him in our estima-tion.

As a rule, when Greville was asked (and he often was) to Merton, he politely excused himself. So anxious was Sir William for his presence that he actu-ally assured him of Nelson's " love," whereas Nelson, as we know, misliked the cold-blooded caster-off of his paragon. Greville, however, perpetually sent his warmest messages to the whole party, including his old acquaintance Mrs. Cadogan. With Greville, by hook or crook, a strange scheme was now to be concocted.

Failing the princely aid of the previous spring, a bargain after his own heart was being revived.

It will be recollected that Beckford, wearied of solitary magnificence, had offered Sir William a large annuity if he could induce royalty to grant a peerage to Hamilton with a reversion to himself. The Marquis of Douglas, heir of the ninth Duke of Hamilton and head of the clan, had shown symptoms of attachment to Euphemia, Beckford's daughter, whom in the end he married. If this attachment could be played upon for the purpose by the wary diplomatist, Beckford's object and Hamilton's might be secured. For such a plum Beckford now proposed a life annuity of £2000 that his kinsman might maintain the dignity of the peerage, and after his death one of £500 to Emma; while, as a bribe to ministers, Beckford's "two sure seats" were to be at their disposal.

Hamilton opened his mind the more freely to his "dear Marquis" on this "delicate" business since there existed a "very remarkable sympathy between them." Beckford had actually sent his West India agent to Merton for the management of this affair. Sir William ridiculed the mere notion of himself coveting such empty honours. He might, however, be useful to his friends, and no *éclat* need attend the transaction. Beckford had "strong claims on Government." An idea had struck Hamilton that the Marquis might one day be intimately connected with the Fonthill family. He did not demand definite answers; he was "sensible of its being a delicate point," yet he could not help flattering himself that "the good Duke of H. and myself would readily undertake anything for Emma's and my advantage, provided it could be done *sans vous compromettre trop.*" The Marquis promptly answered his kinsman's "very kind and confidential letter from Merton" by a gentle refusal. He found town very empty, but a select few, his books, papers, and pictures, contented him.   As to the matter in hand, it was, he feared, quite impracticable.   With regard to his own inclinations, " any symptoms of any sort ' which might have ' appeared in any part of his family " were unknown to and unencouraged by him.   Hamilton must convey every kind expression to Lord Nelson and Lady Hamilton; to himself he need not name his regard, and he was and ever should be his affectionate friend.

Poor " Nestor "!   To this pass have art and ambassadorship brought him.   And, alas, poor Emma, that she, too, should enlist her Nelson in such a service!

This disappointment happened in the summer, but in the spring an event occurred which cast real gloom over the Merton household.   In April died, at his favourite Bath, the well-loved father, that kindly, upright English clergyman, whom his great son fondly cherished, and whom he had actually wished to be a permanent inmate of the household.   Nelson's health immediately grew worse.   His first care, however, was for others, for his brother and sisters and his father's old manservant.   Condolences poured in upon him; nor was Emma the least grief-stricken, for this truly Christian soul had treated her with chivalrous charity, had wholly refrained from cruel speculations, and had rather sought to raise the thoughts of this strange incomer into Horatio's life.   While the brother flattered for gain, while every application for Nelson's favour came through her, she had known and felt that Nelson's father, who refused to realise the truth, was wholly good as well as godly.   She was in London at the time, and what she wrote has not survived.   Sir William's letter has.   It is characteristic of his " philosophy "—that of " the best of all possible worlds ":—

PICCADILLY, *April 28,* 1802.

". . . Emma says I must write a letter to you of condolence for the heavy loss your lordship has suffered. When persons in the prime of life are carried off by accident or sickness—or what is, I believe, oftener the case, by the ignorance and mistakes of the physicians—then, indeed, there is reason to lament. But, as in the case of your good father, the lamp was suffered to burn out fairly, and that his sufferings were not great; and that by his son's glorious and unparalleled successes, he saw his family ennobled, and with the probability in time of its being amply rewarded, as it ought to have been long ago—his mind could not be troubled, in his latter moments, on account of the family he left behind him. And as to his own peace of mind at the moment of his dissolution, there can be no doubt, among those who ever had the honour of his acquaintance. . . ."

Before the blow, however, had fallen that saddened Merton, a dinner and musical party was given at which Braham, who was afterwards to sing, amid *furore,* the " Death of Nelson," performed.

Nelson had much offended a society that longed to lionise him by sequestering himself from it altogether. Except at the assemblies of the Hamiltons' friends, he seldom figured at all, and the outraged Lady Nelson's advocates added this to their weightier reproaches against the " horrid " woman at Merton. He preferred even Bohemian routs to the solemnities of Downing Street or the frivolities of Mayfair, though he disliked all gatherings but those of intimate friends.

Among the guests of this evening was their old acquaintance Lord Minto, formerly of Vienna. He was disgusted at the interior with its trophies and portraits, but, above all, with Emma herself. Doubtless the sight of him put her in her most self-assertive vein. The reader must form his own judgment; but at any rate the censor, in this record, seems mistaken in supposing that the Hamiltons were " living on " Nelson. The Merton accounts in the Morrison Collection prove that all expenses were scrupulously shared.   And when he brands Emma's effusiveness to Nelson as flattery, what would he have said had he been able, as we are, to read Nelson's own outpourings to Emma?   If hers was " flattery," then still more was his.   But diplomats are not psychologists, nor have they always insight into such emotional temperaments.

". . . The whole establishment and way of life is such as to make me angry as well as melancholy; but I cannot alter it.   I do not think myself obliged or at liberty to quarrel with him for his weakness, though nothing shall ever induce me to give the smallest countenance to Lady Hamilton.   She looks eventually to the chance of marriage. . . . In the meanwhile, she, Sir William, and the whole set of them are living with him at his expense.   She is in high looks, but more immense than ever.   She goes on cramming Nelson with trowelfuls of flattery, which he goes on taking as quietly as a child does pap.   The love she makes to him is not only ridiculous, but disgusting.   Not only the rooms, but the whole house, staircase and all, are covered with nothing but pictures of her and him, of all sizes and sorts, and representations of his naval actions, coats of arms, pieces of plate in his honour, the flagstaff of *L'Orient,* etc., an excess of vanity which counteracts its own purpose.   If it was Lady H.'s house, there might be a pretence for it.   To make his own a mere looking-glass to view himself all day is bad taste.   Braham, the celebrated Jew singer, performed with Lady H.   She is horrid, but he entertained me in spite of her.   Lord Nelson explained to me a little the sort of blame imputed to Sir Hyde Parker for Copenhagen. . . ."

It was certainly a queer household for seemly self-importance to enter. Without question, there was warrant for worse than such superficial strictures as those in which Elliot here indulged. Emma had deteriorated, and she had never fitted the formalities of English drawing-rooms. Average folk, as will be seen hereafter, she charmed. But the guest, though naturally affronted, was likely to be prejudiced. Emma was wholly offensive to him, and the patronising air of one whom Braham's pathos " entertained " may, after its own manner, have been irritating also. The ambassador was an official type of good taste, and of Emma, it must be thought, there was always overmuch in a room. His looks on this occasion must have been vinegar, and can have ill accorded with that natural sweetness of expression which, by consent of friend and foe alike, distinguished Emma from first to last. Officialism had set itself against Nelson like a flint, and, likely enough, his devotee was supercilious to her enemy, whom probably she mimicked after he had gone, as she certainly used to mimic Nelson's fussy brother. Still, however it may be deplored, the stubborn fact remains that Britain's deliverer loved this woman's *reality*, and misliked the spirit of officialism; that against him were arrayed the pettiest forces at home and the mightiest abroad. Nelson endures in history, and with him Emma, while patterns of the primmest diplomacy have long faded into the vagueness of distance. To appraise Emma, not defence but understanding is requisite. Antipathy, like flattery, is the worst critic; and pedantic antipathy is perhaps its worst form. Burleigh would have made a bad judge of the Queen of Scots, and Cicero of Cleopatra.

Emma's " immensity " had been for some time in

evidence, and was grossened in the caricatures.   She affected to think that fatness became her fine stature and large proportions.   It was due, partly, to the porter which she drank for the sake of her voice, and which, as appears in the earlier letters of the Morrison Collection, had been forwarded by Greville to his uncle long before Emma had entered his life at Naples.

In the June of this year, too, died Admiral Sir John Willet-Payne, who, after sitting in Parliament, had for some time been treasurer of Greenwich Hospital.   Nelson must have known him, and curiosity is aroused as to whether Emma ever saw her first tempter again, and what he thought of her marvellous career.

And in November was to flicker out that sensitive genius and singular being to whom Emma had been so beholden in her girlhood.   Romney, wasting with melancholy, had resought the refuge of the Kendal rooftree and the ministering wife so long neglected.   In one of his conversations with Hayley, he told him that he had always studied " Sensibility " by observing the fibrous lines around the mouth.   It was Emma's mouth that had been a revelation to him.   One cannot help wishing that some final correspondence between them may one day be discovered.

For the summer, Hamilton had planned a driving tour to the Milford property, where the nephew and steward wished to show his uncle the best work of his life—a flourishing settlement of labourers.   Emma and Nelson accompanied him on the Welsh trip, which soon turned into a fresh triumphal progress for the hero of the Nile and of Copenhagen, who shamed the Government by remaining a Vice-Admiral.   Greville's presence may be assumed.   Certainly he was at Milford.   Before they started, William Nelson, who had just returned from bowing to " Billy " Pitt at Cambridge, his wife and their young Horatio, were added to the group of travellers. It is strange on this occasion to find the triple alliance of Nelson and the Hamiltons reinforced by Greville, before whom, Nelson had told Emma, conversation must be restrained; in his official presence they could not speak freely " of kings and beggars." This journey, like its continental predecessor, was certainly not calculated to allay irritation in high places.

They started on the 9th of July with Box Hill once more—" a pretty place, and we are all very happy." They went on to Oxford, where Nelson received the freedom of the city in a fine box to the music of finer orations, and where the Matchams joined the caravan. It was here that on a visit to Blenheim the Marlboroughs infuriated Emma by declining to receive her. She was determined to appeal, for herself and her hero, to the Cæsar of the people. She performed her music both for the select and the vulgar. Everywhere Emma beat the big drum of popular enthusiasm. The long highroads, the swarming streets, the eager villages from Burford to Gloucester, from Gloucester to Ross, from Ross to Monmouth, Caermarthen and Milford, from Milford to Swansea, from Swansea to Cardiff, were thronged with stentorian admirers. On the return journey, from Cardiff to Newport and Chepstow, and so to Monmouth again, on to Hereford, Leominster, Tenbury, Worcester, Birmingham, Warwick, Coventry, Dunstable, Watford, and Brentford, all turned out like one man to cheer the postilioned carriages. Bells were rung, factories and theatres visited, addresses read, speeches made, the National Anthem and " Rule Britannia " sung by the shouting crowds. Wherever they went, the neighbouring magnates loaded Nelson and his friends with invitations, and Payne-Knight implored Emma for a visit. And everywhere this exuberant daughter of democracy led

and swelled the chorus. Her Nelson *should* " be first."
" Hip, hip, hip ! " " God Save the King ! " " Long
live Nelson, Britain's Pride ! "

> " Join we great Nelson's name
> First on the roll of fame,
>   Him let us sing;
> Spread we his praise around,
> Honour of British ground,
> Who made Nile's shores resound—
>   God save the King ! "

It was Naples over again, and Emma was in her
true element. Let the whole official brotherhood look
to themselves and dare their worst. They were routed
now. The *people* were on the side of those who had
toiled hard, of those who had really borne the brunt,
who had risked their lives to save their homes from the
bogey of Europe. " Hip, hip, hip, *in excelsis!* " No
wonder that, when all was over and, hoarse but happy,
Emma reposed at Merton once more, awaiting a fresh
but private jubilation on Nelson's approaching birthday, she took up her pen with triumph :—

" We have had a most charming Tour which will
Burst *some* of THEM. So let all the enimies of the
GREATEST man alive [perish?] ! And bless his
friends." In this same letter her native goodness of
heart breaks out with equal vehemence about the death
of " poor Dod," one of Nelson's countless protégés :
" Anything that we can do to assist the poor widow
we will." How this *" we "* reminds us of the " we "
before Sir William married her, which had so annoyed Legge ! And the sensation of this progress still
tingled in the air. In October Lord Lansdowne
begged in vain for a visit, should they stay again at
Fonthill. While Banks sympathised with Greville's
sigh of relief, Ball told Emma of his interest, smiled

over her huzzaings, and recalled her kindness to the Maltese Deputies. Her enthusiasm was still contagious.

But this trip did not close without a conjugal breeze easily raised and easily calmed.

Emma insisted on recruiting her health by her old remedy of sea-baths, probably at Swansea; Hamilton, however, longed to get home. He was exhausted, and she was petulant, as the following little passage at arms bears witness:—

"As I see it is pain to you to remain here, let me beg of you to fix your time for going. Weather I dye in Piccadilly or any other spot in England, 'tis the same to me; but I remember the time when you wished for tranquillity, but now all visiting and bustle is your liking. However, I will do what you please, being ever your affectionate and obedient E. H." On the back of it Sir William wrote:—

"I neither love bustle nor great company, but I like some employment and diversion. . . . I am in no hurry, and am exceedingly glad to give every satisfaction to our best friend, our dear Lord Nelson. Seabathing is usefull to your health; I see it is, and wish you to continue a little longer; but I must confess that I regret, whilst the season is favourable, that I cannot enjoy my favourite amusement of quiet fishing. I care not a pin for the great world, and am attached to no one as much as you." On its fly-leaf Emma added, "I go, when you tell me the coach is ready," to which Hamilton retorted: "This is not a fair answer to a fair confession of mine." So ended the last of their tiny quarrels. Nestor was reconciled to Penelope.

The sands of his life were fast running down, and he was soon to have that euthanasia which he had praised to Nelson. Emma's heart smote her as she beheld his fading powers. He suffered no pain, but he gradually sank. He was removed to Piccadilly, and by the March of 1803 it was clear that his end was in sight. Both Emma and Nelson were constant in their attendance and attention. It had been Nelson who, in his passionate outpouring, occasionally speculated on "my uncle's" demise; but Emma, apart from gratitude and a sense of the wrong that she had done him, well knew that his death would remove a real friend and a loving counsellor. All the past rose up vividly, from the days of the selfishness of Greville, who was now again half-hardening himself against her, to those of the loving husband who had trusted and shielded her. Some feeling of sorrow, compunction, and forlornness possessed her. However grievously she had erred, she did her duty at the last. And at the last the old man's mind had wandered.

On April 6, 1803, at eleven o'clock, Nelson wrote this hurried note to Davison:—

"Our dear Sir William died at 10 minutes past Ten this morning in Lady Hamilton's and my arms without a sigh or a struggle. Poor Lady H. is as you may expect desolate. I hope she will be left properly, but I doubt."

Greville had once more succeeded.

Nelson would not so have written if Emma had not so felt. His feelings were coloured by hers. Among Nelson's papers remains one in Emma's handwriting intended for no eye but his, and to which no hypocrisy can be imputed:—

"*April* 6.—Unhappy day for the forlorn Emma. Ten minutes past ten dear blessed Sir William left me."

In all her private answers to condolence the refrain is the same—" What a man, what a husband." It can scarcely be called falsetto. Not until she had lost him did she realise all that he had been to her, and how she had wronged him. Strange as it may sound, she was stricken indeed.

And yet her attitudinising heart soon alternated between different moods. She cut off her flowing locks and wore them *à la* Titus in the fashionable mode of mourning. When Madame Le Brun met her a few months afterwards, she sat down and sang a snatch at the piano. On a later occasion the French paintress noticed that she had put a rose in her hair, and inquiring the reason, was told, " I have just received a letter from Lord Nelson." Later on, she consented to oblige Madame Le Brun by privately showing before a few of the *noblesse émigrée* some of her " Attitudes," which she had never been willing to display in London.

" On the day appointed," notes the artist in her chronicle, " I placed in the middle of my drawing-room a very large frame, with a screen on either side of it. I had a strong lime-light prepared and disposed, so that it could not be seen, but which would light up Lady Hamilton as though she were a picture. . . . She assumed various attitudes in this frame in a way truly admirable. She had brought a little girl with her, who might have been seven or eight years old, and who resembled her strikingly. One group they made together reminded me of Poussin's ' Rape of the Sabines.' She changed from grief to joy, and from joy to terror, so that we were all enchanted."

Such a " lime-light," perhaps revealing without being seen, was Emma's own organisation unconsciously " lighting up " the possibilities of others. Her " Attitudes " were the expression of her successive and often self-deceiving emotions. In the old Indian music, we are told, are certain selected notes, called " ragas," that, separately and without harmonised relations, strike whole moods into the heart of the listener.

Such, it seems to me, was her temperament, and such its function.

Sir William Hamilton was buried by the side of his first wife, as he had promised her twenty-five years before.

A month after his decease the will was read in Piccadilly before the assembled relations—the Grevilles, the Cathcarts, the Meyricks, the Abercorns, and the rest. Nelson forwarded the announcement to Davison by Oliver. He had suggested the advisability of reading Sir William's deed of gift of the furniture to Emma before a full conclave, as it might otherwise " be supposed that Mr. C. Greville *gives* Lady H. the furniture," which her money had bought for Sir William. The will itself proved Nelson's suspicion of Greville's influence not altogether unfounded, and the fact " vexed " him sorely. Though Hamilton had forestalled income, his means were ample; even Elliot was astonished at the inadequate provision for his widow.[1] To his " dear wife Emma " he bequeathed a sum of £300, and an annuity of £800, to include provision for her mother. In a codicil he recites that as he had promised to pay her debts, amounting to £700, but of this sum had only paid £250, Greville was to pay her in advance the current annuity of £800, for herself and Mrs. Cadogan, while the unpaid remainder of her debts she was to recover as a charge upon the arrears of pension owed him by the Government. The last arrangement was nugatory on the face of it. The Government that had disregarded Sir William was unlikely to re-

---

[1] *Minto Life and Letters,* vol. ii. p. 283. "Worse off than I imagined." He adds: "She talked very freely of her situation with Nelson, and of the construction the world may have put upon it, but protested that her attachment was perfectly pure which I can believe, though I declare it is of no consequence whether it is so or not." Maria Carolina also deplored her "indifferent provision."

gard his widow. It is but just towards Greville, who had been always at his uncle's elbow, to relate that within a week of Sir William's demise he urged his dying wishes on the then Foreign Secretary in the strongest terms, while at the same time he repeated his (Hamilton's) previous strictures on the Government's past treatment. " I *know*," he concluded, " that the records of your office confirm the testimony of their Sicilian Majesties by letter as well as by their Ministers of circumstances peculiarly distinguished and honourable to her, and at the same time of high importance to the public service." But Emma was thus left with no capital except the furniture, of uncertain value, and with an income diminished by a debt which her husband had promised to discharge, but of which only one-quarter had been settled. Greville and his brother, the Colonel, were declared executors, the first being residuary legatee. To Nelson he gave an enamel of Emma " as a very small token of the great regard I have for his lordship, the most virtuous, loyal, and truly brave character I ever met with. God bless him, and shame fall on all those who do not say Amen."

This avowal does Hamilton honour. Poor Nestor! —however reluctant his submission, whatever his misgivings, he steeled himself against them to the last. I do not think that Hamilton was wholly befooled, but how could the Nelson that he loved reconcile to his conscience such tributes of trust from one whom he had long cherished with more than esteem? He and Emma must both have felt a pang of shame and remorse. They had skated on thin ice together. Though their duplicity, uncongenial to the frankness of both, had been imposed on them by their united care for each other's interest, and Horatia's, it had also imposed upon others. Bearing in mind every extenuation, one would fain forget this unlovely spectacle; apart from extenuation it is hideous. Their falsity towards Hamilton cannot be condoned. Their sin had impaired Emma's sense, and Nelson's principle, of truth.

Neither of them lost time in besetting the authorities for a grant both of pension and of compensation which might clear her of debt. To Addington she wrote herself. She was " forced to petition." She was " most sadly bereaved." She was now " in circumstances far below those in which the goodness " of her " dear Sir William " allowed her " to move for so many years." She pleaded for his thirty-six years' efforts for England at Naples. " And may I mention," she added, in words to be carefully scanned as the first expression of her claims, " what is well known to the then administration at home—how I too strove to do all I could towards the service of our King and Country. The fleet itself, I can truly say, could not have got into |Sicily but for what I was happily able to do with the Queen of Naples (and through her secret instructions so obtained), on which depended the refitting of the fleet in Sicily, and with that, all which followed so gloriously at the Nile. These few words, though seemingly much at large, may not be extravagant at all. They are, indeed, true. I wish them to be heard only as they can be proved; and being proved, may I hope for what I have now desired." Addington professed to Lord Melville, who spoke to him on the matter, that he would give the whole circumstances a favourable consideration. But Nelson from the first counted little on his assistance, though of Pitt, for the moment, he seemed rather more sanguine.

But already, amid all these agitations, the supreme one of renewed severance from Nelson threatened. He had always prophesied that the truce of Amiens would not endure. In May Napoleon divined the safe moment for breaking it. Russia was then friendly, and

Austria hesitating. It was not till the following year, when his murder of the Duc d'Enghien scandalised Europe, that Russia contrived the third coalition, which Prussia and Austria joined. Napoleon now prepared to invade Naples: his troops were soon to occupy Hanover. Our Ambassador, Lord Whitworth, was recalled from Paris. Maria Carolina assured Emma of her delight at the prospect of Nelson's renewed Mediterranean command, and Acton, who had by now assumed the superintendence of Bronte, looked forward to seeing his old associate once more.

Death, doubt, and despair confronted Emma together, but she did not quail. Her faults were many, but cowardice was never one of them. Her hero would win fresh victories and once more save his country. She little recked how long that absence was to last. For the first time he had been with her for eighteen months, unparted.

A wedding and a christening signalised the month of his departure, and showed Nelson and Emma together in public.

In May, at the Clarges Street house, to which Emma had then been forced to remove, Captain Sir William Bolton married his cousin, the daughter of Nelson's sister and Emma's friend, Mrs. Thomas Bolton. Emma was afterwards to be godmother to their first-born, " Emma Horatia." Sir William, for whose promotion Nelson always exerted himself, proved somewhat of a booby, to Nelson's amused chagrin.

And three days before he said farewell, Horatia was baptized in the same Marylebone church which had witnessed her mother's marriage. The nurse had already brought the two years old child from time to time to see them at Merton. Nelson and Emma stood by the font as god-parents of their own child, and two clergymen officiated at the christening of " Horatia Nelson

Thomson." Now, at least, she might soon find her home at Merton. Nelson gave her a silver cup, a cup by which hangs a sad tale, and which, years afterwards, had to be sacrificed to poverty.

Greville hardly behaved well. He harshly denied her a moment longer than the end of April in the Piccadilly house. She applied to him, in the third person, to ascertain the precise limit of her stay, as she must "look out for lodgings" and "reduce her expenses." Nelson, however, now resolved to allow her £100 a month for the upkeep of Merton, but unfortunately, though mainly residing at her "farm," she could not refrain from still renting a smaller town house in Clarges Street.

An altercation ensued, it is said, between Nelson and Greville. At any rate, Greville's continued hardness towards Emma, soon to be accentuated by his deduction of the income-tax from her annuity, evoked the following from Nelson more than two years afterwards:—

"Mr. Greville is a shabby fellow. It never could have been the intention of Sir William but that you should have had seven hundred pounds a year neat money. . . . It may be law, but it is not just, nor in equity would, I believe, be considered as the will and intention of Sir William. Never mind! Thank God, you do not want any of his kindness; nor will he give you justice."

At four o'clock on the morning of May 18, the postchaise drew up before Merton Place: only one trunk was in it. Before any one was astir, Nelson had bidden his passionate adieu, and had driven off with the dawn. From Kingston, on his road, he despatched the familiar line of consolation:—

"Cheer up, my dearest Emma, and be assured that I ever have been, and am and ever will be, your most faithful and affectionate." He had hardly reached his destination when he resumed: "Either my ideas are altered, or Portsmouth. . . . It is a place, the picture of desolation and misery, but perhaps it is the contrast to what I have been used to. . . . When you see my *élève,* which you will when you receive this letter, give her a kiss from me, and tell her that I never shall forget either her or her dear good mother." Two days later he again gave comfort from the *Victory* :— "You will believe that although I am glad to leave that horrid place Portsmouth, yet the being afloat makes me now feel that we do not tread the same element. I feel from my soul that God is good, and in His due wisdom will unite us. Only, when you look upon our dear child, call to your remembrance all that you think I would say, was I present. And be assured that I am thinking of you every moment. My heart is full to bursting. May God Almighty bless you is the fervent prayer of, my dear beloved Emma, your most faithful, affectionate Nelson."

The old trio had been dissolved, and a new trio reigned in its stead. Horatia now sanctified his existence, her portrait already adorned his cabin. Emma becomes Calypso no more, but Penelope—a Penelope, moreover, with repulsed suitors. On Greville's life— even on Hamilton's—she had been but an iridescence, but to Nelson she is light, air, and heat in one; and what she was to him, that Nelson remains to her in perpetuity.

CHAPTER XIII

PENELOPE AND ULYSSES

June, 1803—January, 1806

IT is a far cry from Merton to the Mediterranean, but for Nelson the one was nearly as important as the other: the heart of Ulysses was with his Penelope.

Estranged Greville straightway took up his uncle's mantle, exchanging learned disquisitions with Banks about "mud volcanoes in Trinidad." Davison was trying to curb Emma's extravagant schemes for Merton improvements, though he himself was now in election scrapes, and a few years later was, unfortunately, to rival St. George himself as a fraudulent contractor. Penelope (fretted and ailing), whether at Merton, Southend, Clarges Street, or Canterbury, by turns with the Matchams, Boltons, or Nelsons, sent daily reports to her wandering Ulysses. She tattled alike of her conflicting emotions, of the dukes and princes, her suitors, and of her exertions to secure berths for countless applicants. All Nelson's nephews and nieces constantly found themselves a happy family under her roof, and Merton was now Merton Academy for Charlotte. Strange as it seems, Emma's relations and Nelson's were on affectionate and equal terms, her cousin, Sarah Connor, being now governess to the Bolton children, while Mrs. Matcham, Nelson's pet sister, actually wished to find a new house near Merton. "Our good Mrs. Cadogan," too, was beloved by his family and his friends, whom she provided from the dairy. She was the Merton economist, kept all too busy checking the accounts of the rapacious Cribb.[1] Such was Penelope's chronicle.

Nelson had only three thoughts—Emma, Horatia, and the French fleet. During the next three years, whether at Gibraltar or Naples, Toulon or, afterwards, La Rosas, and eventually off Boulogne, he mused on these, and these alone, by day; he dreamed of them at night; they possessed him in fierce concentration. He was an inspired monomaniac, and the flame of his fanaticism both burnt and fired him to achievement. Different kinds of self-forgetful ardour animate every prophet. Adoration of his country, a woman, and a child, animated Nelson. In this he contrasts with all his colleagues and predecessors, who did their duty like stolid Spartans, unwarmed and unenticed by any dangerous glow. To the sober-minded, Emma is his will-of-the-wisp; to him, she was his beacon. He calls her his " Alpha and Omega "; he beseeches her not to fret. Her and the French fleet—" to these two objects tend all his thoughts, plans, and toils," and he will " embrace them so close " when he " can lay hold of either the one or the other, that the devil himself should not separate " them. He longed " to see both " in their " proper places "—the one at sea, the other " at dear Merton, which, in every sense of the word," he expects " to find a paradise." He still deemed none worthy " to wipe her shoes." He vowed not to quit his ship till they could meet again. " From Ambassatrice to the duties of domestic life " he has never seen her equal; her " elegance, . . . accomplishments, and, above all, goodness of heart," are " unparalleled,"

---

[1] He was a sort of steward at Merton, but he also supplied the green-groceries. He encouraged the extravagant expense of the Merton improvements.

and he is devoted to her " for ever and beyond it."
Eagerly he treasured the slenderest tidings of her from
officers returning to or from England.

Each night, as Scott, his chaplain—Scott, with his
lightning-struck head—relates to Emma, he toasted
their Guardian Angel, with a tender look towards her
portrait, and a side glance, doubtless, at the smiling
face of the child below it. To Horatia he addressed
the first *whole* letter that he had written to her. He
bought her a gold watch through Falconet of Naples,
and forwarded it as a reminder of her liking to listen
to his own; he sent her a pretty picture-book of " Spanish dresses," bidding her be always good and obedient
to her " Guardian Angel, Lady Hamilton." When,
for the second time, he ensured such a settlement for
Horatia's future as no imprudence could undo, he commended " the dear little innocent " to Emma, as certain
to train her in the paths of religion and virtue.
Emma's every concern interested him. In her letters
he finds the " knack " of hitting off and picturing topics
to a marvel. Over her cousin, Charles Connor, now a
midshipman under his charge, he watched like a
father. As he passed Capri, recollection " almost over-
powers " his feelings. He enclosed for her the new entreaties of her old friends the King and Queen of
Naples, while she transmitted to him Maria Carolina's
letter to her, protesting the usual sympathy and gratitude. Amid his many engrossments he followed the
projected improvements at Merton as if he were there
—the new rooms and porch, the new road, the dike to
fill up a part of the " Nile," the surrender of a strip to
" Mr. Bennett, which will save £50 a year," the acquirement of another field, the " strong netting " to
surround the rivulet for little Horatia's safety. Davison had remonstrated over the expense; Nelson directed
him to proceed. He expressly enjoined her—a fact

afterwards important—not to pay for them out of her *income*. He little guessed what a millstone she was hanging round her neck; she was right to have her way; all was right always that she did, wrote, or thought. He commended her to Davison's tenderest care. He chose her presents of shawls and chains from Naples. He recovered some of her lost furniture both at Malta and Palermo. He enclosed £100— for herself and the poor at Merton, together with gifts to Miss Connor, Mrs. Cadogan, and Charlotte, "a trifling remembrance from me, whose whole soul is at Merton"; and her "good mother" is always sure of his "sincerest regard."

Emma's heart, too, was across the sea. She watched every wind, chance, and disappointment. When at Southend, where she met her old friend Jane Powell, the actress, she thought of little but Nelson and Horatia. She was in ill health; but she was still "patroness of the navy," forwarding each officer's requests to, and his interest with, her Nelson. If she diverted herself with concerts, or teased her ogling suitors, at the same time she begged Davison to introduce her to Nepean, for her hero's sake. She kept the "glorious first of August" with her friends, and only regretted that the Abbé Campbell must be absent. She looked anxiously for letters,—"despatches and sea breezes will restore you," wrote Mrs. Bolton. She bought and sent off his very boots—a size, it would seem, too small. He has warned her never to spend her money "to please a pack of fools," nor to let her native generosity empty her purse even for his sisters, as she so often did; not to hunt for a legacy from "Old Q."—Nelson (repeating her own phrase) "would not give sixpence to call the King my uncle." He regretted Addington's hard-heartedness in begrudging her an annuity, but Addington's tether was fast

coming to an end. He got the Queen to address the
Government on Emma's behalf, though he placed little
reliance on the letter's efficacy or her friendship.
When, nearly eighteen months later, he was baulked,
as he usually was, of his prize-money, Emma char-
acteristically wrote to Davison:—" The *Polyphemus*
should have been Nelson's, but he is rich in great and
noble *deeds,* which t'other, poor devil, is not. So let
dirty wretches get pelf to comfort them: victory belongs to Nelson. Not but what I think money necessary for comforts; and I hope *our, yours,* and *my* Nelson will get a little, for all Master O." [1] How well
does this accord with Nelson's own avowal to her of
" honourable poverty "! " I have often said, and with
honest pride, what I have is my own; it never cost the
widow a tear or the nation a farthing. I got what
I have with my pure blood from the enemies of my
country. Our house, my own Emma, is built upon a
solid foundation."

In September, so wretched was she away from him,
that she implored him to let her come out and see him.
" Good sense," he replied, " is obliged to give way to
what is right, and I verily believe that I am more likely
to be happy with you at Merton than any other place,
and that our meeting at Merton is more probable to
happen sooner than any wild chase in the Mediterranean." " It would kill you," he repeated, " and myself to see you. Much less possible, to have Charlotte,
Horatia, etc., on board ship." And as for living in
Italy, " that is entirely out of the question. Nobody
cares for us there ": it would cost him a fortune to go
to Bronte, and be " tormented " out of his life. Indeed at this very moment he had serious thoughts of re-
linquishing Bronte altogether.

Nelson was never self-indulgent; he was unselfish,

[1] Sir John Orde. This letter is of January, 1805.

if not selfless, in devotion, even where he went most
astray. Under dispiritments innumerable, and morti-
fications doubly galling to one of his temperament,
through a catalogue of hardships which rival the
apostle's, in weary wakefulness, in headache, eye-ache,
toothache, and heartache, constantly sea-sick in the
newly painted cabins which he abhorred, with a body,
as he said, unequal to his spirit, he was always thinking of and caring for others; and it is this that endears
him to us even more than his glory.   At this very time
he bade Emma do her utmost for General Dumouriez,
the brave enemy turned into a friend—*their* friend;
not a sailor in the service but was proud of one of his

> " . . . nameless, unremembered acts
> Of kindness and of love,"

and his considerate maintenance of their health was his
perpetual boast.

There was, moreover, something dæmonic about this
wonderful man.   At a glance he sweeps the horizon,
intuitively discerning the danger and its preventives.
At Naples once more he renewed the royal gratitude,
incited Acton, now rapidly falling into disfavour, and
forecast the French designs at a time when Ferdinand
wrote to him, " the hand of Providence again weighs
heavy on us," when the Sicilians themselves, and even
the Queen, were on the verge of turning towards Napoleon's risen sun, and our old acquaintance Ruffo, now
ambassador, was off on the wonted wild-goose chase to
Vienna.   As in public, so in private, Nelson seems always to hear voices prompting him.   He believes in a
star that will guide him to victory and home.   " My
sight is getting very bad," he wrote, " but I *must not*
be sick till after the French fleet is taken," at the very
moment when it seemed further off than ever.   Small
wonder that, with such a leader, Davison ejaculated his

certainty that sooner or later Buonaparte's Boulogne flotilla would " go to old Nick."

Nelson this autumn retailed all the Neapolitan gossip for Emma. Napoleon had dictated to Maria Carolina the dismissal of her ex-favourite, Acton. She herself, surrounded by French minions, had relapsed into the peccadillos of a date prior to Emma's arrival, of which Acton used to tell them such amazing stories. The King had thrown the last shred of love for her to the winds. It would not be long before Napoleon pounced on and annexed Naples; before the royalties were once more exiles in Sicily. The Princess Belmonte was mischief-making in London, and Emma must be careful of encountering her. All Sir William's old dependants were cared for; one of his servitors, Gaetano, was already in Nelson's service, and preferred it to home. Hugh Elliot was now ambassador, friendly to Emma's claims. One of the Hamiltons' old abodes had become an hotel. Their ancient friend, Lord Bristol, was dead at Rome. He had once promised them the bequest of a table, but now, " There will be no Lord Bristol's table. He tore his last will a few hours before his death."

These are trifles, but before reverting to Emma, let us rapidly glance at Nelson's doings during this year of 1804, during his tedious task of guarding the Mediterranean and watching Toulon ("blockading" he would never term it: he hated blockades). He was endeavouring to decoy the French to sea—to " put salt on their tails," but save for a brief spurt in May, endeavouring in vain. As the French fleet was " in and out," so he was up and down—at Malta, Palermo, and when Spain rejoined the fray, at Barcelona, where the Quaker merchant " Friend Gaynor " became a fresh intermediary with Emma. His " time," as he said, " and movements depended on Buonaparte." Impa-

tient by nature, he could play the waiting game to perfection. Though his cough and swelled side continu-
ally troubled him, he was as indefatigable out of action
as in it, and he disdained the mean advantage offered
by any subordinate's breach of strict neutrality. He
still hoped to force those unconscionable ships out of
port. Tréville was now the Toulon Admiral, and
Nelson " owed him one " for landing the Grenadiers at
Naples in 1792. Amid the discouragements of long
delays and the customary official threat to supplant
him, he could look forward to eating " his Christmas
dinner at Merton." Although, when his birthday came
round, he was farther off from consummation than
ever, and reminded Emma of his " forty-six years of
toil and trouble," he refused to appear downcast. The
accession of Pitt to power in the spring of 1804 cheered
him, both on England's account and hers. He still regularly drank her health and " darling " Horatia's. Her
letters still brought before him the tranquillity of their
days; he rejoiced in her many acts of kindness, not
only to his friends and relations, but to grateful
strangers. He welcomed a tress of her beautiful hair,
and treated it as a pilgrim does a relic. Even while
he sat signing orders, he wrote to her, " My life, my
soul, God in heaven bless you." He remembered the
birthday of the " dear beloved woman " with emphasis.
He instructed her to buy pieces of plate for their new
and joint god-children. Even in his wrath at the capture of a vessel bringing her portrait and letters, he
made merry over the admiration of them by the French
Consul at Barcelona.

While Emma was occupied with Horatia and her
young charges from Norfolk, all had suddenly to be
dismissed. Nelson's second daughter, " Emma," was
born may be at the close of February. The reader will

recall Nelson's torrent of passionate love and anxiety in the ebullition cited [1] as applicable to his feelings at the time of Horatia's birth. At this very moment Horatia was unwell also, and her illness added to his " raging fever " of emotion as he awaited Emma's news. Before July, the second infant of his hopes was dead. Thorns there were besides roses at Merton.

All this while the correspondence of the Boltons and Matchams, both young and old, with Lady Hamilton, breathes affectionate regard, unfeigned admiration, and real respect. She is the best of friends; her coming is eagerly awaited, her going keenly deplored. Eliza and Anne Bolton find in her a confidante, a trusted and trustworthy counsellor, the acme of the accomplishments that she knows how to impart to them. With the William Nelsons it was the same, though here, perhaps, the motives were less disinterested. Charlotte adores her benefactress and educatress. As for the Navy, Louis and others, in their letters, look up to her almost with veneration. If Emma had the power of offending, that also of conciliating was hers. These are facts which cannot be wholly ascribed to the exaggerations of homely admirers, or to the self-interest of office-seekers. These people seem, none of them, ever to have relinquished their fondness.

Nothing can exceed the variety of contrasts in a nature to which it lends fascination. Emma's tissue is spangled homespun, but the spangles mainly overlie it. Let us examine it on both sides.

We watch her throughout these letters, on the one hand, simple, homely, sympathetic, with no good or humble office beneath her, working in and for her house and her friends; a Lady Bountiful dignifying the trivial round, and generous not only with her purse but with her time, her praise, and her exertions—a true

[1] Cf. chapter xi.

Penelope by her spinning-wheel.   And yet, on the other hand, we view her inhaling the fumes of homage, whether from the suitors or the crowd.   We see her courting the flutter of Bohemia, while she cherishes her household gods, and hugging flattery though she has a keen scent for the flatterer.   In like manner she borrows with far less consideration than she gives; nor does debt cause her a pang until its consequences are in sight.   To the end she remains far more lavish to her lowliest kinsfolk and associates than to herself, while she conceals her unsparing generosity quite as much as her waste.   So far from " affecting to be unaffected " —that " sham simplicity which is a refined imposture " —she rather affects affectation, whether from whim or in self-defence.   Devoid of the petty vanities of fashion, she is vain of her power.   Tender in excess to her friends, to her foes she can be overbearing.   Enjoying the recognition of rank, of her own kindred she is proud; and if she is not gentle, she is never genteel, though in her flush of pride at the royal licence to wear her Maltese honours, she can stoop to bid Heralds' College invent the " arms of Lyons."   Lyon's arms, forsooth!   Had her blacksmith father but known of this, surely he would have thrown up his own brawny arms in astonishment.   Compassionate and sensitive, to such as thwart or suspect her she can be coarse and obdurate.   Natural and outspoken to a fault, she is unscrupulous wherever her connection with Nelson is concerned, in double-speaking and double-dealing. Piquing flirtation, to Nelson she abides steadfast as a rock.   When least virtuous, she never loses a sense of and reverence for virtue.   A tender, if unwise, mother, her moods drive her into outbursts with the child she adores.   Big schemes of expenditure always allure her; to little economies she attends, and she will squander by mismanagement in the mass what her man-

agement saves in detail.   Constantly ailing, she is always energetic, but though never idle, she is often indolent.   Passionate and even stormy, she battles hard
with a temperament which repeatedly masters her.
She is at once home-loving and pleasure-loving, careful and careless, sensible and silly, kind and cruel, modest and unblushing, calm and petulant, natural and artificial; and through all these phases runs the thread of
individuality, of self-consciousness, of independence, of
insurgent and infectious courage and enthusiasm.

The letters speak for themselves.   Little Miss
Matcham, at " Pappa's " request, indited a prim little
note to her dearest Lady Hamilton.   Miss Anne Bolton, often at loggerheads with her morbid sister Eliza,
wrote to her at Ramsgate, where she was recruiting her
health with Charlotte and Mrs. William Nelson :—

" I would have thanked you sooner for the few affectionate lines you sent me by Bowen, tho' indeed the
life we lead is so uniformly quiet, that tho' we are perfectly happy and comfortable, it is very unfavourable
to letter writing. . . . It gives me much pleasure to
find that Miss Connor is not to come into Norfolk, till
you go.   I should not know what to do without her.
She is so companionable to me, who, you know, would
have none without her, for Eliza, when most agreeable,
I consider as nothing, and my father is very much in
town.   She is so good, she seems quite contented with
the very retired life we lead.   We have got our instrument, which, with books and work, form our whole
amusement.   Sometimes, by way of variety, we have
the old woman come down, who behaves extremely well
and is become quite attached to Miss Connor.   Sometimes we sing to her till the poor thing sheds tears, and
we are obliged to leave off.   I am glad I have got over
the horror I once felt in her presence, because it is in
my power, the short time I am here, to contribute a

little to her comfort.   We have beautiful walks in this
neighbourhood, which Miss Connor and I enjoy, and
you, dearest Lady Hamilton, are often the subject of
our conversation.   I live in the pleasing hope of seeing you once more, before we begin our journey, which
will not be till the 22nd of August.   But possibly, as
you are so well and happy, you may prolong your stay
at Ramsgate.   I was delighted at the account Bowen
gave me of you.   I made him talk for an hour about
you, and, indeed, to do him justice, he seemed as fond
of the subject as myself.   And thank you for the
darling pin-cushion, which is treasured up, and only
taken out occasionally to be kissed.   A few nights ago
I had an alarming attack of the same complaint which
was very near killing me a year and a half ago.   I
fainted away and terrified them all.   Eliza declares
she began to consider what she could do without me.
Thank God, and my father's skill, I am again well.
Pray write to me; if it is but such a little scrap as I
have hitherto had from you, I shall be content.   How
often we long to have a peep at you. . . . Miss Connor and Eliza desire their best love to you, as would
daddy, were he at home.   God bless you, most dear
Lady Hamilton. . . ."   Eliza Bolton, who at Merton
had learned music from Emma and Mrs. Billington,
also reports her own progress.

Nor, meanwhile, in Clarges Street, did Emma neglect the interests of the Boltons.   For Tom, she
solicited Nelson's cautious and official friend George
Rose, already busied over her own suit with the new
Ministry:—" It will make Nelson happy," she tells
him; " I hope you will call on me when you come to
town, and I promise you not to bore you with my own
claims, for if those that have power will not do me
justice, I must be quiet.   And in revenge to them, I
can say, if ever I am a Minister's wife again with the

power I had then, why, I will again do the same for
my country as I did before.   And I did more than any
Ambassador ever did, though their pockets were filled
with secret service money, and poor Sir William and
myself never got even a pat on the back.   But indeed
the cold-hearted Grenville was in then."   She adds that
Pitt would do her justice if he could hear her story:
she calls him " the Nelson of Ministers."

When Emma proposed spending the 1st of August
with the Nelsons at Canterbury, Nelson, during a fresh
scare of French invasion, evinced playful anxiety at
her neighbourhood to the French coast.   But the 1st
of August was always her fête.   She begged her constant and learned ally, Dr. Fisher, to join their " turtle
and venison."   " I wish," she concludes, " you would
give heed unto us, and hear us, and let our prayers prevail."   Doubtless the long, thin beakers and pink cham-
pagne of our ancestors were brought out at Canterbury to celebrate the anniversary of the Nile, while
" Reverend Doctor " bowed his best, and Emma raised
the glass with a tirade in honour of the distant hero.
It was not the French fleet that interrupted this festivity: a worse epidemic than invasion was abroad—that
of smallpox.   Poor little Horatia caught the disease,
though lightly, and Emma was in great distress.   Nelson's anxiety was as keen:—" My beloved," he wrote,
" how I feel for your situation and that of our dear
Horatia, our dear child.   Unexampled love never, I
trust, to be diminished, never: no, even death with all
his terrors would be jubilant compared even to the
thought.   I wish I had all the small-pox for her, but
I know the fever is a natural consequence.   Give Mrs.
Gibson a guinea for me, and I will repay you.   Dear
wife, good, adorable friend, how I love you, and
what would I not give to be with you at this moment,
for I am for ever all yours."   Relieved by better ac-

counts, he sighed for long years of undivided union
—" the thought of such bliss delights me "—" we shall
not want with prudence."

Horatia could at last be " fixed " at Merton, to his
intense delight, though she was not definitely installed
there till about May of the next year. Nelson now
despatched to Emma a strange announcement, evidently designed as a circular note of explanation for
the enlightenment of over-curious acquaintances. It
bears date *Victory*, August 13, 1804:—" I am now going to state a thing to you, and to request your kind assistance, which, from my dear Emma's goodness of
heart, I am sure of her acquiescence in. Before we
left Italy, I told you of the extraordinary circumstance
of a child being left to my care and protection. On
your first coming to England, I presented you the child,
dear Horatia. You became, to my comfort, attached
to it, so did Sir William, thinking her the finest child
he had ever seen. She is become of that age when
it is necessary to remove her from a mere nurse, and
to think of educating her. Horatia is by no means
destitute of a fortune. My earnest wish is that you
would take her to Merton, and if Miss Connor will
become her tutoress under your eye, I shall be made
happy. I will allow Miss Connor any salary you may
think proper. I know Charlotte loves the child, and
therefore at Merton she will imbibe nothing but virtue,
goodness, and elegance of manners, with a good education to fit her to move in that sphere of life which
she is destined to move in." Not long afterwards he
added that his dearest wish was that Horatio Nelson
when he grew up, " if he behaves," should wed Horatia,
and thus establish his posterity on Emma's foundation
as well as his brother's, and this wish he embodied in
one of his numerous wills.

In these mysteries of melodrama it is impossible not

to discern Emma's handiwork.　As a girl she had de-
voured romances and been thrilled by the strokes and
stratagems of the theatre.　The same leaning that had
prompted the secret passage episode at Naples,
prompted this also; and from her Nelson caught the
pleasures of mystification.　Nor can impartiality acquit her of planting some of her relatives on Nelson's
bounty.　Sarah Connor's salary is one instance;
Charles Connor's naval cadetship is another.　At this
very time the youth, who was to end in madness, was
discoursing to "her Ladyship" of Nelson's "unbounded kindness."　It is true that the unworthier
members of this family, especially Charles and Cecilia,
took advantage of Emma to the close, and that she had
to support all of them, including their parents; but it is
also true that Nelson's charities temporarily lightened
her burdens.

Nelson was now nearing the end of his Mediterranean vigil.　The King and Queen of Naples
despaired at his departure.　Acton, in disgrace, had
thoughts of taking his new wife to England.　Nelson
had tarried long enough in the scenes of his memories.
"Nothing, indeed," he tells his "dearest Emma," "can
be more miserable and unhappy than her poor Nelson."
From February 19, 1805, he had been "beating" from
Malta to off Palma, where he was now anchored.　He
could not help himself; none in the fleet could "feel"
what he did; and, "to mend his fate," since the close
of November all his letters had gone astray, and he
was without even the solace of news.

And yet his energy was never more indispensable
than at this moment.　The French strained every nerve
to meet the renewed vigour which characterised Pitt's
brief and final accession to power.　Directing their
fleet to the West Indies, they hoped to strike Britain
where she was most vulnerable, her colonies.　Eight

months' strenuous activity dejected but could not sub-
jugate Nelson. "I never did," he assured Davison,
"or ever shall desert the service of my country, but
what can I do more than swim till I drop? If I take
some little care of myself, I may yet live fit for some
good service." He was dying to catch Villeneuve.
Irritated at the command of Sir John Orde, destitute of
"any prize-money worthy of the name," he could still
waft his thoughts and wishes beyond the waves. It
was not only each movement at Merton that he followed; he cared for poor blind "Mrs. Nelson," while
he sat beside the sick-bed of many a man in his own
fleet. Nor did his vigilance concerning each veriest
trifle that might profit his country ever diminish.
Scott's descendants still cherish the two black-leathered
and pocketed armchairs, ensconced in which, night by
night, Nelson and his secretary waded through the
polyglot correspondence, and those "interminable papers" which engrossed him. "His own quickness,"
writes one of the latter's grandsons, "in detecting the
drift of an author was perfectly marvellous. Two or
three pages of a pamphlet were generally sufficient to
put him in complete possession of the writer's object,
and nothing was too trivial for the attention of this
great man's mind when there existed a possibility of its
being the means of obtaining information." Nelson
insisted on examining every document seized in prize-
ships, and so tiring proved the process that "these
chairs, with an ottoman that fits between them, formed,
when lashed together, a couch on which the hero often
slept those brief slumbers for which he was remarkable." At the end of March he heard that the French
were safe in port. Within three days his fleet was
equipped and refreshed. He scoured every quarter,
ransacked every corner, to sight the enemy—in vain.
Villeneuve had left Toulon to form his junction with

the Spaniards and effect his great design; Orde retired
from Cadiz, where the junction was effected. Nelson
ground his teeth and cursed his luck. By mid-April
the French were reported as having passed Gibraltar
with their colours flying. Nelson chased them once
again, foul winds and heavy swells hampering his
course. "Nothing," he wrote, "can be more unfortunate than we are in our winds. But God's will
be done! I submit. Human exertions are absolutely
unavailing. What man can do, I have done." Orde's
remissness in taking no measures for ascertaining their
course over-exasperated Nelson. At last he heard of
their East Indiaward direction. Though they outnum-
bered him greatly in ships, and entirely in men, he
swore that he would track them "even to the Antip-
odes." Though, by the opening of May, the elements
still defied him off Gibraltar, and the linen had been
actually sent on shore to be washed, while the officers
and men had landed, their observant commander perceived some indication of an east wind within twenty-
four hours. Without hesitation he took the risk of his
weatherwise observation. "Off went a gun from the
Victory, and up went the Blue-peter." The crew was
recalled, "the fleet cleared the gut of Gibraltar, and
away they steered for the West Indies." He hurried
with unexampled expedition to Martinique and Bar-
badoes—thus revisiting, in the last year of his life, the
two scenes associated respectively with his love and his
marriage. By the West Indies he was hailed as a deliverer, and it was their joy that first warned the
French of the approach of the sole commander whom
they dreaded. Nelson did not stay even to water his
ships. The shrewd Villeneuve, who had once escaped
from Egypt, hastened to escape once more, and his
superior force fled like a hare from Nelson's fury.

And Emma, meanwhile, was in an agony of suspense. To the incessant inquiries of Nelson's sisters, she could give no answer, for she could glean no news. At last letters arrived. He was longing to fly to "dear, dear Merton." He dared not enclose one of his "little letters," for fear of "sneaking and cutting," but he published for all to read "that I love you beyond any woman in the world, and next our dear Horatia." As for her, she paid visits. She threw herself into London distractions—again she sought retirement. But the hard fact of debt stared in the face of all her emotions. Just before her return to Merton, her mother wrote to her: "I shall be very glad to see you to-morrow, and I think you quite right for going into the country to keep yourself quiet for a while. My dear Emma, Cribb is quite distrest for money, would be glad if you could bring him the £13 that he paid for the taxes, to pay the mowers. My dear Emma, I have got the baker's and butcher's bills cast up; they come to one hundred pounds seventeen shillings. God Almighty bless you, my dear Emma, and grant us good news from our dear Lord. My dear Emma, bring me a bottle of ink and a box of wafers. Sarah Reynolds thanks you for your goodness to invite her to Sadler's Wells."

While Emma lingered, bathing at Southend, Mrs. Tyson, returning from a visit to her there, described a pleasant day spent at "charming Merton" with "dear Mrs. Cadogan": "She, with Miss Lewold" (Emma always left her mother a companion) "did not forget to drink my Lord's and your health. Tom Bolton was of the party. We left them six o'clock, horseback, but, alas! I am got so weak that the ride is too much for me. . . . I am, my dear Lady Hamilton, wishing all the blessings your good and charming disposition should have in this life. . . . Your Ladyship, I beg, will pardon this and please give it to Nancy.

. . . I will be much obliged to look for a pair of silk
stockings marked H.S. or only H., as they were given
me at Bath, changed in the wash. . . . She has been
very pert about them, and I will not pay her till I hear
from you." Nor did old sailors forget to show Emma
their appreciation. Captain Langford brought back
for her from Africa a crown-bird and a civet cat, which
must have astonished the Mertonites.

Far removed from such trivialities Nelson still struggled to come up with that fleeing but unconquered
fleet. Once more at Cadiz he gained fresh advices: it
had been seen off Cape Blanco. He rounded Cape Vincent, the scene of his earliest triumphs. Collingwood,
steering for the Straits' mouth, reported Cape Spartel
in sight; but still no French squadron. Anchored
again at Gibraltar, Nelson could descry not a trace of
them. He went ashore, as he recounts, for the first
time since June 16, 1803, and although it was "two
years wanting ten days" since he had set foot in the
Victory, still he would not despair. The French
destination might be Newfoundland, for aught he
knew; Ireland, Martinique again, or the Levant; each
probability had its chance. He searched every point
of the compass. He inquired of Ireland. He secured
Cadiz. He sailed off to Tetuan. He reinforced Corn-
wallis, lest the combined ships should approach Brest.
At last he heard of Sir Robert Calder's brilliant encounter, but problematic victory, sixty leagues west of
Cape Finisterre. Pleasure mingled with disappointment; at least and at last he was free. On August 17
he rode off Portland, at noon off the Isle of Wight. He
anchored at Spithead on the following morning at nine,
and with a crew in perfect health, despite unfounded
allegations of the need of quarantine, he landed.

All his family were gathered at Merton with Emma,
who had sped from Southend to greet him. The next

day saw him in Emma's and Horatia's arms. This
was his real reward. The society that resented his
isolation rushed to honour him. London was jubilant.
Deputations and gratitude poured in on his privacy.
But, rightly or wrongly, Merton was his Elysium, and
from Merton he would not budge.

"Thank God," wrote her lively cousin Sarah to
Emma the day after his arrival, " he is safe and well.
Cold water has been trickling down my back ever since
I heard he was arrived. Oh! say how he looks, and
talks, and eats, and sleeps. Never was there a man
come back so enthusiastically revered. Look at the
ideas that pervade the mind of his fellow-citizens in
this morning's post. Timid spinsters and widows are
terrified at his foot being on shore; yet this is the
man who is to have a Sir R. Calder and a Sir J. Orde
sent to intercept his well-earned advantages. I hope
he may never quit his own house again. This was my
thundering reply last night to a set of cowardly women.
I have lashed Pitt . . . to his idolatrice brawler. I
send you her letter. The public are indignant at the
manner Lord Nelson has been treated." Outside his
family he received friends like the Perrys. With reluctance he acceded to the Prince's command that he
would give him audience before he went.

He had not long to remain. On September 13, little
more than three weeks after his arrival, the *Victory*
was at Spithead once more, preparing to receive him.
Villeneuve must be found, and the sole hope of the
French at sea shattered. Nelson's "band of brothers " were to welcome the last trial of the magic " Nelson touch." Emma is said to have chimed with, and
spurred his resolve for, this final charge. Harrison's
recital of this story has been doubted, but she herself
repeated it to Rose at a moment, and in a passage,
that lend likelihood to sincerity. Moreover, in a strik-

ing letter of self-vindication to Mr. A. J. Scott, Nelson's trusted intimate, she thus delivered herself in the following year, assuming his own knowledge of the fact :—" Did I ever keep him at home, did I not share in his glory? Even this last fatal victory, it was I bid him go forth. Did he not pat me on the back, call me brave Emma, and said, ' If there were more Emmas there would be more Nelsons.' "

Together with his assembled relatives she shrank from bidding him adieu on board. One by one all but the Matchams departed. On that Friday night of early autumn, at half-past ten, the postchaise drew up, as he tore himself from the last embraces of Emma and Horatia, in whose bedroom he had knelt down and solemnly invoked a blessing. George Matcham went out to see him off, and his final words were a proffer of service to his brother-in-law. At six next morning he sent his " God protect you and my dear Horatia " from the *George* at Portsmouth.

A familiar and pathetic excerpt from his letter-book bears repetition:—

Friday, Sept. 13, 1805.

" Friday night, at half-past ten, drove from dear, dear Merton, where I left all that I hold dear in this world, to go to serve my King and country. May the great God whom I adore enable me to fulfil the expectations of my country, and if it is His good pleasure that I should return, my thanks will never cease being offered up to the throne of His mercy. If it is His good providence to cut short my days upon earth, I bow with the greatest submission, relying that He will protect those so dear to me that I may leave behind. His will be done. Amen. Amen. Amen."

The humility of true greatness rings through this valediction.

He seems to have felt some foreboding—and his last letters confirm it—that he would never return. During the two days on board before he weighed anchor, each moment that could be spared from business was devoted to the future of Emma and his child. His thoughts travelled in his letters to every cranny of his homestead. A few hours after he stepped on deck, he asked Rose, come from Cuffnells, to bring Canning with him to dinner. Canning was not present when Nelson engaged his friend in a parting conversation about Bolton's business, and also the prosecution of Emma's claims, though she maintained eight years later that she understood them to have given their joint assurances on her behalf. He purposely embarked from the bathing-machine beach to elude the populace. To Davison, in sad privacy, while he was off Portland, he gave his last mandate for mother and child. He twice answered Emma's last heart-broken notes. " With God's blessing we shall meet again. Kiss dear Horatia a thousand times."—" I cannot even read your letter. We have fair wind and God will, I hope, soon grant us a happy meeting. We go too swift for the boat. May Heaven bless you and Horatia, with all those who hold us dear to them. For a short time, farewell." The next day, off Plymouth, he entreated her to " cheer up," they would look forward to many, many happy years," surrounded by their " children's children." There are tears, and a sense of tragedy, in all these voices.

Passing the Scilly Islands, three days later, he again conveyed his blessings to her and to Horatia. At that very time Miss Connor wrote prettily of her young charge to Charlotte, whose family the mother had joined at Canterbury. " She is looking very well indeed, and is to me a delightful companion. We read about twenty times a day, as I do not wish to confine

her long at a time. . . . We bought some shoes and
stockings and a hat for the doll. She is uncommonly
quick. . . . I told her she was invited to see a ship
launched; every morning she asks if it is to be *to-day,*
and wanted to know if there will be any firing of
guns." How these trifles contrast with the coming
doom, and lend a silver lining to the dark cloud hanging over the sailor-father! Poor child, there was soon
to be firing of guns enough, and a great soul, as well
as a ship, was to be launched on a wider ocean. Emma
forwarded this letter to Nelson:—" I also had one
from my mother, who doats on her, and says that she
could not live without her. What a blessing for her
parents to have such a child, so sweet; altho' young, so
amiable. . . . My dear girl writes every day in Miss
Connor's letter, and I am so pleased with her. My
heart is broke away from her, but I have now had her
so long at Merton, that my heart cannot bear to be
without her. You will be even fonder of her when you
return. She says, ' I love my dear, dear Godpapa, but
Mrs. Gibson told me he killed all the people, and I was
afraid.' Dearest angel she is! Oh! Nelson, how I
love her, but how do I idolise you,—the dearest husband of my heart, you are all in this world to your
Emma. May God send you victory, and home to your
Emma, Horatia, and paradise Merton, for when you
are there, it will be paradise. My own Nelson, may
God preserve you for the sake of your affectionate
Emma." [1]

[1] Morrison MS. 844, 845, October 4 and 8 respectively. These
two letters only escaped destruction because Nelson never lived
to receive them. In the last Emma also says: " . . . She now
reads very well, and is learning her notes, and French and
Italian. The other day she said at table, ' Mrs. Cadoging, I
wonder Julia [a servant] did not run out of the church when
she went to be married, for I should, seeing my squinting husband come in, for . . . how ugly he is, and how he looks

It was not for that paradise that Nelson was reserved.

There is no need to recount the glories of Trafalgar.
Let more competent pens than mine re-describe the
strategy of the only action in which Nelson ever appeared without his sword.   When he explained to the
officers " the *Nelson touch*," " it was like an electric
shock.   Some shed tears, all approved "; " it was new,
it was singular, it was simple."—" And from Admirals
downwards, it was repeated—it must succeed if ever
they will allow us to get at them."   Again he had been
stinted in battleships.

Nelson ascended the poop to view both lines of those
great ships.   He directed the removal of the fixtures
from his cabin, and when the turn came for Emma's
portrait, " Take care of my Guardian Angel," he exclaimed.   In that cabin he spent his last minutes of retirement in a prayer committed to his note-book.
" May the great God whom I worship, grant to my
country, and for the benefit of Europe in general, a
great and glorious victory; and may no misconduct in
any one tarnish it, and may humanity after victory be
the predominant feature in the British fleet!   For myself individually, I commit my life to Him that made
me, and may His blessing alight on my endeavours for
serving my country faithfully.   To Him I resign myself, and the just cause which is entrusted to me to defend.   Amen.   Amen.   Amen."

And then he entrusted to his diary that memorable
last codicil, witnessed by Blackwood and Hardy, re-
counting his Emma's unrewarded services, and com-
mending her and Horatia (whom he now desired to

cross-eyed; why, as my lady says, "he looks two ways for
Sunday."'   Now Julia's husband is the ugliest man you ever
saw; but how that little thing cou'd observe him; but she is
clever, is she not, Nelson?"

bear the name of " Nelson " only [1]) to the generosity
of his King and country :—" These are the only favours
I ask of my King and Country at this moment when I
am going to fight their battle. May God bless my King
and Country and all those I hold dear. My relations
it is needless to mention; they will, of course, be amply
provided for." On his desk lay open that fine letter to
Emma, the simple march of whose cadences always
somehow suggests to one Turner's picture of the
Téméraire :—

" My dearest, beloved Emma, the dear friend of my
bosom, the signal has been made that the enemies' combined fleet is coming out of port. May the God of
Battles crown my endeavours with success; at all events
I will take care that my name shall ever be most dear
to you and Horatia, both of whom I love as much as
my own life; and as my last writing before the battle
will be to you, so I hope in God that I shall live to
finish my letter after the battle. May Heaven bless
you prays your Nelson and Bronte. . . ." [2]

As in a vision, one seems to behold that huge *Santis-
sima Trinidad,* that mighty *Bucentaur,* that fatal *Re-
doubtable,* the transmission of that imperishable
" Duty " signal; the *Victory* nigh noon, hard by the
enemy's van. One hears the awful broadside—the
" warm work " which rends the buckle from Hardy's
shoe—Nelson's words of daring and comfort. One
heeds his acts of care for others and carelessness for
himself.

---

[1] The King duly gave his licence to that effect. Morrison MS.
[2] October 19. The original was prominent in 1905 at the
British Museum with Emma's indorsement :—" This letter was
found open on His desk, and brought to Lady Hamilton by
Captain Hardy. ' Oh, miserable, wretched Emma! Oh, glorious
and happy Nelson!' "

His four stars singled him out as a target for the
deathblow that " broke his back " fifteen minutes afterwards.   He fell prone on the deck, where Hardy raised
him :—" They have done for me at last, Hardy." And
then, as he lies below, in face of death—" Doctor, I told
you so ; doctor, I am gone " ; the whisper follows, " I
have to leave Lady Hamilton and my adopted daughter
Horatia as a legacy to my country."   He feels " a gush
of blood every minute within his breast."   His
thoughts are still for his officers and crew.   " How
goes the day with us, Hardy ? "   *His* day is over.   " I
am a dead man . . . come nearer to me."   Over his
filming eyes, assured of conquest,[1] hover but two pres-
ences, but one place.   " Come nearer to me.   Pray
let my dear Lady Hamilton have my hair, and all other
things belonging to me."   And next, raising himself in
pain, " Anchor, Hardy, anchor ! "   Not Collingwood
but Hardy shall give the command ; " for, if I live, *I*
anchor."—" Take care of my poor Lady Hamilton,
Hardy.   Kiss me, Hardy." [2]—" Now I am satisfied."
While his throat is parched and his mouth agasp for
air, his oppressed breathing falters once more to Scott :
" *Remember* that I leave Lady Hamilton and my
daughter [now there is no " adopted "] to my country.''
Amid the deafening boom of guns, and all the chaos
and carnage of the cockpit, while the surgeon quits him
for five minutes only on his errands of mercy, alone,
dazed, cold, yet triumphant, with a spirit exulting in
self-sacrifice, and wavering ere its thinnest thread be

---

[1] Scott's account (cf. App., Part II. F. (2)) brings a striking
detail into prominence.   "He died," he says, *" as the battle
finished, and his last effort to speak was made at the moment of
joy for victory."*
[2] Hardy, in a letter to Scott of March 10, 1807, protesting his
continued esteem for Lady Hamilton, declares that Nelson's *last*
words to him were, "Do be kind to poor Lady H." Cf. *Life of
Rev. Dr. Scott* (1842), p. 212.

severed, around the distant dear ones, he dies. " Thank God," he " has done his duty " ! Can man do more, or love more, than to lay down his life for his friends?

Bound up with Britain, the son who saved, ennobled, and embodied her, rests immortal. Ministers, who used him like a sucked orange, might disregard his latest breath. With such as these he was never popular. But wherever unselfishness, and valour, and genius dedicated to duty, are known and famed, there will he be remembered. *" The tomb of heroes is the Universe."*

Sad and slow plodded the procession of fatal victory over the waters *homeward*. Long before the flagship that formed Nelson's hearse arrived, Scott, his chaplain, broke the news to Emma at Clarges Street through Mrs. Cadogan :—" Hasten the very moment you receive this to dear Lady Hamilton, and prepare her for the greatest of misfortunes. . . . The friends of my beloved are for ever dear to me." Nine days elapsed before she realised the worst. She was stunned and paralysed by the blow. For many weeks she lay prostrate in bed, from which she only arose to be removed to Merton. Her nights were those of sighs and memories; her mother tended her, wrote for her, managed the daily tasks that seemed so far away. Quenched now for ever was

> " The light that shines from loving eyes upon
> Eyes that love back, till they can see no more."

And when at length she revived, her first thought was to beseech the protection of the Government, not for herself, but for the Boltons. If George Rose could forward Nelson's wishes for them, it would be a drop of comfort in her misery. She kept all Nelson's letters—" sacred," she called them—" on her pillow."

She fingered them over and over again. Her heart, she told Rose, was broken. "Life to me now is not worth having. I lived but for him. His glory I gloried in; it was my pride that he should go forth; and this fatal and last time he went, I persuaded him to it. But I cannot go on. My heart and head are gone. Only, believe me, what you write to me shall ever be attended to." Letters purporting to be Nelson's regarding his last wishes had leaked out in the newspapers. She was too weak to "war with vile editors." "Could you know me, you would not think I had such bad policy as to publish anything at this moment. My mind *is not a common one,* and having lived as confidante and friend with such men as Sir William Hamilton and dearest, glorious Nelson, I feel superior to vain, tattling woman." She was desolate. She had lost not only the husband of her heart and the mainstay of her weakness, but herself—the heroine of a hero. She was "the same Emma" no longer, only a creature of the past. The receptive Muse had now no source of inspiration left, nor any commanding part to prompt or act. Yet her old leaven was still indomitable. She would fight and struggle for herself and her child so long as she had breath.

Messages of sympathy poured in from every quarter, but she would not be comforted. Among others, Hayley, writing with the new year, and before the funeral, entreated her to make "affectionate justice to departed excellence a source of the purest delight." He rejoiced in the idea that his verses had ever been "a source of good" to her, and the egotist enclosed some new ones of consolation. She told him she was most unhappy. "No," she "must not be so," added the sententious "Hermit"; "self-conquest is the summit of all heroism." While Rose and Louis importuned her for mementoes—and Emma parted with all they asked—the Abbé Campbell, writing amid the third overthrow at Naples, was more delicate and sympathetic. His "heart was full of anguish" and commiseration. "I truly pity you from my soul, and only wish to be near you, to participate with you in the agonies of your heart, and mix our tears together." Goldsmid sent philosophic consolation, and tried to get her an allotment in the new loan. Staunch Lady Betty Foster and Lady Percival were also among her consolers, and so too was the humbler Mrs. Lind. The Duke of Clarence—Nelson's Duke—inquired after her particularly. And later Mrs. Bolton wrote:—" For a moment I wished myself with you, and but a moment, for I cannot think of Merton without a broken heart, even now can scarcely see for *tears*. *How I do feel for you* my own heart can tell; but I beg pardon for mentioning the subject, nor would it have been, but that I well know your thoughts are always *so*. My dear Horatia, give my kindest love to her. The more I *think*, the dearer she is to me."

At length the *Victory* arrived at Spithead. Hardy travelled post-haste with his dearest friend's note-books and last codicil to Rose at Cuffnells. Blackwood assured Emma that he would deliver none of them to any person until he had seen her; all her wishes should be consulted. Scott wrote daily to her all December, as he kept watch over the precious remains of the man whom he worshipped. He took lodgings at Greenwich, where they now reposed. Rooted to the spot, throughout his solitary vigil he was ever inquiring after Emma, whom Tyson alone had seen. From the Board Room of Greenwich Hospital the body was deposited in the Painted Chamber. It was the saddest Christmas that England had known for centuries. The very beggars, Scott wrote to Emma, leave their stands, neglect the passing crowd,

and pay tribute to his memory by a look. " Many "
did he see, " tattered and on crutches, shaking their
heads with plain signs of sorrow." The Earl had
been there with young Horace, who shed tears:—
" Every thought and word I have is about your dear
Nelson. Here lies Bayard, but Bayard victorious.
. . . So help me God, I think he was a true knight
and worthy the age of chivalry. One may say, *lui
même fait le siècle*—for where shall we see another? "
In all things she might command him; he only wished
for her approval. He could not tear himself away; he
was rowed in the same barge that bore the hero's
Orient-made coffin to the Admiralty. He watched by
it there, and thence attended it to St. Paul's. He bitterly resented being parted from it by his place, next
day, in the procession. " I honour your feelings," he
exclaimed in the tumult of grief, " and I respect you,
dear Lady Hamilton, for ever."

Who can forget the scenes of that dismal triumph of
January the 10th? Not a shop open; not a window
untenanted by silent grief. The long array of rank
and dignity wends its funeral march with solemn pace.
But near the catafalque draped with emblems and
fronted with the *Victory's* figurehead, are ranged the
weather-beaten sailors who would have died to save
him.

Fashion and officialdom, as distasteful to Nelson living as he was to them, press to figure in the pomp
which celebrated the man at whom they sometimes
jeered, and whom they often thwarted and sought to
supersede. Professed and unfeigned sorrow meet in
his obsequies.

Every order of the State is represented. Yet as
the deep-toned anthem—half-marred at first—swells
through the hushed cathedral, two forms are missing
—that of the woman whom certainly he would never

have forsworn had her wifehood ever meant real affection, and that of the other woman who beyond
measure had loved and lost him.   Can one doubt but
that, when all was over, when form and ceremony
were dispersed, Emma stood there, silent, their child's
hand clasped in hers, and shed her bitter tears beside
his wreaths of laurel, into his half-closed grave?

CHAPTER XIV

THE IMPORTUNATE WIDOW IN LIQUIDATION

February, 1806—July, 1814

WHILE the nation was to vote £90,000 and £5000 a year for the earldom of the clergy-man whose brother died only a Viscount and Vice-Admiral, in receipt of an annual grant not exceeding £2000; while Lady Nelson, soon to wrangle over the will, received that same annuity, not only were Emma's claims disregarded, but the payment of Nelson's bequest to her depended on a fluctuating rental. She retired for a space to Richmond, and at once begged Sir R. Barclay to be one of a committee for arranging her affairs and disposing of Merton. Not apparently until next November did she address Earl Nelson, urging him in the strongest terms, as his brother's executor, to legalise Nelson's last codicil; and nearly a year after he had received the pocket-book containing it from Hardy, he returned her a civil and friendly answer. Her finances were now more straitened than has been supposed. Her income from all sources (including Horatia's £200 a year) has been estimated as over some £2000. This estimate counts Hamilton's and Nelson's annuities, of £800 and £500 respectively, as if they were paid free of property-tax, her Piccadilly furniture as realised and invested intact at five per cent., together with Nelson's £2000 legacy, and Merton as rentable at £500 a year. The tax alone, however, seems to have been some ten per cent., the furniture should surely be reckoned at half-price, Merton was unlet, and with difficulty sold at last, while large inroads had been made by debt and interrupted Merton improvements. Her available capital must have been small. Her net income may be taken as under some £1200, apart from Nelson's annuity payable half-yearly in advance. Had this been so paid regularly from the first, another £450, after deducting property-tax, would have been hers. But I have discovered that Earl Nelson, on the excuse that the money he actually received from the Bronte estate up to 1806 was for arrears of rent accrued due before Nelson's death, never apparently allowed her a penny until 1808, and then, after consulting counsel, haggled over the payment in advance directed by the codicil, and in fact never paid her annuity *in advance* until 1814. The receipt for the first payment in advance still exists. This surely puts a somewhat different complexion on her "extravagance," since a year's delay in the receipt of income by one already encumbered would prove a dead weight. Imprudent and improvident she continued; embarrassed by anticipated expectations, eager, indeed, to compound with creditors she became much sooner than has hitherto been imagined. She remained absolutely faithful to Horatia's trust up to the miserable end. Within three years from Nelson's death Emma and Horatia were to become wanderers from house to house; treasure after treasure was afterwards to be parted with or distrained upon; and the Earl, who had flattered and courted Emma in her heyday, and still protested his willingness to serve her, and his hopes that Government would yield her "a comfortable pension," had joined the fair-weather acquaintances who left her and her daughter in the ditch. On the income, even apart from her variable annuity and the furniture proceeds, she might have been comfortable, if she had been content to retire at once into decent obscurity. She could not bring herself to forfeit the flatteries of worthless pensioners and cringing tradesmen; and, moreover, I cannot help suspecting that Nurse Gibson may not have rested satisfied with the occasional extra guineas bestowed on her, and that whether by her or by servants who had guessed the secret of Horatia's birth, continual hush-money may possibly have been extorted.

From December 6, 1805, when he received his brother's "pocket-book" or "memorandum-book" (in the letters it is named both ways) from Hardy, the new Earl held in his hands the "codicil" on which hung Emma's fate and Horatia's.

Only once do Earl Nelson's papers cast direct light on its adventures, but two of them about his wishes for the national vote, hint his attitude, though I think that she misconstrued and exaggerated its motives.

From December 6 to December 12 it seems to have been kept in his own possession. He then took it to Lady Hamilton's friend, Sir William Scott, at Somerset House, where she was led by him to believe that its formal registration with Nelson's will was in favourable process. Before Pitt's death in the ensuing January it was determined that the memorandum-book should be sent to the Premier. Pitt died at an unfortunate moment, and Grenville became Prime Minister. After consultation with persons of consequence, the Earl resolved in February to hand it over to Lord Grenville, and in Grenville's keeping it actually remained till so late as May 30, 1806. If even, as is possible, the "pocket-book" and the "memorandum-book" mean two separate things, and what Grenville retained was only the latter, referring to the "codicil" in the first, still the undue delay was no less shabby; and Nelson's sisters agreed with Emma, whose warm adherents they remained, in so entitling it.   Grenville was the last person in the world to act favourably towards Emma, but of course it was for him to decide from what particular source, if any, Government could satisfy Nelson's petition.

Up to February 23, 1806, the Earl's letters were more than friendly, and even many years afterwards they professed goodwill and inclination to forward her claims for a pension, but in the interval a quarrel ensued.

Emma subsequently declared that, after so long withholding the pocket-book, the Earl, as her own guest at her own table, tossed it back to her " with a coarse expression."   She then registered the codicil herself.   She added that the reason for its detention was that the Earl desired nothing to be done until he was positive of the national grant to him and his family.

For such meanness I can see no sufficient reason. To put his motives at the lowest, self-interest would tempt him to forward Emma's claims to some kind of Government pension.   But I do think that his course was ruled solely by a wish for his own safe self-advantage.   He did not choose to risk offending Grenville.   The codicil was not proved till July 4.

Earl Nelson certainly never erred on the side of generosity.   Despite his assiduous court to Emma during Nelson's lifetime, and his present amicable professions, he himself, as executor, went ferreting for papers at that Merton where he had so often found a home, and whose hospitality his wife and children still continued gratefully to enjoy; though he was probably angered when the shrewd Mrs. Cadogan proved his match there and worsted him.   With reluctance, and " with a bleeding heart," he conceded Emma's " right " to the " precious possession " of the hero's coat, as the document concerning its surrender, in his wife's handwriting, still attests. In the future, only two years after declaring, "No one can wish her better than I do," he was to begrudge one halfpenny of the expenses after her death. Only a few months before it, his behaviour caused her to exclaim in a letter which has only this year seen the light, and which is one of the most piteous yet least complaining that she ever wrote, "He has never given the dear Horatia a frock or a sixpence." He squabbled over Clarke and M'Arthur's *Life* of his brother. And long after Emma lay mouldering in a nameless grave, he declined to put down his name for the book of a brother clergyman, on the ground that for books he had long ceased to subscribe. If Emma rasped him by overbearing defiance (and she never set herself to conciliation), it would excuse but not justify him, since Horatia's prospects were as much concerned as Emma's in the fulfilment of the last request of the departed brother, to whom he and his owed absolutely everything.

The worst was yet far distant. But harassing vexations already began to cluster round the unhappy woman, who was denied her demands by ministers alleging as impediments long lapse of time and the inapplicability of the Secret Service Fund, though Rose and Canning afterwards acknowledged them to be just. Pitt's death with the dawning year rebuffed anew, as we have seen, the main hope of this unfortunate and importunate widow. Hidden briars beset her path also. Her once obsequious creditors already clamoured, and were only staved off temporarily by the delusive promises of Nelson's will. For a time one at least of the Connors [1] caused her secret and serious uneasiness

---

[1] Ann, who, with the touch of madness peculiar to the whole family, and at this time dangerous in Charles, associated herself now with Emma "Carew," whose pseudonym she took, as Lady

by ingratitude and slander; while the whole of this
extravagant family preyed on and "almost ruined"
her. But, worse than all, the insinuations of her
enemies began at length to find a loud and unchecked
outlet. "How hard it is," she wrote of her de-
tractors, during a visit to Nelson's relations, in a letter of September 7, 1806, to her firm ally the departed
hero's friend and chaplain, "how cruel their treatment
to me and to Lord Nelson! That angel's last wishes
all neglected, not to speak of the fraud that was acted
to keep back the codicil. . . . It seems that those that
truly loved him are to be victims to hatred, jealousy,
and spite. . . . We have, and had, what they that per-
secute us never had, his unbounded love and esteem,
his confidence and affection. . . . If I had any influence over him, I used it for the good of my country.
. . . I have got all his letters, and near eight hundred
of the Queen of Naples' letters, to show what I did

Hamilton's daughter. "How shocked and surprised I was, my
dear friend," writes Mrs. Bolton. "Poor, wretched girl, what
will become of her? What could possess her to circulate such
things? But I do not agree with you in thinking that she ought
to have been told before, nor do I think anything more ought
to have been said than to set *her right.* . . . I am sure I
would say and do everything to please and nothing to fret."
—Morrison MS. 896, Friday, October 11, 1806. In her "will"
of 1808 Emma records:—"I declare before God, and as I hope
to see Nelson in heaven, that Ann Connor, who goes by the
name of Carew and tells many falsehoods, that she is my
daughter, but from what motive I know not, I declare that
she is the eldest daughter of my mother's sister, Sarah Connor,
and that I have the mother and six children to keep, all of
them except two having turned out bad. I therefore beg of my
mother to be kind to the two good ones, Sarah and Cecilia.
This family having by their extravagance almost ruined me, I
have nothing to leave them, and I pray to God to turn Ann
Connor *alias* Carew's heart. I forgive her, but as there is a
madness in the Connor family, I hope it is only the effect of
this disorder that may have induced this bad young woman to
have persecuted me by her slander and falsehood."—Morrison
MS. 959.

for my King and Country, and prettily I am rewarded." For glory she had lived, for glory she had
been ready to die. In seeking to rob her of glory by
refusing to acknowledge her services, and by traducing
her motives her foes had wounded her where she
was most susceptible. Pained to the quick, yet as
poignantly pricked to defiance, she uplifted her voice
and spirit above and against theirs:—

"Psha! I am above them, I despise them; for,
thank God, I feel that having lived with honour and
glory, glory they cannot take from me. I despise
them; my soul is above them, and I can yet make
some of them tremble by showing how he despised
them, for in his letters to me he thought aloud." The
parasites were already on the wing. "Look," she resumed, "at Alexander Davison, courting the man he
despised, and neglecting now those whose feet he used
to lick. Dirty, vile groveler." She meets contumely
with contumely.

But her warm and uninterrupted intercourse with
Nelson's sisters and their families proved throughout a
ray of real sunshine. She stayed with them—especially the Boltons—incessantly, and they with her at
Merton. The Countess Nelson herself, even after
her husband's unfriendliness, was her constant visitor.
Horatia was by this time adopted "cousin" to all
the Bolton and Matcham youngsters. Nothing could
be further from the truth, as revealed in the Morrison
Autographs, than the picture of Emma, so often given,
as now a broken "adventuress." She led the life
at home of a respected lady, befriended by Lady Elizabeth Foster and Lady Percival. Lady Abercorn
begged her to bring Naldi and perform for the poor
Princess of Wales. But her heart stayed with Nelson's kinsfolk, with Horatia's relations. She stifled
her sorrow for a while with the young people, who

still found Merton a home, as Mrs. Bolton tenderly ac‑ knowledged. Charlotte Nelson was still an inmate, and Anne and Eliza Bolton were repeatedly under its hospitable roof. Emma's godchild and namesake, Lady Bolton's daughter, was devoted to Mrs. Cadogan —they all " loved " her, she called her " grandmama." The Cranwich girls reported to " dearest Lady Ham‑ ilton " all their tittle-tattle, the country balls, their mu‑ sical progress, the matches, the prosperous poultry, their dishes and gardens. They awaited her Sunday letters—their " chief pleasure "—with impatience. They never forgot either her birthday or Mrs. Cado‑ gan's. When in a passing fit of retrenchment she meditated migration to one of her several future lodg‑ ings in Bond Street, who so afraid for her inconveni‑ ence as her dear Mrs. Bolton? When the ministry, after Pitt's demise, brought Canning to the fore, who again so glad that George Rose was his friend and hers, so convinced that the " new people who shoot up " as petitioners were the real obstacles to her suc‑ cess? And so in a sense it proved, for one of the min‑ istry's excuses may well have been that a noble fam‑ ily had been ten years on their hands. Mrs. Bolton still hoped—even in 1808—that the " good wishes of one who is gone to heaven will disappoint the wicked." Mrs. Matcham, too, who " recalled the many happy days we have spent together," was always soliciting a visit: " It will give us great pleasure to fête you, the best in our power." She longed—in 1808 again—to pass her time with her, though it might be a " selfish wish." But Emma preferred the Bolton household. She and Horatia went there immediately after the " codicil " annoyances, and twice more earlier in that same year alone. Emma, they repeated, " was beloved by all." And her affection extended to their friends at Brancaster and elsewhere. Sir William Bolton re‑

mained in his naval command, and Lady Hamilton kept her popularity with the navy. Anne and Eliza Bolton, together with their mother, hung on her lightest words, and followed her singing-parties at " Old Q.'s," in 1807, with more than musical interest. Eliza, indeed, one regrets to recount, confided a dream to Emma, a dream of " Old Q.'s " death and a thumping legacy. " There is a *feeling* for *you* at this heart of mine," wrote Anne Bolton, just before the crash, " that will not be conquered, and I believe will accompany me wherever I may go, and last while I have life." Surely in Emma must have resided something magnetic so to draw the hearts of the young towards her —even when, as now, she seemed to neglect them. Those who judge, or misjudge her, might have modified their censoriousness had they experienced the winning charm of her friendship.

But all this while, and under the surface, Emma continued miserable, ill, and worried. Her importunities with the Government were doomed to failure; her monetary position, aggravated by reckless generosity towards her poverty-stricken kinsfolk, grew more precarious; but her pride seems not to have let her breathe a syllable of these embarrassments to the Boltons or the Matchams.

For a while she removed to 136 Bond Street as a London *pied-à-terre*. One of her letters of this period survives, addressed to Captain Rose, her befriender's son. Horatia insisted on guiding Emma's hand, and both mother and daughter signed the letter. " Continue to love us," she says, " and if you would make Merton your home, whenever you land on shore you will make us very happy." To Merton, so long as she could, she and her fatherless daughter still clung.

To carry out Nelson's wishes with regard to Horatia's education was her main care. but her ideas of education began and ended with accomplishments. Horatia's precocities both delighted and angered her. Of real mental discipline she had no knowledge, and her stormy temper found its match in her child's.

Her restless energy, bereft of its old vents, found refuge in getting Harrison to write his flimsy life of the hero; in trying to dispose of the beloved home, which she became hourly less able to maintain; in coping with her enemies; in dictating letters to Clarke, another of the throng of dependants with whom she liked to surround herself; in hoping that Hayley would celebrate her in his *Life of Romney*. An un-published letter from her to him of June, 1806—a portion of which has been already cited—depicts her as she was. She is " very low-spirited and very far from well." She was " very happy at Naples, but all seems gone like a dream." She is " plagued by law-yers, ill-used by the Government, and distracted by that variety and perplexity of subjects which press upon her," without any one left to steer her course. She passes "as much of her time at dear Merton as possible," and " always feels particularly low " when she leaves it. She tries hard to gain " a mastery over herself," but at present her own unhappiness is as in-vincible as her gratitude to her old friend who so often influenced her for good. She is distraught, misin-terpreted, the sport of chance and apathy.

> " L'ignorance en courant fait sa roide homicide,
> L'indifférence observe et le hasard décide."

Two years later again, when misfortunes were thick-ening around her, she thus addressed Heaviside, her kind surgeon:—". . . Altho' that life to myself may no longer be happy, yet my dear mother and Horatia will bless you, for if I can make the old age of my good mother comfortable, and educate Horatia, as

the great and glorious Nelson in his dying moments
begged me to do, I shall feel yet proud and delighted
that I am doing my duty and fulfilling the desires and
wishes of one I so greatly honoured." And in the
same strain she wrote in that same year to Greville,
who had then relented towards her. She strove, she
assured him, to fulfil all that "glorious Nelson"
thought that she "would do if he fell"—her "daily
duties to his memory." Of "virtuous" Nelson she
writes perpetually. On him as perpetually she muses.
For till she had met him she had never known the
meaning of true self-sacrifice. In his strength her
weak soul was still absorbed. Remembrance was now
her guiding star; but it trembled above her over
troubled waters, leading to a dismal haven. Nor, in
her own sadness, was she ever unmindful of the misery and wants of others.

Before the year 1808, which was to drive her from
"dear, dear Merton," had opened, she received one
more letter which cheered her. Mrs. Thomas, the
widow of her old Hawarden employer, the mother of
the daughter who first sketched her beauty, and whom
Emma always remembered with gratitude, wrote to
condole with her on the misconduct of some of the
Connors. She alluded also to that old relation, Mr.
Kidd, mentioned at the beginning of our story, who
from being above had fallen beyond work, but who
still battened on the bounty of his straitened benefactress:—

". . . I am truly sorry that you have so much
trouble with your relations, and the ungrateful return
your care and generosity meets with, is indeed enough
to turn your heart against them. However, ungrateful as they are, your own generous heart cannot see
them in want, and it is a pity that your great generosity
towards them shou'd be so ill-placed. I don't doubt

that you receive a satisfaction in doing for them, which will reward you here and hereafter. I sent for Mr. Kidd upon the receipt of your letter. I believe he has been much distressed for some time back. . . . As he observes, he was not brought up for work." In her opinion, the less pocket-money he gets, the better; it " will onely be spent in the ale-house." The Reynoldses, too, had been living upon Emma, and another relation, Mr. Nichol, Kidd's connection, expected ten shillings a week. Emma had provided Richard Reynolds with clothes, and a Mr. Humphries with lodging. They all imagined her in clover, and she would not undeceive them. When her " extravagance " is brought up against her, these deeds of hidden and ill-requited generosity should be remembered. She was more extravagant for others than for herself. She even besought the Queen of Naples to confer a pension on Mrs. Gräfer, though she besought in vain. And all the time she continued her unceasing presents to Nelson's relations, and to poor blind " Mrs. Maurice Nelson."

But these were the flickers of a wasting candle. By April, 1808, Merton was up for sale. The Boltons had not the slightest inkling of her disasters. They missed the regularity of her letters; they had heard that she was unwell, and fretting herself, but they were quite unaware of the cause. Indeed, Anne Bolton was herself now at Merton with Horatia, under the care of Mrs. Cadogan, who was soon ill herself under the worries so bravely withheld.

Maria Carolina, still in correspondence with her friend, was, however, unable, it would seem, or unwilling to aid her since she had written the reluctant plea on her behalf to the English ministers four years previously. Indeed, it may be guessed that one of the reasons alleged for disregarding the supplication of

Nelson, was that its discussion might compromise the Neapolitan Queen. This, then, was the end of the royal gratitude so long and lavishly professed. When Emma in this year besought her, not for herself, but for Mrs. Gräfer (then on the eve of return to Palermo), she told Greville that she had adjured her to redeem her pledge of a pension to their friend " by the love she bears, or *once* bore, to Emma," as well as " by the sacred memory of Nelson." If the Queen was at this time in such straits as precluded her from a pecuniary grant once promised to the dependant, she might still have exerted herself for her dearest friend. But " Out of sight, out of mind." In despair, while Rose returned to his barren task of doing little elaborately, Emma betook herself to Lord St. Vincent. If her importunities could effect nothing with the gods above, she would entreat one of them below. Perhaps Nelson's old ally could melt the obdurate ministers into some regard for Nelson's latest prayers; perhaps through him she might draw a drop, if only of bitterness, with her Danaid bucket from that dreary official well.

She conjures him by the " tender recollection " of his love for Nelson to help the hope reawakened in her " after so many years of anxiety and cruel disappointment," that some heed may be paid to the dying wishes of " our immortal and incomparable hero," for the reward of those " public services of importance " which it was her " pride as well as duty to perform." She will not harrow him by detailing " the various vicissitudes " of her " hapless " fortunes since the fatal day when " Nelson bequeathed herself and his infant daughter, expressly left under her guardianship, to the munificent protection of our Sovereign and the nation." She will not arouse his resentment " by reciting the many petty artifices, mean machinations,

and basely deceptive tenders of friendship" which
hitherto have thwarted her. She reminds him that
he knows what she did, because to her and her husband's endeavours she had been indebted for his friendship. The widow of Lock, the Palermo Consul, had
an immediate pension assigned of £800 a year, while
Mr. Fox's natural daughter, Miss Willoughby, obtained one of £300. Might not the widow of the
King's foster-brother, an Ambassador so distinguished,
hope for some recognition of what she had really done,
and what Nelson had counted on being conceded?

At the same time both she and Rose besought Lord
Abercorn, who interested himself warmly in her
favour. In Rose's letter occurs an important passage,
to the effect that Nelson on his last return home had,
through him, forwarded to Pitt a solemn assurance
that it was through Emma's "exclusive interposition
that he had obtained provisions and water for the English ships at Syracuse, in the summer of 1798, by which
he was enabled to return to Egypt in quest of the
enemy's fleet"; and also that Pitt himself, while staying with him at Cuffnells, had "listened favourably"
to his representations. Rose had previously assured
Lady Hamilton that he was *convinced* of the "justice
of her pretensions," to which she "was entitled both
on principle and policy."

And not long afterwards, when, as we shall shortly
see, kind friends came privately to her succour, she
forwarded another long memorial to Rose, in whose
Diaries it is comprised, clearly detailing both services
and misadventures. "This want of success," she repeats, and with truth, "has been more unfortunate
for me, as I have incurred very heavy expenses in completing what Lord Nelson had left unfinished at Merton, and I have found it impossible to sell the place."
She might have added that Nelson entreated her not

to spend one penny of income on the contracts; he never doubted that this cost at least the nation would defray. "From these circumstances," she resumes, "I have been reduced to a situation the most painful and distressing that can be conceived, and should have been actually confined in prison, if a few friends from attachment to the memory of Lord Nelson had not interfered to prevent it, under whose kind protection alone I am enabled to exist. My case is plain and simple. I rendered a service of the utmost importance to my country, attested in the clearest and most undeniable manner possible, and I have received no reward, although justice was claimed for me by the hero who lost his life in the performance of his duty. . . . If I had bargained for a reward beforehand, there can be no doubt but that it would have been given to me, and *liberally*. I hoped then not to want it. I do now stand in the utmost need of it, and surely it will not be refused to me. . . . I anxiously implore that my claims may not be rejected without consideration, and that my forbearance to urge them earlier may not be objected to me, because in the lifetime of Sir William Hamilton I should not have thought of even mentioning them, nor indeed after his death, if I had been left in a less comparatively destitute state."

Yet the latter was the excuse continuously urged by successive Governments. Both Rose and Canning, more than once, admitted the justice of her claims, and even Grenville seems by implication not to have denied it. Rose always avowed his promise to Nelson at his "last parting from him" to do his best, and he did it. But he well knew that the real obstacle lay not in doubt, or in lapse of time, or in the quibble of how and from what fund it would be possible to satisfy her claims, but solely in the royal disinclination to favour one whom the King's foster-brother had married against his will, and whose early antecedents, and later connection with Nelson, alike scandalised him. The objections raised were always technical and parliamentary, and never touched the substantial point of justice at all. The sum named—£6000 or £7000—would have been a bagatelle in view of the party jobbing then universally prevalent; and no attentive peruser of the whole correspondence from 1803-1813 can fail to grasp that each successive minister—one generously, another grudgingly—at least never disputed her claims even while he refused them. It was not *their* justice, but justice itself that was denied, and the importunate widow was left pleading before the unjust judge who had more advantageous claimants to content. Pitt's death, in January, 1806, was undoubtedly a great blow to Emma's hopes. During his last illness she must often have watched that white house at Putney with the keenest anxiety. So early as the beginning of 1805, Lord Melville, whom Nelson had asked to bestir himself on Emma's behalf during his absence, told Davison that he had spoken to Pitt personally about " the propriety of a pension of £500 " for her. Melville himself spoke " very handsomely " both of her and her " services." Pitt, if he had survived more than a year and had been quit of Lord Grenville, might have risked the royal disfavour, as in weightier concerns he never shrank from doing. The luckless Emma sank apparently between the two stools of social propriety and official convenience, while the hope against hope, that no disillusionment could extinguish, constantly made her the victim of her anticipations.

For a moment a purchaser willing to give £13,000 for Merton had been almost secured. But debts and fears hung around her neck like millstones. They interrupted her correspondence and sapped her health, now in serious danger. By June, 1808, she told her surgeon, Heaviside, that she was so "low and comfortless" that nothing did her good. Her heart was so "oppressed" that "God only knows" when that will mend,—"perhaps only in heaven." He had "saved" her life. He was "like unto her a father, a good brother." In vain she supplicated "Old Q." to purchase Merton and. she would live on what remained: he had named her in his will, and that sufficed. With her staunch servant Nanny, and her faithful "old Dame Francis," who attended her to the end she and Horatia retired to Richmond, where for a space the Duke allowed her to occupy Heron Court, though this too was later on to be exchanged for a small house in the Bridge Road. She herself drew up a will, bequeathing what still was hers to her mother for her life, and afterwards to "Nelson's daughter," with many endearments, and expressing the perhaps impudent request that possibly she might be permitted to rest near Nelson in St. Paul's, but otherwise she desired to rest near her "dear mother." She begged Rose to act as her executor, and she called on him, the Duke, the Prince, and "any administration that has hearts and feelings," to support and cherish Horatia.

All proved unavailing, and she resigned herself to the inevitable liquidation. After a visit to the Boltons in October, she returned to arrange her affairs in November.

A committee of warm friends had taken them in hand. Many of them had powerful city connections. Sir John Perring was chairman of a meeting convened in his house at the close of November. His chief associates were Goldsmid, Davison, Barclay, and Lavie, a solicitor of the highest standing, and there were five other gentlemen of repute.

A full statement had been drawn up. Her assets

amounted to £17,500, " taken at a very low rate," and independent of her annuities under the two wills and her " claim on the Government," which they still put to the credit side. Her private debts, of which a great part seems to have been on account of the Merton improvements, amounted to £8,000, but there were also exorbitant demands on the part of money-lenders, who had made advances on the terms of receiving " annuities." To satisfy these, £10,000 were required.

Everything possible was managed. All her assets, including the prosecution of those hopeless claims, were vested in the committee as trustees, and they were realised to advantage. Goldsmid himself purchased Merton. £3700 were meanwhile subscribed in advance to pay off her private indebtedness.

At this juncture Greville reappears unexpectedly upon the scene. In her sore distress he thawed towards one whom his iciest reserve and most pettifogging avarice had never chilled. He had evidently asked her to call, though he never seems to have offered assistance. She answered, in a letter far more concerning her friend Mrs. Gräfer's affairs than her own, that an interview with her " trustees " must, alas! prevent her:—" I will call soon to see you, and inform you of my present prospect of Happiness at a moment of Desperation"; you who, she adds, " I thought neglected me, Goldsmid and my city friends came forward, and they have rescued me from Destruction, Destruction brought on by *Earl Nelson's* having thrown on me the Bills for finishing Merton, by his having secreted the Codicil of Dying Nelson, who attested in his dying moments that I had well served my country. All these things and papers . . . I have laid before my Trustees. They are paying my debts. I live in retirement, and the City are going to bring forward my claims. . . . Nothing, *no power*

The death of Admiral Nelson at the battle of Trafalgar.
"Thank God, I have done my duty."

From the Painting by W. H. Overend.

on earth shall make me deviate from my present *system,"* she concludes, using the very word which
Greville used concerning his methods with womankind in the first letter which she ever received from
him. Goldsmid had been an " angel "; friends were
so kind that she scarcely missed her carriage and
horses.

Emma had every reason to be grateful. She was
clear of debt. She could still retain the valuables that
were out of Merton. With Horatia's settlement, she
could count on her old revenue when the " annuities "
had been discharged. Somehow they never were, and
they again figure largely during her last *débâcle*. The
mysteries of her entanglements baffle discovery; so
does her sanguine improvidence which, to the end,
alternated with deep depression. In a few years she
and Horatia, like Hagar and Ishmael, were to go forth
into the wilderness; but even then she was still buoyed
up with this mirage of an oasis in her tantalising
desert.

Relieved for the moment, she resumed the tenor of
her way at Richmond. She frequented concerts, and
sometimes dances, in the fashionable set of the Duke
and the Abercorns. In June, 1809, Lord Northwick
begged her to come to the Harrow speeches, and afterwards meet a few " old Neapolitan friends " and her
life-long friend the Duke of Sussex at " a fête in his
house." The fame of Horatia's accomplishments
added the zest of curiosity. All were eager to meet
the " interesting *élève* whom Lady Hamilton has
brought up " with every grace and every charm. The
Duke of Sussex looked forward to the encounter with
pleasure; Emma had not yet lost her empire over the
hearts of men. Of this invitation Emma took advantage to do a thoughtful kindness for an unhappy
bride who had just married the composer Francesco

Bianchi. Twelve days earlier she had tried apparently to heal the breach between them.

The Bohemians, therefore, were always with her. She continued to receive the Italian singers as well as their patrons; she still saw Mrs. Denis and Mrs. Billington, whose brutal husband, Filisan, was now threatening her from Paris; while Mrs. Gräfer, on the very eve of return to Italy, continued to beset her with importunities. Nor did her old friends, naval, musical, and literary, spare the largeness of her hospitality or the narrowness of her purse.

But, in addition to these diversions, she still overtasked herself with Horatia's education—so much so, that Mrs. Bolton wrote beseeching her to desist. Sarah Connor had now transferred her services to the Nelson family, and Emma eventually took the musical but far less literate Cecilia for Horatia's governess.

" Old Q.," her patron, now in the last year of his self-indulgent life, was busy making a new will every week. His friendship for Emma, however, had been truly disinterested, and even calumny never coupled their names together. When he died next year, he left her an annuity of £500, which, however—such was her persistent ill luck—she never lived to receive, for the old voluptuary's will was contested, it would seem, till after Lady Hamilton had paid the debt of nature. Even if she had survived the litigation, it would probably have absorbed a portion of the bequest.

The autumn of 1809 saw, too, the end of Greville. Since his mean and heartless treatment of her after Hamilton's death, Emma, save for the glimpse of reconciliation afforded by the remarkable communication of 1808 just quoted, had never so much as breathed his name in any of her surviving letters. The collector of stones had, till that moment of compunction, himself been petrified. In 1812 his crystals, for which he had so long ago exchanged Emma, together with the paintings which his cult of beauty at the expense of the beautiful had amassed, were sold at Christie's. "The object of this connoisseur," writes M. Simond, an eye-witness of the auction, "was to exhibit the progress of the art from its origin by a series of pictures of successive ages—many of them very bad." And perhaps the faultiest of his pictures had been himself.

From 1810, when they left Richmond, onwards, Emma and Horatia owned no fixed abode. They moved from Bond Street to Albemarle Street, thence, after perhaps a brief sojourn in Piccadilly again, to Dover Street, thence to two separate lodgings at the two ends again of Bond Street, where Nelson for a brief space after Sir William's death had also lodged. Lady Bolton, with her daughter, the godchild Emma, who had failed to find her at the opening of the year, expressed their keen disappointment: "You cannot think how melancholy I felt when we passed the gate at the top of Piccadilly, thinking how often we had passed it together. . . . Emma sends her best love and kisses to you, and Horatia, and Mrs. Cadogan. When I told her just now how if we had gone two houses further we should have seen you, she looked very grave. At last she called out: 'Pray, Mama, promise me to call as we go back to Cranwich.' . . . My love to Mrs. Cadogan, Miss Connor, and my dear Horatia. . . . God bless you, my dear Lady Hamilton."

But the worst blow was yet to fall. By the opening of the new year her mother lay on her deathbed.

Her old admirer, Sir H. Fetherstonehaugh—and nothing is more curious in this extraordinary woman's life than the way in which the light lover of her first girlhood re-emerges after thirty years as a respectful friend—began a series of sympathising letters. He was much concerned for her health, and ill as she was, she forgot her own ailments in the terrible trial of her mother's malady. "As I am alive to all nervous sensations," he wrote, "be assured I understand your language."—"I trust you will soon be relieved from all that load of anxiety you have had so much of lately, and which no one so little deserves."

Mrs. Cadogan died on the same day as the date of this letter, and Emma with Horatia now drifted forlorn and alone in a pitiless world. Emma's mother had endeared herself to all the Nelson and Hamilton circle, as well as to her own humble kindred. "Dear Blessed Saint," wrote Mrs. Bolton to Lady Hamilton, "was she not a mother to us all! How I wish I was near you!" She was buried in that Paddington churchyard which she and Emma had known so well in the old days at Edgware Row.

Emma was paralysed by the blow. More than a year afterwards she wrote that she could feel "no pleasure but that of thinking and speaking of her." In sending to Mrs. Girdlestone—whose family still possesses so many relics of Nelson—the box which the Duke of Sussex had presented to Mrs. Cadogan in Naples, the bereaved daughter concluded a touching letter as follows: "Accept then, my dear Friend, this box. You that are so fond a mother, and have such good children, will be pleased to take it as a token of my regard, for I have lost the best of mothers, my wounded heart, my comfort, all buried with her."

"Endeavour," wrote Mrs. Bolton, "to keep up your spirits: after a storm comes a calm, and God knows you have had storm enough, and surely the sun must shine sometimes."

The sun was never to shine again. This very year two more staunch friends, to whom Emma had been indebted for many kindnesses, made their exit, the old Duke and the generous Abraham Goldsmid, who, in despair at the failure of the recent Government loan, died by his own hand. It was a year of tumult. The din and riot of Burdett's election endangered the streets; abroad it was the year of Napoleon's second marriage, of the great battle of Wagram preluding the Russian campaign. Maria Carolina was an exile once more. Austria and the allies were worsted and rabid. Whichever way Emma's distraught mind turned, despair and misery were her outlook, and Nelson seemed to have died in vain.

The sum raised for her relief had been soon exhausted. In removing to Bond Street she intended really to retrench, but everything was swallowed up by the crowd of parasites who consumed her substance behind her back. Her landlady, Mrs. Daumier, pressed for payment. And yet Lady Hamilton's own requirements seem to have been modest enough. It was Mrs. Bianchi, Mrs. Billington, the person, whoever he may have been, who filched her papers from her afterwards, and the battening Neapolitans that rendered economy impossible and swarmed around her to the close. Nor would old dependants of Nelson believe that she was impoverished. One, " William Nelson," importuned her for another from Bethnal Green; Mr. Twiss, Mrs. Siddons's nephew, urged her influence for his solicitations to gain a " commissionership of Bankruptcy "— an ominous word for Emma. The Kidds, Reynoldses, and Charles Connor still lived *on,* the girl Connors *with* her. Their conduct ill contrasted with that of the once " poor little Emma "; for the unacknowledged Emma " Carew," after disdaining dependence on her prosperity, was now, in adversity, bidding her a last and loving farewell. Sir William Bolton still entreated her good offices with the royal dukes for " poor

Horace "; so did Mrs. Matcham with Rose. She
could not even now refrain from maintaining appearances, and keeping open house. She could not bring
herself to let those debonair royal dukes know that
one whom they fancied all song and sunshine was on
the brink of beggary. She could not hold the promise,
repeated to her befrienders, of living in tranquillity
and retirement. Nor would she desist from making
presents. She still visited fashionable resorts like
Brighton. She still enjoyed the friendship of Lady
Elizabeth Foster, by now the new Duchess of Devonshire. She still flattered herself, and listened to the
flatteries of others. She still trusted to chance—to her
elusive claims and her elusive legacy.

The old Duke had left Miss Connor a legacy also,
but all his bequests were long postponed. While Mrs.
Matcham was congratulating Emma on accessions of
fortune, while elderly, complimentary, Frenchified
Fetherstonehaugh rejoiced at the Queensberry "mite
out of such a mass of wealth," forwarded her "*envoies
de gibier*" and promised her "a view of old Up Park
dans la belle saison," the widow's cruse was wellnigh
drained. Nor after Greville's death, was his brother,
as trustee, always regular in his payments of her forestalled revenue. With reason, as well as with excuses,
Lord Mansfield warned her not to increase her expenditure till her "affairs were settled." Sir Richard
Puleston, inviting her from Wrexham to revisit the
scenes of her childhood, could still gloat over her
"*fairy palace* in Bond Street."

In extreme need, she revived her desperate petitions
to the new Government. Her fashionable friends
called her "a national blessing," and cried shame on
the deniers of her suit. But Mrs. Bolton well said to
her that she feared the friendly Rose was "promising
more than he could procure"; and amid these dubious

hopes two tell-tale pieces of paper in the Morrison Collection speak volumes. They are bills drawn on Emma by Carlo Rovedino, an Italian, for £150 each.

Even Cecilia Connor, with whom she had quarrelled but who owed her everything, dunned " her Ladyship " for the salary due for such education as she had given " dear Horatia." This was the last straw.

The Matchams and Boltons invited her yet again, but she did not come. She concerted fresh petitions with a fresh man of the pen. He hastened at Emma's bidding from his " Woodbine Cottage " at Wootton Bridge. He worked " like a horse." During his absence his wife was ill. Emma could not rest for thinking of her. She inquired of her from a common friend. She wrote to her herself: " You do not know how many obligations I have to Mr. Russell, and if I have success it will be all owing to his exertions for me. Would to God you were in town. What a consolation it would be to me." All smiles to the world, full of wretchedness within, she could not, as she wrote so many years ago, " divest " herself " of her natural feelings." But her uniform love of excitement—of which these hazardous petitions were a form—peeps out at the close of this little note: " It must be very *dull,* alltho' your charming family must be such a comfort to you."

The crash came suddenly with the opening of the new year, and just as Miss Matcham was begging her to repose herself with them at Ashfield Lodge. Horatia had whooping-cough. Emma, who was never without a companion, had replaced Cecilia Connor by a Miss Wheatley. For the sixth time she had failed in moving the ministers, but her tenacity was inexpugnable. She owed it to her kind committee, to Nelson's memory, to Horatia, to herself. The creditors, however, at last perceived that the asset on which they had built their hopes had vanished. In vain she prayed for time; the royal dukes would not see her draggled in the dust. Royal dukes, however, were not cash, thought the creditors, when they promptly arrested her for debt. It was the first time such a calamity had even entered her mind, but it was not to be the last, as we shall soon discover. She implored none of her grand friends. From the disgrace of prison she saved herself. Ill, with the ailing Horatia, she found a scant lodging at 12 Temple Place, within the rules of the King's Bench. To her old Merton friend, James Perry, afterwards proprietor of the *Morning Chronicle,* and through thick and thin her warm upholder, she addressed the following scrawl—

"Will you have the goodness to see my old Dame Francis, as you was so good to say to me at once at any time for the present existing and unhappy circumstances you wou'd befriend me, and if you cou'd at your conveaneance call on me to aid me by your advice as before. My friends come to town to-morrow for the season, when I must see what can be done, so that I shall not remain here; for I am so truly unhappy and wretched and have been ill ever since I had the pleasure of seeing you on dear Horatia's birthday, that I have not had either spirits or energy to write to you. You that loved Sir William and Nelson, and feel that I have deserved from my country some tribute of remuneration, will aid by your counsel your ever affectionate and gratefull. . . ." [1]

And to the Abbé Campbell, who had just left for Naples:—

". . . You was beloved and honour'd by my husband, Nelson, and myself; knew me in all my former splendours; you I look on as a dear, dear friend and relation. You are going amongst friends who love

[1] Morrison MS. 1042, January 3, 1813.

you; but rest assured none reveres you nor loves more than your ever, etc. *P.S.*—Poor Horatia was so broken-hearted at not seeing you. Tell dear Mr. Tegart to call on me, for I do indeed feil truly forlorn and friendless. God bless you. As glorious Nelson said, Amen, Amen, Amen."

Her stay in these purlieus was not long. Perry, and probably the Mertonite Alderman Smith, must have bailed her out. But during these few weeks of restricted liberty she slaved at new petitions, was visited by friends, and continued her correspondence with the Boltons and the Matchams, who begged hard for Horatia, whom they would meet at Reigate if Emma " could not manage to come " with her. They forwarded her presents of potatoes and turkeys from the country, and their letters evidently treat her just as if she were at large.

All her energies were bent on the two final memorials so often referred to in these pages—that to the Prince Regent, and that to the King. Rose now at last espoused her cause with real warmth, and Canning favoured her, despite his pique at her exaggerated account of what Nelson understood from their last interview. All, however, ended in smoke. Perceval, whom she had persuaded into benefiting one of Nelson's nephews, had been shot in the previous year, and Lord Liverpool trod in the footsteps of Lord Grenville.

Whither she repaired on liberation is unknown, though by the summer of the year she managed to reinstate herself in Bond Street.[1] There is no heading to the strange remonstrance which the distressed

---

[1] No. 150. This is manifest from the inventory and sale catalogue of the following July sold at Sotheby's on July 8, 1905. It is dated " Thursday, July 8, 1813." Her last refuge was at Fulham with Mrs. Billington.

mother penned, in one of her fitful moods, to Horatia
on " Easter Sunday " [1] of this year :—

" Listen to a kind, good mother, who has ever been
to you affectionate, truly kind, and who has neither
spared pains nor expense to make you the most
amiable and accomplished of your sex. Ah! Horatia,
if you had grown up as I wished you, what a joy, what
a comfort might you have been to me! For I have
been constant to you, and willingly pleas'd for every
manifestation you shew'd to learn and profitt of my
lessons. . . . Look into yourself·well, correct yourself of your errors, your caprices, your nonsensical
follies. . . . I have weathered many a storm for your
sake, but these frequent blows have kill'd me. Listen
then from a mother, who speaks from the dead. Reform your conduct, or you will be detested by all the
world, and when you shall no longer have my foster-
ing arm to sheild you, woe betide you, you will sink
to nothing. Be good, be honourable, tell not falsehoods, be not capricious." She threatened to put her
to school—a threat never executed. " I grieve and
lament to see the increasing strength of your turbulent
passions; I weep, and pray you may not be totally lost;
my fervent prayers are offered up to God for you. I
hope you may become yet sensible of your eternal welfare. I shall go join your father and my blessed
mother, and may you on your deathbed have as little
to reproach yourself as your once affectionate mother
has, for I can glorify, and say I was a good child.
*Can Horatia Nelson say so? I am unhappy to say
you cannot.* No answer to this! I shall to-morrow
look out for a school for your sake to *save you,* that
you may bless the memory of an injured mother.
P.S.—Look on me as gone from this world."

Six months later she again blamed her for her

[1] April 18, 1813. Cf. Morrison MS. 1047.

"cruel treatment." It may well be that the poor young girl, bandied about with Emma's fortunes, and with her driven from pillar to post, complained of hard treatment. "If my poor mother," once more exclaimed Emma, who had, at any rate, been a most dutiful daughter, "If my poor mother was living to take my part, broken as I am with greif and ill-health, I should be happy to breathe my last in her arms. I thank you for what you have done to-day. You have helped me nearer to God and may God forgive you." In two days "all will be arranged for her future establishment." She will summon Colonel and Mrs. Clive, Colonel and Mrs. Smith, Mr. and Mrs. Denis, Dr. Norton, Nanny the old servant, Mr. Slop, Mr. Sice, Annie Deane, all the gossips from Richmond, to "tell the truth" if she "has used her ill." "Every servant shall be on oath." "The all-seeing eye of God" knows "her innocence."

Of these two ebullitions, it is impossible not to discern in the first a fear lest her own errors should be repeated in her daughter. And it should not be forgotten that, through the connivance of Haslewood, Nelson's solicitor, Horatia to the last refused to believe that Lady Hamilton, whom she tenderly nursed and comforted at the close, was her real mother. Some such denials of Emma's motherhood may have caused these outbursts, proportioned in their violence to the intense and unceasing love that Emma fostered for Nelson's child, on her real relationship to whom she here—and here only within four walls—laid such vehement stress.

She had been compelled to part with Horatia's christening-cup, Nelson's own gift, to a Bond Street silversmith. Sir Harris Nicolas declared that he had seen a statement in her handwriting to the effect that "Horatia's mother" was "too great a lady to be mentioned." It has been assumed that his ambiguous phrase pointed to the Queen of Naples, who so late as 1808 was in friendly correspondence with Emma. This, however, remains uncertain. Nelson's own action had constrained her to envelop their joint offspring in mystery, for Horatia's benefit as well as their own. It is just as probable that the words "too great a lady" were used of herself, for the same words are used of her by Mrs. Bolton in 1809.

Things went rapidly from bad to worse. The smaller fry of her creditors were emboldened by the complete neglect of her last "memorials" into renewed action. At the instance of an exorbitant coach-builder, with a long bill in his hands, she was re-arrested, and in Horatia's company she found herself, towards the end of July, 1813, for the second time in the bare lodgings at Temple Place. All her remaining effects in Bond Street were sold. The articles offered were by no means luxurious, and included the remnants of Hamilton's library; many of them were bought by the silversmith, whom she still owed, and by Alderman Smith, her most generous benefactor. The city remained her champion.

She could still see her friends, Coxe and George Matcham among them, and she was permitted, such was her miserable health, to drive out on occasion. But the game, spiritedly contested to the last, was now up. Mrs. Bolton's death in the preceding July added one more to the many fatalities that thronged around her. The Matchams, themselves poor, were unwearying in their solicitude, and three years earlier a small windfall had enabled them to contribute £100 to her dire necessities. Alderman Smith came for the second time to the rescue, and once more stood her bail.

But before even this alleviation was vouchsafed, and while she had been for three months confined to her

bed, a crowning trouble beset her. Through the perfidy of some dependant [1] Nelson's most private letters
to her had been abstracted some years before, and were
now published to the world. This is the invaluable
correspondence on which these pages have so frequently drawn. It was not their revelation of the
"Thomson" letters that prejudiced her: her enemies
were always willing to insinuate even that she had
foisted Horatia on Nelson. It was the revelation of
the Prince of Wales episode of 1801, that scandalised
the big world, and destroyed the last shred of hope
for any future "memorials." It was insinuated that
she herself had published the volume. "Weather
this person," she told Mr. Perry, "has made use of
any of these papers, or weather they are the invention
of a vile mercenary wretch, I know not, but you will
oblige me much by contradicting these falsehoods."
"I have taken an oath and confirmed it at the altar,"
the much-harried Emma was to write to the press in
the next September, after she had crossed the Channel, "that I know nothing of these infamous publica-
tions that are imputed to me. My letters were stolen
from me by that scoundrel whose family I had in
charity so long supported. I never once saw or knew
of them. That base man is capable of forging any
handwriting, and I am told that he has obtained money
from the [Prince of Wales] by his impositions. Sir
William Hamilton, Lord N., and myself were too much
attached to his [Royal Highness] ever to speak ill or
think ill of him. If I had the means I would prosecute
the wretches who have thus traduced me." In still
another of her last letters she is even more specific on
this sore subject. "I again before God declare," she
avers, "I know nothing of *the publication* of these
stolen letters."

[1] Harrison; cf. Horatia's letter, *Cornhill*, June, 1906.

These statements point to Emma's truthfulness. All that she asserts is her ignorance of the contents of the volume, and how they came to be published. The Prince of Wales letters in this collection are undoubtedly genuine, corroborated, as they are, by many of their companions in the Morrison Manuscripts. The letters had been purloined by a rascal, and their publication blasted her last chances with the Prince whom in her will she had begged to protect Horatia after she was gone, while it also disclosed for the first time her dishonour of her husband.

Her sin had found her out; but her sin had been born of real devotion, and surely it should not harden us against her lovableness, or alienate us from charity towards the weight of temptation, and from pity for the tragedy of her lot.

She had abstained from reading the book. If she meant to deny the *authenticity* of these letters, then indisputably she must be taken to have lied. But even so, she was driven to bay and at the end of her tether. The perjury would have been exceptional. It would not have been Plato's "lie in the soul": it would have been a lie in defence of the dead and the living.

"The lips have sworn: unsworn remains the soul."

CHAPTER XV

July, 1814—*January,* 1815

SHORT and evil were the few days remaining. "What shall I do; God, what shall I do!" had been her exclamation thirty-two years ago to Greville. As she began, so she closed.

Mrs. Bolton's death in the late summer of 1813 left her more desolate than ever at Temple Place. The Matchams resumed their warm invitations; alas! she could not leave; she was still an undischarged bankrupt. The Matchams themselves were breaking up the last of their many establishments. They all wished to join Emma and Horatia, when possible, in some "city, town, or village abroad." This proposal probably suggested the idea of retiring to Calais when her present ordeal in the stale air of stuffy Alsatia should come to an end.

But even in tribulation she had celebrated, as best she could, the "glorious 1st of August." I have seen a letter inviting a few even then—not "pinchbeck," she calls them, "but true gold"—round that little table in Temple Place, to drink for the last time to the hero's memory.

The few surviving records unite in proving her genuine anxiety that through her no creditor should suffer. Though imprudence, as she confessed, had not a little contributed, her main disasters were due to a crowd of worthless onhangers whom she had recklessly maintained. She herself had gone bail " for a person " whom she thought "honourable." This " person " was probably one Jewett, a young friend of the Russells, in whom she had taken a warm interest. " I should be better," she had written to her " kind, good, benevolent Mr. and Mrs. Russell," " if I could know that this unfortunate and, I think, not guilty young man was saved. He has been a dupe in the hands of villains. . . . I have never seen him, for I could not have borne to have seen him and his amiable wife and children suffer as they must." She employs the same phrase—" dupe of villains "—about herself in a long epistle of this very date to Rose.

All her property was surrendered; with the exception of a few sacred relics, everything unseized had been sold, even Nelson's sword of honour. Her just creditors lost not a penny. The sole extortioners she would not benefit were those annuitant Shylocks who had preyed upon her utmost need, and who had well secured themselves by insuring her life in the Pelican Insurance Company.

James Perry and Alderman Smith exerted themselves to the utmost on her behalf. A small further sum was collected for her in the city, and by the last week of June, 1814, her full discharge was obtained from Lord Ellenborough. She was now free—with less than fifty pounds in her pocket.

But she soon gleaned the fact that these merciless " annuitants " purposed her re-arrest. Without dishonour, she prepared for exodus to France.

It was a flight requiring management and secrecy to elude the new writs about to be issued: it was her last thrill. How different from that memorable flight to Palermo sixteen years earlier, which had earned the admiration of Nelson, the gratitude of a court, and the praise of Britain!

About the last day of June she and Horatia, unattended, embarked at the Tower. The stormy passage thence to Calais took three days. Her single thought was for Horatia's future, but she still buoyed herself up by believing that an ungrateful ministry would at length provide for her daughter. Sir William Scott, she wrote, assured her that there were " some hopes " for her " irresistible claims." She fancied, moreover, that she had some disposing power over the accumulations of arrears on her income under her husband's will, so long withheld and intercepted by greedy annuitants. " If I was to die," she told Greville's brother and executor, imploring him at the same time for £100 on account, " I should have left that money away, for the annuitants have no right to have it, nor can they claim it, for I was most dreadfully imposed upon by my good nature. . . . When I came away, I came with honour, as Mr. Alderman Smith can inform you, but mine own innocence keeps me up, and I despise all false accusations and aspersions. I have given up everything to pay just debts, but [for] annuitants, never will."

She at first lodged at Dessein's famous hotel—the inn where Sterne (of whom Romney, his first portrayer's pupil, must have often told her) started on his *Sentimental Journey,* by the confession over a bottle of Burgundy that there was " mildness in the Bourbon blood "; and where the " Englishman who did not travel to see Englishmen " first inspected, in his host's company, the ramshackle *désobligeante* which was to be the vehicle of his whimsies.

Dessein's, however, was expensive as well as sentimental. It was not long before she inhabited the smaller " Quillac's " and looked out for a still humbler abode. Her " Old Dame Francis " was soon to join her as housekeeper.

She thus describes their manner of life to George Rose:—

". . . Near me is an English lady, who has resided here for twenty-five years, who has a day-school, but not for eating or sleeping. At eight in the morning I take Horatia, fetch her at one; at three we dine; she goes out till five, and then in the evening we walk. She learns everything—piano, harp, languages grammatically. She knows French and Italian well, but she will still improve. Not any girls, but those of the best families go there. Last evening we walked two miles to a *fête champêtre pour les bourgeois*. Everybody is pleased with Horatia. The General and his good old wife are very good to us; but our little world of happiness is ourselves. If, my dear Sir, Lord Sidmouth would do something for dear Horatia, so that I can be enabled to give her an education, and also for her dress, it would ease me, and make me very happy. Surely he owes this to Nelson. For God's sake, do try for me, for you do not know how limited I am. . . . I have been the victim of artful, mercenary wretches." [1]

Dis aliter visum; it was not to be. Nothing but the pittance of Horatia's settlement remained. Rose bestirred himself, but Lord Sidmouth continued impervious to the importunate widow, herself slowly recovering from the jaundice.

When "Dame Francis" arrived, they tenanted a farmhouse two miles distant in the Commune of St. Pierre—"Common of St. Peter's," as Lady Hamilton writes it—and from this farmhouse, not long afterwards, they again removed to a neighbouring one. It

---

[1] Cf. Rose's *Diaries,* vol. i p. 272; and cf. Morrison MS. 1055. "Horatia is improving in person and education every day. She speaks French like a French girl, Italian, *German,* English," etc. —September 21.

belonged to two ladies who had lost a large sum by
the refusal of their sons to join Napoleon's invading
army. Its rooms were large, its garden extensive.
She could at length take exercise in a pony-cart. She
and Horatia were regular in church attendance: the
French prayers were like their own. Provisions were
cheap: turkeys two shillings, partridges fivepence the
brace; Bordeaux wine from five to fifteen pence. Occasionally a stray visitor passed their way. Lord Cathcart, Sir William's old friend and relative, had visited
them, and spied out the nakedness of the land. It was
well known at Calais that the celebrated Lady Hamilton was in retreat: a real live " milord " must have flut-
tered the farmhouse dovecote. For a time there was
a brief spell of cheerful tranquillity, but the gleam
was transient. It was only a reprieve before the final
summons. " If my dear Horatia were provided for,"
she wrote to Sir William Scott, " I should dye happy,
and if I could only now be enabled to make her more
comfortable, and finish her education, ah God, how I
would bless them that enabled me to do it! " She was
teaching her German and Spanish; music, French,
Italian, and English she " already knew." Emma
" had seen enough of grandeur not to regret it ";
" comfort, and what would make Horatia and myself
live like gentlewomen, would be all I wish, and to live
to see her well settled in the world." It was of no
avail that her illness was leaving her. " My Broken
Heart does *not* leave me." " Without a pound in "
her " pocket," what could she do?—" On the 21st of
October, fatal day, I shall have some. I wrote to
Davison to ask the Earl to let me have my Bronte
pension quarterly instead of half-yearly, and the Earl
refused, saying that he was too poor. . . . Think,
then, of the situation of Nelson's child, and Lady Hamilton, who so much contributed to the Battle of the

Nile, paid often and often out of my own pocket at Naples . . . and also at Palermo for corn to save Malta. Indeed, I have been ill used. Lord Sidmouth is a good man, and Lord Liverpool is also an upright Minister. Pray, and if ever Sir William Hamilton's and Lord Nelson's services were deserving, ask them to aid me. Think what I must feel who was used to give God only knows [how much], and now to ask!"[1] Such was the plight of one who had gladly lavished care and money on the son and daughter of Earl Nelson. That new-made Earl, who had canvassed her favour, and called her his "best friend," was now calmly leaving her to perish, and his great brother's daughter to share her carking penury and privation.

Lawyers' letters molested even the seclusion of St. Pierre. The English papers published calumnies which she was forced to contradict. Their little fund was fast dwindling, and as late autumn set in they were forced to transfer their scanty effects to a meagre lodging in the town itself.

In the Rue Française—No. 111—and even there in its worst apartments, looking due north, the distressed fugitives found themselves in the depth of a hard winter.

They were not in absolute want, but, had their suspense been protracted, they must ere long have been so. At the beginning of December the "annuitants'" attorneys were in close correspondence with the Honourable Colonel Sir R. Fulke Greville. Proceedings, indeed, were being instigated in Chancery, which were only stopped by Lady Hamilton's unexpected demise. An embargo was laid on every penny of Emma's income. Even Horatia's pittance was not paid in advance, till she herself begged for a trifle on account from her uncle, Earl Nelson.

[1] Lady Hamilton to Sir William Scott—September 12, 1814.

Under the strain of uncertainty, Emma, worried out of her wits, and drawn more closely than ever to the daughter who absorbed her fears, her sorrow, and her affection, at length collapsed. The strong and buoyant spirits, which had brought her through so many crises, including Horatia's own birth, and the coil of its consequences, failed any longer to support her. A dropsical complaint, complicated by a chill, fastened upon her chest. By New Year's Day, 1815, her state of pocket, as well as of health, had become critical. Some ten pounds, in English money, her wearing apparel, and a few pawn tickets for pledged pieces of plate, were the sole means of subsistence until Horatia's next quarter's allowance should fall due. In 1811 the Matchams had sent all they could spare; they may have done so again. If the mother, denuded of all, asked for anything, it was for Horatia that she pleaded. At her *début,* Greville had noticed that she would starve rather than beg : it proved so now. Only seven years ago she had implored the Duke not to let their " enemies trample upon them." Those enemies had trampled on them indeed. A new creditor was knocking at her door, the last creditor—Death.

One can picture that deserted death-scene in the Calais garret, where the wan woman, round whom so much brilliance had hovered, lay poverty-stricken and alone. Where now were the tribes of flatterers, of importuners for promotion, or even the crowd of true and genial hearts? Her still lingering beauty had formed an element of her age, but now only the primitive elements of ebbing life remained intact—the mother and her child. By her bedside stood a crucifix —for she had openly professed her faith. Over her bed hung, doubtless, the small portraits of Nelson and of her mother—remnants from the wreck. Nelson was no longer loathed at Calais; a Bourbon sat on the throne, and not even wounded pride angered the French against the man who had delivered the sister— now dead herself—of Marie Antoinette. Perhaps Emma is trying to dictate a last piteous entreaty to the hard-hearted Earl, and sad Horatia writing it at the bare table by the attic casement. Perhaps, while she gasps for breath, and calls to mind the child within her arms, she strives but fails to utter all the weight upon her heart. Horatia sobs, and kisses again, may be, and again that " guardian " whom now she loves and trusts with a daughter's heart. Sorrow unites them closely; here " *they* and sorrow sit."

Of her many tragic " Attitudes " (had Constance ever been one?) the tragedy of· this last eclipses all. She, whose loveliness had dazzled Europe, whose voice and gestures had charmed all Italy, and had spell-bound princes alike and peasants; whose fame, whatever might be muttered, was destined to re-echo long after life's broken cadence had died upon the air; she whose lightest word had been cherished—*she* now lay dying *here*. Nelson, her mother, her child, these are still her company and comfort, as memories float before her fading eyes. Ah! will she find the first again, and must she lose the last?

A pang, a spasm, a cry. The priest is fetched in haste. She still has strength to be absolved, to receive extreme unction from a stranger's hands. Weeping Horatia and old " Dame Francis " re-enter as, in that awful moment, shrived, let us hope, and reconciled, she clings, and rests in their embrace.

It had been her wish to lie beside her mother in the Paddington church. This, too, was thwarted. On the next Friday she was buried. The hearse was followed by the many naval officers then at Calais to the cheerless cemetery, before many years converted into a timber-yard. Had she died a Protestant—such was the revival of Catholicism with monarchy in France—intolerance would have refused a service: only a few months earlier, a blameless and charming actress had been pitched at Paris into an unconsecrated grave. It was these circumstances that engendered the fables, soon circulated in England, of Emma's burial in a deal box covered by a tattered petticoat.

Earl Nelson and the Mr. Henry Cadogan, who has been mentioned earlier, came over before the beginning of February—the former to bring Horatia back, the latter to pay, through Alderman Smith's large-heartedness, the last of the many debts owing on the score of Lady Hamilton. None of them were defrayed by the Earl, who had never given his niece so much as " a frock or a sixpence." It was soon known that the " celebrated Emma " had passed away. Polite letters were exchanged between Colonel Greville and the " Prefect of the Department of Calais " as to the actual facts, and Greville's executor was much relieved to feel that Emma's departure had spared him the bother of a long lawsuit.

Horatia owed nothing to her uncle Nelson's care: she stayed with the Matchams until her marriage, in 1822, to the Reverend Philip Ward of Tenterden. She became the mother of many children, and died, an octogenarian, in 1881.

The research of these pages has tried to illumine Lady Hamilton's misdeeds as well as her good qualities, to interpret the problems and contrasts of a mixed character and a mixed career. It has tracked the many phases and vicissitudes both of circumstance and calibre that she underwent. We have seen her as a girl, friendless and forsaken, only to be rescued and trained by a selfish pedant, who collected her as he collected

his indifferent pictures and metallic minerals. We
have seen her handed on to the amiable voluptuary
whose torpor she bestirred, and for whose classical
taste she embodied the beautiful ideal. We have seen
her swaying a Queen, influencing statesmen and even
a dynasty, exalted by marriage to a platform which
enabled her to save, more than once, a situation critical
alike for her country, for Naples, and for Europe.
We have seen her rising not only to, but above, the
occasions which her highest fortunes enabled. We
have followed her conspicuous courage, from its germs
in battling with mean disaster, to a development which
attracted and enthralled the most valiant captain of
his age. We have marked how her resource also enhanced even his resourcefulness. We have watched
her swept into a vortex of passionate love for the hero
who transcended her dramatic dreams, and sacrificing
all, even her native truthfulness, for the real and un-
shaken love of 'their lives. We have shown that she
cannot be held to have detained him from his public
duty so long as history is unable to point to a single
exploit unachieved. And eventually, we have found
that the infinite expressiveness which throughout rendered her a muse both to men of reverie and of action,
rendered herself a blank, when the personalities she
prompted were withdrawn and could no more inspire
her as she had inspired them. We have viewed her
marvellous rise, and we have traced her melancholy
decline, from the moment of the prelude to Horatia's
birth to the years which involved its far-reaching and
inevitable sequels. We have found, despite all the re-
sulting stains which soiled a frank and fervid but un-
schooled and unbridled nature, that she never lost a
capacity for devotion, and even self-abandonment;
while her kindness and bounty remained as reckless
and extravagant as the wilfulness of her moods and

the exuberance of her enthusiasm. We have found her headstrong successively, and resolute, bold and brazen, capricious and loyal, vain-glorious, but vainer for the glory of those she loved; strenuous yet inert, eminently domestic yet waywardly pleasure-loving; serviceable yet alluring, at once Vesta and Hebe. We have tracked her, as catastrophe lowered, tenaciously beating the air, and ever sanguine that she could turn stones—even the stones flung at her—to gold. We have tracked also the cruelty and shabbiness of those that were first and foremost in throwing those stones, whose propriety was prudence, and whose virtue was self-interest. We have marked how long this woman of Samaria's wayfare was beset by bad Samaritans. We have felt the falsities to which they bowed as falser than the genuine idolatry which held her from a nobler worship, and from an air purer than most of her surrounders ever breathed. It was in Nelson's erring unselfishness that her salvation and her damnation met. And in her semi-consecration of true motherhood, springing at first from wild-animal devotion to her first child, we can discern the refinement of instinct which at length led the born pagan within the pale of reverence. Astray as a girl, she had found refuge in her own devotion, with which she invested Greville's patronage. An outcast at the close, she turned for shelter to a worthier home. And above all, implanted in her from the first, and ineradicable, her unwavering fondness for her mother has half-erased her darkest blot, and made her more beautiful than her beauty. May we not say, at the last, that because she loved much, much shall be forgiven her: *quia multum amavit.*

The site of her grave has vanished, and with it the two poor monuments rumoured to have marked the spot; the first (if Mrs. Hunter be here believed) of wood, "like a battledore, handle downwards"; the second, a headstone, which a *Guide to Calais* mentions in 1833.[1] Its Latin inscription was then partially decipherable :—

> " . . . Quae
> . . . Calesiae
> Viâ in Gallicâ vocatâ
> Et in domo C.VI. obiit
> Die xv. Mensis Januarii. A.D. MDCCCXV.
> Ætatis suae LI." [2]

It was perhaps erected by some officer of that navy which, long after she had gone, always remembered her unflagging zeal and kindness with gratitude. Her best epitaph may be found in the touching lines indited by the literary doctor Beattie (not Nelson's Sir William Beatty), after visiting her grave on his return from attending William IV. and his wife in Germany. They were published in 1831, and have been quoted by Pettigrew.

> " And here is one—a nameless grave—the grass
> Waves dank and dismal o'er its crumbling mass
> Of mortal elements—the wintry sedge
> Weeps drooping o'er the rampart's watery edge;
> The rustling reed—the darkly rippling wave—
> Announce the tenant of that lowly grave.
>
> .   .   .   .   .   .
>
>   . . . Levelled with the soil,
> The wasting worm hath revelled in its spoil—
> The spoil of beauty! This, the poor remains
> Of one who, living, could command the strains
> Of flattery's harp and pen. Whose incense, flung
> From venal breath upon her altar, hung,
> A halo; while in loveliness supreme
> She moved in brightness, like th' embodied dream

---

[1] Pettigrew, vol. ii. p. 636. The "battledore" bore the inscription, "Emma Hamilton, England's friend"
[2] *i. e.* In the fifty-first year of her age.

Of some rapt minstrel's warm imaginings,
The more than form and face of earthly things.

.   .   .   .   .   .

Few bend them at thy bier, unhappy one!
All know thy shame, thy mental sufferings, none.
All know thy frailties—all thou wast and art!
But thine were faults of circumstance, not heart.
Thy soul was formed to bless and to be bless'd
With that immortal boon—a guiltless breast,
And *be* what others *seem*—had bounteous Heaven
Less beauty lent, or stronger virtue given!
The frugal matron of some lowlier hearth,
Thou hadst not known the splendid woes of earth:
Dispensing happiness, and happy—there
Thou hadst not known the curse of being fair!
But like yon lonely vesper star, thy light—
Thy love—had been as pure as it was bright.
I've met thy pictured bust in many lands.
I've seen the stranger pause with lifted hands
In deep, mute admiration, while his eye
Dwelt sparkling on thy peerless symmetry.
I've seen the poet's—painter's—sculptor's gaze
Speak, with rapt glance, their eloquence of praise.
I've seen thee as a gem in royal halls
Stoop, like presiding angel from the walls,
And only less than worshipp'd! Yet 'tis come
To this! When all but slander's voice is dumb,
And they who gazed upon thy living face,
Can hardly find thy mortal resting-place."

THE END

Lightning Source UK Ltd.
Milton Keynes UK
UKHW03f1159300318
320279UK00001B/36/P

9 780898 753745